Teaching and Learning in Environmental Law

THE IUCN ACADEMY OF ENVIRONMENTAL LAW SERIES

Founding Series Editors: Kurt Deketelaere, *University of Leuven, Belgium* and Zen Makuch, *Imperial College London, UK*

Editorial Board
Zen Makuch, *Imperial College London, UK* (Editor in Chief)
Jamie Benidickson, *University of Ottawa, Canada* (Editor in Chief)
Natasha Affolder, *University of British Columbia, Canada*
Javier de Cendra, *IE Law School, Spain*
Veerle Heyvaert, *London School of Economics, UK*
Francesco Sindico, *Strathclyde University, UK*

As environmental law increases in importance as an area of legal research, this series brings together some of the most current research carried out by the IUCN Academy of Environmental Law, a global network of environmental law scholars. Each volume in the series addresses an important issue in the field and presents original research analysis and assessment, along with a much-needed synthesis of the state of environmental law. Directions as to the positive role that environmental law can play at a global level are also emphasized. This series provides essential reading for scholars throughout the world with an interest in cutting edge environment-related issues, and will no doubt play an important role in shaping future debate.

Titles in this series include:

The Search for Environmental Justice
Edited by Paul Martin, Sadeq Z. Bigdeli, Trevor Daya-Winterbottom, Willemien du Plessis and Amanda Kennedy

Implementing Environmental Law
Edited by Paul Martin and Amanda Kennedy

Energy, Governance and Sustainability
Edited by Jordi Jaria i Manzano, Nathalie Chalifour and Louis J. Kotzé

The Law and Policy of Biofuels
Edited by Yves Le Bouthillier, Annette Cowie, Paul Martin and Heather McLeod-Kilmurray

Protecting Forest and Marine Biodiversity
The Role of Law
Edited by Ed Couzens, Alexander Paterson, Sophie Riley and Yanti Fristikawati

Courts and the Environment
Edited by Christina Voigt and Zen Makuch

The Impact of Environmental Law
Stories of the World We Want
Edited by Rose-Liza Elsma-Osorio, Elizabeth A. Kirk and Jessica Steinberg Albin

Teaching and Learning in Environmental Law
Pedagogy, Methodology and Best Practice
Edited by Amanda Kennedy, Anél du Plessis, Rob Fowler, Evan Hamman and Ceri Warnock

Teaching and Learning in Environmental Law

Pedagogy, Methodology and Best Practice

Edited by

Amanda Kennedy

Professor of Law, Faculty of Law, Queensland University of Technology, Australia

Anél du Plessis

Professor of Law, Faculty of Law, North-West University, South Africa

Rob Fowler

Adjunct Professor, Law School, University of Adelaide, Australia

Evan Hamman

Adjunct Senior Lecturer, Queensland University of Technology School of Law, Australia

Ceri Warnock

Professor, Faculty of Law, University of Otago, New Zealand

The IUCN Academy of Environmental Law

Edward Elgar
PUBLISHING

Cheltenham, UK • Northampton, MA, USA

Published by
Edward Elgar Publishing Limited
The Lypiatts
15 Lansdown Road
Cheltenham
Glos GL50 2JA
UK

Edward Elgar Publishing, Inc.
William Pratt House
9 Dewey Court
Northampton
Massachusetts 01060
USA

Paperback edition 2023

A catalogue record for this book
is available from the British Library

Library of Congress Control Number: 2021938822

This book is available electronically in the **Elgar**online
Law subject collection
http://dx.doi.org/10.4337/9781789908534

ISBN 978 1 78990 852 7 (cased)
ISBN 978 1 78990 853 4 (eBook)
ISBN 978 1 0353 1342 6 (paperback)

Printed and bound by CPI Group (UK) Ltd, Croydon, CR0 4Y

Contents

List of contributors   viii

1   From 'marginality' to 'mainstream': the evolution of
    teaching and learning in environmental law   1
    *Rob Fowler, Ceri Warnock, Amanda Kennedy, Anél du
    Plessis and Evan Hamman*

PART I   VALUES-BASED DIMENSIONS OF
            ENVIRONMENTAL LAW

2   Engendering hope in environmental law students   22
    Lynda Collins and Brandon D. Stewart

3   Bringing the 'heart' into environmental law teaching   35
    Karen Bubna-Litic

4   Placing natural resources law: preliminary thoughts on
    decolonizing teaching and learning about people, places, and law   49
    Estair Van Wagner

PART II   FORMATS AND METHODOLOGIES FOR
            TEACHING ENVIRONMENTAL LAW

5   Is your textbook (still) really necessary?   69
    Stuart Bell

6   Techniques for enhancing the lecture format in teaching
    environmental law   83
    Tracy Bach

7   Teaching and learning environmental law using small
    group teaching methodologies   96
    Ben Boer

8   Enhancing learning in environmental law through
     assessment design   113
     Ceri Warnock, James Higham, Sara Walton, Lyn Carter
     and Daniel Kingston

9   Environmental law clinics in Australia and the United
     States: a comparison of design and operation   129
     Evan Hamman and Jill Witkowski Heaps

PART III   THE TEACHING OF INTERNATIONAL
           ENVIRONMENTAL LAW

10   Game on! Game-based learning as an innovative tool for
     teaching international environmental law   144
     Alexandre Lillo and Thomas Burelli

11   Teaching international environmental law as a story   164
     Chris McGrath

PART IV   ENVIRONMENTAL LAW AT THE
           POSTGRADUATE LEVEL

12   The emergence of specialist postgraduate coursework
     programs in environmental law   182
     Heather McLeod-Kilmurray

13   Enriching the postgraduate environmental law classroom:
     combining mixed cohorts and intensive mode teaching   197
     Erika Techera

14   Doctoral research in environmental law (Part 1): rationale
     and some supervision challenges   210
     Willemien du Plessis and Anél du Plessis

15   Doctoral research in environmental law (Part 2): the
     student-supervisor relationship   225
     Anél du Plessis and Willemien du Plessis

PART V   CHALLENGES FOR TEACHING
         ENVIRONMENTAL LAW

16   Of density and decline: reflections on environmental
      law teaching in the UK and on the co-production of
      environmental law scholarship   241
      Steven Vaughan

17   Never mind the platform, here's the pedagogy: e-learning
      in environmental law   253
      Amanda Kennedy and Amy Cosby

18   Teaching environmental law in Thailand   276
      Chacrit Sitdhiwej and Rob Fowler

Index   289

Contributors

Tracy Bach, Professor of Law and Visiting Professor, Washington University in St. Louis, United States of America

Stuart Bell, Dean of the Faculty of the Social Sciences and Professor of Law, University of York, United Kingdom

Ben Boer, National Distinguished Professor, Wuhan University, China and Emeritus Professor, University of Sydney, Australia

Karen Bubna-Litic, Adjunct Associate Professor of Law, UniSA Justice and Society, University of South Australia, Australia

Thomas Burelli, Associate Professor of Law, Co-director of the Centre for Environmental Law and Global Sustainability, University of Ottawa, Canada

Lyn Carter, Senior Lecturer, Te Tumu School of Māori, Pacific & Indigenous Studies, University of Otago, New Zealand

Lynda Collins, Full Professor of Law, Centre for Environmental Law and Global Sustainability, University of Ottawa, Canada

Amy Cosby, Research Fellow, Institute for Future Farming Systems, CQUniversity Australia, Rockhampton, QLD, Australia

Rob Fowler, Adjunct Professor, Law School, University of Adelaide, Australia

Evan Hamman, Adjunct Senior Lecturer, Queensland University of Technology School of Law, Australia

James Higham, Professor of Tourism, Faculty of Law, University of Otago, New Zealand

Amanda Kennedy, Professor of Law, Faculty of Law, Queensland University of Technology, Australia

Daniel Kingston, Senior Lecturer, School of Geography, University of Otago, New Zealand

Alexandre Lillo, Postdoctoral Fellow and Part-time Professor of Law, Centre for Public Law, University of Ottawa, Canada

Chris McGrath, Adjunct Associate Professor at the University of Queensland Global Change Institute, University of Queensland, Australia

Heather McLeod-Kilmurray, Full Professor, Centre for Environmental Law and Global Sustainability, Faculty of Law, University of Ottawa, Canada

Anél du Plessis, Professor of Law, North-West University, South Africa

Willemien du Plessis, Professor of Law, North-West University, South Africa

Chacrit Sitdhiwej, Lecturer, Faculty of Law, Thammasat University, Thailand

Brandon D. Stewart, (LL.M, J.S.D. (Yale)) is an Instructor at the Schulich School of Law, Dalhousie University, Nova Scotia, Canada

Erika Techera, Professor of Law, University of Western Australia Law School, University of Western Australia, Australia

Estair Van Wagner, Assistant Professor of Law, Osgoode Hall Law School, York University, Canada and Co-Director of the Osgoode Environmental Justice and Sustainability Clinic and the Joint Master in Environmental Studies and *Juris Doctor* programme, Osgoode Hall Law School, York University, Canada

Steven Vaughan, Professor of Law and Professional Ethics, Faculty of Laws, University College London, United Kingdom

Sara Walton, Associate Professor of Business and Management, Department of Management, University of Otago, New Zealand

Ceri Warnock, Professor, Faculty of Law, University of Otago, New Zealand

Jill Witkowski Heaps, Assistant Director, Environmental Advocacy Clinic, University at Buffalo School of Law, United States of America

1. From 'marginality' to 'mainstream': the evolution of teaching and learning in environmental law

Rob Fowler, Ceri Warnock, Amanda Kennedy, Anél du Plessis and Evan Hamman

Why produce a book on teaching environmental law? There are three principal reasons that we offer.

First, environmental law has emerged since the 1970s as a widely embraced component of the undergraduate law curriculum in many countries. It is also a specific focus within numerous postgraduate legal studies and research programs. Whether it has become a part of the mainstream of legal education or remains a marginal component is open to debate, and the answer may vary from one country to another. We examine this matter further below, but, irrespective of the conclusion, this development in itself justifies a specific examination of the teaching of environmental law. We believe that this book is the first to be devoted entirely to the subject of teaching environmental law and hope that it will provide both inspiration and practical guidance to legal scholars who are seeking to take up, or improve, their teaching of this subject. We also hope that it will encourage further discussion and debate amongst environmental law scholars about how best to do so.

Second, there is a widespread recognition amongst environmental law scholars that teaching environmental law involves a number of distinctive challenges. Arguably, the inherent characteristics of environmental problems create more acute challenges for environmental law teaching than for many other legal subjects. Environmental law is of great scope and it is hard to delineate clear boundaries for the subject. The law changes rapidly, forced by advances in scientific knowledge, technological processes and political concern. In many nations, environmental law presents as a predominantly statute-based subject – which creates its own pedagogical challenges – but environmental scholars also have to contend with the legal relevance of policy, planning instruments and other forms of 'soft law'. The emergence of environmental law principles (such as sustainable development and the precautionary principle) create a tension between legal formalism and new approaches to legal reasoning. In addition, alongside these challenges, the subject is characterised by great factual complexity, bringing into play interdisciplinarity and the need to consider the relationship between law and science, law and economics, and law and socio-cultural concerns. Accordingly, determining the purpose, scope and content of the subject can prove challenging. As a result, it is desirable to examine the difficulties that teachers may encounter in designing and delivering an environmental law course and how best to address these. We will elaborate further on these challenges later in this chapter. Many of the contributions also do so and provide suggestions as to how to overcome them.

Third, environmental law has provided a vehicle in a number of countries for considerable innovation in legal teaching methodology. Whether this innovation is a necessary response to the distinctive nature of the subject (e.g., its interdisciplinary and polycentric characteristics) is also a matter for debate, and these are explored further in this introduction. Irrespective of the reasons for such innovation, the presentation in this book of a range of distinctive teaching methodologies that reach beyond the entrenched, lecture-based paradigm for legal education may inspire their adoption more widely, not only by environmental law teachers but also, where appropriate, in other subjects within the general law curriculum. In this respect, an examination of environmental law teaching may provide some constructive insights for legal teaching methodology more generally.

SOME PRELIMINARY QUALIFICATIONS

In presenting this introduction, and in editing the contributions to this book, we have been conscious of the need to avoid generalised statements and assumptions that ignore differing circumstances across the world of legal education. In particular, we acknowledge that the conditions for the provision of legal education, including environmental law, vary considerably around the world and that some of the teaching methodologies described in the following chapters may be difficult or impossible to adopt, or even to relate to, where resources and facilities are inadequate. Our aim, in presenting these methodologies, is not to provide a prescriptive template for how to teach an environmental law course. Rather, we seek to present a range of methodological alternatives to the lecture-based paradigm that are particularly suited to the teaching of environmental law and which may serve to help environmental law teachers to think differently about what they do, and why. It is possible that many of these methodologies may be utilised elsewhere in the legal curriculum where circumstances permit.

We note also that the contributions to this book largely reflect experience with the teaching of environmental law in Western, developed countries. This was not a deliberate editorial choice but rather an unintended consequence of the manner in which we have assembled the book. While we 'commissioned' several chapters in order to ensure a treatment of some fundamental aspects of the general topic, most have come from a response to our call for contributions. The quality and quantity of this response has been impressive, reflecting a commendable vitality and commitment within the international community of environmental law scholars to the teaching of the discipline. We note however, with regret, that we have not succeeded in attracting many suitable contributions from environmental law scholars working in countries with a developing or emerging economy. Whether this reflects the marginality of environmental law within the legal curriculum in these countries, a shortage of scholars experienced in environmental law teaching and scholarship, a lack of confidence on the part of these scholars in submitting contributions, or other factors, is unclear. Whatever the reasons, there is a critical need to explore further the particular opportunities and challenges related to the teaching of environmental law in these parts of the world.

Finally, we acknowledge that a shortage of legal scholars with appropriate expertise in environmental law may constitute a significant impediment to the teaching of the subject in some countries, especially those with less developed economies.[1] It is not possible for a book of this nature to address this significant problem, as the solution lies primarily in providing access for legal scholars, particularly those from developing countries, to training or a formal, postgraduate education in environmental law. Nevertheless, we hope that this book can serve as a guide and inspiration to those who are relatively new to the teaching of environmental law, wherever they may be located, especially as they set about the challenging task of developing a course on the subject for the first time.

THE STRUCTURE AND CONTENTS OF THIS BOOK

We have allocated the 18 selected contributions to five separate Parts, with the aim of providing a coherent and logical order to their presentation. This will also enable readers to choose, if they wish, which contributions to focus on more closely.

Part I comprises three contributions that reflect on the values-based and emotional dimensions of environmental law. In Chapter 2, Lynda Collins and Brandon Stewart explore how to engender hope in students confronting the impacts of climate change. In Chapter 3, Karen Bubna-Litic argues for the adoption of a values-based approach to teaching environmental law that serves to inspire students. In Chapter 4, Estair Van Wagner adopts a somewhat con-

---

[1]   For a description of the challenges in this regard in Thailand, see Ch.18.

trary perspective by suggesting that there is a need to provide some discomfort to students in a natural resources law course through place-based learning that involves an effort to 'decolonise' its teaching.

These contributions provide differing perspectives in the environmental law context on some broader questions concerning the general approach to legal education. On the one hand, environmental law intertwines inescapably with values-based ideas and perspectives that are difficult, and arguably undesirable, for environmental law teachers to ignore or avoid. On the other hand, there are good reasons why law teachers should avoid adopting polemical attitudes and approaches in the classroom.[2] Finding the right balance between these two perspectives is a delicate challenge for environmental law teachers.

An equally difficult, emerging challenge for environmental law teachers involves placing environmental law in the context of the rapidly expanding scientific evidence of impending ecological collapse, in particular because of climate change, but also through the loss of terrestrial biodiversity and the demise of ocean ecosystems. The overall picture of environmental destruction and potential ecological collapse can be a source of mental depression for students that their teachers may need to keep in mind. Lynda Collins and Brandon Stewart argue in Chapter 2 that there are compelling psychological reasons for providing a hopeful perspective to students concerning the role of environmental law in avoiding serious collapse. But an equally forceful argument has been made that younger students can emotionally handle the emerging evidence of impending collapse, and need to be provided with a frank and unsparing assessment of the future through their teachers.[3] This debate deserves much greater attention in university education generally, not just in the context of environmental law scholarship.

Part II is very much the core of the book, in which the various formats and methodologies that have been employed in the teaching of environmental law are examined. As noted above, environmental law has engendered considerable innovation in teaching methodology as a result in part of its interdisciplinary and values-based character. In particular, it offers an opportunity for its teachers to utilise approaches to the delivery of their course that extend beyond

---

[2]   The issue of poor-quality environmental scholarship associated with 'the need to promote a certain ideology' is discussed in E. Fisher, B. Lange, E. Scotford and C. Carlarne, 'Maturity and Methodology: Starting a Debate about Environmental Law Scholarship'(2009) 21:2 *Journal of Environmental Law* 213 at 223–4.

[3]   See R. Read and S. Alexander, *This Civilisation is Finished,* The Simplicity Institute, Melbourne, 2019, at 49–51 (Ch.12, 'The role of a "teacher" in a dying civilisation'), available at https://www.researchgate.net/publication/334067990_This _civilisation_is_finished_Conversations_on_the_end_of_Empire_-_and_what_lies _beyond, accessed 28 April 2021.

the conventional lecture format and that promote student-centred learning outcomes.

In Chapter 5, Stuart Bell explores the role of open access textbooks and other open pedagogies in helping learners rethink their own learning, encouraging them to become producers rather than simply consumers of knowledge. In a similar vein, Ceri Warnock and others, in Chapter 8, describe their use of multidisciplinary approaches to teaching climate law to a mixed cohort of students, with corresponding innovative assessment design. They suggest this can enable a move beyond the 'didactic methods of teaching prevalent in many law schools, where the aim is to deliver a large amount of substantive content through a traditional lecture format'.

In Chapter 7, Ben Boer examines the rationale for the use of small-group teaching methodologies, both generally and within an environmental law class, and then outlines how group-based activities can range from structured discussion and report back activities to self-directed, free form and brainstorming forms of discussion. He also describes other possible applications of the small-group format, including drafting assignments, role-plays, case studies and comparative law exercises.[4] As we have noted above, the deployment of these teaching methodologies, either as alternatives or in addition to the conventional lecture format, may depend on a range of factors. These include class size, teaching facilities and even, in some countries, prescriptive requirements by universities or their law schools concerning the use of the lecture method.[5] Nevertheless, as this contribution demonstrates, there is great potential for the use of innovative approaches to the teaching of environmental law as a means of fostering student-centred learning techniques.

Even where lecturing remains the principal format for the delivery of an environmental law course, there remains room for innovation. As Tracy Bach demonstrates in Chapter 6, it is possible to enhance the student learning experience in a large class by using active learning exercises, video, guest lectures and, where facilities permit, by breaking these classes into smaller groups on occasions. Again, this chapter reflects how the embrace of alternative, creative

---

[4]   The various small-group teaching methodologies identified in this chapter have been the subject of demonstration and discussion in the Training the Teachers (TTT) program developed and delivered by the IUCN Academy of Environmental Law (with support, inter alia, from the Asian Development Bank) in a range of Asian countries between 2012–18. See further, R.J. Fowler, 'The Role of the IUCN Academy of Environmental Law in Promoting the Teaching of Environmental Law' (2017) 8 *IUCNAEL e-Journal*, available at https://www.iucnael.org/en/e-journal/previous -issues/86-journal/issue/640-issue-2017#, accessed 28 April 2021.

[5]   Ibid., at 39.

teaching methodologies by environmental law scholars provides examples that may have a wider application in the field of legal education.

Another context in which environmental law teaching has been at the forefront of innovation in legal education in a number of countries is the development of environmental law clinics. In Chapter 9, Evan Hamman and Jill Heaps provide a survey of the experience with such clinics in Australia and the United States that demonstrates both the popularity and learning benefits of this particular teaching methodology for students. Elsewhere in this book, various contributions identify other methodologies adopted in the course of teaching environmental law, including field trips (see Chapters 3, 4 and 8), and the reflective journal (see Chapter 2).

While mindful of our earlier caution against broad generalisations, the conclusion that we draw from these contributions to this book is that innovation and experimentation with teaching methodologies that constitute alternatives to the conventional lecture has been a distinctive feature of environmental law teaching across many countries. This, in turn, reflects an intellectual dynamism within the discipline of environmental law that we suggest is both impressive and commendable.

The next two parts of the book delve into other contexts for the teaching of environmental law besides an elective or core course on national environmental law within the basic legal curriculum. Part III considers the teaching of international environmental law as a separate subject. The two contributions each examine the use of innovative tools. Alexandre Lillo and Thomas Burelli discuss game-based learning in Chapter 10 and Chris McGrath explores the use of stories in bringing international environmental law to life for students in Chapter 11. There are valuable insights here particularly for those who have focused their scholarship and teaching on international rather than domestic environmental law.

In Part IV, there are four chapters devoted to the emergence of environmental law as a subject of study at the postgraduate level. As noted earlier, this trend has been another distinctive feature of the overall development of environmental law scholarship, particularly as it affords environmental law scholars the opportunity to engage at an advanced level in the classroom with their students. In Chapter 12, Heather McLeod-Kilmurray provides an expansive review of the emergence of specialist postgraduate coursework programmes in environmental law. In Chapter 13, Erika Techera examines how to teach a postgraduate environmental law course to a mixed cohort (that is, classes with both legal and other qualifications) and the use of intensive teaching modes (that is, courses delivered over a short time space). The remaining two chapters in this Part (Chapters 14 and 15), written by Willemien du Plessis and Anél du Plessis, provide a timely examination of the various issues and challenges associated with the supervision and conduct of doctoral research in environmental law. These contributions also provide some broader messages and learnings for general legal scholarship at the doctoral level.

Finally, in Part V, there are three contributions that identify challenges related to the teaching of environmental law and, in the case of Chapter 17, some opportunities for new approaches centred around e-Learning. In Chapter 16, Steve Vaughan and a cohort of his students collectively present the results of a survey conducted by them of environmental law teaching in the United Kingdom that suggests the subject remains marginal in the legal curriculum, and is either static or in decline in terms of its popularity with students and its place in the curriculum. This situation may be particular to the UK, but it may also be a harbinger of developments elsewhere. Universities and law schools in the developed world appear to be facing financial constraints that may give rise to contractions in support for both teaching and research. The COVID-19 global pandemic, which has had an economic impact on universities in many countries, may have exacerbated these constraints. In this changing climate for universities, the established place of environmental law in the legal curriculum could become vulnerable if scholarship and teaching contracts to other areas considered more essential or foundational.

Chapter 18, by Chacrit Sitdhiwej and Rob Fowler, raises similar issues with respect to the teaching of environmental law in Thailand, where the subject struggles still to find a place in the law curriculum and where there is also a shortage of legal scholars with the necessary expertise to teach it. It is difficult to determine to what extent the situation described in Thailand is indicative of a problem on a much wider scale globally, particularly in developing countries, but there is evidence that it is at least representative of the situation in a considerable number of other Asian countries.[6] There is a strong argument for devoting greater attention to the promotion of environmental law scholarship and teaching in countries where it presently lacks recognition or status within the law curriculum. The IUCN Academy of Environmental Law has accepted this challenge by developing and delivering a Training the Teachers (TTT) project in Asia, but this work needs to extend elsewhere also.[7]

In Chapter 17, Amanda Kennedy and Amy Cosby examine the place for e-Learning in environmental law. They contend that environmental law is suited to the online teaching medium for a variety of reasons, not least of which is its potential to lower energy usage and reduce the carbon footprint of students (where travel to campus and use of physical lecture spaces is minimised as a consequence). Online learning platforms can facilitate the sharing of rich multimedia content with students, which is particularly apposite in the

---

[6]   *Supra*, fn.4.
[7]   Ibid.

context of environmental law given the wealth of content available online from documentaries to interactive mapping tools that enable students to better visualise the sites and spaces of the cases they are learning about. E-Learning may also assist in enabling access to study for those who may otherwise be prevented from attending a physical campus; a benefit which has become considerably more relevant in a COVID-19-affected world that has seen the forced closure of university classrooms in many places, and a move to online teaching techniques to enable the continuation of classes. This raises questions, as Kennedy and Cosby note, around the conscious design of learning activities that are suitable for the digital medium, as well as access to the required technical resources by both teachers and students. This chapter provides a valuable and highly topical insight to how this technique can be effectively utilised in the delivery of an environmental law course.

Each of the chapters in this book help to paint a picture of environmental law teaching taking place around the world now. However, they also suggest possibilities for the future and raise important questions for continuing debate amongst the scholarly community. In an attempt to draw the threads together, the rest of this introductory chapter summarises some of the core issues prompted by the contributions to this book.

THE STATUS OF ENVIRONMENTAL LAW IN LEGAL EDUCATION: MARGINAL V MAINSTREAM ACTIVITY?

A contestable but critically important issue concerning environmental law is its perceived 'marginal' status in the legal curriculum. Marginality suggests that a subject sits at the fringes of the discipline of law, is inconsequential, and is seen as a luxury rather than an essential component of a good legal education. There are certain ramifications that flow from the perceived marginality of a subject, not least that its continuing place in the curriculum may be particularly vulnerable to differing ideologies and political undercurrents at state, institutional and even faculty level.

Although the perception of environmental law as having only a marginal disciplinary status may be more prevalent in certain legal cultures as opposed to others, this view has been extended to both its scholarship and its teaching. In an article published in 2009, Fisher et al advanced a vigorous argument concerning the perceived marginality of environmental law, as part of a wider exploration of the 'maturity' of environmental law scholarship.[8] They suggested that environmental law scholars regard the subject as marginal to

---

[8]   *Supra*, fn.2.

mainstream legal scholarship and offer in support explanations that are partly specific to the British situation (a relatively low number of environmental law scholars; and a low output in generalist legal journals) and partly of a more general nature. In the latter regard, they point to the values-based nature of the subject and its connections to alternative politics and new social movements, and to its disconnection from mainstream legal scholarship, which they link to a considerable demand for environmental law teaching from non-law students.[9] While this critique represents an internal, rather than an external assessment by other legal scholars or practitioners, this does not exclude the possibility that the perception may be more widely shared within the legal education system.

The marginality view has also found expression with respect to the teaching of environmental law. In 2018, Scotford and Vaughan observed that:

> Environmental law dominantly being an option suggests that it is an 'extra' to the core of legal learning, a 'nice to have' for students if they care about the environment and can forgo other subjects often perceived as more relevant for their future careers.[10]

In a subsequent publication, Vaughan et al (2019) have argued that 'environmental law is marginal in a number of ways', including a decline in environmental law teaching and static student numbers revealed in their recent survey of British environmental scholars.[11] They also attribute low student interest in the subject to a consideration of their future employability prospects, given that practising lawyers in Britain apparently do not perceive the subject as important in practice.[12] These are important observations that may resonate with environmental law scholars in other countries and they deserve serious consideration. In particular, environmental law remains an outlier in certain countries, especially in some parts of the developing world, as evidenced by the study in this book of the teaching of environmental law in Thailand.

However, it is necessary also to bear in mind our earlier caution about broad generalisations. There are other, contrary indications that environmental law

---

[9] Ibid., at 221–3.

[10] E. Scotford and S. Vaughan, 'Environmental Law and the Core of Legal Learning: Framing the Future of Environmental Lawyers', OUPBlog, 15 August 2018, available at https://blog.oup.com/2018/10/environmental-law-core-legal-learning/, accessed 28 April 2021.

[11] S. Vaughan, et al., 'Of Density and Decline: State of the Nation Reflections on the Teaching of Environmental Law in the UK', (2019) Faculty of Laws University College London Law Research Paper No. 5/2019, available at SSRN: https://ssrn.com/abstract=3395220, accessed 28 April 2021 (a condensed version of this article appears in this book at Chapter 16).

[12] Ibid., at 17–18.

has become a part of mainstream legal scholarship, or is progressing steadily towards this status, in many other parts of the world.[13] Particularly in North America and many parts of Europe, domestic and international environmental law classes, despite their elective status, have a well-established place in the basic legal curriculum and continue to attract relatively large enrolments. In law schools in the United States, there are numerous specialist environmental law clinics[14] and over 80 specialised environmental law journals;[15] in addition, there are various national rankings of law schools for their environmental law programs.[16] In other countries as diverse as South Africa, Australia, Brazil and New Zealand, strong communities of environmental law scholars also are engaging enthusiastically in teaching and research in the field of environmental law. Besides being taught routinely as an elective in the core legal degree, many law schools around the Western world also have established an extensive array of postgraduate coursework Masters' programs in environmental law.[17] The overall picture therefore is of a new and dynamic sub-discipline of law that is evolving by establishing a substantial presence in legal education across many parts of the world.

It is also undesirable to assume there is a direct nexus between the elective status of a subject and its marginality (think of the widespread recognition of family law, human rights law, intellectual property law, taxation law and labour law as legitimate areas of teaching and research within the global legal

---

[13] In fairness to Vaughan et al, we acknowledge that their critique focuses on the UK and does not intend to present a broader picture with respect to environmental law teaching elsewhere.

[14] For a description of the experience with environmental law clinics in the USA and Australia, see Chapter 9.

[15] This figure is cited at fn.117 in M. Blumm, '*Environmental Law* at 50: Cutting-Edge Journal Examining the Central Issues of our Time' (2020) 50 *Env. Law* 1.

[16] See, e.g., *Top Law Schools – Environmental Law* (2019), available at https://www.kaptest.com/study/lsat/best-10-law-schools-for-environmental-law/, accessed 28 April 2021. There is also a thriving and highly active community of environmental law scholars that has its own listserv (ENVLAWPROFESSORS), administered by Professor John Bonine from the Law School, University of Oregon.

[17] A 2020 global ranking of Masters in Environmental Law Courses lists ten courses from the USA, the UK, Australia, the Netherlands and Canada: see LLM Guide, *Top LL.M Programs for Environmental Law 2020,* available at https://llm-guide.com/lists/top-llm-programs-by-speciality/top-llm-programs-for-environmental-law, accessed 28 April 2021. A separate guide for the USA by the same source lists 49 Masters programs in environmental law and related areas in that country alone: see LLM Guide, *LLM Programs in Environmental Law / Energy Law / Resources Law - United States,* available at https://llm-guide.com/schools/usa/concentration/environmental-law-energy-law-resources-law, accessed 28 April 2021. For a discussion of the development of postgraduate coursework programs in environmental law, see Chapter 12.

academy). In addition, while environmental law still may be an elective in many countries, it is moving gradually towards becoming a 'core' subject in the basic legal curriculum in some parts of the world. Interestingly, this is occurring most often in countries outside the Western world,[18] including four of the most populous: India, China, Indonesia and the Philippines. There is no reliable information to assist in determining whether this is a trend confined to the Asian region or that extends elsewhere as well. However, insofar as it has manifested in Asian countries with developing or emerging economies, this may reflect that legal education has been undergoing a rapid expansion in these countries that has allowed greater flexibility in the design of legal curricula than is possible in much of the Western world.

We note also that environmental law scholars are convening together in various parts of the world with increasing regularity to share their scholarship and engage in discussions concerning approaches to the teaching of environmental law. The IUCN Academy of Environmental Law (IUCNAEL) has provided a particular impetus in this regard by convening an annual colloquium that on occasions has attracted several hundred participants, with both a teaching and a research workshop usually preceding the main event. This volume is the result of a project initiated by the Teaching and Capacity-Building Sub-Committee of IUCNAEL, of which all of the editors are members. Within particular countries and regions, meetings of environmental law scholars also are becoming commonplace, reinforcing the growing recognition of environmental law as a legitimate and dynamic new field of legal scholarship. Many of these activities have either emerged or expanded considerably since Fisher et al invited a debate about environmental law scholarship just over a decade ago.

Finally, we note the burgeoning body of publications in the field of environmental law. There is now a wide range of specialist environmental law journals to which scholars in this field regularly contribute articles. In addition, textbooks and specialist treatises on particular aspects of environmental law have found willing publishers across the world. These include the publisher of this volume, Edward Elgar Publishing, which has an entire section of its legal publications dedicated to environmental law, publishes the edited proceedings of the IUCNAEL Colloquia and has commissioned the first Encyclopaedia of Environmental Law. Arguably, environmental law ranks favourably alongside many other areas of law in producing a large and creative publication output,

---

[18]   A notable exception is Australia, where two Law Schools (at the University of Southern Cross (see https://www.scu.edu.au/study-at-scu/courses/bachelor-of-laws-3007083/ accessed 28 April 2021) and the University of South Australia (see https://study.unisa.edu.au/degrees/bachelor-of-laws-honours#section-degree   accessed   28 April 2021)) have designated environmental law as a core subject within their LL.B curriculum.

if we consider these additional avenues for publication alongside generalist legal journals.

Given all these considerations, and embracing our earlier self-caution against making broad or generalised assertions, a qualified conclusion is that environmental law has found a place in the mainstream of legal scholarship and education in many parts of the world. The qualifications are, first, that some significant exceptions exist in this regard, particularly in developing countries, and second, that there is also a perceivable risk that this mainstream status could decline in the near future, or is already declining, in some countries.

Finally, even if the status of environmental law within the law curriculum remains questionable in some places, we suggest that the conception of what represents the core elements of a legal education should not remain static and should reflect contemporary concerns and challenges for human society. From this perspective, environmental law deserves recognition worldwide today as a mainstream area of legal study, given the increasing severity of environmental problems on a global scale that are giving rise to the suggestion of a new epoch named the Anthropocene.[19]

DESIGNING AN ENVIRONMENTAL LAW COURSE (PURPOSE, SCOPE AND CONTENT)

For legal scholars engaged in the teaching of environmental law, whether they are doing so only recently or have been involved in this vocation for many years, there are some significant challenges that they must address in designing their course. We examine these next.

A fundamental task at the outset is to determine the **purpose** (often described as the aims and objectives) of an environmental law course. This involves an issue that has long been the subject of debate in legal education more generally: is the aim to provide a 'scientific', vocational education for the students that they may utilise later in the workforce or is it to provide a 'liberal arts' education that explores the subject matter from related social, political, economic, ethical and other perspectives?[20] This translates into a choice for environmental law teachers whether to present a 'survey' course that covers a relatively wide range of environmental laws or to undertake a deeper examination of one or a few specific aspects of environmental law (e.g., environmental impact assessment, pollution control, hazardous substances or

---

[19]   See C. Hamilton, C. Bonneuil and F. Gemenne, *The Anthropocene and the Global Environmental Crisis, Rethinking Modernity in a New Epoch*, Routledge, 2015.
[20]   For a detailed history of this debate, see J. Krook, 'A Brief History of Legal Education: A Battle between Law as a Science and Law as a Liberal Art' (2017) 17:2 *Legal History* 30, particularly at 42–3.

nature conservation laws). The latter approach can involve the consideration of governance principles, regulatory theory, economics or other perspectives that extend beyond a conventional legal analysis.

The risk for teachers, in opting for a survey approach, is that their students will find themselves buried in a mass of legislative detail without gaining any real appreciation of how the multitudinous provisions operate in practice. This situation prompted the late Professor Joseph Sax to describe American environmental law 30 years ago as '… an encounter with statutes of numbing complexity and detail'.[21] Given also the frequent amendment of most environmental laws in many countries, this assessment is equally pertinent today. On the other hand, the pursuit of relatively sophisticated, social science perspectives to examine the operation of particular aspects of environmental law may involve an excursion into unfamiliar and challenging intellectual territory for students within a basic legal programme and might be better suited to more advanced, postgraduate coursework studies.

A pragmatic middle ground to defining the purpose of an environmental law course might involve examining not only the key regulatory or other elements of whatever aspects of environmental law are selected by the teacher for coverage, but also exploring with students the implementation and effectiveness of these laws. These are two related, but distinct, aspects of the operation of environmental law that can be examined from a relatively non-theoretical perspective, by referring to relevant reports, independent assessments or other evaluations. With respect to implementation, the aim could be to examine the extent to which those responsible for the administration of the relevant legislation and those whose activities are directly regulated or otherwise influenced by it, are complying with their statutory obligations. It can extend also to considering the sanctions or remedies that are available to compel compliance (in particular, through proceedings in the courts or specialist environmental tribunals) and their use in practice. Effectiveness involves an examination of the type of environmental problem that particular environmental legislation seeks to address and whatever evidence exists as to whether the legislation is achieving its stated goals.

This pragmatic approach to defining the purpose of an environmental law course affords students the opportunity to examine the operation of particular laws in a wider political, economic and social context, with a view to considering deeper questions concerning efficiency and accountability. This can extend or supplant traditional methods of legal learning that often focus on the examination of statute and (at least in common law jurisdictions) case law. While

---

[21]　Joseph Sax, 'Environmental Law in the Law Schools: What We Teach and How We Feel About It' (1989) 19 *Environmental Law Report* 10251 at 10251.

this may prove to be uncomfortable territory for some students, for most it is a refreshing opportunity to stretch themselves beyond the confines of much of their other legal studies.

It might also be preferable for students to study environmental law towards the end of the legal curriculum, after they have completed core subjects such as constitutional, administrative, property, criminal and torts law, all of which can have some relevance and application to environmental law. Whether any, or all, of these subjects should be designated as prerequisites is a matter for those designing an environmental law course to consider carefully at the outset and may be determined by the particular course design and content that they adopt.[22]

The **scope** of an environmental law course depends primarily on two factors: first, the purpose and objectives identified for the course (as just discussed), which may influence the extent to which it involves a survey of a wide range of environmental laws; and second, the identification of what laws fall within the ambit of this area of the law. No agreed definition of environmental law exists that can authoritatively determine its ambit, but we suggest there are some broad 'streams' that are readily identifiable and which should be considered when designing the content of an environmental law course. These include:

- Environmental planning laws, which can encompass traditional land-use planning law (though this is often taught separately as a stand-alone, elective subject) and environmental impact assessment law;
- Environmental protection laws covering pollution (air, water, noise and wastes) and various types of environmental risk regulation (concerning chemicals, site contamination and potentially hazardous technologies such as genetic engineering);
- Laws designed to conserve and protect particular aspects of the natural environment (e.g., biodiversity, terrestrial and marine protected areas, endangered species and wetlands) and various forms of 'heritage' (natural, built, cultural and indigenous), many of which provide for the identification, listing and protection of highly-valued components;
- More recently, the new stream of climate change law (which usually requires the study also of particular aspects of energy law), which also may

---

[22] To go a step further, it is arguable that a considerable proportion of the commonly identified 'core' of the law curriculum is teachable from an environmental perspective. See, e.g., Scotford and Vaughan, *supra*, fn.10, where the following question is posed: 'Might we want to restructure some parts of legal degrees to teach key legal concepts and reasoning more explicitly through the framework of environmental problems…?'

be taught in more detail as a separate, stand-alone subject, particularly at the postgraduate, coursework level.

Finally, there is a substantial stream of laws relating to natural resources management which some would argue constitutes a separate and distinct area of scholarship from environmental law. These laws cover the ownership, allocation and utilisation of natural resources such as land, soils, water, forests, minerals, oil and gas (including unconventional gas) and fisheries. However, it is possible to examine some aspects of these laws from an environmental perspective, in particular how and to what extent their traditional objective of promoting the orderly allocation of such resources has been modified by the inclusion of objectives and mechanisms designed to prevent over-allocation of these resources. It is possible also to examine how these laws provide for the management of the environmental and social impacts associated with the extraction or taking of particular resources and the relationship between these measures and the more general environmental planning and protection laws that fall within the first stream mentioned above. Within a 'survey' style of environmental law course, it is still possible to include a component that examines at least selected aspects of natural resources management law (e.g., water resources management law).

With these streams in mind, the environmental law teacher must decide upon the exact **content** of their course. In so doing, several other themes or perspectives of a more general nature also need to be considered, in particular:

–   Whether, in presenting a course on national environmental law, to include some consideration of relevant **international or regional perspectives** (e.g., the nature of relevant environmental problems on these larger scales), the efforts through international and/or regional environmental laws to address these problems, and the extent to which relevant national laws are based upon international or regional treaty commitments;[23]

–   To what extent to explore, possibly at the outset of the course, the underlying **'foundations' of environmental law**, in particular the identification of an over-arching goal such as sustainable development[24] and general legal principles (e.g., precaution, inter-generational equity, polluter pays, pollution prevention etc.) that may have relevance across the various streams;[25]

---

[23]   These considerations may be particularly important when teaching environmental law in countries within the European Union, but could also apply elsewhere, for example within the ASEAN or South Pacific regions.

[24]   See, e.g., D. French and L.J. Kotze (eds), *Sustainable Development Goals: Law, Theory and Implementation*, Edward Elgar Publishing, 2018.

[25]   Australian Panel of Experts in Environmental Law (APEEL), Technical Paper 1, *The Foundations of Environmental Law: Goal, Objects, Principles and Norms* (2017),

- Whether to explore **'normative' aspects of environmental law**, in the form of general environmental rights (e.g., to a clean and healthy environment) arising from human rights[26] and constitutional laws[27] and general environmental duties (e.g., to prevent or minimise environmental harm); and
- Whether to include an examination of the **ethical and philosophical dimensions of environmental law**, including recent literature proposing its substantial re-design as 'wild law'[28] or 'ecological' law[29] or through the recognition of rights for nature.[30]

Finally, there is also the challenge of the **interdisciplinary nature of environmental law**, which involves questions for the teacher about how, and to what extent, to introduce content from other disciplines into an environmental law course. Techera describes the possibilities in this regard as follows:

> Many other disciplines are also relevant, including the physical and social sciences, environmental studies, politics and international relations. It is clear that graduates of environmental law programmes, whether practising lawyers or not, will need to develop an understanding of the role of other disciplines in addressing environmental issues in order to contribute positively to this growing field.[31]

---

available at https://static1.squarespace.com/static/56401dfde4b090fd5510d622/t/58e5f
852d1758eb801c117d8/1491466330447/APEEL_Foundations_for_environmental
_law.pdf accessed 28 April 2021; see also N. de Sadeleer, *Environmental Principles: From Political Slogans to Legal Rules*, Oxford University Press, 2002.

[26] See, e.g., United Nations, Human Rights Council, *Report of the Special Rapporteur on the issue of human rights obligations relating to the enjoyment of a safe, clean, healthy and sustainable environment*, A/HRC/37/59, available at https://undocs .org/en/A/HRC/37/59, accessed 28 April 2021.

[27] See, e.g., J.R. May and E. Daly, *Global Environmental Constitutionalism*, Cambridge: Cambridge University Press, 2014.

[28] See C. Cullinan, *Wild Law, A Manifesto for Earth Justice*, 2nd ed., Green Books, 2017; also, P. Burdon, *Exploring Wild Law, the Philosophy of Earth Jurisprudence*, Wakefield Press, 2011.

[29] See K. Bosselman and P. Taylor, *Ecological Approaches to Environmental Law*, Edward Elgar Publishing, 2017; note also the activities of the Ecological Law and Governance Association (ELGA): see https://www.elgaworld.org/, accessed 28 April 2021.

[30] See R.F. Nash, *The Rights of Nature*, University of Wisconsin Press, 1990; and D.R. Boyd, *The Rights of Nature: A Legal Revolution That Could Save the World*, ECW Press, 2018. There are other, human-centred perspectives that also may be explored, in particular the concept of environmental justice which finds recognition in the principle of intra-generational equity, and the related concept of inter-generational equity.

[31] E.J. Techera, (ed) *Environmental Law, Ethics and Governance*, ID Press, Oxford UK, 2010; UWA Faculty of Law Research Paper No. 2012-04. Available at https://ssrn .com/abstract=2177408 , accessed 28 April 2021.

Within the broad ambit of the social sciences, both economics and governance have particular relevance. For example, the role of economic instruments as an alternative or supplement to legal regulation is a significant issue that may warrant attention in a range of contexts.[32] In addition, environmental governance studies provide insights that can assist students to understand how environmental law operates in practice.[33] Thus, there are multiple disciplinary dimensions that can be addressed in an environmental law course, alongside the various streams and themes identified above.

Many environmental law scholars recognise and accept the interdisciplinary nature of the subject, but there is relatively little discussion concerning how best to approach this aspect in designing and delivering an environmental law course. The obvious limitation for teachers of environmental law is that they are unlikely to have expertise across all of the other relevant disciplines, and cannot expect their students to be capable of embracing these in substantial depth. However, it may still be possible to tackle the interdisciplinary dimensions of the subject in a way that opens the minds of students to different ways of thinking about how environmental law operates, or how it might be re-designed in the future.

To take one example, in considering various forms of risk regulation, it is possible to explore the differences in the legal and scientific conceptions of proof that may arise in such contexts and whether persons with the relevant scientific expertise should make regulatory decisions or whether community input and engagement also is appropriate. Likewise, in teaching climate change law, it is possible, even necessary, to examine the weight of scientific evidence concerning the causes and impacts of climate change, as a background to the study of various legal measures. In these ways, interdisciplinary considerations can be part of a wider exploration of the rationale for particular environmental laws and the examination of their effectiveness, which we have suggested should be a strong focus within an environmental law course.

---

[32] See N. Gunningham and P.N. Grabowsky, *Smart Regulation: Designing Environmental Policy,* Clarendon Press, 1998; also N. Gunningham, 'Environmental Law, Regulation and Governance: Shifting Architectures' (2009) 21:2 *Journal of Environmental Law* 179. Economics also may provide a deeper understanding of principles of environmental law that have been adopted from it, such as the polluter pays principle, and of approaches such as command and control regulation that rely upon the idea of a 'rational economic person' responding in a particular way to maximise utility.
[33] See C. Holley, N. Gunningham and C. Shearing, *The New Environmental Governance,* Earthscan, 2012.

CHALLENGES IN TEACHING ENVIRONMENTAL LAW IN THE FUTURE

To conclude this introduction, we offer some thoughts on two major challenges in relation to the future direction of environmental law teaching that warrant further attention.

The first is the need to expand the number of legal scholars who are equipped to teach environmental law in countries, particularly in the less-developed world, where currently there is a shortage of such experience. In this regard, the further deployment of 'training-the-teachers' programmes, such as that developed by IUCNAEL and subsequently delivered across a range of Asian countries, should be a high priority. Alongside adding to the teaching ranks, such programmes can demonstrate and promote participatory and innovative teaching practices of the kind described in this book. In addition, there is also a need to address the lack of specialised teaching resources (textbooks, specialist journals) and of access to digital teaching materials and technologies in many countries.

The fundamental challenge therefore is to find the resources to help address these deficiencies, whether it is through internal funding by governments, international funding through aid agencies and development banks, or with the support of philanthropic foundations. The global community of environmental law scholars should where possible promote this agenda to potential funders, and organisations such as IUCNAEL should continue to lead efforts in this regard.

The second challenge relates to the impact of technological innovation on the teaching of environmental law. At the most basic level, as has just been noted, this involves providing expanded access to digital teaching technologies in the classroom, especially in many lesser-developed countries. However, this technology-related challenge goes much further. The COVID-19 global pandemic has resulted in the closure of face-to-face teaching in universities around the world and forced many students to rely largely on digital, distance-learning technologies and materials to continue their studies, where these are available.[34] Whether this proves to be a temporary measure, or becomes a longer-term trend in teaching delivery for the many universities that are identifying cost-cutting measures in the wake of the pandemic, remains to be seen.[35] Reliance upon digital technologies for distance learning, rather

---

[34] See International Association of Law Schools, *Transitioning to Online Legal Education: The Student Voice,* July 2020 (copy on file with the authors).

[35] For an argument that it may be unsafe for law teachers to resume classroom teaching while the coronavirus continues to circulate, see T. Duane, *Teaching Law in*

than the delivery of face-to-face teaching, may represent a far more common approach to the teaching of law, including environmental law, in the future.[36]

Other consequences of recent technology innovation also are likely to require consideration in the near future. Specifically, with respect to environmental law, teachers may need to explore with their students the particular application of technologies such as remote sensing, modelling and data analytics in the operation of environmental law. More generally, legal education will need to come to terms with the emergence of artificial intelligence, algorithms, machine learning, big data and analytics in relation to the operation of the legal system and the practice of law in the future. These are challenges for legal education and environmental law in a rapidly changing world that demand greater attention in the near future.

CONCLUSION

At the beginning of this chapter, we offered three justifications for the publication of this book, to which we will now return with some concluding remarks.

First, we suggested that the emergence of environmental law over the past 50 years as a significant new area of legal scholarship justifies a closer examination of how it is taught. Fisher et al have argued that environmental law suffers from an intellectual 'incoherence' that often reduces courses on the subject to 'superficial surveys'.[37] An alternative perspective, which may be supported by the contributions to this book, is that environmental law presents a rich intellectual 'diversity' that provides both challenges and rewards for those engaged in scholarship and teaching in this exciting field.

Second, we noted a range of challenges that are particular to the teaching of environmental law that deserve closer attention, including the identification of the purpose and content of an environmental law course. In addressing this challenge, teachers of the subject may need to acquire sufficient expertise across all of the potential legal streams and themes mentioned earlier to feel confident in making suitable choices with respect to their course content.[38] An

---

the Time of COVID-19, unpublished paper circulated by the author on the envlawprofs listserv, 7 July 2020.

[36] This may be just one part of a wider social trend that involves people working from home more often and avoiding gatherings in larger groups for social, entertainment, sporting or other activities.

[37] *Supra*, fn.2.

[38] The difficulty in doing so is exacerbated by the fact that many, if not most, scholars will be expected to be involved in teaching one or more core areas of the legal curriculum, with which they must therefore keep pace alongside their environmental law scholarship.

acceptable alternative, now adopted by many environmental law scholars, is to focus their scholarship on particular areas within the discipline and to reflect this in the way in which they design and deliver their own environmental law course.

Third, we highlighted the use of innovative and distinctive teaching methodologies by environmental law teachers. We have sought to present many of these methodologies through the contributions to this book. We hope it will provide ideas and inspiration to all who are involved in, or about to embark upon, teaching a course in environmental law and that its audience will extend to legal educators more generally.

PART I

Values-based dimensions of environmental law

2. Engendering hope in environmental law students

Lynda Collins and Brandon D. Stewart

I. INTRODUCTION

As law professors interested in sustainability, one of our most important jobs is to educate and motivate the next generation of environmental advocates and decision-makers. In particular, we should strive to create *effective* environmental lawyers and policy-makers. To do this, we must support our students in cultivating their mental health and happiness. Scientific research demonstrates that happy workers are more creative, proactive, collaborative, committed and effective.[1] In contrast, unhappy workers are more likely to experience health problems, absenteeism and burnout.[2] The deliberate cultivation of happiness is therefore crucial for every environmental lawyer – from plaintiff-side litigators to those who work for corporate clients or the government. However, legal education has too often failed to assist students in maintaining their mental health, and has in fact tended to do the opposite.[3]

Students in environmental law courses may face additional mental health challenges compared to their counterparts, as they confront daunting environmental issues, such as climate change, that invariably raise existential concerns for those who take them seriously.[4] Thus, the need to increase competency in mental health skills may be even more pronounced in the environmental law classroom. This chapter will argue that environmental law professors urgently

---

[1] C D Fisher, 'Happiness at Work' (2010) *International Journal of Management Reviews* at 399; S Cote, 'Affect and Performance in Organizational Settings' (1999) 8 *Current Directions in Psychological Science* at 65–8.

[2] Ibid.

[3] See generally Todd David Peterson and Elizabeth Waters Peterson, 'Stemming the Tide of Law Student Depression: What Law Schools Need to Learn from the Science of Positive Psychology' (2009) 9 *Yale Journal of Health Policy & Ethics*.

[4] Molly S Casstelloe, 'Coming to Terms with Ecoanxiety' (2018) Psychology Today, on-line: https://www.psychologytoday.com/gb/blog/the-me-in-we/201801/coming-terms-ecoanxiety, accessed 28 April 2021.

need to embrace a pedagogy of hope, consciously teaching an approach to environmental law that is psychologically sustainable over time.

II.   THE CHALLENGE: ANXIETY AND DEPRESSION IN ENVIRONMENTAL LAW STUDENTS

Students and practitioners of public interest environmental law enjoy an important advantage with respect to career happiness; they tend to have a strong sense of purpose, which has been positively associated with increased happiness and job satisfaction.[5] But environmental law students and lawyers are also at risk: the complex, severe and stubborn nature of environmental problems such as climate change gives rise to real challenges to mental health. As Koger et al. explain, '[i]t is well known that depressive symptoms including feelings of anxiety, paralysis, and lack of motivation occur when the causes of events are seen as unchangeable and global; this is particularly relevant to issues of environmental degradation'.[6] The resulting phenomenon of 'burnout' is well known in the environmental community.[7] As with the general population, students who focus on the complexity and immensity of global environmental challenges run the risk of becoming cynical, immobilized, anxious or depressed. On the other hand, those who focus on a positive vision of sustainable societies and the solubility of environmental problems are arguably more likely to take effective action to address them:[8]

> It seems crucial to build motivation from a positive, rather than a negative, source. Consider the civil rights movement: 'Martin Luther King Jr.'s "I have a dream" speech is famous because it put forward an inspiring, positive vision that carried a critique of the current moment within it…[H]ad King given an "I have a nightmare" speech instead' the movement might have turned out differently. Comparably, Roszak, the [founder] of Ecopsychology, warned about the 'green guilt and ecological overload' conveyed by many environmental initiatives.[9]

In addition to the mental health problems that may affect any environmentalist, environmental law students also struggle with the significant stresses created

---

[5]   Michael F Steger et al., 'Measuring Purpose at Work: the Work and Meaning Inventory' (2012) 20 *Journal of Career Assessment* 322.

[6]   Susan M Koger et al., 'Climate Change: Psychological Solutions and Strategies for Change' (2011) 3(4) *Ecopsychology* 227 at 228 (internal citations omitted).

[7]   See Jeff Warren, 'Environmentalist and the Mind' (2013) Psychology Tomorrow, on-line: http://psychologytomorrowmagazine.com/environmentalism-and-the-mind/, accessed 28 April 2021.

[8]   Koger *supra* note 6; see also, David Boyd, *The Optimistic Environmentalist* (Toronto: ECW Press, 2015).

[9]   Koger, ibid., at 228 (internal citations omitted).

by law school. Substantial empirical research from the developed world has shown that law students suffer a significant deterioration in mental health during law school, and the high incidence of anxiety, depression and substance abuse continues into legal practice.[10] In the developing world, specific research on law student mental health is generally lacking, but there is strong evidence of mental health challenges among university students[11] and students in professional schools in particular.[12] There is also significant anecdotal evidence of mental health challenges among lawyers in the developing world.[13] To summarize, available data suggests that legal education (and the practice of law) as we know it seems to undermine the health and happiness of our students. However, research has also shown that effective strategies exist for improving student mental health generally,[14] and law student mental health in particular.[15]

---

[10]   Adele Bergin and Kenneth Pakenham, 'Law Student Stress: Relationships Between Academic Demands, Social Isolation, Career Pressure, Study/Life Imbalance and Adjustment Outcomes in Law Students' (2015) 22(3) *Psychology, Psychiatry and the Law* 388; Catherine M Leahy et al., 'Distress Levels and Self-Reported Treatment Rates for Medicine, Law, Psychology and Mechanical Engineering Tertiary Students: Cross-Sectional Study' Australia and New Zealand Journal of Psychiatry on-line: https://doi.org/10.3109/00048671003649052, accessed 28 April 2021.

[11]   See e.g., Caleb J Othieno et al., 'Depression Among University Students in Kenya: Prevalence and Sociodemographic Correlates' (2014) 165 *Journal of Affective Disorders* 120; Atieq Ul Rehman, 'Academic Anxiety Among Higher Education Students in India' (2016) 5(2) *International Journal of Modern Social Sciences* 102; 'Depression Among Chinese University Students: Prevalance and Socio-Demographic Correlates' (2013) PLoS One. 2013;8(3):e58379. doi: 10.1371/journal.pone.0058379. Epub 2013 Mar 13.

[12]   See e.g., M Dafaalla, A Farah, S Bashir et al., 'Depression, Anxiety, and Stress in Sudanese Medical Students: A Cross Sectional Study on Role of Quality of Life and Social Support' (2016) 4 *Am J Educ Res* at 937–42; A Obarisiagbon, et al., 'Clinical Anxiety Among Final Year Dental Students: The Trainers and Students Perspectives' (2013) 16 *Sahel Med J* 64–70.

[13]   Govind Manoharan, 'The Impaired Lawyer: Why we Need to Talk about Mental Health in the Legal Profession' (2016) on-line: https://caravanmagazine.in/vantage/mental-health-legal-profession, accessed 28 April 2021.

[14]   See e.g., Bernedeth Ezegbe et al., 'Impacts of Cognitive-behavioral Intervention on Anxiety and Depression Among Social Science Education Students: A Randomized Controlled Trial' (2019) *Medicine (Baltimore)*, on-line: https://www.ncbi.nlm.nih.gov/pubmed/30985642, accessed 28 April 2021.

[15]   Ian Ayres et al., 'Anxiety Psychoeducation for Law Students: A Pilot Program' (2017) 67(1) *Journal of Legal Education* 118.

III.   SOLUTIONS 101: IMPROVING STUDENT WELLBEING IN LAW SCHOOLS

Many law faculties and professional organizations now provide extensive mental health support to students, including professional counselling (whether on-line or in-person), peer support, mindfulness training, free fitness classes, etc.[16] Some law schools also offer specialized for-credit courses in mental health and wellness in the law.[17] Environmental law students should be encouraged to take advantage of these resources wherever they exist. Moreover, like all law students, environmental law students should be strongly encouraged to invest in good relationships, physical fitness, fun and leisure, and anything else that will promote their overall life satisfaction, as this will increase both academic success and general wellbeing.[18]

Given the central importance of mental health in the study and practice of environmental law, professors and students alike should also consider taking advantage of the significant body of free, web-based courses on wellbeing that have been made available by major universities.[19] The University of California at Berkeley, for example, has created a free on-line course entitled 'Foundations of Happiness at Work' that identifies the basic prerequisites

---

[16]   See e.g., Centre for Innovation in Campus Mental Health, 'Ontario Law Student Mental Health Initiative: Enhancing the Mental Health Outcomes of Ontario's Law Students', on-line: https://campusmentalhealth.ca/initiatives/ontario-law-student -mental-health-initiative/, accessed 28 April 2021; American Bar Association 'Mental Health Resources [for students]' https://abaforlawstudents.com/events/initiatives-and -awards/mental-health-resources/ accessed 28 April 2021; Canadian Bar Association, 'JustBalance', on-line: https://www.justbalance.ca/resources/ accessed 28 April 2021; Stanford Law School, 'WellnessCast' on-line: https://law.stanford.edu/media/ wellnesscast/ accessed 28 April 2021.

[17]   See e.g., the University of California at Berkeley, 'Mindfulness for Lawyers: Understanding the Legal Mind for Greater Effectiveness and Wellbeing in the Study and Practice of Law', on-line: https://www.law.berkeley.edu/students/mindfulness -at-berkeley-law/courses/ accessed 28 April 2021; see also 'Western law students being taught how to relax' on-line https://www.cbc.ca/news/canada/london/western -university-mindfulness-mediation-thomas-telfer-1.4583836 accessed 28 April 2021.

[18]   Susan Antaramian, 'The Importance of Very High Life Satisfaction for Students' Academic Success' (2017) 4(1) *Cogent Education*.

[19]   See e.g., the Yale College course, 'Psychology and the Good Life', which focuses on happiness and has become the most popular course in Yale's history (Mara Leighton, 'Yale's most popular class ever is now available for free online — and the topic is how to be happier in your daily life', Business Insider (April 4, 2019), on-line: https://www.businessinsider.com/coursera-yale-science-of-wellbeing-free -course-review-overview, accessed 28 April 2021). An on-line version of the course is now available for free under the name 'The Science of Wellbeing' (see, https://www .coursera.org/learn/the-science-of-well-being, accessed 28 April 2021).

for sound mental health in the workplace and includes practical instruction in accessible techniques that students, professors and practitioners can use to improve their own happiness at work immediately and over the long term.[20] These resources are particularly relevant to students and faculty in developing world universities that may not currently offer for-credit courses in these areas, and may provide less institutional support for mental health due to resource limitations.[21]

Moreover, as professors of environmental law, we can make specific, evidence-based pedagogical choices to improve our students' mental health and motivation.

IV.   SOLUTIONS 102: TEACHING HOPE IN ENVIRONMENTAL LAW

As educators, we have the power to influence environmental law students to choose hope over despair. Many environmental law professors may intuitively sense the importance of modelling positive attitudes and sharing stories of environmental law's many successes, but some might not be aware of the excellent resources available to assist them in adding hope to the environmental law curriculum. Below we offer two concrete options for integrating mental health and wellbeing into the teaching of environmental law.

A.   The Pedagogy of Hope

In their ground-breaking interdisciplinary research, Martin and Rand found that 'hope predicts both academic performance and psychological wellbeing…'.[22] Fortunately, relevant research also demonstrates that law professors can effectively 'engender' hope in their students by making specific pedagogical changes.[23] In particular, student academic performance and mental health improve when professors implement the following principles:

> A) help law students formulate appropriate goals [specifically those focused on learning outcomes, rather than grades] B) increase student autonomy [eg by pro-

---

[20]   On-line: https://www.edx.org/course/the-foundations-of-happiness-at-work, accessed 28 April 2021.

[21]   See 'MOOCs are benefiting developing countries the most', on-line: https://www.qs.com/moocs-are-benefiting-who/, accessed 28 April 2021.

[22]   Allison D Martin and Kevin L Rand, 'The Future's So Bright, I Gotta Wear Shades: Law School Through the Lens of Hope' (2010) 48 *Duquesne Law Rev* 203 at 205.

[23]   Ibid. See also Rachael Field and James Duffy, 'Better to Light a Single Candle than to Curse the Darkness: Promoting Law Student Well-being through a First Year

viding choices in methods of evaluation] C) model the learning process D) help law students understand grading as feedback rather than pure evaluation [of a student's intelligence or worth] E) model and encourage [positive] thinking.[24]

A substantial body of scholarship on the legal 'pedagogy of hope' exists to assist environmental law professors who wish to learn and implement these techniques.[25] But we would emphasize that the pedagogy of hope does not necessarily require a radical re-visioning of existing syllabi and can be gradually implemented, beginning with the basic awareness of how we talk about our subject-matter and a continuous effort to choose more positive framing of both the process of learning law and the potential of environmental law practice. The science of positive psychology also demonstrates that simple, daily practices (such as those taught in the on-line courses discussed above) can increase the mental health and efficacy of law students and the lawyers they become.[26] Environmental law professors may wish to consider familiarizing themselves with these basic techniques and teaching them in their classes.

In addition to these cross-cutting pedagogical approaches, environmental law professors should highlight the many and dramatic successes of environmental law and policy.[27]

B.   The Power of Success Stories

Imagine that an aluminium plant begins operations in a new community. The plant employs many local residents, but its emissions drift onto nearby orchards owned by fruit growers, damaging their crops. The fruit growers hire a lawyer who sues the plant, seeking damages to cover the past crop losses and an injunction requiring the plant to install pollution controls. Years later, the fruit growers win at trial and the plant is directed to install a pollution control technology system. The fruit growers' lawyer is then retained by property owners across the country for their litigation with other facilities. Public

---

Law Subject' (2012) 12(2) *QUT Law and Justice Journal* 133; Nancy Schultz, 'Lessons from Positive Psychology for Developing Advocacy Skills' (2013) 6 *John Marshall L J* 103; Carol L Wallinger, 'Autonomy Support 101: How Using Proven Autonomy Support Techniques Can Increase Law Student Autonomy, Engender Hope and Improve Outcomes' (2010) 48 *Duquesne Law Rev* 385.

[24]   Martin and Rand, *supra* note 22.

[25]   See e.g., Julia Glencer et al., 'The Fruits of Hope: Student Evaluations' (2010) 48 *Duquesne Law Rev* 233; Schultz, *supra* note 23.

[26]   See e.g., Wendy Kersemaekers et al., 'A Workplace Mindfulness Intervention May Be Associated with Improved Psychological Wellbeing' (2018) 9 *Frontiers in Psychology* doi:10.3389/fpsyg.2018.00195, accessed 28 April 2021.

[27]   See, *infra* note 34.

concern over pollution increases and legislation is passed requiring facilities to install the best available pollution control technology. Given his past work, the lawyer is appointed as a state's assistant attorney general to help negotiate with facilities to ensure their compliance with the new legislation.[28]

While some environmental law students might aspire to the same type of successful career as the fruit growers' lawyer, most would be surprised to learn that this story is true.[29] Indeed, many of our most dramatic environmental success stories are missing from modern environmental law curricula. Students instead survey the main environmental law statutes, regulations, policies and judicial decisions in the field and discuss 'hot topics' like climate change.[30] And like many law school courses, the instruction students receive is problem-oriented, which invites,[31] and even rewards,[32] a certain level of pessimism.

Creating an environmental law curriculum that embraces optimism is not as challenging as it may at first seem. There are several helpful resources that highlight the many successes of environmental law and policy.[33] For example,

---

[28]   Adapted from the detailed hypothetical (and true story) in Douglas A Kysar, 'The Public Life of Private Law: Tort Law as a Risk Regulation Mechanism' (2018) 9 *EJRR* 48 at 58–61.

[29]   Ibid., at pp 62–3, citing *Renken v. Harvey Aluminum Inc*, 226 F Supp 169 (D Or 1963).

[30]   This is often out of necessity since environmental law is 'simply too large, too sprawling, and too complex' to be taught 'soup to nuts' (Michael Robinson Dorn, 'Teaching Environmental Law in the Era of Climate Change: A Few Whats, Whys, and Hows' (2007) 82 *Wash L Rev* 619 at 632).

[31]   Yale Law Professor, E Donald Elliott, explains the problem in this way:
   American culture is very critical, both of ourselves and of others. We sometimes overlook our successes in our effort to use law and regulation to better manage the relationship between human beings and the natural environment and focus exclusively on our continuing challenges, which are also many
(E Donald Elliott, 'U.S. Environmental Law in Global Perspective: Five Do's and Five Don'ts from Our Experience' (2010) 5(2) *NTU L Rev* 143 at 145).
We add that it is easy to forget our historical successes in the face of existing problems. This is why Purdy argues that professors should use historical materials to understand 'the defining commitments of…[major environmental]…statutes and their significance in the development of…[our]…ideas of nature' (Jedidiah Purdy, 'The Politics of Nature: Climate Change, Environmental Law, and Democracy' (2010) 119 *Yale LJ* 1122 at 1204).

[32]   See Martin E P Seligman et al., 'Why Lawyers are Unhappy' (2001–2002) 23 *Cardozo L Rev* 33, finding that pessimistic law students had higher levels of achievement, in terms of GPA and law journal success, than their more optimistic peers.

[33]   See Oliver A Houck, *Taking Back Eden: Eight Environmental Law Cases that Changed the World* (Washington, DC: Island Press, 2010); Jane Goodall, *A Reason for Hope – A Spiritual Journey* (New York: Warner Books, 1999); David Suzuki and Holly Dressell, *Good News for a Change: How Everyday People are Helping the Planet*

David R Boyd's *The Optimistic Environmentalist*[34] presents several inspiring, but widely under-acknowledged, success stories – such as the dramatic recovery of many endangered species and the global triumph over ozone depletion[35] – to demonstrate our capacity to overcome environmental challenges and achieve a 'bright green future'.[36] Boyd also mentions a success story that continues to gain global attention: the recognition of the right to a healthy environment. Since the 1970s, there has been an 'environmental rights revolution', resulting in the constitutionalization of the right to a healthy environment in the majority of the world's nations. Constitutional environmental rights have created real environmental change, particularly in regions where citizens have meaningful access to justice.

For example, the Supreme Court of India ordered the City of Delhi to convert its huge fleet of diesel buses to compressed natural gas to ameliorate air quality, saving many thousands of lives as a result.[37] In the Philippines, the judiciary imposed detailed, ongoing and ambitious remedies resulting in massive remediation efforts that cleaned up the most polluted watershed in that nation.[38] In a similar case from Argentina concerning the highly polluted Matanza-Riachuelo river basin, the Supreme Court required the government to conduct a comprehensive environmental assessment of the river, to inspect all polluting facilities, close illegal dumps, clean up the river banks, improve the storm water, sewage and wastewater systems, and develop a regional environmental health plan.[39] Hundreds of thousands of people now enjoy access to safe drinking water and sanitation as a result of these judgments.[40]

(Vancouver: Greystone Books, 2002); Tony Oposa, *Shooting Stars and Dancing Fish: A Walk to the World We Want* (Cebu City, the Philippines: RAFI, 2017).

[34]   Boyd, *supra* note 8.

[35]   Ibid., at pp 3–25, 89–99.

[36]   Ibid., at xi, xxiii.

[37]   U Narain and R Bell Greenspan, *Who Changed Delhi's Air? The Roles of the Court and the Executive in Environmental Policymaking* (Washington, DC: Resources for the Future, 2005).

[38]   *Manila v. Concerned Residents of Manila Bay* [2008] 171947-48 (Supreme Court of the Philippines).

[39]   *Beatriz Silvia Mendoza et al. v. National Government et al. (Damages stemming from contamination of the Matanza-Riachuelo River)*, M. 1569, July 8, 2008, Supreme Court of Argentina.

[40]   Boyd, *supra* note 8 at 94.

How can environmental law professors integrate success stories like these into the classroom? Psychology professors Russo-Netzer and Ben-Shahar suggest this approach:

> Stories form an important part of every class…regardless of whether they are personal stories or stories about other people. Each of the topics discussed in the course includes presenting a story as an introduction to research on the topic, followed by an application. In other words, the story 'sets the stage' for a study or a theory, which in turn leads to action—the implications of the ideas presented and how they can be implemented in 'real-life'.[41]

Law professors can 'set the stage' in a number of ways that complement their method of instruction and evaluation, course content and classroom dynamic. For example, they might: (1) use a success story to introduce each major topic covered in a course; (2) discuss a success story for certain challenging topics, such as those related to climate change; (3) have students identify and then present a weekly success story as part of a participation or discussion exercise; and/or (4) invite guest speakers to share their own success stories.

The study of environmental success stories serves several important purposes. First, it may provide psychological benefits to students. Positive psychologists report that storytelling can help students cope with anxiety and depression.[42] Writing positive, personal stories has also been found to increase optimism in students,[43] which itself is associated with mental and physical health benefits.[44] Existing studies, however, do not evaluate legal stories and/or case studies and further research is required to determine whether the above results may be replicated in the environmental law classroom. We remain hopeful that studying success stories will increase student optimism around environmental problems and, at the very least, serve as a buffer against the

---

[41]   P Russo-Netzer and T Ben-Shahar, 'Learning from Success: A Close Look at a Popular Positive Psychology Course' (2011) 6 *Positive Psychology J* 468 at 472.

[42]   Daniel J Tomasulo and James O Pawelski, 'Happily Ever After: The Use of Stories to Promote Positive Interventions' (2012) 3(12) *Psychology* 1189 at 1191–4.

[43]   See, e.g., Madelon L Peters et al., 'Manipulating Optimism: Can Imagining a Best Possible Self be used to Increase Positive Future Expectancies?' (2010) 5(3) *Positive Psychology J* 204.

[44]   For example, optimism has been found to benefit law students' health (see Suzanne C Segerstrom and Sandra E Sephton, 'Optimistic Expectancies and Cell-Mediated Immunity: The Role of Positive Affect' (2010) 21(3) *Psychol Sci* 448 (finding that optimism about law school boosted immunity)).

steady stream of negative stories emanating from the media,[45] expert reports[46] and critical environmental law scholarship.[47]

Second, a deep familiarity with environmental law success stories[48] should help students develop problem-solving skills.[49] Research in cognitive psychology demonstrates that having a familiarity with similar problems improves problem-solving skills.[50] As students gain exposure to success stories, they

---

[45] Media coverage in general trends overwhelmingly toward the negative, with significant psychological consequences for consumers. See Stuart Soroka and Stephen McAdams, 'News, Politics and Negativity' (2015) 32 *Political Communication* 1; J Singal, 'What all this Bad News is Doing to Us', *New York,* Aug 8, 2014.

[46] See, e.g., Intergovernmental Panel on Climate Change, 'Special Report: Global Warming at 1.5°C' (United Nations, October, 2018), online: https://www.ipcc.ch/sr15/, accessed 28 April 2021, finding that even if the commitments under the *Paris Agreement* are met, urgent and unprecedented action is still required over the next 12 years to limit global warming to 1.5°C above pre-industrial levels; see also, Carl Bruch et al., 'Environmental Rule of Law: First Global Report' (UN Environment, January 2019), online: https://wedocs.unep.org/bitstream/handle/20.500.11822/27279/Environmental_rule_of_law.pdf?sequence=1&isAllowed=y, accessed 28 April 2021, concluding that while environmental laws have significantly increased since 1972, there is a widespread failure to enforce these laws globally.

[47] See, e.g., David Boyd, *Unnatural Law: Rethinking Canadian Environmental Law and Policy* (Vancouver: UBC Press, 2003) (detailing the legal system's role in Canada's weak environmental performance); Stepan Wood, et al., 'What Ever Happened to Canadian Environmental Law?' (2010) 37 *Eco LQ* 981, explaining why Canada has become a laggard in both legal reform and environmental policy; Bruce A Ackerman and Richard B Stewart, 'Reforming Environmental Law' (1985) 37 *Stan L Rev* 1333 at 1333, critiquing America's environmental regulatory system; Douglas A Kysar, 'What Climate Change Can Do About Tort Law?' (2011) 40 *Environmental Law* 1, reviewing the doctrinal hurdles facing climate change tort plaintiffs and concluding that the pessimism of legal scholars is justified. But see, Daniel C Esty, 'Red Lights to Green Lights: From 20th Century Environmental Regulation to 21st Century Sustainability' (2017) 47 *ELR* 1, (calling for a shift in U.S. environmental policy that highlights environmental leaders over laggards.

[48] Students may also benefit from an even broader approach that situates environmentalism in the history of public interest movements and litigation.

[49] See, e.g., Martha C Munroe and Stephen Kaplan, 'When Words Speak Louder Than Actions: Environmental Problem Solving in the Classroom' (2010) 19(3) *JEE* 38, finding that case studies of successful solutions to environmental problems and encouraging discussions of actual problem-solving experiences were the most effective teaching strategies for developing environmental problem-solving skills among high school and college students; see also, Martha Minow, 'Stories in Law' in Rickie Solinger et al. (eds), *Telling Stories to Change the World: Global Voices on the Power of Narrative to Build Community and Make Social Justice Claims* (New York: Routledge, 2008) 249 at 250, noting that some writers advocate for the use of stories to teach practical problem-solving.

[50] Munroe and Kaplan, ibid., at 38.

should be able to identify key features that characterize an environmental opportunity, such as the presence of an organized movement to support law reform and litigation measures, relatable environmental communication that engages the sympathies of decision-makers[51] and financial motivations to draw advocates[52] or governments to a cause.[53] Armed with this critical practical skill, students would be better prepared to be successful environmental lawyers.[54]

Finally, exposing students to these success stories might serve a more fundamental and ambitious purpose: to help build optimistic environmentalists – what Boyd describes as citizens who are ecologically literate and inspired to act in ways that support and achieve a sustainable future.[55] As one of us has argued elsewhere, the journey 'from crisis to sustainability' is as much an intellectual, ethical and social process as it is a technical, legal and economic one.[56] Students need to know that real change is possible in order to play a meaningful role in effecting such change. Bardwell expresses this same idea – and the importance of students knowing what success looks like – using a cognitive psychology framework:

> Active participation in environmental issues depends on several factors: how one understands the issues, how competent one feels about doing something about

---

[51]   For example, courts have been receptive to rights-based arguments in recent climate change litigation in North America, Europe and Latin America,(see, Jacqueline Peel and Hari M Osofsky, 'A Rights Turn in Climate Change Litigation?' (2017) 7 *Transnational Env L* 37; see also, Grace Nosek, 'Climate Change Litigation and Narrative: How to Use Litigation to Tell Compelling Climate Stories' (2018) 42 *Wm & Mary Envtl L & Poly* 733). There is also a growing body of literature on the science of science communication and how to overcome conflict or inaction around climate change, see, Dan M Kahan, 'Making Climate-Science Communication *Evidence*-based: All the Way Down' in Deseria A Crow and Maxwell T Boykoff (eds), *Culture, Politics and Climate Change: How Information Shapes Our Common Future* (New York: Routledge, 2014), 203–20.

[52]   Toxic tort litigation can be immensely profitable, particularly when there is scientific consensus on the harmfulness of a product or substance.

[53]   See, Martin Olszynski et al., 'From Smokes to Smokestacks: Lessons from Tobacco for the Future of Climate Change Liability' (2017) 30 *Georgetown Envtl L Rev* 1 at 9–14, recounting how Canada and the U.S. attempted to recover billions in public health care costs against tobacco manufacturers.

[54]   This might help address the concern that graduating law students are not well-equipped to practise law – especially specialized fields like environmental law – competently (Dorn, *supra* note 30 at 625).

[55]   Boyd, *supra* note 8 at xxiii, 199.

[56]   Lynda Collins and Lorne Sossin, 'Approach to Constitutional Principles and Environmental Discretion in Canada' (2019) 52 *UBC L Rev* 293 at 327, citing James Gustave Speth, *The Bridge at the Edge of the World: Capitalism, the Environment, and Crossing from Crisis to Sustainability* (New Haven: Yale University Press, 2008).

them, and what kinds of imagery one has for what to do...Success stories hold promise in terms of helping people build more adequate [cognitive] models about environmental problems and their role in addressing them. While acknowledging environmental realities, these stories establish norms for seeing those realities as challenges [instead of eventualities].[57]

Success stories therefore have the potential to empower students to imagine a sustainable future and spur action to bring that future about.

The study of environmental success stories is not without some challenges. Environmental law courses already cover a substantial amount of material and law professors must carefully balance substantive, theoretical and practical content. Adding success stories requires sacrificing some of this content. What to cut is a personal choice for each law professor, but we argue that the potential benefits of this pedagogical approach for students make the effort worthwhile.

Another pitfall is if law professors focus disproportionately on success stories or their impact, which might create unrealistic student expectations about the challenges faced by environmental advocates – expectations that might face a harsh reality after graduation. This risk is easy to manage if law professors practise what Rosen calls 'flexible optimism' – that is, using optimism only when it is helpful, while still allowing room for healthy scepticism and critical dialogue.[58] Moreover, the use of success stories should be complemented by the more general mental health skills discussed above, so as to improve resilience in environmental law students. The core goal should be to create an atmosphere where students feel encouraged to pursue meaningful careers in environmental law and policy, where they know how to succeed as environmental lawyers *and* have the emotional skills to cope when they fail. The key is to maintain balance in course content, contextualize success stories honestly and frankly and empathetically address student questions and concerns.[59]

---

[57] Lisa Bardwell, 'Success Stories: Imagery by Example' (1991) 23(1) *JEE* 5 at 10.

[58] Corie Rosen, 'Creating the Optimistic Classroom: What Law Schools Can Learn from Attribution Style Effects' (2011) 42 *McGeorge L Rev* 319 at 336–8.

[59] See, e.g., Maria Ojala, 'Hope in the Face of Climate Change: Associations with Environmental Engagement and Student Perceptions of Teachers' Emotion Communication Style and Future Orientation' (2015) 46(3) *JEE* 133, finding that constructive hope in Swedish high school students was positively associated with: (1) a teacher's positive communication style and respect for students' negative emotions concerning societal issues; and (2) environmental engagement. The author concludes (at p. 144) that 'if teachers want to promote constructive hope concerning climate change, it is wise to take into account negative emotions evoked by information about this problem among the students, to take these emotions seriously, and to use them as teachable moments'.

V.   CONCLUSION

Environmental law students face significant mental health challenges beyond the typical stresses of law school, as they are consistently confronted by formidable environmental problems like climate change. In order to maximize their potential as environmental advocates, our students will need to acquire competence in managing their own mental health. To this end, we have offered two concrete options for supporting students' mental health and happiness in the environmental law classroom: (1) 'engendering' hope in students through specific pedagogical changes, such as helping students formulate goals focused on learning outcomes, increasing student autonomy, and modelling and encouraging positive thinking; and (2) cultivating student optimism by highlighting the significant successes of environmental law and policy. These options do not require radical changes to the existing environmental law curriculum, but they may call for important changes within ourselves. As environmental law professors, we must invest time and energy to increase our own optimism by studying environmental success stories, cultivating good work-life balance and tending to our own mental health. We cannot impart to students what we do not have; we will have to cultivate hope and happiness in ourselves if we wish to graduate effective, optimistic environmental lawyers who carry in their hearts the hope of a sustainable future.

3. Bringing the 'heart' into environmental law teaching

Karen Bubna-Litic

I. INTRODUCTION

Many environmental disputes are multi-stakeholder disputes with each stakeholder holding entrenched and value laden positions. In Australia, examples include the ongoing Adani mine dispute, disputes over the positioning of wind farms, the Gloucester mining dispute, the potential of drilling in the Great Barrier Reef and the eco-tourist resort proposed to be built in the National Park on Kangaroo Island.

Stakeholders involved in environmental disputes often have emotion as the central core of their position in their dispute and this emotion plays a large part in the process of dispute resolution. Traditionally 'thinking like a lawyer' has embodied reasoning and rationality, leaving emotions out of the legal lexicon.[1] Environmental law practitioners, in addition to understanding the law, need to understand the position of all the relevant stakeholders. Student learning can be enhanced by students being able to critically examine the assumptions and values behind their thinking. Emotions can have a transformative effect in relation to the learning of law, having both a powerful effect on both the student and the teacher.[2] The use of reflective journals and deep ecology workshops are two teaching methodologies that can help students in this process.

This embodiment of values in environmental law is unique within the law discipline. When a government accepts that science is objective and disinterested, this allows it to rely on science to proclaim a connection between scientific description and moral prescription and thus implement policies without consulting citizens.[3] Glenna argues that this technocratic approach to managing

---

[1]   Jones, E., 2018, 'Transforming legal education through emotions', *Legal Studies* 38, 450–79, 450.

[2]   Ibid., 452, 459.

[3]   Glenna, L., 2010, 'Management and environmental conflicts – the case of the New York City Watershed Controversy', *Science, Technology and Human Values*, 35(1), 81, 82.

environmental problems is not just that scientific facts replace public participation. The problem is that it ignores how 'values and value-laden assumptions enter into the formulation of the issue before the "facts" are even established'.[4]

A 2005 report[5] investigated the role of values in the resolution of scientific disputes. It argued that many of these disputes pitted environmentalists against anti-environmentalists, scientific against unscientific and ethical against unethical. Instead of this dualism, it has been argued that 'environmental conflicts often emerge not because one side is unethical, antiscientific, or anti-environmental but because the competing sides often appeal to different primary ethical traditions'.[6] This hypothesis was tested in a conflict in New York City regarding the city's drinking water, which concluded that technocratic management of environmental problems is laden with value assumptions, and that environmental conflicts may indeed reflect different ethical and value perspectives.[7]

A.   The Application of Affective Self-understanding into Environmental Law Pedagogy

Recognizing that environmental law disputes are value-laden, my last 20 years of environmental law teaching[8] have included two techniques which allowed my students to understand their own emotions and values with the aim of gaining awareness of them.[9] The basis of both of these techniques has been the element of reflective practice leading to the application of self-regulating strategies.[10] Emotional self-understanding has been the subject of extensive research within the psychology discipline,[11] with the educative assumption

---

[4]   Ibid., 82.

[5]   Council for Agricultural Science and Technology (CAST). 2005. Issue Paper: Agricultural Ethics. November (29): 1–12.

[6]   Glenna (n 3).

[7]   Ibid., 103–4.

[8]   My teaching has included undergraduate and postgraduate teaching of environmental law to law, science and business students, climate change and energy law, environmental forensics law and environmental dispute resolution.

[9]   Reflective journals have been included as an essential assessment item in each of these courses. Full deep ecology workshops have been included in courses undertaken by science and business students, although elements of deep ecology practice have been included more widely throughout all courses.

[10]   Mortari, L., 2015, 'Emotion and education: Reflecting on the emotional experience emotion and education', *European Journal of Educational Research,* 4(4), 157–76. doi: 10.12973/eu-jer.4.4.

[11]   Dyment, J.E. and O'Connell, T.S., 2011, 'Assessing the quality of reflection in student journals: a review of the research', *Teaching in Higher Education* 16(1), 81–97, 82.

grounding this experience being 'that the daily writing increases the capability to reflect on one's inner experience and, in particular, on one's emotional experience, and then to gain a meaningful comprehension of it'.[12] This then allows the reflective practitioner to be able to understand the values underlying all other stakeholders in an environmental dispute.

Emotions are often thought of as irrational and arguably excluded from rational understanding and pedagogical discourse, especially in a legal context. Recognizing that environmental disputes are value laden, it becomes necessary to examine what theories would support a pedagogical discourse about emotions.[13] The irrational conception of emotion posits that emotions are merely physical, not mental phenomena, subjecting us to the mind/body dualism and induced reductionist reasoning. Framed this way, would make it impossible to conceive of an education about emotional life.[14] Thankfully, there is recent philosophical thinking that has developed a view whereby emotions have a cognitive component.[15] This can fit well into the teaching of environmental law.

Nussbaum's philosophical theory posits a cognitive conception of emotion, through which she affirms that emotions are infused by thoughts, maintaining that emotions are 'intelligent responses to the perception of value'.[16] She writes:

> an emotion embodies a thought about an object, and this thought is constituted by a propositional content of an evaluative kind as regards the object; this evaluation exerts a performative power on the way of being of the person. The emotions 'embody not simply ways of seeing an object, but beliefs – often very complex – about the object'.[17]

Mortari argues that:

> if we acknowledge that emotional life is suffused with thoughts, meaning that it has 'rich cognitive/intentional content', it is possible to assume that the emotions are objects of a reflective process through which, by investigating their thoughtful component, one can reach an understanding of them.[18]

---

[12] Mortari (n 10) 158.
[13] Ibid., 159.
[14] Ibid.
[15] Nussbaum, M.C., 2001, *Upheavals of Thought: The Intelligence of Emotions*, Cambridge: Cambridge University Press; Jones (n 1) 456.
[16] Ibid., 1.
[17] Ibid., 28, as cited in Mortari (n 10) 159.
[18] Mortari (n 10) 160.

What follows from this is a cognitive/evaluative theory of emotions which legitimizes the conception of experiences aimed at including emotions into the processes of a reflection that aims at understanding.[19] This cognitive theory of emotions implies that education is possible because we can understand emotions by identifying their cognitive components and the actions they induce,[20] and this practice of affective self-understanding can help students reach a better understanding of how they relate to others.[21]

II.   THE REFLECTIVE JOURNAL IN LAW SCHOOLS

The use of reflective journals in law schools has not been well documented. As one legal scholar remarked more than 20 years ago:

> This absence of academic dialogue on the use of journals in the literature on legal education is remarkable for several reasons. First, the use of journals as a pedagogical tool enjoys over two thousand years of recorded history. Second, our colleagues in other academic disciplines have been using journals extensively and there is much to learn from their analysis and experience.[22]

Since 1996, when this was written, the use of reflective journals in law schools has increased but few are employed to understand student emotions and values, despite the use of reflective journals being one way of understanding our emotions and how they connect into our values.[23]

Reflective journals can be used in the context of understanding emotions because they allow students to examine their beliefs, values, experiences and assumptions about the subject matter at hand.[24] The use of a reflective journal in higher education has the potential to help to facilitate deep reflection and be very useful in a variety of contexts.

One of these contexts is within the discipline of nursing. The discipline of nursing has embraced reflection as a teaching and learning method[25] and

---

[19]   Ibid.

[20]   Ibid.

[21]   Ibid., 163.

[22]   Ogilvy, J.P., 1996, 'The use of journals in legal education: a tool for reflection', *Clinical Law Review* 3(1), 55–108, 55.

[23]   Chirema, K., 2007, 'The use of reflective journals in the promotion of reflection and learning in post-registration nursing students', *Nurse Education Today* 27, 192–202.

[24]   Ibid.

[25]   Ibid.; Mahlanze, H.T. and Sibiya, M.N., 2017, 'Perceptions of student nurses on the writing of reflective journals as a means for personal, professional and clinical learning development', *Health SA Gesondheid* 22, 79–86.

journal writing has been the tool used to foster this reflection.[26] It has been seen as a necessary tool for nursing practitioners who have to act autonomously and make critical clinical decisions. The use of the reflective journal in nursing has been seen as valuable because of its ability to allow practitioners to explore their experience, think about it, and evaluate it which can lead to new understandings.

Reflective journals can be used to achieve a number of purposes and it must first be made clear to the student what this purpose is. They can include cultivating life-long self-directed learning; improving critical thinking and problem-solving skills; promoting reflection; and raising self-awareness, amongst others.[27] However, there is a danger that some students will never achieve the aim of deep learning and reflection. In order to ensure students do achieve a level of deep learning and reflection, educators need to recognize and avoid potential pitfalls, many of which revolve around instructions to students, because often they are asked to reflect without any structure being provided.[28] Ethical dilemmas can arise where personal revelations written by students are read and assessed by educators. How can you grade a personal reflection? Some students feel that they are 'journaled to death' and that journals are 'a pointless ritual wrapped in meaningless words'.[29]

Studies have shown that reflection does not flourish spontaneously[30] and that most students are not particularly reflective, their tendency being to write mainly descriptive accounts of events. I found this particularly evident in my experience of using reflective journals amongst law students, as opposed to business and science students. Student feedback at the end of their courses was particularly instructive in improving the continued use of reflective journals.[31]

If the aim of the process is to ensure a substantial quality of introspection and reflection,[32] how can this be achieved? Effective deep student learning is conditioned by their perceptions of the appropriateness and relevance of the

---

[26]   Boud, D., Keogh R., et al, 1985, *Reflection: Turning Experience into Learning*, Kogan Page, London.

[27]   Ogilvy (n 22).

[28]   Mills, R., 2008. '"It's just a nuisance": Improving college student reflective journal writing', *College Student Journal*, 42(2), 684–90.

[29]   Dyment and O'Connell (n 11) 82.

[30]   Rue, J., Font, A. and Cebrian, G., 2013, 'Towards high quality reflective learning amongst law undergraduate students: analysing students' reflective journals during a problem-based learning course', *Quality in Higher Education* 19(2), 191–209, 195.

[31]   They required a lot of detailed feedback throughout the process as well as clear instructions up front. Employing these strategies improved the quality of the reflection in later years.

[32]   Ogilvy (n 22) 59.

tools and strategies used for their learning.[33] Fairness of the assessment tasks
is also an important factor,[34] as is the need for clear expectations, clear briefs,
clear assessment criteria[35] and detailed feedback.[36] The relationship of trust
has been found to be a key factor in achieving high levels of deep reflection.[37]
Self-confidence is also important as it allows students to reflect and write
'freely about their thoughts, feelings and fears and, in turn, it empowers them
to write deeper personal accounts'.[38] The assessment regime plays a major
role in the quality of the reflection. For example, in my classes, employing an
assessment regime where the main outcome was to ensure adherence to the
process rather than the content of the journals saw an increase in more effective reflections. These strategies are teased out in more detail in the following
section.

Dyment and O'Connell summarised seven factors[39] that can inhibit or
enable reflective writing and it is useful to take note of these before looking
at the use of reflective journals in my environmental law classes. Most of the
journals reviewed were mandatory but there is an argument that an optional
journal would result in deeper reflections from those that actually opt in. This
is a valid observation depending on what the purpose of the reflective journal
is. In my classes, they needed to be mandatory, as it was the process rather than
the content which was the main purpose of the reflective journal. Secondly,
grading can be a powerful student learning motivator, but as is explained later
in this chapter, grading my journals was not a viable option. I had to find an
assessment option that would ensure that each student was achieving a high
quality of introspection and reflection. It has been suggested that frequent
reflective journal entries coupled with regular feedback and training may

---

[33]   Struyven, K., Dochy, F., Janssens, S. and Gielen, S., 2005, 'Students' perceptions about evaluation and assessment in higher education: a review', *Assessment and
Evaluation in Higher Education*, 30(4), 325–41.

[34]   Ibid., 333.

[35]   Ibid., 334.

[36]   Ogilvy (n 22) 59.

[37]   Dyment and O'Connell (n 11).

[38]   Rue et al (n 30) 195.

[39]

  1. Optional or mandatory;
  2. assessment criteria;
  3. frequency and duration of the entries;
  4. training and support;
  5. feedback;
  6. clarity of instructions;
  7. relationship of mutual trust between educator and student.
Dyment and O'Connell (n 11) 93.

develop deeper reflective skills over time.[40] This was one of the findings from my experience. Countering this was the experience that students may get bored writing journals and therefore deep reflections might decrease over time. Length of the reflection needs to be negotiated with the students. It is logical that training and support would enhance the quality of the reflections. This too is borne out from my experience in environmental law teaching. Timely and appropriate feedback on student journals can support students to write more reflectively in subsequent journals. Those students whose journals were submitted on multiple occasions might be in a better position to be journaling more deeply and reflectively than their counterparts who were not provided with feedback.[41]

Another technique used to develop deep reflection is to encourage students to adopt questioning as a part of the reflective process as it helps students mirror their thoughts and feelings.[42]

A.   The Use of and the Assessment of the Reflective Journal

One of the basic reasons for getting students to write a reflective journal is the demonstrated connection between writing and learning, leading students to engage with the material in a deeper and more critical manner, thus enhancing their critical thinking skills.[43]

Fajans and Falk use what they call, a *reading journal* to help students become more active and critical readers of legal text,[44] whereby students are instructed to record their personal associations, reactions, evaluations, interpretations and questions and then to reflect upon it, allowing them to move from summarizing or paraphrasing what they read toward real analysis of the text.[45]

In my environmental law class the educative aim was for students to achieve deep learning through understanding the values they held in relation to the environment and to various contested environmental issues, enhancing their critical thinking skills.[46] Examples of these contested issues include waste (plastic? food? recycling?); energy (renewable? mining? coal? gas? wind-farms? solar? hydro? nuclear?); water (usage? groundwater? agricultural?

---

[40]   Ibid.

[41]   Ibid., 94.

[42]   Rue et al (n 30) 197.

[43]   Ogilvy (n 22) 64.

[44]   Fajans, E. and Falk, M.R., 1993, 'Against the tyranny of paraphrase: talking back to texts' *Cornell L. Rev.*, 78, 163, as cited in Ogilvy, ibid., at 66.

[45]   Ibid.

[46]   Ogilvy (n 22) 76.

recycled?). All of these examples carry contested views and values amongst the wider community.

It is important for students to understand these contested values in order to be able to evaluate stakeholder positions in environmental disputes, particularly in order to help resolve disputes without recourse to the court process, which in Australia has limited power to actually stop environmentally damaging projects once a decision for approval has been made.[47] In order to understand the differing values of various stakeholders, it is essential to understand one's own values. The process of using a reflective journal as a teaching tool has the ability to help achieve this outcome.

The philosophy set out by Schon and Ogilvy grounds the approach taken in my environmental law classes to incorporate a reflective journal where students reflect on their emotional response to a series of readings in order to perceive their environmental values and to develop their critical thinking skills.

Students were instructed to write a reflection on one of their prescribed readings each week. They were instructed to write about how they felt in response to that particular reading. They were to handwrite it in a journal. No word limit was imposed but there was a guide of 200–500 words per entry. I reiterated that it was not a piece of analytical or descriptive or critical writing. Students had to reflect on how they were feeling about what they had read. I emphasized that the use of questions would help in the process of reflection.

I used this reflective journal for many years, in teaching environmental law to law students, business students and science students and I found it was the law students who had the most difficulty in reflecting on their feelings and some were quite hostile to the use of reflective journals, seeing it as a waste of time and having nothing to do with the law. There are many reasons why the students may resist the use of a reflective journal. They may not understand the value of reflection or they may have encountered them in other subjects and had an unsatisfactory experience and therefore are hostile to the idea.[48] They may see it as not very 'lawyer like', they may be anxious about self-revelation and they may not be naturally reflective.[49] All these concerns can be overcome by clear guidance and support and usually once they begin to reflect, their hostility abates.

As self confidence and trust have been identified as being critical to achieving deep and personal reflections, it was crucial that students were constantly

---

[47]   The ability for merits review is extremely limited in Australia. In some Australian jurisdictions, third-party appeals are also limited.

[48]   Ogilvy (n 22) 87.

[49]   Ibid.

encouraged and supported and I employed the following strategies to engage them and accomplish this outcome.

1. They would tell me that they had used reflective journals in other classes and their task in those classes was to critically analyse articles. I would constantly explain that this reflective journal was different because environmental issues are so value laden with stakeholders having emotional connections to their values on different issues. I would give examples such as wind farms; climate change; contested water use; building large infrastructure projects, such as dams or mining projects; and explain that reflecting on their feelings would help them identify and understand the values each of them holds in relation to some of these issues. This, in turn, would help them understand other stakeholder values.

2. To counter the concern of privacy, confidentiality and self-revelation, I told them they were reflecting for themselves and that no one else would be reading their reflective journal except me, and I was not going to read it for content, only for process to ensure they were reflecting on how they felt about what they had read. Students must be assured of the confidentiality of their reflections. I also explained that I keep a reflective journal of my teaching and explained the rationale for doing so. I was prepared to share some of my reflections with them, which seemed to confirm the value of these journals.

3. I prescribed the types of words they needed to use. First, they should write in the active voice. That is, in the first, not third person. They must never use the words, 'I feel that…' or 'I believe that…' because although they use the word, 'feel', this is not reflecting on how they are actually feeling. I gave them some examples of the sort of things they could write. E.g., 'I feel sad…', 'I am very angry at…', 'I am furious …', 'I feel frustrated…', 'I feel happy…'. Often they would look at me still unconvinced so I employed the following for the first week's reflection.

4. For the first week of reflections, I ask them to reflect on an environmental experience they had encountered, disconnected to anything to with the law and reflect on how it made them feel. I told them they had to write their reflection and for that week only, they had to be prepared to come to class and read their reflection aloud. This was so I could give them public feedback and the whole class could begin to understand what was expected in relation to this assessment.

5. I employed a further element of feedback. Halfway through the semester, I collected the journals and gave feedback to those who were not reflecting on their feelings, giving them examples of phrasing that would help them. If they improved in the second half of the semester, they would not be penalised in their assessment.

Students are very concerned with assessment regimes but because the reflective journal is about the process, not the content of the reflection, I allocated 10 per cent of the total mark to the reflective journal. I then gave each student full marks if they completed their reflections. Because I collected their reflections twice throughout the ten-week semester, for those students who were not reflecting on their feelings, but who took on my feedback and improved, these students gained full marks. The students who never reflected on their feelings, even after feedback, and there were very few of those, would fail this component of the course.

Another issue that arises concerns the amount of time spent by the educator in administering the reflective journal. A large amount of time is devoted to collecting, reading, commenting on and returning the student journals. However I have found that the benefits of using these reflective journals in my environmental law classes far outweigh the costs. Reading the student journals and keeping a reflective journal myself enabled me to continuously improve my environmental law teaching from year to year.

B.   The Student Experience

The student evaluations gave very positive feedback on the use of the reflective journal. It helped the students gain a solid understanding of the values they held in relation to various environmental issues. Anecdotally, from my observations via some of the role plays conducted later in the semester and class discussions, I saw a deep understanding of various stakeholder values and an ability to argue well from their own value perspectives. I also noticed that in discussions of highly contentious issues, with different opinions amongst the students, many students were able to reflect on why those differing opinions were held and were able to apply a less emotional response to them. These types of responses have been borne out in other studies of the use of journals that reflect on emotional responses.[50]

III.   DEEP ECOLOGY WORKSHOPS

Deep ecology is a philosophy established by the Norwegian philosopher, Arne Naess in 1972.[51] Its basic tenets are the interconnectedness of all living beings and recognition of the intrinsic value of nature. Deep ecology workshops

---

[50]   Mortari (n 10) and Ogilvy (n 22).
[51]   Naess, A., 1972, 'The shallow and the deep, long range ecology movement', *Inquiry* 16, 95.

were first developed by Joanna Macy with the underlying philosophy of deep ecology in her practice of 'the work that reconnects'.[52]

I first introduced deep ecology workshops into my environmental law teaching when I was teaching environmental law to business students in the mid-1990s. This was a time in university life in Australia when students were less pressured and they had less external time pressures on their studies. This enabled me to take the students away for two days on a deep ecology workshop as part of their environmental law in business course. I had recently completed a deep ecology workshop with Joanna Macy, and participated in a Council for All Beings with John Seed.[53] The deep ecology workshop also drew on the philosophy of Aldo Leopold[54] and his theory of a land ethic.

I based this teaching technique on the many writers who advocated that by establishing a heart connection to the environment, we would start to take action to help heal the planet – and what better cohort to start with than the business leaders of the future.

This deep ecology workshop had success in achieving this aim. One student approached me at their graduation, with their parents, telling me how they were going to employ sustainability practices into their family businesses when they took over. I made the students reflect on this deep ecology workshop after we returned to the city and I was overwhelmed by their responses to spending two days and nights in silence in the bush. At first, they had found it difficult to maintain silence being in the midst of a group of other students. Some had only experienced 'nature' in their backyard and others had no experience in simple food preparation. During these workshops, they had, for a short period of time, connected with nature and it had an incredible heart shifting effect on their relationship to nature. They had happily given up one of their weekends in addition to their 39 hours of class time and they had loved the experience.

It was difficult logistically within the university constraints but was a successful application of Joanna Macy's deep ecology workshops which aim to effect social change by transforming apathy into constructive action, seeing 'our world as our larger living body'.[55] The exercises I employed were improvisational and synergistic and effective when done in a group setting.

---

[52] Macy, J., 1995, 'Working through environmental despair', in Roszak, T., Gomes, M.E. and Kanner, A.D., (eds), *Ecopsychology: Restoring the Earth, Healing the Mind*, San Francisco, CA: Sierra Club Books, 240–59; Macy, J., 2007, *World as Lover, World as Self: Courage for Global Justice and Ecological Renewal*, Berkeley, CA: Parallax Press.

[53] Seed, J., Macy, J., Fleming, P. and Naess, N., 1988, *Thinking Like a Mountain, Toward a Council of All Beings*, Gabriola Island BC Canada: New Society Publishers.

[54] Leopold, A., 1949, *A Sand County Almanac*, Oxford University Press.

[55] Macy (2007) (n 52).

The aim of Macy's work is to help people trust their raw experience and give voice to what they see and feel is happening to their world.[56]

The theory behind these workshops is based on deep ecology, systems thinking, Gaia theory and Buddhist and spiritual teachings. In 1991, she wrote:

> Life on our planet is in trouble....It is hard to go anywhere without being confronted by the wounding of our world...a world that can end....How do we deal with our unique place in history as participants in an era that offers no certainty that there will be a future for humans? Our children and theirs will inherit the Earth. Herein lies my pressure, my responsibility, our responsibility. How can we make a difference?[57]

There are four steps in her process, and her writings set out a variety of exercises to be used in this process.[58]

The exercises are about developing trust and letting go. The deep ecology workshop that I incorporated into my environmental law teaching was based on Macy's four part spiral being, 'coming from gratitude, honoring our pain for the world, seeing with new eyes, and going forth'.[59]

At the centre of her teachings is the view that we must not shy away from the hurt, suffering and despair we feel:

> Don't ever apologize for the sorrow, grief, and rage you feel. It is a measure of your humanity and your maturity. It is a measure of your open heart, and as your heart breaks open, there will be room for the world to heal. That is what is happening as we see people honestly confronting the sorrows of our time. And it is an adaptive response.[60]

The purpose of her work and John Seed's work and what I tried to incorporate into my teaching is to change students' perception of nature from something outside the self to being one with the self. For parts of nature to be 'no longer removed, separate, disposable objects pertaining to a world out there',[61]

---

[56]   Ibid.

[57]   Ibid.

[58]   Work that Reconnects Network https://workthatreconnects.org/spiral/ (page accessed 5 May 2021).

[59]   Macy (2007) (n 52).

[60]   Macy, J., 1990, 'The greening of the self', in Hunt Badiner, A. (ed), *Dharma Gaia: A Harvest of Essays in Buddhism and Ecology*, Parallax Press, Earth Day, 53–64, 57.

[61]   Ibid., 54.

thereby shifting one's concept of self, generating a profound interconnected-ness with all life. As Naess says:

> In this process, notions such as altruism and moral duty are left behind. It is tacitly based on the Latin term 'ego' which has as its opposite the 'alter'. Altruism implies that the ego sacrifices its interests in favor of the other, the *alter*. The motivation is primarily that of duty. It is said we *ought* to love others as strongly as we love our self. There are, however, very limited numbers among humanity capable of loving from mere duty or from moral exhortation.
>
> Unfortunately, the extensive moralizing within the ecological movement has given the public the false impression that they are being asked to make a sacrifice—to show more responsibility, more concern, and a nicer moral standard. But all of that would flow naturally and easily if the self were widened and deepened so that the protection of nature was felt and perceived as protection of our very selves.[62]

The exercises employed in the two-day deep ecology workshop revolved around the four steps in the spiral as outlined by Macy. It also involved living in silence, except when asked to engage during activities or in response to lectures during the two days. Food preparation and eating and cleaning were all conducted in silence. This was challenging for some students, as was the fact that their mobile phones were out of range. When silence was broken the importance of keeping a silent retreat was continuously explained and over the two days, the students began to embrace the silence. Feedback from the students indicated an appreciation for reflection that the silence offered. The exercises helped to break hearts open, to connect with the pain, and the silence and reflection allowed the opportunity to plan and move forward.

Over the ensuing years, I was committed to continue to embed the use of these workshops into my environmental law teaching. However things changed dramatically within the education system from the mid-1990s to the present time. The financial burden shifted from the government to the student and with most students having to now fund their time at university, two things changed. They became driven by attaining the best marks to obtain the best jobs and they became time poor with attendance numbers dropping in order for students to be able to work to fund their university studies. Some saw spending two days at a deep ecology workshop as a waste of time and those who saw value in this were, alas unable to afford the time to attend.

This resulted in a modification within my environmental law teaching to transfer Joanna Macy's workshops into a half-day field trip where we went on bushwalks into nature to try to encapsulate some of the theory and a care for nature ethic. The students reflected on this process and many saw value in this. However, the result was not as powerful as the two-day workshops.

---

[62] As cited, ibid., 62.

Today we have come full circle and there is a much greater concern amongst the mainstream of environmental issues including mass extinctions and climate change. The recent rise of XR (extinction rebellion) and the climate change law suits around the world[63] are evidence of this.

IV.   CONCLUSION

Although I have been bringing the 'heart' into environmental law teaching for more than 25 years through the use of reflective journals and deep ecology workshops, these two techniques seem to have more relevance and importance today than ever before. Their natural link to the environment is well established and now is the time to mainstream these pedagogical tools into all environmental law teaching.

As has been borne out in this chapter, reflective journals have an easier path in terms of incorporating them into the curriculum. Both Ogilvy and Mortari confirm the therapeutic value of reflective journals which give students the opportunity to reflect on their emotions and careful instruction and support and trust need to be employed to enable the most effective outcomes.

As she reaches 90 years of age, there has been a recent resurgence of interest in the work of Joanna Macy. Her 'Work that Reconnects' seems to answer the call for help from those feeling despair at the state of the planet. This does not exclude environmental law practitioners and I see her deep ecology workshops as an important pedagogical tool to enable environmental law students to understand the interconnectedness of all things, leading to eco-centric approaches to law and policy. Arguments will have to be made to overcome university administrative barriers to these overnight field trips but the experience to the students will be invaluable.

Both reflective journals and deep ecology workshops involve extensive time commitment on the part of the educator but as I hope I have demonstrated, the cost in terms of time is far outweighed by the benefits resulting to the student and educator alike.

---

[63]   https://www.vox.com/energy-and-environment/2019/2/22/17140166/climate -change-lawsuit-exxon-juliana-liability-kids (page accessed 5 May 2021).

4. Placing natural resources law: preliminary thoughts on decolonizing teaching and learning about people, places, and law

Estair Van Wagner

INTRODUCTION

This chapter is a reflection on the role place-based teaching and learning can play in working towards decolonization of legal education. Confronting issues about ownership of, and jurisdiction over, land and resources must be at the heart of any meaningful attempt to transform relations between settler and Indigenous peoples in Canada. How we respond to both historic and contemporary challenges to colonial ownership and governance frameworks by Indigenous peoples is one of the central challenges facing lawyers, governments, and academics today. As Cree legal scholar Jeffery Hewitt plainly puts it, 'Law schools may either reinvent to become locations where Indigenous laws are fully valued and taught alongside common and civil law traditions or risk being left behind.'

My focus in this chapter is on teaching and learning natural resource law; however, the discussion below has implications for all land use and environmental law subjects. Learning and teaching about land law, environmental law, or natural resource law is always necessarily learning and teaching about Indigenous law and relations with the earth – either as a form of continued erasure in their absence from the curriculum, or as an uncomfortable and complicated attempt to engage with the original laws of the land, confront our history, and think about how we can do things differently. Further, as Anishinaabe legal scholar John Borrows points out, '[r]econciliation between Indigenous peoples and the Crown requires our collective reconciliation with the earth'.[1] Yet, traditional legal education not only fails to prepare students to engage with the complex social, ecological, and cultural contexts of environmental and natural resource decision making, it may actively contribute to environmental crises and ongoing colonialism. Australian property and environmental law scholar Nicole Graham argues, legal education in its present form may itself be a 'negative influence on the adaptive capacity of society'.[2] Borrows argues, '[o]ne source of rapprochement can be facilitated by the resurgence of Indigenous peoples' own laws and life ways', which have 'rich and vibrant insights and include deep intellectual and social resources that can help us care for the natural world'.[3] This requires what Hewitt calls 'work of a different kind than is currently taught in law schools'.[4] This chapter considers the role of the natural resource classroom in supporting this broader project of decolonizing the law school. It does so in the spirit of critically thinking through my own role as a settler legal academic – one who teaches areas of law integrally linked with colonial violence and the dispossession of Indigenous land and resources. There are no clear answers or formula in what follows. My hope is that in reflecting on my own experience this chapter will contribute to difficult but necessary conversations about our responsibilities as legal educators in the context of both colonization and environmental crises.[5]

PLACING MYSELF

My own relationship with the lands in which I live and work and the benefits I enjoy as a result of my ancestors uninvited arrival on this territory come with responsibilities. One of these is to learn and teach about the legal structures that continue to enable colonial dispossession and violence. And, more hopefully,

---

[1]   Nicole Graham, 'This Is Not a Thing: Land, Sustainability and Legal Education' (2014) 26 *JEL* 395, 401.

[2]   Ibid., 398.

[3]   John Borrows, 'Earth-Bound: Indigenous Resurgence and Environmental Reconciliation' in Michael Ash, John Burrows and James Tully (eds), *Resurgence and Reconciliation: Indigenous-Settler Relations and Earth Teachings* (University of Toronto Press 2018) 49.

[4]   Jeffery G Hewitt, 'Decolonizing and Indigenizing: Some Considerations for Law Schools' (2016) 33 *Windsor YB Access Just* 65, 72.

[5]   These conversations are ongoing in different forms and venues in Canada, see, e.g., the blog *Reconciliation Syllabus*, which invites: 'law professors across Canada (and lawyers? and students?) to gather together ideas about resources and pedagogies that might support recommendation #28 of the [Truth and Reconciliation] Calls to Action: the call for us to rethink both what and how we teach in our schools. And to respond to the #CallsforJustice' from the National Inquiry into Murdered and Missing Indigenous Women and Girls. https://reconciliationsyllabus.wordpress.com, accessed October 20, 2019.

to learn and teach about how we might use law to transform settler-Indigenous relations and our relations with the lands on which we teach and learn. This includes working through the implications of Indigenous ownership and jurisdiction and possibilities for 'co-existence' to define our relations with, and with respect to, lands and resources.[6]

As a settler legal academic my relationship with Canada, and the Great Lakes Region in particular, originates with my Dutch ancestors who arrived in the lands they called New Amsterdam in the 17th century and moved North to eventually settle in southwestern Ontario as United Empire Loyalists. The Two Row Wampum between the Dutch and the Haudenosaunee, and then later with the British, establishing the agreement for peaceful and respectful coexistence is thus a source of direct obligation and relationship.[7] These relations are overlayed with relationships and obligations with Anishinaabe treaty partners in the territory in which I live and work now and the other areas of Ontario where my Scottish ancestors settled in the 19th century. These include not only historic treaties with the British, but also the pre-existing treaties between Anishinaabe and the more-than-human world, and between Indigenous nations, such as the Common Dish or Dish One Spoon treaty between the Anishinaabe and the Haudenosaunee to care for and share the land and common resources.[8]

For me, this is where teaching natural resource law begins: A sense of strong and deep connection to the lands and waters and a commitment to honour the legal obligations and relationships my ancestors took on so many generations ago to both the human and more-than-human worlds of this place. These obligations have been left unfulfilled and the relationships have been grossly one-sided, as the violent dispossession of Indigenous lands and resources has benefited my family and communities for generations. This truth must be the foundation of my teaching and learning. As legal anthropologist Michael Asch concludes:

> the point of reconciliation…is to reconcile our practices today with the certain knowledge that we have acted wrongly (even on our own ethical terms), accept

---

6   Deborah McGregor, 'Traditional Ecological Knowledge and the Two—Row Wampum' (2002) 3 *Biodiversity* 8, 9.

7   Jon Parmenter, 'The Meaning of Kaswentha and the Two Row Wampum Belt in Haudenosaunee (Iroquois) History: Can Indigenous Oral Tradition Be Reconciled with the Documentary Record?' (2013) 3 *Journal of Early American History* 82; Darlene M Johnston, 'Quest of the Six Nations Confederacy for Self-Determination, The' (1986) 44 *U Toronto Fac L Rev* 1.

8   Leanne Simpson, 'Looking after Gdoo-Naaganinaa: Precolonial Nishnaabeg Diplomatic and Treaty Relationships' (2008) 23 *Wicazo Sa Review* 29; Alan Corbiere, 'Their Own Forms of Which They Take the Most Notice' in Alan Corbiere and others (eds), *Anishinaabewin Niiwin: Four Rising Winds* (Ojibway Culture Foundation 2014).

responsibility for the harms our actions have caused, and work to ensure that our actions and values in the future come into accord.[9]

As he notes, the promises made through treaties between Indigenous nations and European settlers are 'inviolate, for to violate these promises is to invalidate our right to be here'.[10]

NATURAL RESOURCES LAW: WHAT IS IT AND WHERE DOES IT FIT IN THE LAW SCHOOL CURRICULUM?

Natural resource law governs the ownership and jurisdiction over the acquisition, use, and management of parts of earth systems for human benefit. In Canada and other common law jurisdictions this has traditionally included subjects like water rights, mining, forestry, agriculture, energy, and fish and wildlife. Since the 1950s, it has grown to include law related to less extractive human uses of the environment, such as conservation of land and waters and parks, as well as species protection.

Natural resource law is rooted firmly in property law – who owns what and who can acquire various forms of property and use rights for particular resources and lands. It is shaped profoundly by colonial determinations of ownership and jurisdiction over land, property rights, and the exploitation of various elements of the environment.[11] Indeed, resource exploitation for settlement and private commercial gain has defined Canada's legal, economic, and cultural context since Europeans first arrived in these lands.[12] Laws governing public lands and resources were from the outset, and remain, a central component of colonial nation building in Canada. Historically the primary function of these laws was privatization through direct grants for settlement, railway development, or resource exploitation.[13] Necessarily then, natural resource law is at the heart of the settler-colonial project in Canada, requiring the erasure of Indigenous relationships with lands and resources to facilitate and justify ongoing settler claims despite the prior ownership and governance

---

[9]   Michael Asch, 'Confederation Treaties and Reconciliation: Stepping Back into the Future' in Asch, Borrows and Tully (n 3) 30.

[10]   Ibid., 45.

[11]   Elaine Lois Hughes, Arlene J Kwasniak and Alastair R Lucas, *Public Lands and Resources Law in Canada* (Irwin Law 2016) 53.

[12]   Ibid., 102–3; Laurel Sefton MacDowell, *An Environmental History of Canada* (UBC Press 2012); David Wood, *Making Ontario* (McGill-Queen's Press 2000).

[13]   Hughes, Kwasniak and Lucas (n 11) 89.

of Indigenous peoples. It is an essential part of 'the way we tell our story' in Canada.[14]

As Harold Innis pointed out with his staples theory of Canadian economic development, Canada has been historically dependent on the exploitation of resources for foreign export.[15] Indeed, while economic diversification has resulted in greater secondary processing of primary resources, the Canadian economy and political imagination are still firmly rooted in natural resource exploitation. According to Michael Howlett and Keith Brownsey, only Ontario and Quebec rely on non-resource sectors for the majority of their economic trade and exports.[16] As I write, the new Premier of the oil-producing province of Alberta is challenging federal environmental assessment jurisdiction perceived as standing in the way of oil and gas development and pursuing a public inquiry into the activities of environmental groups opposed to development of the oil sands.[17] Despite repeated commitments to addressing climate change,

---

[14]   Asch (n 9) 31.

[15]   Harold Innis, *Essays in Canadian Economic History* (University of Toronto Press 2017).

[16]   Michael Howlett and Keith Brownsey, *Canada's Resource Economy in Transition: The Past, Present, and Future of Canadian Staples Industries* (Toronto: Emond Montgomery Publications 2008).

[17]   James Keller, 'Alberta challenges Ottawa's environmental assessment law, arguing it encroaches on province's power' *The Globe and Mail* (Calgary, 10 September 2019) https://www.theglobeandmail.com/canada/alberta/article-alberta-challenges -ottawas-environmental-assessment-law-arguing-it/ accessed 20 October 2019. See also, Martin Olszynski and Nigel Bankes, 'Setting the Record Straight on Federal and Provincial Jurisdiction Over the Environmental Assessment of Resources in the Provinces' (*University of Calgary Faculty of Law Blog*, 24 May 2019) https://ablawg .ca/2019/05/24/setting-the-record-straight-on-federal-and-provincial-jurisdiction-over -the-environmental-assessment-of-resource-projects-in-the-provinces/, accessed 20 October 2019. For details of the inquiry, see the website for the Public inquiry into anti-Alberta energy campaigns: https://www.alberta.ca/public-inquiry-into-anti-alberta -energy-campaigns.aspx, accessed October 20, 2019. See also Martin Olszynski, 'Everything You Wish You Didn't Need to Know About the Alberta Inquiry into Anti-Alberta Energy Campaigns' (*University of Calgary Law Blog*, 17 October 2019) https://ablawg.ca/2019/10/17/everything-you-wish-you-didnt-need-to-know-about-the -alberta-inquiry-into-anti-alberta-energy-campaigns/ accessed 20 October 2019. See also Cree legal scholar Darcy Lindberg's comment on social media noting the link between the $30 million budget for a new social media 'war room' to combat 'misinfor- mation' about the oil sands and reductions to the Alberta Indigenous Relations budget in the same amount, @Darcy13Lindberg:

> AB budget: 'Indigenous Relations' operating expense is budgeted at $190 million for 2019–20, $188 million in 2020–21, and $176 million for 2021–22 and 2022–23.' 30 million cutback over 4 years. Where has 30 mil come up before, oh yeah... (Twitter Post, 24 October 2019) <https://twitter.com/Darcy13Lindberg/ status/1187482830940491777> accessed 29 October 2019.

the federal government purchased an oil pipeline intended to move oil sands resources to port for export in 2018 after the regulatory approval was success-fully challenged by Indigenous nations and environmental groups and private sector interest waned.[18] Control over natural resource exploitation thus remains a key issue in the Canadian legal and political imagination.

NATURAL RESOURCES LAW IN LEGAL EDUCATION

The emergence of Natural Resources Law courses was explained by Clyde O Martz in 1949 as a response to 'a new burst of activity in natural resource exploitation', which he argued, required 'grounding the law student in the stat-utory and case law governing the acquisition, development, and conservation of mineral oil and gas, water, and land resources'.[19] Natural resources law was originally, as Robert L Fischman describes, 'a variation on the property law course'.[20] In Canada natural resource law also requires significant engagement with our constitutional structure and the division of powers between federal and provincial governments, which includes provincial government ownership of public lands and the vast majority of resources.[21] In this dominant version of Canadian natural resource jurisdiction, constitutional protection of Aboriginal rights may shape and complicate federalism, but it is ultimately about the divi-sion of powers between the federal and provincial governments.[22] Discussions of Indigenous jurisdiction are focused on the Crown's duty to consult about impacts on constitutionally protected rights and title rather than questioning the presumption of Crown sovereignty, unsettling ownership of land and resources, and addressing the exclusion of Indigenous nations from the con-

---

[18]   'Ottawa Is Buying Trans Mountain. What Does That Mean? A Guide' *The Globe and Mail* (Canada, 29 May 2018) https://www.theglobeandmail.com/canada/article-ottawa-buys-trans-mountain-from-kinder-morgan-explainer/ accessed 20 October 2019.
[19]   Clyde O Martz, 'Study of Natural Resource Law, The' (1948) 1 *J Leg Ed* 588, 589.
[20]   Robert L Fischman, 'What Is Natural Resources Law?' (2007) *U Colo L Rev* 717, 718.
[21]   The British North America Act, 1867, ss 91, 92. Section 109 grants the original provinces ownership of the lands and resources they brought into confederation. While the prairie provinces entered confederation on different terms and the federal govern-ment owned the lands and resources this was altered in the Natural Resource Transfer Agreements in the 1930s. The territories now have a mixture of control over their lands and resources with a significant amount of federal control remaining in the Northwest Territories and Nunavut. The vast majority of public lands are owned by the provincial crown.
[22]   Dwight Gordon Newman, *Natural Resource Jurisdiction in Canada* (LexisNexis Canada Incorporated 2013) 2.

stitutional structure. As Canadian legal scholar Janet Mosher has noted, legal education tends to treat the existing social, political, and economic order as given: 'In doing so, legal education communicates to students that, as lawyers, their role is not to seek substantive change to the existing order, but to get what they can for their clients within that order.'[23] Natural resource law has been no exception.

By the 1970s, administrative law began to be overlayed on the crucial property law foundations of natural resource law, particularly with respect to emerging demands for environmental protection and conservation to be built into resource management: 'whereas once mining, logging, and even road-building were merely matters of perfecting the appropriate property rights, today agencies play a crucial role in conditioning resource use'.[24] Teaching natural resource law now requires dealing with a complex combination of established common law principles about property rights in resources, early statutory frameworks dealing with land and resource dispositions, and contemporary regulatory schemes attempting to balance a range of values and interests related to the environment and resources. Foundational concepts of property must be taught alongside principles of judicial review as statutory frameworks authorizing dispositions and governing extraction and use are characterized by 'profound and pervasive discretion at every level of decision making'.[25]

Despite some overlap with the more recent development of courses in environmental law, natural resource law is still where lawyers and law students grapple directly with the rules about how resources are extracted for transformation into goods and services – what Fischman terms, 'the stuff of consumption'.[26] As he points out, '[N]atural resources law is dominated by this "resource-ist", utilitarian approach' rather than approaches emphasizing the intrinsic value of aspects of the environment or attempting to deal with the effects of secondary uses of resources, such as pollution.[27] Despite shifts towards 'sustainability' and 'sustainable management' in statutory frameworks and policy guidance, economic interests continue to dominate natural

---

[23]   Janet E Mosher, 'Legal Education: Nemesis or Ally of Social Movements' (1997) *Osgoode Hall L J* 613, 625.

[24]   Fischman (n 20) 718.

[25]   Lynda Collins and Lorne Sossin, 'In Search of an Ecological Approach to Constitutional Principles and Environmental Discretion in Canada' (2019) 52 *UBCL Rev* 293, 295.

[26]   Fischman (n 20) 731.

[27]   Ibid., 733.

resource decision making in Canada.[28] One of the few natural resource law texts available notes, 'Canada's approach [to sustainable development] has been inconsistent and relatively weak.' Indeed, the authors note sustainability discourse has created an opportunity for 'wealth creation aspects of resource use to once again regain dominance over the need for environmental protection and reduced consumption'.[29] As Graham sums up the continued domination of property law in land use decision making: 'To put it simply, the influence of property law on land use practice and natural resource management is greater than the influence of environmental law, even where the latter explicitly prohibits certain land use practices and actions.'[30] Thus while natural resource and environmental law teaching may have some subject areas in common, they continue to serve distinct functions in legal education. In my view they also offer distinct possibilities for the transformation of legal education. Natural resource law, with its grounding in colonial property and constitutional relations, and its ongoing role in attempts to sever Indigenous people-place relations through both dispossession and ecological devastation, is a particularly important site of intervention.

NATURAL RESOURCES LAW AS A SITE FOR DECOLONIZATION AND RECONCILIATION

In 2015, the Truth and Reconciliation Commission of Canada (TRC) issued a series of Calls to Action following from a national inquiry process into residential schools in Canada. Law schools were specifically included in the Calls to Action. This included Recommendation 28, which directly addressed action from law schools:[31]

> We call upon law schools in Canada to require all law students to take a course in Aboriginal people and the law, which includes the history and legacy of residential schools, the *United Nations Declaration on the Rights of Indigenous Peoples*, Treaties and Aboriginal rights, Indigenous law, and Aboriginal–Crown relations. This will require skills-based training in intercultural competency, conflict resolution, human rights, and anti-racism.

Recommendation 28 has received considerable attention, including from my own law school, which instituted an Indigenous and Aboriginal Law

---

[28] David R Boyd, *Cleaner, Greener, Healthier: A Prescription for Stronger Canadian Environmental Laws and Policies* (UBC Press 2015).

[29] Hughes, Kwasniak and Lucas (n 11) 114.

[30] Graham (n 1) 401.

[31] Truth and Reconciliation Commission of Canada, 'Calls to Action' (2015) http://trc.ca/assets/pdf/Calls_to_Action_English2.pdf accessed 20 October 2019.

Requirement in 2018, requiring all students to 'complete a course for credit that focuses primarily on Indigenous and Aboriginal legal issues and engages in a substantial way with Indigenous laws, Aboriginal law, and aspects of professionalism and practice skills related to serving indigenous clients'.[32]

However, as Hewitt has noted, law schools must also attend to Recommendation 50 and its call for 'deeper institutional structural change and meaningful partnerships with Indigenous organizations'.[33] Recommendation 50 states:

> 50. In keeping with the *United Nations Declaration on the Rights of Indigenous Peoples*, we call upon the federal government, in collaboration with Aboriginal organizations, to fund the establishment of Indigenous law institutes for the development, use, and understanding of Indigenous laws and access to justice in accordance with the unique cultures of Aboriginal peoples in Canada.

Recommendation 50 is a call for broad institutional change. For example, Hewitt calls on Canadian law schools to 'offer a degree in the Indigenous legal traditions as a necessary reshaping of the master narrative'.[34] Nonetheless, changing the way we teach key areas of the existing curriculum can be part of laying the foundation for the broader transformation of legal education and contribute to the sustainability of institutional change. It can open up possibilities to link research in the legal academy to Indigenous-driven research agendas and methodologies. Perhaps more profoundly it can create spaces where law students and teachers can heed the Chair of the TRC Senator Murray Sinclair and learn to listen.[35]

Taking engagement with Indigenous law. We must confront jurisdiction seriously requires rethinking the very premise of natural resource law and its grounding in a colonial property law narrative not only grounded in racist assumptions justifying dispossession, but also the treatment of the earth and ecological systems as a set of resources whose primary, if not only, value derives from their use and consumption for human benefit. Natural Resources Law courses provide an important site for disruption of dominant narratives of Canadian constitutionalism through engagement with Indigenous laws and assertions of jurisdiction *as law*.[36] This includes acknowledging the long

---

[32] Degree requirements are listed online: https://www.osgoode.yorku.ca/programs/juris-doctor/jd-program/degree-requirements accessed 20 October 2019.

[33] Hewitt (n 4) 70.

[34] Ibid., 80.

[35] Ibid., 80–81.

[36] Hadley Friedland and Val Napoleon, 'Gathering the Threads: Developing a Methodology for Researching and Rebuilding Indigenous Legal Traditions' (2015) 1 *Lakehead Law Journal* 16, 20; Joseph Williams, 'The Harkness Henry Lecture Lex

history of Crown's engagement with Indigenous law and practice, but also the treatment of a full range of Indigenous law, legal practices, and sources of law as valid and relevant to contemporary law making and conflict resolution.[37]

Indigenous leaders and scholars have noted that any meaningful transformation of settler-Indigenous relations requires us to grapple with the land question.[38] As Hewitt makes plain, 'Indigenous peoples are partners in Confederation – the partner who contributed all of the lands and natural resources.'[39] In the territory where I live and teach, as in many parts of Canada, this partnership is documented in the historic treaties that made Canadian confederation possible. In the words of legal anthropologist and treaty expert Michael Asch, 'one can not have Confederation until there is a home on which to build it, and without treaties we have no home here…our legitimacy arises from the agreements we made with those who were already here when we first arrived'.[40] Yet, a traditional approach to natural resource law taught through the overlapping lenses of colonial property concepts, the 1867 division of powers, and contemporary administrative law, such as the procedural duty to consult, serves not only to reinforce the existing constitutional structure, but to reproduce it by preparing students 'to work within the existing order, marginally, incrementally modifying it through litigation'.[41] Grounding courses about how we regulate our relationship to places and to the more-than-human world in the traditional understanding of Canadian constitutionalism does important work in upholding the colonial 'master narrative' of Indigenous inferiority, which as Hewitt argues, clears the way for settler appropriation of lands and resources.[42] The presumption of Crown sovereignty as a non-justiciable feature of the Canadian legal system underpins what Sarah Morales and Joshua Nichols call

---

Aotearoa: An Heroic Attempt to Map the Maori Dimension in Modern New Zealand Law' (2013) 21 *Waikato L Rev: Taumauri* 1; Jacinta Ruru, 'First Laws: Tikanga Maori in/and the Law' (2018) *V U W L R* 211; Carwyn Jones, *New Treaty, New Tradition: Reconciling New Zealand and Maori Law* (UBC Press 2016).

[37]   John Borrows, 'Wampum at Niagara: The Royal Proclamation, Canadian Legal History, and Self-Government' in Michael Asch (ed), *Aboriginal and Treaty Rights in Canada* (UBC Press 1998); Corbiere (n 8).

[38]   Glen Sean Coulthard, *Red Skin, White Masks: Rejecting the Colonial Politics of Recognition* (Taylor & Francis 2014) http://www.tandfonline.com/doi/pdf/10.1080/2325548X.2016.1145982#page=57 accessed 22 March 2017; Jeffery G Hewitt, 'Land Acknowledgment, Scripting and Julius Caesar', *The Supreme Court Law Review: Osgoode's Annual Constitutional Cases Conference* (2019); Arthur Manuel and Grand Chief Ronald M Derrickson, *Unsettling Canada: A National Wake-up Call* (Between the Lines 2015).

[39]   Hewitt (n 4) 66.

[40]   Asch (n 9) 42.

[41]   Mosher (n 23) 626.

[42]   Hewitt (n 4).

the 'thick' version of sovereignty, leaving little space for Indigenous law and jurisdiction as Indigenous peoples are 'subjects (or even wards) of the Crown' rather than 'equal partners in Confederation'.[43]

Yet, serious and meaningful engagement with Indigenous law 'as law' and as an equal source of jurisdiction in relation to lands, waters, animals, plants, and earth systems is not only crucial to decolonization of the law school; it is central to effectively teaching students about the legal and relational frameworks governing natural resource decisions and disputes on the ground.[44] This kind of deep engagement with indigenous law and environmental jurisdiction is at the core of the most groundbreaking work in natural resource law in Canada and beyond. Recognition of Māori relationships with lands and waters is for example central to the transformative land use frameworks being implemented in Aotearoa New Zealand.[45] Recognition of legal personality for the Whanganui River and the declaration of former National Park Te Urewea as a legal entity are rooted in Māori law and the jurisdiction of local iwi [tribe]. Joint decision making regimes are also emerging in Canada, such as the *Kunst'aa guu-Kunst'aayah Reconciliation Protocol*, which authorizes the Haida Gwaii Management Council to make decisions about forestry and heritage preservation.[46] As Dayna N Scott and Andrée Boisselle observe, while co-management can reinscribe state authority, negotiation of these frameworks 'can be a process through which settler institutions are forced to explicitly

---

[43]   Sarah Morales and Joshua Nichols, 'Reconciliation beyond the Box' (Center for International Governance Innovation 2018) Special Report 8–9 https://www.cigionline .org/person/sarah-morales accessed 20 October 2019.

[44]   Deborah Curran, 'Putting Place in Law: Field School Explorations of Indigenous and Colonial Legal Geographies' in Deborah Curran and others (eds), *Out There Learning: Critical Approaches to Off-Campus Study Programs* (University of Toronto Press 2018).

[45]   Te Awa Tupua (Whanganui River Claims Settlement) Act 2017; Te Urewera Act 2014; James D K Morris and Jacinta Ruru, 'Giving Voice to Rivers: Legal Personality as a Vehicle for Recognising Indigenous Peoples' Relationships to Water' (2010) 14 *AILR* 49; Jacinta Ruru, 'A Treaty in Another Context: Creating Reimagined Treaty Relationships in Aotearoa New Zealand' in John Borrows and Michael Coyle (eds), *The Right Relationship: Reimagining the Implementation of Historical Treaties* (University of Toronto Press Toronto 2017); Katherine Sanders, '"Beyond Human Ownership"? Property, Power and Legal Personality for Nature in Aotearoa New Zealand' (2017) 30 *JEL* 207; Carwyn Jones, 'Tūhoe-Crown Settlement – Tūhoe Claims Settlement Act 2014; Te Urewera Report of the Waitangi Tribunal' (2014) October *Maori LR* 13; Linda Te Aho, 'Ruruku Whakatupua Te Mana o Te Awa Tupua – Upholding the Mana of the Whanganui River at Māori Law Review' (2014) May *Maori LR*.

[46]   See Haida Nation and British Columbia (Minister of Aboriginal Relations and Reconciliation) 'Kunst'aa guu–Kunst'aayah Reconciliation Protocol' (2009) Schedule B   http://www.haidanation.ca/wp-content/uploads/2017/03/Kunstaa-guu_Kunstaayah _Agreement.pdf accessed 20 October 2019.

recognize the authority and legitimacy of Indigenous governance systems'.[47] These forms of 'intersocietal law' are a product of legal systems coming together, often in confrontation and without a clear path to reconciliation, and they require lawyers who are equipped to do this complex and difficult work.[48]

Taking the task of preparing students for this work seriously requires a shift from both traditional approaches to natural resource law in particular and dominant legal pedagogies more broadly in core law school curricula such as property, contract, and constitutional law. As Hewitt notes, we need to engage each other in difficult and uncomfortable conversations 'to develop plans for the return of the lands and establishing sustainable ways to "peaceably share"'.[49] While as a non-Indigenous scholar trained in Canadian law I am not qualified to teach Indigenous law, I can require students to think about what it means to recognize those pre-existing legal orders as core parts of our system of natural resource governance and challenge them to take assertions of ownership and jurisdiction seriously as matters of day-to-day relevance in natural resource transactions. I can engage with Indigenous methodologies and create and sustain relationships with Indigenous communities, and this can inform my approach to teaching.[50] Elsewhere I have focused on the potential for place-based approaches to address concerns about environmental law teaching failing to address, or even perpetuating, the underlying conditions of ecological crises. I concluded that place-based approaches can be adapted to the law school environment to effectively shift away from the placelessness of traditional legal education to provide students with tools for thinking critically and contextually about land use conflicts.[51] Below I reflect on the potential of place-based approaches to law teaching and learning to contribute to, however modestly, this work of decolonizing legal education.

---

[47]   Dayna Nadine Scott and Andrée Boisselle, 'If There Can Only Be "One Law", It Must Be Treaty Law. Learning From Kanawayandan D'aaki' [2019] Articles & Book Chapters 2745 https://digitalcommons.osgoode.yorku.ca/scholarly_works/274, accessed on 20 October 2019, Forthcoming, UNB Law Review, Special Issue on Puzzles of Pipelines and Riddles of Resources.

[48]   Brian Slattery, 'The Generative Structure of Aboriginal Rights' (2007) 38 *Supreme Court Law Review* 595; Williams (n 35).

[49]   Hewitt (n 37) 43.

[50]   Hewitt (n 4) 72.

[51]   Estair Van Wagner, '"Seeing the Place Makes It Real": Place-Based Teaching in the Environmental and Planning Law Classroom' (2017) 34 *EPLJ* 522; Estair Van Wagner, 'Innovation in a New Zealand Law School's Resource Management Curriculum' (2017) 13 *Resource Management Theory and Practices*.

A MODEST PROPOSAL FOR PLACE-BASED LAW SCHOOL LEARNING: LINKING PLACE WITH DECOLONIZATION

The roots of natural resource law lie in the dephysicalized conceptualization of colonial property law imported to Canada and other countries settled by European colonizers. As such, in some ways it imports the abstract, place-lessness of colonial law prevalent in law schools.[52] However, in other ways natural resource law teaching lends itself to place-based teaching because the subjects of the course are themselves rooted in place. As Fischman notes, natural resource problems are generally *in situ*, requiring decision making to respond to the conditions of a particular location and context.[53] In this sense, natural resource law is particularly situated as an area of law through which students can be engaged meaningfully in place-based legal orders, regulatory frameworks, and governance models. Canadian legal scholar Deborah Curran argues the 'inherently place-based' nature of these issues requires direct engagement with the specific places in which they take place.[54] It is, in many ways, the perfect law school course in which to attend not only to *what* we teach and learn, but *how* and *where*.[55] As Borrows notes, 'Law lives "on the ground"; it is present in physical and social relationships.'[56] Yet too often legal education filters out the broader material and social relations in which legal cases are embedded.[57] This is particularly problematic in the context of conflicts about Indigenous relations to land where technical legal tests are taught in classrooms without an understanding of the 'specific lands, waters, and Indigenous governance systems from which the jurisprudence arose'.[58] The land and resources governed by Canadian law 'serve as sources of law for many Indigenous peoples, such as the Anishinaabe'.[59] As Borrows notes, Anishinaabe law 'can be seen as literally being written on the earth'. He describes learning from an Elder in his community, Dr Basil Johnston:

> Thus, Basil, emphasized that standards for making judgments can be found in the natural world as described in Anishinaabemowin, our language. He said that author-

---

[52] Curran (n 43); Van Wagner, 'Seeing the Place Makes It Real', ibid.; Van Wagner, 'Innovation in a New Zealand Law School's Resource Management Curriculum', ibid.

[53] Fischman (n 20) 734.

[54] Curran (n 43).

[55] John Borrows, 'Outsider Education: Indigenous Law and Land-Based Learning' (2016) 33 *Windsor YB Access Just* 1.

[56] Ibid., 4.

[57] Curran (n 43) 135.

[58] Ibid., 138.

[59] Hewitt (n 4) 66.

ity, precedent, and rules are triggered by observing the winds, waters, rocks, plants and animals, and describing what we see in this light.[60]

Therefore to effectively understand the legal frameworks engaged by land use disputes, students must not only understand the law as understood by Canadian courts and law schools, they must understand it as 'rooted in specific ecosystems and cultural contexts'.[61]

My own approach to place-based law teaching is informed by David Gruenwald's 'critical pedagogy of place', which: 'aims to (a) identify, recover, and create material spaces and places that teach us how to live well in our total environments (reinhabitation); and (b) identify and change ways of thinking that injure and exploit other people and places (decolonization)'[62]. However, I note McInerney et al.'s caution that simply adding place to education, legal or otherwise, will not necessarily foster transformative thinking.[63] Indeed Eve Tuck and K Wayne Yang have noted concerns about 'settler moves to innocence' and I am conscious of the ways in which place-based approaches may map onto these 'diversions, distractions, which relieve the settler of feelings of guilt or responsibility, and conceal the need to give up land or power or privilege'.[64] I agree with Curran who argues place-based initiatives must be consistent with the 'decolonization imperative' by foregrounding local voices and experiences while explicitly attending to power relations.[65] She notes four place-based best practices: (1) a relational integration of the topics in the course; (2) immersion experiences; (3) being in the places shaped by and shaping law; and (4) interacting with participants and decision makers and understanding the complexity of the issues they face.[66] The final section below reflects on place-based teaching and learning in the context of the natural resource law classroom.

---

[60]   Borrows, 'Earth-Bound' (n 3) 51.

[61]   Curran (n 43) 139.

[62]   David A Gruenewald, 'The Best of Both Worlds: A Critical Pedagogy of Place' (2008) 14 *Environmental Education Research* 308, 310.

[63]   Peter McInerney, John Smyth and Barry Down, '"Coming to a Place Near You?" The Politics and Possibilities of a Critical Pedagogy of Place-based Education' (2011) 39 *Asia-Pacific Journal of Teacher Education* 3, 9–11.

[64]   Eve Tuck and K Wayne Yang, 'Decolonization Is Not a Metaphor' (2012) 1 *Decolonization: Indigeneity, Education & Society* 21 http://decolonization.org/index .php/des/article/view/18630 accessed 3 June 2014.

[65]   Curran (n 43) 142.

[66]   Curran (n 43).

LINKING PLACE WITH ACTION: REFLECTIONS ON TEACHING NATURAL RESOURCES LAW

I first taught Resource Management and Natural Resource Law in Aotearoa New Zealand as a lecturer at the Victoria University of Wellington. Elsewhere I have provided a detailed description of my experiences of developing a place-based approach to these courses.[67] Through field trips, guest speaker selection, and a novel assessment model linked to community-based resource management issues, I provided students with an alternative, community-engaged learning experience in these land use law subjects. In addition to incorporating place-based approaches, I attempted to build on some of the insights and tools developed by educators in clinical education settings.[68] Another key part of the development of the place-based elements of these courses was engagement with Māori legal concepts and practices both in the classroom, and through field trips and community-based projects. A qualitative survey of students identified a number of positive learning outcomes were associated with the place-based aspects of the course and the assessment.[69]

Since my arrival at Osgoode and my return to Canada, my teaching has focused on land use law courses, including natural resources law, the Environmental Justice and Sustainability Clinic, as well as a mandatory first year property law course. I have also been involved as a participant and an organizer of our Anishinaabe Law Camps. These provide an immersion experience in a local Anishinaabe community under the guidance of Indigenous legal scholars such as Professors John Borrows, Heidi Stark, Jeff Hewitt, and Lindsay Borrows, and a number of community Elders and Knowledge Keepers. Neyaashiinigmiing, the home of the Chippewas of Nawash Unceded First Nation, has hosted Osgoode faculty and students for four days in September

---

[67]   Van Wagner, 'Seeing the Place Makes It Real' (n 50); Van Wagner, 'Innovation in a New Zealand Law School's Resource Management Curriculum' (n 50).

[68]   Christine Zuni Cruz, '[On the] Road Back in: Community Lawyering in Indigenous Communities' (1998) 5 *Clinical L Rev* 557; Andrea M Seielstad, 'Community Building as a Means of Teaching Creative, Cooperative, and Complex Problem Solving in Clinical Legal Education' (2001) 8 *Clinical L Rev* 445; Shin Imai, 'A Counter-Pedagogy for Social Justice: Core Skills for Community-Based Lawyering' (2002) 9 *Clinical L Rev* 195; Anthony V Alfieri, 'Educating Lawyers for Community' (2012) *Wis L Rev* 115; Juliet M Brodie, 'Little Cases on the Middle Ground: Teaching Social Justice Lawyering in Neighborhood-Based Community Lawyering Clinics' (2008) 15 *Clinical L Rev* 333; Karen Tokarz and others, 'Conversations on Community Lawyering': The Newest (Oldest) Wave in Clinical Legal Education' (2008) 28 *Wash U J L & Pol'y* 359; Mosher (n 23).

[69]   Van Wagner, 'Seeing the Place Makes It Real' (n 50); Van Wagner, 'Innovation in a New Zealand Law School's Resource Management Curriculum' (n 50).

for the last six years.[70] The Chippewas of Rama in Mnjikaning have hosted a second camp with Osgoode for three years. Participants are introduced to Anishinaabe legal concepts and principles, systems of governance and diplomacy, and pedagogies and modes of reasoning. Interactive lectures are held outside, beside lakes and rivers and under the Niagara escarpment as we are taught from the fundamental text of the Anishinaabe intellectual tradition: the land itself. Through engagement with Anishinaabe stories we learn to draw out some of the principles they contain for living in community and resolving conflicts, including in relation to land and resources. Historic and current conflicts and relationships are explained and contextualized in place during the Law Camps, which helps students to contextualize Indigenous-settler relations more broadly during their legal education. While my focus here is on a Natural Resources Law course, the discussion reflects my thinking on teaching and learning in each of these contexts.

Natural Resources Law is an upper year elective course, which I have explicitly designed from a place-based perspective and to complement these other offerings at Osgoode. The materials focus on Ontario rather than surveying statutory frameworks from across Canada, and particularly the Great Lakes Region. This focus guides the substantive content of the course and the course projects discussed below. For example, we spend substantial time on forestry, mining, freshwater, and biodiversity protection and only touch on the marine environment and oil and gas briefly. Further, while students are encouraged to examine the Indigenous legal orders relevant to all the cases and issues we discuss, and to situate them in their material and social contexts, the course materials and projects engage specifically with Anishinaabe law. This emphasis reflects both that Osgoode is situated in the Anishinaabe territory, the current Treaty holders being the Missisaugas of Credit, and that Osgoode has developed specific opportunities for students and faculty to engage with Anishinaabe law and Knowledge Keepers. It also reflects my own goal of learning and engaging with Anishinaabe law. To be clear, I am not teaching my students Anishinaabe law in the course, nor are they learning to practice Anishinaabe law. As noted above, I am not qualified to do so. I am drawing students' attention to relevant Indigenous laws and practices *as law* and providing textual and non-textual resources for us, including videos and podcasts, to work together to better understand how they shape and inform resource management law in particular places. As with my courses in New Zealand,

---

[70]   The law camp was developed by Professor Borrows and the Borrows family in partnership with Professor Andrée Boisselle.

I have drawn on colleagues or guests who are experts in Anishinaabe law to provide guest lectures to supplement our learning.[71]

Students in both Natural Resources Law and the EJS Clinic select their research projects from a list of topics I develop with lawyers and community partners in advance of the course. While the topics list in my courses at VUW and in the EJS Clinic have included research for both Indigenous and non-Indigenous organizations, the Osgoode Natural Resources Law course has involved research topics specifically related to Indigenous natural resource governance in partnership with both communities directly and lawyers working with Indigenous communities. In the first class in 2018–2019 enrolment was small and students chose from two topics. Students were invited by Elder and Counsellor Anthony (Miptoon) Cheghano, one of the Elders and community teachers in the law camp at Neyaashiinigmiing, to write papers about Indigenous jurisdiction and endangered species protection in the context of the Saugeen (Bruce) Peninsula where his community is located. This project is part of my efforts to ensure that our relations with the community at Neyaashiinigmiing are reciprocal, with the law students and faculty using our skills to support the work of the community. Students were also invited to support an ongoing community-based research project with Professor Dayna N Scott on the development of the Ring of Fire, a valuable mineral deposit in the Far North of Ontario.[72] Professor Scott has worked in partnership with community-based researchers in a number of First Nations in the Far North, including Kitchenuhmaykoosib Inninuwug, Neskantaka, and Eabametoong First Nations as mining infrastructure projects have been proposed and developed. These two projects continue in 2019–2020 and students will build on the earlier projects. However, with larger enrolment I also reached out to law firm Olthius, Kleer, Townshend who specialize in Indigenous governance and work exclusively for First Nations communities. Lawyers there identified three areas of research that would support their clients' ongoing land and resource management work: (1) Recent reforms to environmental law in Ontario, particularly the Endangered Species Act and the reforms to the planning law framework; (2) the treatment of cumulative effects in environmental assessment and planning; and (3) models for co-governance of freshwater resources. Student research papers and projects are provided to the partners at the end of the course after being assessed and edited as required. Last year the research

---

[71] In particular, I am grateful to Dr Carwyn Jones, Dr Maria Bargh, Maia Wikaria, and Professor Deborah McGregor for their wonderful contributions to my classes in Canada and Aotearoa New Zealand.

[72] Scott and Boisselle (n 46); Rachel Ariss and John Cutfeet, 'Kitchenuhmaykoosib Inninuwug First Nation: Mining, Consultation, Reconciliation and Law' (2011) 10 *Indigenous Law Journal at the University of Toronto, Faculty of Law* 1.

projects directly informed submissions to major legislative reform processes on planning and environmental law.

My commitment to place-based learning has also meant building field trip experiences into the course. Each year we have been to the Art Gallery of Ontario early in the class to explore the ways in which art and representation shape, and are shaped by, settler-Indigenous relations and our relations with the more-than-human world. In 2018–2019 we visited the Anthropocene exhibit and had a follow up discussion about Indigenous perspectives on the Anthropocene concept based on the work of Métis scholar Zoe Todd.[73] In 2019–2020 we visited the J S Mclean Centre for Indigenous & Canadian Art with Indigenous art educator, Charlotte Big Canoe, who discussed a number of Indigenous and non-Indigenous pieces with the class. Students working with Counsellor Cheghano were also invited to visit Neyaashiinigmiing, where we spent the day learning about Anishinaabe relationships with plant and animal species and the impacts of development and climate change on the community's territory in order to better understand Anishinaabe environmental governance. In 2019–2020 students working on the OKT projects were also invited to attend this field trip, which included Elder and Knowledge Keeper Lenore Keeshig, who is also a story teller and naturalist with expertise in the geological history of the Great Lakes Region. In future years, I hope to build each project around a field experience, ensuring that the research is grounded in 'a real understanding of the importance of place in Aboriginal and Indigenous law and how that embeddedness drives the approach to and resolution of specific legal issues'.[74] This will take time as these partnerships must be built and founded on a sense of trust and reciprocity.

CONCLUSION: CAUTIONS AND HOPES

The decolonization imperative requires transformative shifts in the way we think about relationships with the more-than-human world. It requires fundamental change in the constitutional relationships between Indigenous and settler governments. As a teacher it is not only my personal willingness to sit with discomfort that is required, but to knowingly draw students in my course into uncomfortable spaces, without the promise of resolution or comfort at the end of the class or the semester. As Canadian law teacher Nicole O'Byrne

---

[73]   Zoe Todd, 'Indigenizing the Anthropocene' (2015) in Heather Davis and Etienne Turpin (eds), *Art in the Anthropocene: Encounters among aesthetics, politics, environments and epistemologies* 241; Heather Davis and Zoe Todd, 'On the Importance of a Date, or Decolonizing the Anthropocene' (2017) 16 *ACME: An International E-Journal for Critical Geographies*.

[74]   Curran (n 43) 139.

reflects about her own attempts to grapple with decolonization in the law school classroom: 'emotional reactions to the course materials are to be expected and [that] there is nothing easy about the decolonization process.'[75] Indeed, that is the point – if it is easy it is not moving towards decolonization. In my view, place-based pedagogy has a crucial role to play in this work.

The above said, I am cautious about using the language of decolonization in the context of law teaching. As Tuck and Yang have noted, the term decolonization has been 'superficially adopted into education and other social sciences' as a substitute for social justice language and to signal awareness of Indigenous scholarship and relevant issues being confronted by communities.[76] However, as they note, decolonizing requires more than symbolic gestures: 'decolonization in the settler colonial context must involve the repatriation of land simultaneous to the recognition of how land and relations to land have always already been differently understood and enacted; that is *all* of the land, and not just symbolically'.[77] The conversations required to meaningfully engage with Tuck and Yang's understanding of decolonization will be difficult and uncomfortable. Yet, it is clearly a set of conversations in which future lawyers working in land use law, and particularly natural resources law, will be required to engage. As law teachers it is our job to help them develop the knowledge and tools to do so; and, perhaps most importantly the humility to listen before they do so – to Indigenous colleagues, scholars, and communities, and to the earth itself.

---

[75] Nicole O'Byrne, 'Teaching Aboriginal Law in an Age of Reconciliation' (2019) 9 *Antistasis* 65, 60.

[76] Tuck and Yang (n 61) 2.

[77] Ibid., 7.

PART II

Formats and methodologies for teaching environmental law

5. Is your textbook (still) really necessary?[1]

Stuart Bell

The title of this chapter is taken from 1970 and a typically swashbuckling and sweetly provocative piece by William Twining which ostensibly reviewed the third edition of a popular textbook on Jurisprudence.[2] In gently but purposefully dismantling the specific approach taken in the book, Twining took a swipe at textbooks generally in setting out an argument that they were: 'too narrow, too philistine and generally too restrictive to be suitable as a vehicle for many kinds of scholarly communication'.[3] His argument was principally that textbooks were bad for students and for academics. For the former they discouraged independent critical thought and for the latter they were a waste of intellectual energy. Underlying his critique was a broader reflection on a 'number of ailments' in legal education which were not 'easy to diagnose, let alone cure'.[4] Twining saw the rapid growth in sub-standard textbooks as a canary in the coal mine of a liberal legal education. In asking purposive questions about textbooks, he was also asking normative questions about legal education generally. Although written over 50 years ago, the themes and arguments have a familiar ring to them.[5]

---

[1] I first presented an outline of the ideas in this chapter at the *Annual Journal of Environmental Law Workshop* in November 2018 on 'Environmental Law and the Academy' and the accompanying Blog Post at https://blog.oup.com/2018/09/environmental-law-textbook/. I am grateful for the feedback from participants at the Workshop and in particular the thoughts and ideas of Steven Vaughan and my long-standing colleague and co-author Don McGillivray.

[2] W. Twining, 'Is Your Text-Book Really Necessary' (1970) 11 *J. Soc'y Pub. Tchers. L. N.S.* 81.

[3] Ibid., p.88.

[4] Ibid.

[5] Ibid. In 1970 these ailments included: the rapid expansion of legal education; development of new ideas and methods of communication; the questioning of traditional classifications of legal subjects; and the movement supporting a broader approach to 'law' as a discipline – evidence of the more things change, the more they stay the same.

In contemporary environmental law, writing and using textbooks is not 'where it's at'. By their nature they tend to be descriptive and dependable, conveying the basics of the discipline or sub-discipline in a way that is accessible and straightforward for new learners. They are rarely innovative or 'cutting edge scholarly activity'.[6] Certainly, in terms of environmental law scholarship, all the stimulating action is to be found in the deeper waters of research monographs, academic journal articles, impact activities and even the contemporaneity and directness of social media. There is a prosaic air surrounding the 'unglamorous' and 'unpopular' world of textbook writing. 'The unspoken duty of textbook writers is to be staid' is not a description that exactly lights the academic fires of curiosity, is it?[7]

There is, therefore, an obvious tension in reconsidering the purposes of the 'staid' and dependable textbook in a collection that highlights innovation in environmental law learning and teaching. Indeed, as Twining would no doubt argue, textbooks can undermine innovative approaches because they implicitly promote the comfort of the status quo through the idea that there is a set format and context for learning. Nevertheless, textbooks still represent a key source of information for learners whilst new generations of authors appear to remain committed to the values of a liberal legal education at the same time as wasting their intellectual energies in preparing new editions of long-standing texts.[8] Any suggestion that the textbook is dead is probably an exaggeration.

Perhaps the best way of approaching the role of textbooks in this collection is to ask whether they continue to be fit for purpose? My argument is that we need to rethink the role and purpose of textbooks to address general changes in higher education and make space for innovation and new approaches to learning. In the context of environmental law, there are disciplinary challenges for textbook writers in trying to capture the rapid pace of change and seemingly incessant growth of regulatory and non-legal responses to environmental problems. As our understanding of law's role in addressing the complexity and messiness of these problems grows, the standard descriptive textbook seems both anachronistic and simplistic. Would it be better to redeploy our intellectual and physical energies in other directions in designing more appro-

---

[6]   E. Fisher, B. Lange, and E. Scotford, 'The Glamour of Textbook Writing', Blog Post at global.oup.com/uk/orc/law/environmental/fisher/resources/textbook-writing/, accessed 28 April 2021.

[7]   Ibid.

[8]   The textbook I contribute to is in its ninth edition with new authors joining over the last two editions, see S. Bell, D. McGillivray, O. Pederson, E. Lees and E. Stokes, *Environmental Law* (9th edn, Oxford: OUP, 2017). I started writing the first edition with the late Simon Ball in 1988.

priate learning resources to support, encourage and inspire a new generation of learners?

The chapter is divided into four main sections addressing: two key purposes of textbooks; the challenges to those purposes; and some potential responses to those challenges. In the first section I consider the textbook tradition model, namely the formative purpose of textbooks, considering the impacts of the textbook tradition on legal education generally and more specifically the reflexive relationship between environmental law textbooks and the development of a maturing discipline. In the second section I consider the learning resource model, namely the educational purposes served by textbooks as resources supporting learning. In the third section, I consider the challenges to these models in the context of changes in higher education and supporting innovation in environmental law learning and teaching. In the final section I briefly outline some thoughts on responding to these challenges by looking at some key characteristics that could trigger a reinvention of the textbook to support learners and facilitate, rather than stifle innovation.

I have some pre-emptive apologies/disclaimers/caveats. First, my focus is on pedagogical issues and on the purposes of textbooks in the context of learning environmental *law*. I do not directly consider the economic and social justice issues around the affordability and accessibility of textbooks, although my brief discussion of the role of open educational resources in section 4 should provide an indication of my views. I am also aware of the breadth of literature and thinking about environmental or sustainability education more generally, but I am taking a relatively narrow view.[9] It should be clear from what I have to say that I think that the overlap between learning about law and environmental issues more generally is significant, particularly the range of skills and/or competencies that are required to address environmental challenges – whether through legal or non-legal means.[10] Second, motivation for writing this piece is self-reflective rather than a wholesale critique of textbooks or other authors. Having spent the best part of the last 30 years in writing and rewriting a textbook, I consider that I have enough intellectual investment to ask purposive questions about the nature of the return. There are many textbooks of various shapes and sizes that I admire as being well-written, thoroughly researched and that continue to prove their worth to generations of learners – if there is any criticism, it is primarily directed inwards. Third, most of my references refer to

---

[9]   J. Holder, 'Identifying the Points of Contact and Engagement Between Environmental Education and Legal Education' (2013) 40(3) *J. Law and Society* 541–69.

[10]   A. Wiek, L. Withycombe and C. Redman, 'Key Competencies in Sustainability: A Reference Framework for Academic Program Development' (2011) 6 *Sustain Sci.* 203–18.

the UK (or even English) context. I hope the general principles are applicable more widely. Finally, it should be clear that although the focus is on the role and purpose of textbooks in supporting learning in environmental law, the meta-theme of this chapter is what learners should be learning and how. I do not have the space to develop this theme in detail, but my hope is that other chapters in this collection make up for that omission.

1.   THE FORMATIVE PURPOSE – THE 'TEXTBOOK TRADITION'

One of the points that Twining does not directly address in his article is that textbooks have more than a single purpose. Several writers have highlighted the significance of the 'textbook tradition' in UK legal education and the role such books have played in the development of the way we 'teach, write and think about law' as an academic discipline.[11] In the early days of UK Law Schools, textbooks underpinned the development of law as an academic subject and gave the pioneers of legal education a professional identity in a world where law was seen as a practical and vocational subject.[12] Producing textbooks that set out a taxonomy of legal principles through systematising and codifying case law, was a way of demonstrating that law was a 'proper' science – and could sit happily alongside other academic disciplines within higher education. Under this model, the production of textbooks was driven by a desire to organise by way of elucidating clear principles that brought order from the apparent chaos of reported cases. A side effect of this ordering process was that there was a legitimation of the professional role of academics themselves.

The key point about the textbook tradition is the extent to which there is a normative dimension to a descriptive process. Underlying the organisation and 'structuralisation' was the common-law mind-set portrayed in these textbooks. This mind-set relied heavily upon the idea that there is a 'technique' to learning the law that is 'objective, neutral and apolitical'.[13] The difficulty was that it also created a false impression of the role that social and political factors played in law in everyday life. The common-law mind-set 'tended to obfuscate the role of lawyers, judges and jurists as translators and creators

---

[11]   D. Sugarman, 'Legal Theory, the Common Law Mind and the Making of the Textbook Tradition' in W. Twining (ed), *Legal Theory and Common Law* (Oxford: Blackwell, 1986) pp.26–62.

[12]   J. Rose, 'The Legal Profession in Medieval England: A History of Regulation' (1998) 48 *Syracuse L. Rev.* 31; and R. Abel, *The Legal Profession in England and Wales* (London: Blackwell, 1988).

[13]   Sugarman, n.11, p.27.

of one of our most important political and social discourses'.[14] In this sense, the textbook writers were not educationalists, but 'conceptive ideologists', structuring a concept of law that was not reflected in reality.[15] In ordering, structuring and legitimising, the authors of these textbooks placed law firmly within a case-law shaped box.

This analysis of the textbook tradition provides a context for the important formative role textbooks play in shaping and reinforcing the structure and coherence of emerging disciplines as a distinct area of law. This certainty is useful for learners because it represents a closed model of rationality and knowledge that allows them to link ideas and principles across otherwise unconnected material. This provides a recognisable structure to the complexity and depth of a subject that may otherwise have no discernible shape or internal logic. On the other hand, the textbook tradition also places constraints upon different ways learners think about the role of law in society.

This formative role can be seen in environmental law – a subject where definitions and boundaries are contestable.[16] Certainly the development of environmental law as a separate subject in England and Wales can be traced back to a period between 1970–90 and the dual emergence of new statutes dealing with pollution control,[17] nature conservation[18] and institutional and integrative arrangements;[19] and the first textbooks on the subject. It is interesting to note that elements of what would be later aggregated within the general subject of environmental law, featured in a range of early treatises. These texts, written by pioneers of what would now be described as environmental law set out to describe the law in cognate areas including air pollution,[20] town and country planning[21] and public health law.[22] In 1972, coinciding with early academic interest, a slim volume covering the 'Laws relating to Pollution' was

---

[14]   Ibid., p.54.

[15]   Ibid.

[16]   Z. Plater, 'Environmental Law and Three Economies: Navigating a Sprawling Field of Study, Practice, and Societal Governance in which Everything is Connected to Everything Else' (1999) 23 *Harv Envtl L Rev* 359, and R. Lazarus, 'Environmental Scholarship and the Harvard Difference', (1999) 23 *Harv Envtl L Rev* 327.

[17]   Control of Pollution Act 1974.

[18]   Wildlife and Countryside Act 1981.

[19]   Environmental Protection Act 1990, Environment Act 1995.

[20]   J.F. Garner and R.S. Offord, *The Law on the Pollution of the Air and the Practice of Its Prevention* (London: Shaw and Sons, 1957).

[21]   D. Heap, *An Outline of Planning Law* (London: Sweet & Maxwell, 1955).

[22]   J.F. Garner, *The Law of Sewers and Drains* (London: Shaw & Sons, 1960).

published.[23] This was followed ten years later, by one of the first textbooks clearly aimed at the student market in the UK.[24]

Fast-forward 30 years, and the 'market' for student texts has matured and developed to reflect the growth of the discipline itself. There are traditional textbooks covering both general[25] and subject specific areas[26] and 'source-books' with commentary, cases and materials.[27] There are also jurisdictionally specific texts for each constituent country in the UK[28] along with the truest symbols of academic maturity, 'nutshells', revision guides and non-specialist, very short introductions.[29] The variety of approaches and academic depth appears to provide learners with choice to meet their own needs. The fact that most of them have gone through several editions suggests that they are popular and meet a demand. Perhaps most of all, the maturity in the market for student textbooks suggests that the primary formative battle has been won and that there is a degree of consensus about the nature of the clear and precise legal rules and principles that make up the hierarchically organised sub-system that can be called environmental law.[30] So where does this leave the formative purpose of environmental law textbooks? Once this core becomes accepted, there is then the danger that, as with the common law mind-set, it dominates, constrains and stifles new or different approaches. Path dependency in terms of using textbooks to shape modular and programme design is difficult to move away from.

---

[23]   J. McLoughlin, *The Law Relating to Pollution: An Introduction* (Manchester: Manchester University Press, 1972).

[24]   D. Hughes, *Environmental Law* (London: Butterworths, 1986).

[25]   E.g. Bell et al n.8; S. Wolf, *Wolf and Stanley on Environmental Law* (6th edn, Abingdon: Routledge, 2013).

[26]   E.g. P.-M. DuPuy and J. Vinuales, *International Environmental Law* (2nd edn, Cambridge: CUP, 2018); J. Peel et al., *Principles of International Environmental Law* (4th edn, Cambridge: CUP, 2018); L. Kramer, *EU Environmental Law* (London: Sweet & Maxwell, 8th edn, 2016); and M. Lee, *EU Environmental Law, Governance and Decision-Making* (2nd edn, Oxford: Hart Publishing, 2014).

[27]   E.g. E. Fisher, B. Lange, and E. Scotford, *Environmental Law: Text, Cases and Materials* (2nd edn, Oxford: OUP, 2019; and J. Holder and M. Lee, *Environmental Protection, Law and Policy: Text and Materials* (2nd edn, Cambridge: CUP, 2007).

[28]   F. McManus, *Environmental Law in Scotland: An Introduction and a Guide* (Edinburgh: Edinburgh University Press, 2016).

[29]   E.g. S. Sneddon, *Law Express: Environmental Law* (2nd edn, Harlow: Pearson, 2014); and E. Fisher, *Environmental Law: A Very Short Introduction* (Oxford: OUP, 2017).

[30]   D. Maldonado, 'Environmental Law Scholarship: Systematization, Reform, Explanation, and Understanding', in (ed) O. Pederson, *Perspectives on Environmental Law Scholarship* (Cambridge: Cambridge University Press, 2018) pp.42–3.

Perhaps the focus needs to shift elsewhere? In terms of environmental law scholarship, Fisher and others issued a challenge to diffident academics within the field to cast off the shackles of self-justification and the search for disciplinary distinctiveness and definition.[31] They argued that environmental law is, and always will be, ill-defined, complex and messy and no amount of introverted, intellectual hand-wringing or reductionist scholarship will change those basic characteristics. Their argument was to focus on the *quality* of environmental law research through a 'deeper and more reflective approach to scholarly method'.[32] By analogy, the same argument applies to learning and teaching environmental law and the textbooks that support that learning. As with environmental law scholarship, we need to reconsider the *quality* of environmental law textbooks and ask questions about what outcomes we are wanting learners to achieve when they study environmental law.

2.   THE EDUCATIONAL PURPOSE – THE LEARNING RESOURCES MODEL

The basic educational purpose of textbooks is to provide what is typically a single resource for supporting learning across a module or programme as a whole. This purpose is probably best reflected in the 'innovations' that now seem to separate textbooks from research monographs or professional treatises. Instead of pages of narrative text and footnotes, there are different techniques employed to engage learners and to highlight pedagogical features. For example, in the text book I co-author, there are introductory case studies to set a real-world context; lists of learning outcomes for each chapter; separate text boxes that summarise key points or case law; self-test questions to break up and reinforce blocks of learning and links to generic or bespoke online resources to flesh out the basic coverage in each chapter. Are these sorts of features enough? Returning again to Twining's original article, his critique is presented through the lens of the four 'laws' of textbook writing which still have relevance to textbook writers assessing their own work.[33] Certainly, applying those four laws to my own attempts at textbook writing is both chastening and illuminating and reveals some of the issues that exist when thinking about the educational purposes of environmental law textbooks.

---

[31]   E. Fisher et al, 'Maturity and Methodology: Starting a Debate about Environmental Law Scholarship' (2009) 21 *JEL* 213.

[32]   E. Fisher, 'Back to Basics: Thinking About the Craft of Environmental Law Scholarship' in Pederson, n.30, p.27 – citing S. Vaughan, 'The Law is my Data: The Socio-Legal in Environmental Law' OUP Blog, 4 September 2017 https://blog.oup.com/2017/09/socio-legal-in-environmental-law/, accessed 28 April 2021.

[33]   Twining, n.1 at pp.82–4.

The first Law: *'Cover the Ground, The Whole Ground and Nothing But the Ground'* challenges our disciplinary insecurities. What do we mean by 'covering the ground' when writing textbooks about environmental law? There have been endless paragraphs written about the challenge of defining the core and boundaries of environmental law as a distinctive academic discipline.[34] This ranges from the defensive justification of an emerging subject to attempts to provide a taxonomy or a mapping of the 'canon'.[35] In all this uncertainty, however, there is a degree of consistency of what might be termed the 'core' of the subject.[36]

As with the textbook tradition, an explicit aim for many environmental law textbooks is to lay out distinctive organising principles and techniques to provide internal coherence across different environmental issues. For example, most student texts will analyse the role that environmental principles play in providing a theoretical context and consistency in law and environmental decision-making across different areas.[37] Whilst principles provide the framework and theoretical justification, further shaping of the discipline occurs with the consistent selection of the central classes of subjects that represent environmental *laws*. The groupings of core chapters typically consider different facets of laws on pollution control; the protection and management of nature and biodiversity; and the regulation of industrial processes. An extra layer is often laid over the top of these substantive laws that address overarching or integrative topics, such as the different layers of laws or the relationship between these layers (e.g., transnational environmental law) and subject areas such as natural resources law which can be applied and integrated across the different parts of the core to such an extent that they are not discernibly different from the core.[38] Beyond these core subjects there is then a diversification into areas which reflect broader environmental issues or concerns that perhaps do not fall easily within the defining boundaries of substantive laws. This might include

---

[34]   T. Aagaard, 'Environmental Law as a Legal Field: An Inquiry in Legal Taxonomy' (2010) 95 *Cornell Law Review* 223.

[35]   Classic examples in the UK context include M. Purdue (1991) 54 *MLR* 534; C. Reid (1998) 4 *Jur Rev* 236. In the US, A. Dan Tarlock. 'Is there a There There in Environmental Law?' (2004) 19 *J. Land Use & Envtl. L.* 213; J. Sax, 'Environmental Law in the Law Schools: What we Teach and How we Feel About It' (1998) 19 *Env. L. Rep.* 10251.

[36]   Aagaard, n.34, p.226.

[37]   E.g. Bell et al, n.8, Part I has a range of Introductory Themes covering definitional and structural topics such as values, principles and the role of policy.

[38]   E.g. Bell et al, n.8, in Part II there is coverage of Integrated Themes such as EU Environmental Law, International Environmental Law, Regulatory Approaches, Private Law, Enforcement and Access to Justice.

coverage of transport, international trade and development, energy and the role of technology.

This non-exhaustive list raises several points. First, coverage of these 'peripheral' topics raises the question of the distinction between the study of environmental *laws* and law and environmental *issues*. The key for the textbook writer is that environmental issues may be interesting and important, but they often lack the necessary coherence that is signified by the core. Second, there are difficult decisions to make about drawing the boundaries of the subject. Clearly, as a general category, environmental issues raise a range of questions about the role that law plays in addressing those issues. Nonetheless, there is a risk that, in taking a wide, expansive view of environmental issues and the law, it defeats the very purpose that a textbook serves which is to try to provide a focal point and principled coherence. Third, the proliferation and diversification of these issues over time tends to undermine the idea that there is a basic core at all.

Twining's second Law of textbook writing – '*Be Brief*' is again challenging in the context of environmental law textbooks. As environmental regulation has expanded to address new issues, the tendency has been for textbooks to expand dramatically through different editions.[39] There is a connection between this and the first Law – covering the ground of an expanding field inevitably involves a degree of selection, culling or expansion.[40] In a positive light these changes reflect the ever-changing contours of a vibrant discipline, but in a more negative light, it begs the question as to whether those discarded chapters become irrelevant overnight or whether the 'core' of the subject is changing?

Twining's last two Laws are interlinked and can probably be merged into one. '*Be Reliable and Keep Up To Date*' as a Law is, at least on the surface, uncontroversial. The element of dependability is critical for textbooks but even here, there are challenges. The dynamism and complexity of environmental regulation means that any textbook is bound to be out of date by the time it hits the bookshelf. In terms of reliability, the UK Environmental Law Association (UKELA) has highlighted the overly complex, confusing and uncertain state of environmental regulation in the UK – to the extent that expert practitioners are unclear about the effect and meaning of key statutory provisions.[41] Pity the

---

[39] E.g., the first edition of Bell et al, n.8, was 381 pages in 1991, by the time of the sixth edition in 2006, it had grown to over 900 pages.

[40] In Bell et al, n.8, the banished chapters include Local Controls, Disposal of Waste to Sewers and Landscape Protection, with their newer and shinier replacements including Climate Change, New Technologies and Contaminated Land.

[41] UKELA, 'The State of UK Environmental Legislation in 2011-2012 – Is there a case for Legislative Reform?', available at www.ukela.org, accessed 28 April 2021.

poor textbook writer – particularly with amendment upon amendment tweaking already byzantine statutory provisions.[42]

There are also questions about what 'reliability' means in the context of such a multi-faceted subject? The contrast between 'law in books' and 'law in action' is nowhere starker than in the pages of environmental law texts. Formalist descriptions of specific laws contrast unfavourably with realist versions of what happens in practice. Reliably describing the law does little to help the learner to understand the range of political, scientific, social and economic factors that influence the exercise of discretion in the real world of environmental decision-making.[43]

3.   CHALLENGES TO THE TRADITIONAL PURPOSE OF TEXTBOOKS

In applying Twining's four Laws of textbook writing to environmental law textbooks, we can highlight the *disciplinary* challenges to authors that make it difficult to write a well-defined, brief, reliable and up-to-date account of the breadth and depth of environmental law. With ever expanding yet unclear boundaries and a relentless development of new policies and law, there is complexity and dynamism to environmental law that undermines the basic educational purpose of textbooks. Moreover, there is a tension between providing a formalistic, descriptive account of the principles and substance of environmental laws and the socio-legal realism of the role of law in a strongly normative and interdisciplinary context.[44]

The educational purposes of textbooks under the learning resource model face existential challenges from these changes. If we take the example of the increase in the availability and accessibility of relevant primary sources. A textbook, 30 years ago, provided a convenient secondary source that gathered together and summarised the primary materials. At best, a textbook offered an easier route into a complex subject and represented the basic tools of learning for many learners, acting as a guide to further library-based research.[45]

---

[42]   Take e.g., the Wildlife and Countryside Act 1981, which has been the subject of so many amendments that the Act has a s.12YA but no s.12Y or even ss.12A–X.

[43]   E.g., in the context of enforcement practices in relation to strict liability environmental offences, see E. Lees, *Interpreting Environmental Offences: The Need for Certainty* (Oxford: Hart Publishing, 2015).

[44]   O. Pederson, 'Modest Pragmatic Lessons for a Diverse and Incoherent Environmental Law Scholarship' (2009) 21 *JEL* 213.

[45]   Certainly when I started writing the first edition of *Environmental Law*, the idea of instant access to statutory material and case law was restricted to long sessions logged into the early (and very clunky) Lexis/Nexis Database.

At worst, as Twining pointed out, it prompted rote learning that undermined understanding.[46] Learners today take different approaches to research with immediate access to a much wider range of materials than ever before. For quick answers and summaries, Google can provide an answer to any factual question in seconds and for deeper research there is access to a variety of primary and secondary sources that have been curated and collated for applicability and can be accessed from anywhere through a single link on a Virtual Learning Environment.[47] This context of limitless information threatens text books because it challenges the concept of easy and singular access to relevance as the most efficient route to learning. Historically, textbooks operated to connect the dots of information to provide an overall picture. Technology has moved learners beyond that by giving easier access to many more dots, that can either provide a basic answer quickly or provide a much more complex and richer picture.

Of course, improved accessibility to digital resources does not necessarily correlate to relevance or accuracy. Whereas rote learning from a textbook failed to provide the analytical and evaluative skills required for academic learning, now the challenge for learners is not so much in relying solely on a single source but in sieving, triangulating, re-interpreting and ultimately connecting the multitude of sources available. These connectivist and constructivist approaches to learning do not sit well with textbooks that exist to make those connections for the learner. As access to a wider range of materials becomes easier, the focus for learning is less about the supply of knowledge and content, typically provided by textbooks, but on deeper modes of learning that rely more heavily on better curriculum design and innovation in teaching.

Increased access to information is only part of the picture of change that threatens textbooks. We can see structural changes in higher education which emphasise different modes of learning (e.g., online and blended learning), the development of skills and competencies beyond traditional knowledge and understanding, and innovation in teaching methods suitable for increasingly diverse groups of learners in many different contexts. The traditional textbook that synthesises the core law and policy that addresses environmental problems seems ill-equipped to support learning in this multi-dimensional context.

These changes in technology and the educational experience force us to think about what we are doing in writing textbooks and how we are doing it. This is more than just a question about boundaries and definitions. If the early textbook writers created a common law mind-set which constrained the

---

[46] Twining, n.1, p.82.
[47] B. Wilson, *Constructivist Learning Environments: Case Studies in Instructional Design* (New Jersey: Educational Technology Publications, 1996).

way in which successive generations thought about law's role in society, to what extent do today's environmental textbook writers take responsibility for implicitly imposing similar constraints in the context of law's role in addressing environmental problems? The traditional format of textbooks identifies the nature of environmental challenges and the laws that are designed to address those challenges. Critically, however, it is rare to find the law presented as an active part of a pathway to a solution. In passively describing what law *is* in sufficient detail to provide a basic framework for learners, it is hard to explore what the *potential* for law is or how law may be marshalled to address environmental problems more effectively. This is both a normative and practical point. A settled and identifiable structure both reinforces and constrains the limits of environmental law in the minds of learners. Is that the right vision for these key building blocks for learning? Can we use the integration of law's role in addressing real-world problems and the development of key skills and knowledge to engage, inspire and motivate a new generation of learners? Should we be reframing a new generation of learning resources to explicitly encourage learners to co-produce innovative solutions or pathways to solutions to environmental challenges?

4.   THE FUTURE ROLE OF LEARNING RESOURCES

In identifying what future learning resources might look like we would do better to re-ask ourselves the question – what do we really want learners to learn and how do we want them to develop as learners? Those who design modules and programmes in environmental law ask this question in forming learning objectives and assessment tasks. Textbook writers find it harder to move away from the basic framework of knowledge that underpins traditional approaches. So, in making suggestions about how textbooks might be reinvented, I am, like Twining, also engaging with normative questions about the purposes of legal education generally and learning environmental law specifically. How might innovation in learning and teaching best be supported by environmental textbooks and vice versa? With restricted space, I have limited myself to four key priorities – selected because I consider that they provide the most significant overlaps with the normative issues of what learners should be learning and how.

First, we should consider the format of textbooks. The static and inflexible nature of 'real world' texts has been highlighted in terms of reliability and accuracy in a dynamic and complex legal and policy context. The trend towards open educational resources (OER) in academic publishing would support learners in terms of accessibility, affordability, portability and navigability, but there would also be an opportunity for easy up-dating, customisation and co-production.[48] Open access when coupled with an open pedagogy approach would see a textbook being a tool with which learners can shape their own learning through modifying, reordering and republishing existing texts based upon their own learning experiences.[49] Encouraging learners to network and collaborate within a much wider learning community provides opportunities to become producers and co-creators rather than consumers of knowledge.

Second, we should ensure that open access textbooks promote an inter-disciplinary approach by acting as a hub for relevant resources on how law interacts with other disciplines to address environmental problems. The focus here should be on user-friendly summaries and overviews that support digital literacy by providing a brief analysis and evaluation of a wide range of digital resources in terms of, for example, relevance and accuracy.[50]

Third, we should design texts that recognise that the learning outcomes from studying environmental law should include developing skills and competencies that are relevant to understanding and addressing the real-world context of environmental law. Textbooks could more clearly recognise that learners develop much more than knowledge and understanding during a process of active learning. Whilst knowledge and understanding of legal concepts will always be a fundamental part of any environmental law programme, it should be clear that formalist, descriptive accounts of environmental regulation only provide a small proportion of understanding how law can open up pathways to addressing environmental problems. For example, a fuller understanding of the *realpolitik* of international environmental law might be gained from an explanation of coalition formation and negotiation theory in the process of agreeing the international treaties. Coverage of basic approaches to qualitative and quantitative data analysis could form part of understanding how and why regulation is needed or even how and why regulatory intervention has been (in)effective.

Finally, and leading on from the last point, we could structure texts around the true context for environmental law – realistic, messy, multi-dimensional, interdisciplinary problems that refuse to sit in self-defined silos of knowledge. In this way textbooks can provide supporting resources for thinking broadly about environmental problems across a range of scales – from the local to the

---

48 M. Marques, 'Institution as e-textbook Publisher' JISC at https://etextbook .jiscinvolve.org/wp/, accessed 28 April 2021.

49 For the relationship between open educational resources and open pedagogy see, G. Conole, *Designing for Learning in an Open World* (New York: Springer, 2013) and B. Hegarty, 'Attributes of Open Pedagogy: A Model for Using Open Educational Resources' (2015) *Educational Technology* 3–13.

50 A. Philippopoulos-Mihalopoulos and V. Brooks (eds), *Research Methods in Environmental Law: A Handbook* (Cheltenham: Edward Elgar, 2017).

global – and responses – from legal to extra-legal.[51] Again an approach based around OER and open pedagogy is particularly suited to environmental law. Instead of trying to cover any 'necessary' breadth of topics within the core of a textbook, learners could become more selective, focusing on authentic problems that speak to their own interests and concerns. In this way, learners could use resources to co-create specific and additional content by linking and co-operating with external groups and stakeholders to produce case studies around the application of law in the real world. These case studies then become new resources that can be used by others and the process of adaptation and modification brings a textbook to life through iteration after iteration.

5.   CONCLUSION

Textbooks are as easy a target for criticism today as they were 50 years ago. Perhaps no one would accuse textbooks of undermining the values of a liberal legal education as Twining did (there are more obvious suspects for that nowadays), but we should still be asking normative questions about the purposes of textbooks and learning environmental law. With a relatively well-established substantive core and the development of principles that provide a coherent theoretical framework, the key formative role that textbooks play in structuring and defining an inchoate subject is less important. There is, however, a danger that the structure created by textbooks plays a part in learners developing an unrealistic or formalistic mind-set that constrains their ability to see the potential that law has to address real-world environmental problems. Moreover, the dynamism and complexity of environmental regulation makes even the basic task of providing a straightforward, comprehensive, reliable and up-to-date account of the law challenging. The task for writers interested in what learners learn about environmental law and how, is to finally break free of trying to obey Twining's four Laws and think hard about how open access textbooks and open pedagogies can play a role in helping learners rethink their learning and shift from being consumers to producers of knowledge. Thinking about the textbook as an open educational resource which can evolve to reflect the input and 'real world' experiences of learners provides a flexible set of resources that can support innovation in learning and teaching, whatever form it may take.

---

[51]   See, e.g., D. Farber, 'The Unifying Force of Climate Change Scholarship' in Pederson, n.30, p.162.

6. Techniques for enhancing the lecture format in teaching environmental law

Tracy Bach

INTRODUCTION: WHY ENHANCE YOUR LECTURES?

Lecture is a common method for teaching law subjects, including environmental law. In some countries, the government ministry that regulates curriculum requires this classroom format. In others, the economics of enrolment and staffing lead to large class sizes where lecturing is the only feasible format. Most of the foundational first-year courses in law school are taught via lecture in large lecture halls.

Yet the lecture, while efficient in delivering information to students, is perceived by many as one of the weakest teaching techniques for helping students to understand and retain material. Studies have shown that students remember only 5 per cent of what they hear in a lecture as compared to 10 per cent of what they read, 30 per cent of what they see demonstrated, 50 per cent of what they discuss, 75 per cent of what they practice, and 90 per cent of what they master and teach others.[1] This retention range tracks teaching and learning that is most passive when sitting in a large lecture hall listening to a teacher deliver content to most active when taking knowledge and explaining it to others. This continuum stems from cognitive psychology's theories about four areas of 'meaningful learning', namely information processing, knowledge structure, thinking about thinking, and social processes.[2] In legal education particularly, several recent reports have criticized curriculum as not preparing students to enter their profession ready to apply their knowledge.[3] The 2007 Carnegie

---

[1] National Training Laboratory Institute of Applied Behavioral Science Learning Pyramid, https://www.educationcorner.com/the-learning-pyramid.html accessed 5 October 2019.

[2] Gerald F. Hess and Steven Friedland, *Techniques for Teaching Law* (Carolina Academic Press 1999) 3–5. For example, information processing and retention improves when students both hear and see information. Ibid., at 4.

[3] William M. Sullivan et al., Educating Lawyers: Preparation for the Profession of Law (The Carnegie Foundation for the Advancement of Teaching 2007) http://

Report specifically notes the weaknesses of the Socratic Method used in law school lecturing.[4]

This chapter accepts the utility of lecture for teaching environmental law and offers strategies for improving active learning in large lecture halls. It begins with simple techniques for effective lecturing, like assigning pre-lecture reading, structuring lectures with short periods of information delivery punctuated by active learning exercises, and building in time for student self-reflection in writing. These more active learning techniques[5] encourage individual students to 'construct knowledge'[6] within the larger classroom, as well as to engage in metacognition or thinking about their thinking and learning.[7]

Moving on from the classic reading, listening, and writing learning modes, lectures can use visual learning through short videos that illustrate concepts and invite students to analyse them; guest lecturers who can serve as expert interviewees for the course teacher and students; and case studies based in well-known legal problems or current events. Environmental law lends itself especially well to these teaching techniques, given the many environmental problems that surround any given classroom and reportage about them.

Finally, while it presents the most challenge to time management and course coverage, the lecture can be punctuated by small-group exercises during class time with 'report outs' by rapporteurs from each group or having individual students lead sections of the class lecture discussion, followed by constructive feedback on their performance. These exercises, a form of 'social learning',[8] allow students to learn by doing with their peers, facilitated by the law teacher within the lecture hall.

---

archive.carnegiefoundation.org/pdfs/elibrary/elibrary_pdf_632.pdf accessed 5 October 2019. Roy Stuckey et al., Best Practices for Legal Education (Clinical Legal Education Association 2007) https://www.cleaweb.org/Resources/Documents/best_practices-full .pdf accessed 5 October 2019.

4   Sullivan et al., ibid.

5   Active learning occurs when students do something more than listening, such as discussion, small-group projects, simulations, field work, and writing. Research shows that active learning methods facilitate the development of higher-level thinking, like analysis, synthesis, and evaluation: *see* Gerald F. Hess and Steven Friedland, *Techniques for Teaching Law* (Carolina Academic Press 1999) 13–14; *see also* Cornell University Center for Teaching Innovation, Active Learning https://teaching.cornell .edu/teaching-resources/engaging-students/active-learning accessed 5 October 2019.

6   Yale Poorvu Center for Teaching and Learning, Student Construction of Knowledge https://poorvucenter.yale.edu/ConstructingStudentKnowledge accessed 5 October 2019.

7   Ibid.

8   Ibid.

STEP 1: THREE BASIC BUT CLASSIC TECHNIQUES FOR PROMOTING MORE ACTIVE LEARNING IN LECTURES

The following three techniques provide a relatively easy toehold for bringing more active learning into the lecture hall. The first occurs before the students enter the classroom, while the second and third require recalibrating the use of class time. All three enhancements build on the lecture format and require minimal additional resources.

A.   Assign Pre-lecture Reading

In the U.S. law classroom, students are assigned cases, statutes, and some secondary materials to read before each class. The intent is not to review this material during the lecture period but rather to apply it to new, factual scenarios and thereby model how to 'think like a lawyer'.[9] In reality, most teachers review some of the assigned reading material in class, to draw out a common understanding that students then may apply to posed hypothetical situations. The trick is to assign a combination of pre-lecture reading that students may critically read in advance, knowing that they will be expected to take the next steps with their understanding in class. In this way, law teachers can incorporate cognitive psychology's lessons on meaningful learning by having students read and hear a lecture's core information. This combination can include primary materials, like cases, statutes, and regulations as well as secondary materials, like law review articles.

The case method, endemic to common law countries, seeks to teach students how to read and analyse judicial decisions critically. By learning how to find a court's individual case holding and place it within the fabric of other, similar cases in that jurisdiction, the lawyer in training develops the ability to understand how common law rules develop over time.[10] Case reading in the civil law system is instructive too, to help students see how a court has interpreted a code provision under a set of facts. By assigning a case or two to read and prepare before class, the teacher sets into motion the student's active learning. Learning to read cases requires new skills,[11] as does learning to 'brief' them

---

[9]   This teaching technique, called the Socratic Method for its question and answer approach, was made (in)famous by the 1973 movie, The Paper Chase. *See* https://www.youtube.com/watch?v=wGUfvZU4wiE accessed 5 October 2019.

[10]   The Law School Case Method, https://www.princetonreview.com/law-school-advice/case-method accessed 5 October 2019.

[11]   Leah M. Christensen, 'Legal Reading and Success in Law School: An Empirical Study' https://mylaw2.usc.edu/assets/docs/contribute/ChristensenLegalReadingwithPurpose.pdf accessed 5 October 2019.

for class and use later in exams.[12] Students spend time outside the classroom practicing these skills and then bring that knowledge to the lecture hall, already engaged with the material.

While the case method is particular to common law countries, other primary materials like constitutions, statutes, and regulations are not. Like cases, they require delving beneath a surface reading of individual terms to place them into context.[13] And likewise, this engagement with text sets up testing and application of knowledge in the lecture room. For example, in an environmental law lecture on lead in drinking water, a portion of a country's annotated statute[14] might be assigned along with a relevant section of regulations.[15] The annotations would likely include a case interpreting key terms or standards, which could be explored in the lecture rather than in the assigned reading.

One downside of this method for enhancing the lecture is tiring the students before they enter the classroom or having them come unprepared to class. It is important to establish the readings in advance in a syllabus, and take care not to assign too many pages, especially of primary materials.[16] Offering a short list of guiding questions to help students benchmark what they should take out of assigned reading helps them develop critical reading skills, especially early on. Using lecture to review some of the assigned reading material at the outset of a course helps students internalize the expectations and readies them for their application of the material to hypotheticals. Finally, making class preparation and participation a significant percentage of the final grade (20–30 per cent typically) will encourage students to do the readings.

B.   Structure the Listening

A second way to enhance the law school lecture format is for teachers to speak less and students to speak more. When this happens, students learn to listen to questions posed, process information to answer them, and listen to each other's answers and detect and debate differences. In this way, classroom

---

[12]   Nicole Raymond Chong, 'Reading and Briefing Cases in Law School: Guidelines and Helpful Tips' https://pennstatelaw.psu.edu/sites/default/files/Case%20Briefing %20Article.pdf accessed 5 October 2019.

[13]   5 Tips for Reading Statutes, https://lawschoolacademicsuccess.com/2015/02/03/ statutory-interpretation/ accessed 5 October 2019.

[14]   In the United States, this would be the Safe Drinking Water Act, 42 USC 300f.

[15]   For example, the National Primary Drinking Water Regulations, 40 CFR 141.

[16]   There is little published literature on this point, but plenty of anecdotal information about good and not good practice. *Compare* <https://www.quora.com/How-many -pages-a-day-do-law-school-students-read-on-average accessed 5 October 2019 *with* https://lawstudents.findlaw.com/surviving-law-school/sample-1l-study-schedule.html accessed 5 October 2019.

lecture affirms cognitive psychology's lessons on knowledge structure (by constructing answers to classroom questions) and social processes (via debate with peers' answers) as ways to ensure more meaningful learning.

Whether or not reading is assigned before class, lectures can be composed of short periods of information delivery punctuated by active learning exercises based on questions. One source of questions is the teacher. The practice of 'cold calling' or asking questions of students who have not raised their hands is a staple of the U.S. law school classroom. Although it can feel odd at first, students soon acclimate and law teachers can more easily include everyone in the conversation over the course of the semester. Teachers' questions can focus on the content of the lecture or the assigned readings. They can also move beyond content review to the application of it to hypothetical scenarios. Given the prevalence of environmental issues in the media, often law teachers can bring current events into the classroom as the basis for applying the lecture's legal principles, rather than hypothetical situations.

Although teacher as interlocutor is the more typical classroom lecture stance, having students pose the questions is especially instructive. First, it gives students an opportunity to ask basic content questions and, if the law teacher does not immediately reply but instead asks other students to do so, to hear what their peers have understood. Second, students also have the opportunity to pose their own hypotheticals or bring in real life events, testing where the doctrine they have just learned might go next. Third, as teachers answer questions posed to them, they have the opportunity to model reasoning and communication skills while delivering content. These skills include listening both to surface and underlying questions, providing short, direct answers (yes, no, or maybe in this case, but not in that case), and backing them up with reasoning supported by authority.

One vexing scenario for early career law teachers is getting questions they are not prepared to answer. Sometimes it is only a factual matter that needs to be checked, while other times it may involve a point of law. My approach has always been one of honesty in such situations, telling students that I do not know the answer, will research it, and bring my answer to the next class. Doing so usually engenders respect from students, showing a shared approach to learning. It also models to students what to do when they will inevitably be in the same situation: be honest about the limits to one's expertise, avoid pretending to know an answer, and show engagement in professional self-learning.

C.   Allocate Time for Student Self-reflection

A third technique for enhancing lecture-based learning again cedes class time from the teacher to the student, but this time invests it in written self-reflection. This technique gives students an opportunity to reflect on what they have learned as well as how they have learned it.[17] Writing enables students to capture their metacognition in a more concrete form and reread it over time. Teachers can establish students' reflective practice by setting aside five–ten minutes in class and directing students to reflect on specific questions. These might include ones focused on the content of the lecture's learning objectives (e.g., what are the five key principles outlined in the United Nations Framework Convention on Climate Change (UNFCCC) and how do they shape treaty obligations?) and materials (e.g., what did I learn from Article 3 of the UNFCCC and from the law review article about Article 3?), as well as on the learning itself (how well did I learn this information? what did I miss? how would I approach it differently the next time?). The simplest approach is to ask students to reflect in a private journal, which the teacher can review periodically. The teacher can anonymously share entries that model perceptive and detailed reflection. Written self-reflection need not always include this range of questions. Nor does it have to occur during every class. Including it purposively on a regular basis throughout the semester suffices for students to develop this active learning habit.[18]

STEP 2: TAKING MORE TIME TO ADD VISUAL LEARNING, CASE STUDIES, AND SMALL-GROUP EXERCISES TO LECTURING

This next category of lecture enhancements takes more time to prepare and execute in the classroom, and so is offered as a set of techniques that build on the simpler ones already outlined. Education research chronicles a range of different learning styles anchored in the core four: visual; aural; verbal; and kinesthetic.[19] The first three techniques explored thus far are grounded in the listening (aural) and speaking and reading (verbal) learning styles traditionally associated with legal education. The following three techniques add visual and kinesthetic elements to lecturing.

---

[17]   Engage2Learn, The importance of self-reflection for learning, https://engage2learn.org/blog/2018/05/17/the-importance-of-self-reflection-for-learning/ accessed 5 October 2019.

[18]   *See* Chapter 3, this volume, 'Bringing the "Heart" into Environmental Law Teaching', by Karen Bubna-Litic.

[19]   Nancy Chick, 'Learning Styles, Vanderbilt Center for Teaching' https://cft.vanderbilt.edu/guides-sub-pages/learning-styles-preferences/ accessed 5 October 2019.

A.   Bringing Visuals into the Classroom

While watching short videos could evoke passive 'movie time', using them and also live guest lectures purposively can instead illustrate concepts and invite student analysis in ways that written materials and spoken lectures do not.[20] For example, some law teachers show film or television clips to present the messy facts underlying legal claims or to demonstrate specific lawyering skills, like interviewing and negotiation.[21] Typically students view a scene and are asked to 'spot' the potential legal claims and their constituent elements. By 'reading' these visual texts, law students view the more real-life, chaotic context for the facts they eventually see organized and flattened on the pages of judicial opinions.[22] Other teachers use film scenes to point out the unrealistic portrayal of legal practice, using the counter factual to clarify legal claims and their analytical elements. Finally, a small group of law teachers uses films as one kind of legal storytelling and encourages students to see in them the narrative structures litigators should use when convincing juries to rule for their clients.[23]

Another form of visual learning in the classroom takes place when guest lecturers present lessons learned from the real life practice of law.[24] Frequently in the environmental law classroom this technique revolves around a lawyer presenting on her area of expertise, a scientist presenting his research findings, or an engineer explaining remediation techniques, in person or virtually.[25] It

---

[20]   For the essence of this debate, *see* Melissa Kelly, '11 Pros and Cons of Using Movies in Class', https://www.thoughtco.com/pros-and-cons-movies-in-class-7762 accessed 5 October 2019.

[21]   Justin Myers, '"I'd like to thank the Academy…": Using Movies in the Law School Classroom, Best Practices for Legal Education', https://bestpracticeslegaled .com/2010/01/22/%E2%80%9Ci%E2%80%99d-like-to-thank-the-academy%E2%80 %A6%E2%80%9D-using-movies-in-the-law-school-classroom/ accessed 5 October 2019.

[22]   Dramas are often used this way. E.g., the film, *A Civil Action*, portrays the difficulty of gathering and presenting proof of causation in a toxic torts case, https://www .youtube.com/watch?v=ecBKI_Zi1HU accessed 5 October 2019.

[23]   *See* James R. Elkins, 'Popular Culture, Legal Films, and Legal Film Critics' (2007) 40 *Loy. L.A. L. Rev.* 745, 768–77, https://digitalcommons.lmu.edu/cgi/viewcontent.cgi ?referer=https://www.google.com/&httpsredir=1&article=2573&context=llr accessed 5 October 2019.

[24]   Karen Hughes Miller, 'The Blessings and Benefits of Using Guest Lecturers', *Faculty Focus* https://www.facultyfocus.com/articles/teaching-and-learning/blessings -benefits-using-guest-lecturers/ accessed 5 October 2019.

[25]   Eytan Tepper, 'Guess Who's Coming to Lecture: Using "Virtual Guest Lecture" to Support the Role of the Classroom Professor', https://www.mcgill.ca/law/files/law/ les-paper-eytan_tepper.pdf accessed 5 October 2019.

can become more active learning when these guest lecturers serve as expert interviewees, requiring students to develop relevant questions. Live clients can also serve as another kind of guest lecturer. While students more typically work with clients in the legal clinic setting, an increasing number of law schools are bringing clients and their legal problems into skills courses, like legal research and writing.[26] In the environmental law classroom, these clients are typically environmental agency officials, non-governmental organization leaders, and business people who provide their perspective on a particular issue. All kinds of guest lecturers require teachers to organize and prepare for their presence in the classroom.

Finally, another visual way of learning in the lecture hall can be through role plays. Students grasp more deeply the challenges of multi-party negotiations and litigation when placed in a role within them.[27] The back stories of well-known appellate cases[28] can make their legal principles more vivid, and can provide students a vehicle for kinesthetic learning by acting them out with a group of students. For example, a role play of a point-source water pollution problem would allow students to learn actively about how a typical water pollution statute works, through the lens of the polluter, the government regulator, wildlife biology and water quality experts, and affected downstream residents. Again, this kind of activity takes a measure of preparation beyond writing a lecture. It also requires students to spend time outside the classroom reading, researching, and preparing, which has an impact on the amount of time spent on this assignment topic compared to others. To use this technique effectively, law teachers will need to think through their overall course coverage goals in advance and plan time accordingly.

---

[26] Eduardo R.C. Capulong, 'Working with Actual Clients in the First Year', https://www.youtube.com/watch?v=bkk6ehatYOQ accessed 5 October 2019.

[27] *See* Lara Sanpietro, 'How Negotiation Role-Play Simulations Can Help You Resolve Disputes, Program on Negotiation', Harvard Law School, https://www.pon.harvard.edu/daily/teaching-negotiation-daily/how-negotiation-role-play-simulations-can-help-you-resolve-environmental-disputes/ accessed 5 October 2019; Karl S. Coplan, 'Teaching Substantive Environmental Law and Practice Skills Through Interest Group Roleplaying' (2016) 18 *Vt. J. Env. L* 194. *See also* IUCN Academy of Environmental Law Simulation Resources, https://www.iucnael.org/en/online-resources/climate-law-teaching-resources accessed 5 October 2019.

[28] *See*, e.g., Robert Rabin and Stephen Sugarman, *Tort Stories* (Foundation Press 2003).

B.   Using Case Studies Based on Well-known Legal Problems or Current Events

As the films and simulations already cited suggest, there is no shortage of historical and contemporary environmental degradation cases to draw on in the law school lecture hall. A well-used one in the U.S. is the Woburn, Massachusetts toxic torts case that is the subject of the film, A Civil Action, which has been published in book form for teaching civil procedure.[29] Similar water pollution cases can be found around the world.[30] Case studies provide a rich source of real facts that can be used rather than hypothetical ones, as a means for student application of legal principles learned during lecture. They can also be used for the documents developed within them, like expert reports, witness testimony and affidavits, and complaints and motions. Case studies also can serve as a basis for role plays. Teachers can prepare case studies themselves, locate and use already prepared ones, or assign that research to students as part of a graded exercise. Regardless of how case studies arrive in the environmental classroom, they can be used to promote active learning by helping students connect the legal knowledge learned in lecture to real-world pollution problems.

C.   Reinforcing Lecture Material with Small-group Exercises[31]

Just as posing questions to individual students promotes more active learning, punctuating lectures with small-group exercises brings a measure of social learning to the classroom. Having groups of five students work together makes the lecture hall a more intimate learning environment that can draw more quiet students out. By devoting class time to these 'zones of proximal development', the law teacher increases opportunities for students to communicate their understanding of the material and recognize misconceptions.[32] Working with

---

[29]   Lewis Grossman and Robert Vaughn, *A Documentary Companion to A Civil Action* (4th edn, Foundation Press, 2008).

[30]   *See*, e.g., C.B. Dissaynake et al., 'The Environmental Pollution of Kandy Lake: A Case Study from Sri Lanka' https://www.sciencedirect.com/science/article/pii/0160412082901271 accessed 5 October 2019; N.S. Lakshmana Rao and M. Narayana Rao, 'Pollution in Selected Rivers of India – Three Case Studies', https://www.tandfonline.com/doi/abs/10.1080/00207238708710341 accessed 5 October 2019; Roberto Max Hermann and Benedito Pinto Ferreira Braga Jr, 'Case Study VI* – The Upper Tietê Basin, Brazil', https://www.who.int/water_sanitation_health/resourcesquality/wpccasestudy6.pdf accessed 5 October 2019.

[31]   *See* Chapter 7, this volume, 'Teaching and Learning Environmental Law using Small Group Teaching Methodologies' by Ben Boer.

[32]   Yale Poorvu Center for Teaching and Learning (n 6).

peers who have just shared the lecture experience can also have metacognition benefits by reinforcing what material has been learned and what needs more study.

The substance and output of small-group exercises can take many forms. In its simplest version, the teacher's sequential questions to individual students can instead take the form of simultaneous small-group discussions. By presenting the answers to a series of questions, individual students end up leading sections of the class lecture. The questions can be posed orally or written on the board or a presentation slide. Each group selects a rapporteur at the start, who takes notes and has the responsibility for reporting the answers to the entire class. Teachers can provide group interaction guidelines, like giving everyone a chance to speak, capturing all ideas, analysing and organizing them in a clear answer format, grounding them in the lecture materials, and presenting minority views when the group does not come to consensus. Rubrics should be created and shared so that students know in advance the basis for formative and summative evaluation.

The law school teaching literature suggests many other, creative ways for structuring small-group exercises in the lecture hall. These include panel discussions, knowledge maps, debates, visual lists, and the 'modified fish bowl'.[33] In a panel discussion activity, the output of the group problem solving is every member presenting on the topic as part of a panel and answering questions from other students and the teacher. A knowledge map captures the output more visually, in the form of one map that connects key points to help others understand the topic. In an exercise that results in a debate, the teacher assigns two groups different sides of an issue and has them engage in a structured debate. A visual list requires the small group to create a comprehensive list of the pros and cons of an issue that the students then share with the larger group, whether via posting on a wiki, writing on the board, or sending to the teacher to project for the class.

The modified fish bowl exercise is a particularly creative and engaging exercise. It allows individual students to voice their questions about lecture topics they found difficult and then have small groups work on the answers. These actions are sequenced. Just as individual student-written self-reflection could take place in the last five minutes of class, in this small-group exercise, students would use that time to write down their questions and put them in a fish bowl. Before leaving the lecture hall, two or three student groups pull

---

[33]   Cristina D. Lockwood, 'Improving Learning in the Law School Classroom by Encouraging Students to Form Communities of Practice', 38–9, https://pdfs .semanticscholar.org/ba89/cf1495346e7071b4a19c04415d628fd02a78.pdf accessed 5 October 2019.

questions from the bowl, and present the answers during the next class, using any of the formats just described. While not all questions can be answered this way after each class, given time constraints, over the course of the semester all small groups would have an opportunity to do so. And, of course, the teacher knows the contents of the fish bowl and so can answer questions not answered by students in their next class lecture.

This detailed description of ways to invest lecture time into small-group exercises to promote more active learning inspires while at the same time it exposes the downsides of this type of enhancement. The teacher will need to create materials and capture the output, so that they may evaluate it fairly. Time in class and outside class engaging in the small group discussions will mean focusing on some content more and other content, less or not at all. It will likely take time for students expecting to be talked at in the large lecture hall to adjust to this new set of expectations.[34] As with other lecture enhancement techniques offered in this chapter, the tension over course coverage and competing demands for the teacher's time is always present. That is why trying out just a few techniques over the course of a semester will allow both the teacher and students to adapt to the more dynamic classroom in a measured way.

STEP 3: 'FLIPPING' THE CLASSROOM LECTURE[35]

This technique for achieving active learning entails the most change of all discussed in this chapter. The concept of the flipped classroom[36] has gained currency with the development of on-line teaching materials. The basic idea is to replace all or part of the pre-lecture 'reading' with video or audio lectures and short quizzes, all made available on line before students come to class. With the 'knowledge transfer' taking place this way, the classroom component in the flipped space focuses on problem solving. For example, an experienced U.S. contracts professor created short videos to convey basic doctrine and quizzes to assess understanding of it; students do this work on line before coming to the classroom, where they solve relevant problems posed by the

---

[34] *See* Lockwood, ibid., on this point, including her suggestions for how teachers can facilitate this change.

[35] *See* Boer (n 31).

[36] Lutz-Christian Wolff and Jenny Chan, *Flipped Classrooms for Legal Education* (Springer 2016).

professor.[37] Law teachers in Canada[38] and Australia[39] have also pioneered this technique, using it to promote smaller group learning within the classroom. A common theme of proponents' advocacy for flipping the classroom is how mainstream technology, like cell phone videos and apps, decreases the work of putting lectures and quizzes on line. In this way, the flipped classroom moves beyond assigning traditional written materials before class, using new technology to achieve the aim of more active learning in the lecture hall.

On one hand, this method presents a radical re-conception of how and where learning takes place. It requires both teachers and students to understand and agree that transferring knowledge can take place outside the classroom. It also requires them to see the value in using class time to act on that knowledge, through a variety of different active learning exercises. Curriculum regulators, whether at the faculty or government levels, must also see merit in flipping the traditional lecturing paradigm.

On the other hand, we can see through the organization of this chapter how the flipped classroom represents the next, logical step in the progression to making the lecture hall the site of more active learning. Knowledge transfer, while admittedly in a new location, is still done via lecture, with some likely assigned reading to prepare beforehand and quiz questions to help students master content and assess how they learned it. By shifting it outside the lecture hall, the law teacher and student now have more time to use techniques like visuals, case studies, and group work to cement the learning. As on-line learning becomes more prevalent, the cultural and regulatory barriers to flipping the classroom will likely recede, allowing it to become the norm for some classes within a course or for entire courses.

CONCLUSION

This chapter has sought to describe a range of techniques for making lecture a more active learning experience for environmental law students. Through its organization, it presents enhancements that range from easier to harder in terms of law teacher expertise, student expectations, and costs of time and materials. It also offers a number of resources for learning more about these techniques, from the cognitive psychology they are grounded in to 'how to' videos with

---

[37] Deborah Threedy, 'Flipping Contracts: The Making of Videos' https://vimeo .com/109149855 accessed 5 October 2019.

[38] Philip Preville, 'Why Don't More Law Profs Flip Their Classrooms?' https:// tophat.com/blog/flipped-classroom-law/ accessed 5 October 2019.

[39] Matthew Stubbs, 'Flipping the Public Law Classroom at the University of Adelaide', https://www.youtube.com/watch?v=0vMOD7ZbYj8 accessed 5 October 2019.

specific advice. In this way, environmental law teachers interested in moving beyond their current lecturing skills can pick and choose what works best for them, their students, and the learning environments they work in. Some may become fascinated with progressing through all three steps. Others may see the wisdom in adopting one or two techniques described in the first two. As with all changes, it is important to start small and to assess comfort levels along the way. Regardless of the path chosen, increasing our metacognition about why we teach the way that we do makes us more mindful about the strengths and weaknesses of the lecture format, and more thoughtful about teaching techniques and how they affect learning.

7. Teaching and learning environmental law using small group teaching methodologies

Ben Boer

INTRODUCTION

This chapter examines the benefits of using small groups as a teaching strategy in general, and in particular for environmental law education, both at undergraduate and at postgraduate levels.[1] For the purposes of this analysis, the

---

term 'small groups' can refer to traditional-sized tutorial groups as well as the use of small groups within a larger lecture class. The chapter sets out several justifications for small-group student-centred learning. It does not make a strict distinction between undergraduate and postgraduate studies, as the techniques and methods involved are applicable to both levels. However, the more sophisticated methods might be more suitable to postgraduate studies, if only for the reason that at postgraduate level there is often more flexibility in terms of coverage of subject matter, as well as more time that can be devoted to discussion.

The chapter first canvasses some general points that are applicable to small-group methodology that might be used in any law course. It then goes on to explore the rationale for using this methodology in an environmental law course and provides examples of various exercises and activities that may be employed through this approach. Some of these may be quite familiar to professors[2] who have been in the classroom for some years.

This chapter acknowledges that lecturing is generally the main methodological approach in both larger and smaller law classes in many law schools around the world, that traditional teaching methodologies tend to be reproduced from one generation of professors to the next,[3] and that this is reflected to a great extent in the law curricula as well.[4] Readers might take some heed of the following critique of this methodology: 'lecturing is the process whereby words flow from the mouth of the professor to the page of the student without going through the brains of either of them'.[5] By contrast, when effectively implemented, small-group methods can serve to create stimulating, inspirational learning spaces for the development of legal analytical skills and intensive

---

[2]   'Professor' is used here in the North American sense to refer to teachers, at any level, in universities.

[3]   'Despite its rapidly changing landscape, European legal academia proved extremely resilient in protecting its traditional legal curriculum and teaching methods against disruptive and pervasive phenomena such as digitalization.' Alberto Alemanno and Lamin Khadar (eds), *Reinventing Legal Education: How Clinical Education Is Reforming the Teaching and Practice of Law in Europe* (Cambridge University Press, 2018) 24. There is good reason to think that such sentiments are applicable in many jurisdictions outside Europe.

[4]   Given the dramatic recent transformations to legal professions and justice systems globally, one might expect to witness parallel developments in legal education. Yet despite the urgent need to reform the legal curriculum in light of these unprecedented, seismic developments, the curricula of law schools continue, in many respects, to resemble curricula in the time of law students' ancestors...
Alemanno and Khadar, ibid., 1.

[5]   Quote noted by the author from an Indian professorial participant in 'Trainers in the Teaching of Environmental Law' program at the National University of Singapore (n 1, above). The origin of this aphorism is obscure; see 'Quote Investigator' <https://quoteinvestigator.com/2012/08/17/lecture-minds> (accessed 17 May 2021).

absorption of knowledge. The learning outcomes specified for any particular law course can thereby be considerably enhanced to a level well in advance of what can be achieved through primary reliance on the lecturing methodology.

GENERAL OBSERVATIONS ON THE SMALL-GROUP TEACHING METHODOLOGY

The rationale for the small-group teaching methodology is to encourage students to articulate their ideas and to become used to speaking in public, thus increasing their level of confidence. Many students are reluctant to speak in larger seminar classes, and even more so in large lecture rooms. Small-group techniques are one way to encourage them to do so. The basic philosophy is that intensive discussion of particular questions will assist the learning process and enhance the ability of law students to think critically. If students know that they are expected to speak regularly in class, they should also be motivated to read and critically analyse the prescribed reading materials more intensively. Various scholars have observed that the depth of student learning is enhanced by the use of small groups in a variety of law courses and contexts,[6] as well as in other disciplines. For example, in nursing education: Jackson et al, state 'The benefits of group work include deep, active and collaborative learning and the use of peer processes to help with motivation and enthusiasm of less motivated students.'[7]

The learning outcomes for the teaching of most university law school subjects have a similar rationale. It is widely accepted that the skill of oral communication is a quality that law students must develop as an essential part of their legal education, to be used in subsequent legal work, whether in practice or otherwise and in whatever area of law they might be involved in. It is contended that the way that law is taught and learned can influence the way in which law is practised, through the manner in which lawyers conduct their professional lives, individually and collectively. Obviously, most practising lawyers must engage in discussions and negotiations on a regular basis. Thus if we wish to positively influence the way that the law is practised, we should begin by evaluating the way that it is taught. For this to occur, we need to look

---

    [6]   For example, Adiva Sifris and Elspeth McNeil, 'Small Group Learning in Real Property Law', *Legal Education Review* (Web Page) <http://138.25.65.17/au/journals/LegEdRev/2002/10.html> (accessed 8 March 2020); Nora Markard, 'Clinical Legal Education in Germany' in Alberto Alemanno and Lamin Khadar (eds), n 3 above, at 153.
    [7]   Debra Jackson, Louise Hickman, Tamara Power and Rebecca T Disler, 'Small Group Learning: Graduate Health Students' Views of Challenges and Benefits' (2014) 48(1) *Contemporary Nurse* 118.

at how professors engage in the process of teaching. The narrowness or breadth of their curricula, and the flexibility or inflexibility of the teaching and learning methods used, may well carry through unconsciously into their students' idea of what they perceive being a lawyer entails, how they think about the law and its role in society, and the way that law develops or should develop.

Cantley-Smith notes that communication skills 'are undoubtedly one of the most important tools of a competent, professional lawyer'.[8] She points out that well-developed oral communication skills are not only important in courts, but that these skills 'transcend almost all aspects of legal professional practice'.[9] She also finds that, 'despite the obvious importance to professional legal practice, oral communication skills are seldom taught to undergraduate law students'.[10] It is contended here that small-group teaching methodology, when used as a normal, every-day teaching/learning tool in law schools, is likely to have some bearing on the ways in which lawyers interact with their colleagues, clients, the courts and the general community.

The next contention is that each student is a repository, at some level, of knowledge about the subject matter, both in terms of the applicable legal frameworks and mechanisms and also the information required to understand why those frameworks and mechanisms have been developed. The undergraduate student will generally have less knowledge and experience than the postgraduate student, but the basic point remains the same. As John Biggs has argued: '[l]earners construct knowledge with their own activities, building on what they already know. Teaching is not a matter of transmitting but of engaging students in active learning, building their knowledge in terms of what they already understand'.[11] In other words, students are not simply empty vessels 'to fill with knowledge and to compare with others and with benchmarks in order to rank and classify them'.[12] This 'transmission model' was described by renowned educationist Paolo Freire as the 'banking concept of education':[13] 'Education becomes an act of depositing, in which the students are the depositories and the teacher is the depositor. Instead of communicating, the teacher

---

[8]   Rowena Cantley-Smith, 'Put Down Your Pen: The Role of Oral Assessment in Undergraduate Law Studies' (2006) 13 *James Cook University Law Review* 30, 30.

[9]   Ibid.

[10]   Ibid.

[11]   John Biggs, *Teaching for Quality Learning at University* (Open University Press, 2007) 21.

[12]   Catherine Broom, 'Empowering Students: Pedagogy that Benefits Educators and Learners' (2015) 14(2) *Citizenship, Social and Economic Education* 79, 80.

[13]   Paolo Freire, *Pedagogy of the Oppressed* (Continuum, New York, 1970, 1993) 72.

issues communiqués and makes deposits which the students patiently receive, memorize, and repeat'. In counteracting this concept he wrote:

> In the banking concept of education, knowledge is a gift bestowed by those who consider themselves knowledgeable upon those whom they consider to know nothing. Projecting an absolute ignorance onto others, a characteristic of the ideology of oppression, negates education and knowledge as processes of inquiry. The teacher presents himself to his students as their necessary opposite; by considering their ignorance absolute, he justifies his own existence. The students, alienated like the slave in the Hegelian dialectic, accept their ignorance as justifying the teachers' existence—but, unlike the slave, they never discover that they educate the teacher.[14]

It is argued here that the store of knowledge that each student brings to the class can be particularly capitalised on to promote a richer learning experience, both for the individual student and for the rest of class. The use of small-group methods can further enhance that experience.

A further contention is that small-group teaching methods promote a deeper level of learning on the one hand and a higher level of verbal articulation on the other. In other words, small-group methods can turn the classroom 'on its head'. An emphasis on oral communication can cast the professor primarily as a catalyst for learning and, at various points of a class, can place the student in the 'traditional' role of the professor. In doing so, students come to understand that, by being placed in that role, the depth of their learning is improved. They realise that they must have a much greater understanding of a particular subject matter if they are expected to communicate their knowledge and their views clearly and articulately. As Freire has argued: 'Education must begin with the solution of the teacher-student contradiction, by reconciling the poles of the contradiction so that both are simultaneously teachers and students.'[15]

The use of the interactional forms of learning and teaching involved in small-group methods can be, at least initially, more confronting for both professors and students. However, it can be argued that such experience also can be part of its value. It should mean that teachers must encourage the questioning of every proposition, the querying of every element of an argument, and remain cognisant of both the limitations and the opportunities presented by taking a position with respect to any particular legal concept or problem. While some students will find such teaching and learning situations challenging, these difficulties can be overcome if the professor is aware of them. By paying close attention to group dynamics and one-to-one interactions, she/he

---

[14]   Ibid.
[15]   Ibid.

can make appropriate interventions in order to reduce tensions and actually make the experience positive, comfortable and indeed enjoyable.

The general benefits of the small-group teaching methodology include intellectual stimulation of the maximum number of students for an optimal time; encouragement of more disciplined modes of thinking and interaction; development of closer intellectual relations among students, and between students and professors; avoidance of (perceived or real) authoritarianism of the professor and of the more dominant students; a flattening of the usual hierarchy between professors and students;[16] and reduction of feelings of frustration and alienation, especially for less-confident students.[17]

An essential point is that if a professor is planning to use small-group methods as a regular teaching and learning methodology, the methods need to be thought about when designing the course, and not as an afterthought or optional extra. When coping with larger class numbers, particularly in lecture theatres, many professors may initially find the small-group methodology difficult, if not impossible, to adapt and utilise. However, the small-group discussion activities that will be discussed below can be used both within larger and smaller classes.

A further important aspect of the course design is the use of assessment of class participation as a motivation for deeper learning. An emphasis on oral communication encourages students to take on more responsibility for their learning. When oral communication is assessed through attribution of levels of class participation, as part of the overall assessment scheme for a course, the motivation to communicate effectively within classes can be considerably enhanced. The manner in which this form of assessment can be applied to small-group discussions is discussed further below.

Finally, it should be noted that the small-group teaching methodology has a number of similarities with the 'flipped classroom' approach that has been developed in some law schools in recent years.[18]

---

[16]   As noted by Nora Markard in the context of small groups in clinical law teaching: 'Avoiding hierarchy in our teaching practice encourages in-depth discussions and interactive learning'; Markard (n 6) 154.

[17]   See Emily Finch and Stefan Fafinski, *Legal Skills* (Oxford University Press, 7th ed, 2019) at 197–8, where the authors advise less confident students on how to deal with participation in tutorials.

[18]   This approach is discussed in Chapter 6 of this volume: 'Techniques for enhancing the lecture format in teaching environmental law', by Tracy Bach; it is also described in 'The Flipped Classroom Explained', University of Adelaide, available at https://www.adelaide.edu.au/flipped-classroom/about/:

An engaging series of learning segments, that are closely linked to learning and assessment outcomes, that provide feedback to the learner during each stage. Carefully designed pre-class activities assist students to learn key concepts in

THE RATIONALE FOR USE OF THE SMALL-GROUP METHODOLOGY IN TEACHING ENVIRONMENTAL LAW

The reasons for the use of the small-group methodology specifically in environmental law include that this field is value-laden and is, by its nature, interdisciplinary. The fields of political science, legal and social history, psychology, economics, philosophy and ethics and, most importantly, the fundamentals of the natural physical sciences, are all relevant. The study of environmental law also necessitates the making of value judgements that can involve complex sociological, political, economic and cultural issues and can require an understanding of various legal systems and the meaning of law itself in different cultures. As environmental issues are often politically controversial and socially confronting, environmental lawyers also require well-developed argumentative legal skills alongside expertise that can range across various other disciplinary areas, together with both a broader and a deeper understanding of the ways in which society functions. Small-group methods, adequately designed and used on a regular basis, can allow for intensive discussion of the polycentric issues that are often brought up in environmental matters, at international, national and local levels.

Environmental lawyers also need to be critically aware of the powerful forces that can manifest themselves when decisions are made concerning approvals for development activity. In most legal systems, such decisions must take into account the environmental effects of proposed development as a matter of law. In such decision-making processes, there can be significant power imbalances between development proponents and members of the community who might wish to object to a development, or have it modified to reduce its environmental effects. Maxwell makes the point, in arguing for the development of students' critical awareness, that students 'need to appreciate that the law is not simply a value-free or value-neutral mechanism for dispute resolution…but is also a political mechanism for the acquisition, exercise and defense of power'.[19] This observation is particularly pertinent in the area of environmental law.

---

a self-paced manner, developing their confidence and motivation to engage in peer-led discussions during class that lead to synthesis and application of these key concepts. Post-class assessment activities are clearly connected to pre-class and face-to-face class learning experiences and address 'capabilities that count', making the students' learning relevant, real and sustainable.

[19]   Lucy Maxwell, 'How to Develop Students' Critical Awareness? Change the Language of Legal Education' (2019) 22(1) *Legal Education Review* 99, quoting

Beyond facilitating the practice of environmental law, the interactional approaches involved in small-group teaching and learning can be effective in ensuring that students become starkly aware of the ecological challenges that the world faces, and that the existential crises that we are confronting in the current era are kept front and centre. With those ecological realities in the forefront of their minds, students might be more motivated to speak out, analyse and come up with solutions to the myriad problems that we face on every level across the globe.

PREPARATION FOR SMALL-GROUP ACTIVITIES

It is suggested that for optimal effectiveness of the small-group teaching methodology, whether used in tutorial size classes or in lecture rooms, an important requirement is that the professor develops a style that is simultaneously open, friendly, informative, critical, reflective, questioning and constructive. Some professors possess this teaching style as a natural set of qualities, while there are others for whom these qualities do not come naturally but who can still develop and/or adapt to this style. There will, of course, always be some professors who are quite resistant to changing their teaching style and methods.

For the small-group methodology to be effective, 'buy-in' and collaboration is also needed from students. It is therefore necessary for professors to explain the learning methods in writing as well as in class. In some cultures, it can be challenging to convince students to engage in discussion and to express an opinion, or even just to speak in class. For students who come from educational backgrounds where rote learning is the norm, it can be especially difficult for them to develop their critical abilities, especially in a class context. In situations or cultures where professors may be seen as authorities whose views and opinions are the final word on any particular subject, extra care must be taken to ensure that the students fully understand the rationale for the techniques discussed here.

In order for small-group activities such as those outlined below to be successful, it is essential that both the professor and the students be well prepared. The extent and nature of the students' preparation depends in part on whether the professor intends to assess the oral skills demonstrated by the students in class. In any case, preparation by setting prior reading or the carrying out of other tasks is required in many law schools, whether or not oral skills are assessed.

Stephen Wizner, 'The Law School Clinic: Legal Education in the Interests of Justice' (2001) 70 *Fordham Law Review* 1929, 1930.

USING SMALL GROUPS TO FACILITATE STUDENT DISCUSSION

One of the principal means by which the benefits of small-group learning that have been outlined above can be achieved is to conduct a range of exercises in which students are afforded the opportunity to engage in discussion with each other, usually to be followed by some form of review of the discussion outcomes across the small groups within the class. Discussion activity can take a number of forms, including structured discussion and report-back; self-directed, structured discussion; free-form discussion; and brainstorming. Each of these will be explained further below.

1.   Structured Discussion and Report-back

The most common form of discussion activity within a small-group format is the conduct of a structured discussion followed by a report-back process to the full class. The term 'structured' is used in this context to reflect that the topic of the discussion has been designed by the professor, and possibly has been the subject of a prior lecture presentation or, alternatively, is supported by the provision of relevant reading materials. This activity can be utilised both for seminar-sized classes and in larger classes where lecturing is the normal teaching methodology. Guidelines for structured discussion activities in both contexts will be presented below.

A seminar is normally understood as being an alternative to a lecture or tutorial and can be regarded as a combination of the two. Seminars are often directed to specialist parts of an environmental law curriculum. They are more often conducted for postgraduate students rather than undergraduate students, and usually involve between 15 and 30 students.

The following guidelines concern small-group structured discussion and report-back in a seminar-sized class. The steps outlined should be regarded as flexible, and can be adapted to the size of the seminar class, the cultural background and capacity of the students and the subject matter to be discussed. The technique of a structured discussion can be used once or several times in a class, combined with other techniques such as brainstorming and free-form class discussion. Some educational specialists in small-group teaching recommend that groups of four work well,[20] but in this author's experience, groups of five to six work satisfactorily in law classes. In any case, there is no reason

---

[20]   For an excellent discussion of innovative teaching in the science context, see generally, Carl Weiman, 'Student work in educational settings' in *Improving How Universities Teach Science: Lessons from the Science Education Initiative* (Harvard

not to vary the number of students in the groups from one question or issue to another, or from one class to another.

(a)   For seminars and smaller classes

(i)   In the first class, explain how the class will be conducted, the teaching/ learning methods to be used and whether student participation is to be assessed.

(ii)   If student participation is to be assessed, explain how that will be done, for example, assessment only by the professor or self-assessment by each student. Such assessment can be done by filling out a form (see Appendix).

(iii)   If necessary, begin with a short introduction to the subject matter.

(iv)   Divide the class into groups of five or six students.

(v)   Structured discussion involves each group being given the same question or issue for discussion, or giving them each a different question. If lectures are also used in the course, the question can be based on lecture material that has already been delivered and on articles, legislation or other material that has been set as required reading for the class.

(vi)   Instruct the groups to choose a reporter.

(vii)   The reporter should take notes of the discussion and any conclusions drawn by the group.

(viii) Instruct the groups to ensure that all participants have an opportunity to speak.

(ix)   Depending on the complexity of the question, specify between five and 15 minutes for the small-group discussion.

(x)   At the end of the discussion period, the class should come back into plenary session, and the reporter from each group should be asked to give a short report to the plenary group. If there is sufficient time, this can be done in handwriting on a whiteboard or on PowerPoint.

(xi)   When the reporters have completed their oral reports, where appropriate, invite the other members of each group to add any further comments.

(xii)   Where appropriate, encourage a debate within the full seminar class about specific points of contention or disagreement.

University Press, 2017); and with respect to small groups, see: 'Student Group Work in Educational Settings', ibid. 203–207.

(b)   For larger classes

The structured discussion activity can also be used where class sizes are large.[21] Adaptation of this activity to large classes requires creativity and professorial confidence. Use of this approach, however, can be stimulating and help to avoid the loss of student attention. It also makes the professorial role and the student experience more rewarding because of the satisfaction gained from encouraging the class to be more engaged in the subject matter.

Once again, the following steps should be regarded as flexible, and can be adapted to the size of the class, the cultural background and capacity of the students and the subject matter to be discussed. They can be used in classes conducted in lecture theatres or large seminar rooms.

(i)   In the first class, explain how the class will be conducted, the teaching/ learning methods to be used and, if participation is assessable, how student performance will be assessed.

(ii)   Give a short introduction to the subject matter and, preferably, decide beforehand, the question or issue to be made the subject of discussion in small groups.

(iii)   At an appropriate time after the introduction, divide the whole class into groups. If each group is to report back, divide the class into groups of five or six students. If the class is large, do this by counting them off one to six, one to six etc. around the lecture room. If there is more than one group discussion session, it is more time-efficient to have students form into the same groups as before. If the lecture room is flat and the tables and chairs can be moved, ask the students to move the furniture around as necessary. If the chairs or writing spaces are fixed, divide the groups in such a way that, say, there are three students in one row and three in the row above or below, as the case may be.

(iv)   Give each group a question for discussion. The question can be based on lecture material that has already been delivered and on articles, legislation or other material that has been set as required reading for the class.

(v)   Instruct the class that each group should choose a reporter.

(vi)   The reporter should take notes of the discussion and any conclusions drawn by the group.

(vii)   Instruct the groups to ensure that all participants have an opportunity to speak.

(viii) Depending on the complexity of the question, allocate between five and 15 minutes for the small-group discussion.

---

[21]   James L Cooper and Pamela Robinson, *Getting Started: Informal Small-Group Strategies in Large Classes New Directions for Teaching and Learning* (Jossey-Bass Publishers, no. 81, 2000) 17–24.

(ix)   At the end of the discussion period, the class should come back into plenary session, and the reporter from each group (or reporters from just a few groups) should be asked to give a short report to the plenary group.

(x)   If there is only a limited time for a group session, ask only a few representative groups to report back.

(xi)   When the reporters have finished their report, if appropriate in terms of time or the need to clarify views, invite the other members of each group to add any further comments.

(xii) Where appropriate, encourage debate about specific points of contention or disagreement.

2.   Self-directed, Structured Discussion and Report-back

Self-directed small-group discussion can take a similar form to the structured discussion activity outlined above. The class can be asked to generate its own topics, within the scope of the relevant segment of the course, form into small groups, generate their own questions and discuss them in a set period of time, report back to the plenary group and then, if time allows, engage in broader discussion.

3.   Free-form Discussion

Free-form discussion involves a deliberation in small groups concerning topics or issues raised by the professor and any of the students which are relevant to the subject matter of the course, prior to reporting back to the full class on their discussions. The free-form method allows students to impose their own discipline on their interactions, in order to come up with new insights and further questions. Often, such discussion can be based on daily newspaper articles, weekly journal articles, television programmes or environmental issues arising from the city or region which are relevant to the course. Students should be encouraged to read daily newspapers and weekly journals, or their internet equivalent, and bring relevant material to class for free-form discussion as appropriate.

4.   Brainstorming

Brainstorming refers to the process by which small groups (or the class as a whole if it is not too large) generate a range of ideas on a particular topic, often in an intensive manner. This methodology differs from free-form discussion because it is conducted in a rapid way by the professor or a student volunteer. At the same time, the professor or a volunteer student briefly records the points being made on a whiteboard (alternatively, large sheets of paper, or PowerPoint if technologically possible) so that all students can immediately see the results of the discussions. When the brainstorm is over, the professor can summarise, comment on and add to the points made, as appropriate.

OTHER SMALL-GROUP ACTIVITIES

While discussion exercises are the most common form of small-group activity, there is a wide range of other learning exercises that can also be employed within a course, using the small-group format. In the following section, a description is provided of the following activities: (a) drafting assignments; (b) case studies; (c) role plays; and (d) comparative law exercises.

1.   Drafting Assignments and Report-back

This activity can be a very useful introductory exercise at the beginning of an environmental law course, serving the dual purposes of providing an initial experience of the small-group methodology and enabling students to think for themselves about the scope of the course subject matter. It can involve a range of drafting exercises connected to new environmental legislation, including, for example:

• the preparation of drafting instructions;
• the drafting of a set of statutory definitions; or
• the drafting of a set of statutory objectives.

As another example, a small-group drafting activity can involve drafting a definition of a key word or phrase for insertion into national legislation concerning environmental protection. It should be explained to students that the exercise demonstrates that the definition of a particular word or concept can determine the scope of the legislation. A narrow definition, for example, of 'environment', or 'natural resources' or 'pollution' limits the scope of the legislation, while a broader definition can allow for a wider application of the legislation.

2.   Case Studies and Student Presentations

The professor and/or students can develop a range of case studies[22] concerning specific environmental law issues that can be refined in small-group discus-

---

[22]   The term 'case study' here does not necessarily mean a judicial decision/case but also may include a wider environmental problem or issue that can be examined from a legal perspective.

sions and presented by the small groups to the larger class. For example, cases concerning environmental impact assessment, biodiversity conservation or any type of pollution could be used. If there are judgments available from national courts that are relevant to the subject matter, the facts and law in those judgments can be used. In addition, cases studies from other jurisdictions also can be used to illustrate any points in the class. This can be especially rewarding when students come from a variety of cultural and/or geographical backgrounds.

Case studies can be particularly useful where students are asked to give presentations on specific topics within the course. With such an activity, professors should normally discuss the scope of the topic with the student and ask them to prepare a written outline for distribution to the seminar class. This can be done beforehand by email or social media channels as appropriate. Students can be coached by their professors on their speaking and presentation skills, and be assisted with regard to use of PowerPoint and other visual media.

3.   Role Plays

In a role-play exercise, each small group is asked to represent a different set of interests within a fact situation. If the role play takes the form of a mediation exercise, the groups can represent the different interests involved in the role-play topic, with two or three students appointed to perform the mediator role. If it is a negotiation exercise, each group can be asked to negotiate with the other groups to resolve the fact situation.

The successful conduct of a role-play exercise involves preparation. A set of agreed facts to be used as the basis of the exercise should be generated, which can be distributed in writing or explained in a preceding lecture. Alternatively, the facts can be embedded in separate materials made available to each individual or group taking a role in the exercise. This can include development of detailed preparatory materials by the professor. As a further or additional element, the basic legal and policy issues can be set out on a PowerPoint slide. A map, graphic, photo or drawing to help describe the fact situation can also be very useful.

4.   Comparative Law Exercises

The use of comparative approaches is an important aspect of understanding different ways in which various jurisdictions address environmental law issues. In many universities, especially at postgraduate level, students come from a variety of countries, with common law, civil law or sharia law systems, or sometimes a combination of these. However, comparative exercises of this kind can also be useful in classes where students come from the same or similar backgrounds, especially if the subject matter is regionally or transnationally focused.[23] By devising the appropriate types of questions and exercises, such comparative discussions between students can be invaluable.

Questions and discussion points can involve macro- and micro-comparisons. The macro-comparisons can include the environmental, natural resources, economic, cultural and social contexts, and the constitutional, political and institutional backgrounds. The micro-comparisons can include a detailed comparative analysis of the relevant legislation and regulatory frameworks. This can involve comparisons of legislative objectives, definitions, institutional arrangements, management plans, environment protection mechanisms, planning regimes, etc. In classes with mixed student backgrounds, the report-back sessions from the small group to the full class can often generate a high degree of interest, since the students are called upon to talk about their own countries and, through their comparisons, also to reflect on the quality and level of effectiveness of laws in their home jurisdictions.

FEEDBACK AND ASSESSMENT

1.   Constructive Feedback in Small-group Work

During any kind of small-group work, constructive feedback can be given by the professor and the students on particular points. Feedback promotes the logical development of ideas and the collective understanding of concepts in a way that encourages maximum participation and the building of student confidence concerning their involvement in class discussions. Feedback can also be given as part of the assessment process; see below.

2.   Assessment of Participation in Small-group Activities

Assessment of class participation can be a useful way to promote closer engagement in a class and built into the assessment scheme for the course. All types of participation can be assessed. Students can be assessed on their overall level of discussion, or on oral presentations that they have delivered.

Assessment modes can include assessments by the professor only; self-assessment and assessment of students by students (peer assessment), or a combination of these. The mark is normally no less than 10 per cent and no more than 30 per cent of the total assessment for the course.

---

[23]   For example, the author has used these comparative discussion activities at Master's level in teaching Asian and Pacific Environmental Law to international and Chinese students at Wuhan University.

Some professors build compulsory assessment of oral skills into their overall assessment scheme. In doing so, the following preparation might be expected:

(i)   The professor should, prior to the first class, distribute appropriate reading materials, with indications of what is compulsory reading and what is suggested for extra reading.

(ii)   Written material should be distributed explaining the small-group methods to be used. At postgraduate level at least, this might include background materials on small-group teaching methodology.

In the first class, and whenever appropriate during the course, the professor should explain the methods that will be used, so as to encourage an understanding of the philosophy of those methods and their advantages.

A useful device for assessment is a printed form that identifies the various aspects to be assessed. An example of such a form is found in the Appendix.

CONCLUSIONS

This brief survey has canvassed a variety of small-group activities that can be used in the teaching of any law course, but in particular, the subject of environmental law. It should be clear from this chapter that small-group work entails the professor and the students being willing to work with a variety of activities, being prepared to change or discard those activities that are less successful and to embrace and refine the activities that do work. Keys to success with this methodology are for the professor to be open to constructive feedback from students, be self-critical of their own teaching methodology, not to be afraid to make mistakes, be willing to discuss and share their experiences with their peers, and never give up on opportunities for improvement.

Perhaps the most significant indicators of whether the use of small-group teaching techniques has succeeded are whether the students walk away from the class having enjoyed the experience. It is important that they have been stimulated to think more broadly and deeply about the fundamental role of environmental law in addressing the multifarious environmental issues that the world faces and that they remain enthused about the possible roles they can play in addressing them.

APPENDIX: EXAMPLE OF SELF-ASSESSMENT FORM FOR CLASS PARTICIPATION

Note: the form should be adapted by the professor to reflect actual techniques employed in the course.

ENVIRONMENTAL LAW

Self-assessment of Class Participation

Your name:
Your student number:

As indicated above, 20% of your final mark is comprised of an assessment of your class participation. The criteria for assessing class participation are set out below. Please remember that the mark you give is only a suggestion. The professor will determine the final mark.

Please tick the appropriate box alongside each category:

Range of marks	0-9.5	10-12.5	13-14.5	15-17.5	18-20
Preparation for class					
Listening actively to class discussion					
Contributing to class discussion					
Contribution to small-group discussions					
Asking questions					
Quality of class presentation					

Overall Numerical Self-Assessment Mark for Class Participation

Any comments or factors you wish to be taken into consideration by the professor in determining the final mark:

_____

_____

Comments and numerical assessment by professor:

_____

8. Enhancing learning in environmental law through assessment design

Ceri Warnock, James Higham, Sara Walton, Lyn Carter and Daniel Kingston

1. INTRODUCTION

Assessment is often considered one of the 'most controversial issues in higher education today', as evidenced by a UK quality assurance study that indicated students are most dissatisfied with the assessment and feedback aspects of their higher education experience.[1] Boud suggests this dissatisfaction may be explained by the fact that students can escape the impacts of poor teaching but not of poor assessment.[2] This chapter explores assessment in environmental law courses. Using the development of a new multi-disciplinary environmental law course as a case study, it explores the role of assessment in learning; surveys traditional and emerging forms of assessment in law, particularly those most suited to environmental law pedagogies; and it considers in greater detail student conferences (the method that we chose to employ in our course) and reflexive essays (a method we plan to trial in the future). It also includes data from student and staff evaluations as to the success of our assessment method. The structure of this chapter mirrors the steps that we took in selecting and designing the assessment for our course. However, the process that we followed did not follow a pre-ordained path – it was much more organic: a point that illustrates pedagogy is a product that merges scholarship, experience, experimentation and creativity, and of necessity entails both objective evaluation and subjective reflection.

---

[1]   Lin Norton, 'Assessing Student Learning' in Heather Fry, Steve Ketteridge, and Stephanie Marshall (eds), *A Handbook for Teaching and Learning in Higher Education: Enhancing Academic Practice* (3rd edn, Taylor & Francis Group 2008) 132.

[2]   David Boud, 'Ensuring Assessment Fosters Learning: Meeting the Challenge of More Students with Diverse Backgrounds' in Linda Conrad and Lee Ann Phillips (eds), *Reaching More Students* (Griffith Institute for Higher Education 1995).

2.　　THE CASE STUDY: OUR PEDAGOGICAL CHALLENGE

Over a number of years, law students at the University of Otago pressed for a multi-disciplinary course on climate change. They wanted to understand climate change law in its context in order to better understand the scientific causes; the environmental, socio-cultural and economic impacts of climate change; and how law might play a greater role in providing solutions. And they wanted to work with students from other disciplines to test those solutions. Presciently, the requests from the students reflected that even to 'pose the proper issues for analysis, [environmental] lawyers need an increased sophistication and heightened appreciation' of the physical and social sciences.[3] Further, addressing climate change through law will require future generations of lawyers to be trained in or at least aware of co-producing knowledge based on active relationships between practitioners, researchers, scientists and communities.

In response to the student requests, a research consortium of academics at the University of Otago developed a new advanced course in 2016 for the undergraduate syllabus entitled 'Interdisciplinary Aspects of Climate Change'. This experimental course brings together academics from all divisions of the University – Humanities, Science, Medicine and Commerce – and the course is open to all students, thus offering law students the opportunity to work with peers possessing different expertise, knowledge and skills. Over the first four years, numbers in the course grew from 16 to 31 students, with law students consistently representing about one-third of enrolments (the second biggest cohort were Bachelor of Science majors, then Politics and Commerce majors).

Designing the course presented particular challenges, with the primary concerns being how to surmount barriers between law and other disciplines and how to ensure all aspects of the course-building addressed interdisciplinarity, particularly the assessment. To address these challenges we began by identifying the main objectives and learning outcomes, one of which was:

> [t]o be able to work productively within a peer group comprised of people with different skills and knowledge and have confidence to raise, discuss and debate challenging issues amongst that peer group.

---

[3]　Heidi Robertson, 'Methods for Teaching Environmental Law: Some Thoughts on Providing Access to the Environmental Law System' (1998) 23(2) *Columbia Journal of Environmental Law* 237.

A literature review revealed that the scholarship on involving law students in interdisciplinary courses was limited.[4] However, Robertson noted that the main objective of such a pedagogy is to 'provide opportunities for students *to work together on practical, real-life problems* with students from other disciplines'.[5] Further, the general literature on pedagogy emphasised the importance of assessment in helping to anchor the student learning experience, the role of 'outcome-based assessment' ('OBE') and 'authentic assessment', factors that we discuss in the next part of this chapter. Accordingly, we focused our initial attention on how to foster OBE and authentic assessment in group work as a way of guiding our wider pedagogy. We considered emerging practices of assessment in law (discussed in part 4 of this chapter) and ultimately chose to employ a student conference method (see part 5). We evaluated the success of this assessment method over a number of years, from both our own perspective and through annual student surveys (and report on that data in part 6). Finally, we reflect on how we might improve the assessment method and in doing so, draw on a colleague's experience with reflexive essays (as explained in the final part of this chapter).

3.   THE ROLE OF ASSESSMENT IN LEARNING

While assessment is often a neglected topic in higher education *practice*,[6] a growing body of research addresses: why we assess; what we as academics take from student assessment; and the appropriate quantity and form of assessment. In thinking about assessment, the scholarship suggests that there are a number of core considerations for educators.[7]

---

[4]   For a notable exception see L Godden and P Dale, 'Interdisciplinary Teaching in Law and Environmental Science: Jurisprudence and Environment' (2000) 11 *Legal Education Review* 239.

[5]   Ibid 258.

[6]   Norton (n 1).

[7]   Ibid.

First, assessment is a central influence for both teaching *and* learning.[8] Students adopt an orientation to learning depending on the context, and part of that context concerns the assessment requirements.[9] As Biggs notes:

> [w]e teachers might see the curriculum objectives as the central pillar of teaching in an aligned system, but our students see otherwise: 'From our students' point of view, assessment always defines the actual curriculum'.[10]

Second, assessment involves two distinct activities:[11] summative assessment evaluates student knowledge and learning; formative assessment provides feedback to enable further development by learners. However, Astin suggests that this foci can get blurred in higher education practice. While both summative and formative assessment may lead to learning[12] (and courses may provide both types of feedback), Krause has described the need to shift the balance from 'assessment *of* learning' towards greater use of 'assessment *for* learning'.[13] Further, academics should deliberately design assessment methods to give detailed feedback. Traditional teaching methods in law tend to rely more heavily on summative than on formative assessment, with final examinations taking the form of problem-based written opinions and essays.[14] In those circumstances, the grade provides the only feedback. One scholar has described summative assessment in law as not 'fit for purpose'.[15] Certainly, relying

---

[8]   Odeku Kola, 'Awareness Creation and Effective Communication are Impetus for Entrenching Outcomes Based Education in Law Pedagogy in South Africa' (2018) 16(31) *Global Media Journal* 1.

[9]   Paul Ramsden, *Learning to Teach in Higher Education* (2nd edn, Routledge 2003).

[10]   John Biggs, *Teaching for Quality Learning at University* (2nd edn, Open University Press 2003) 140 quoting Ramsden, ibid., 187.

[11]   Alexander Astin and Anthony Lising Antonio, *Assessment for Excellence: The Philosophy and Practice of Assessment and Evaluation in Higher Education* (2nd edn, Rowman & Littlefield Publishers 2012).

[12]   Boud (n 2).

[13]   Kerri-Lee Krause, 'On Being Strategic About the First Year' (Keynote Address, Queensland University of Technology First Year Forum, Brisbane, October 2006) cited in Sally Kift and Rachael Field, 'Intentional first year curriculum design as a means of facilitating student engagement: some exemplars' (12th Pacific Rim First Year in Higher Education Conference, 2009) eprints.qut.edu.au/30044/ accessed 10 May 2019.

[14]   See, e.g.: Barnes, 'The Functions of Assessment: A Re-Examination' (1990–91) 2 *Legal Education Review* 177; Pauline Collins, Toni Brackin, and Caroline Hart, 'Rocky Rhetoric and Hard Reality: The Academic's Dilemma Surrounding Assessment' (2010) 20 *Legal Education Review* 157; Nathan Ross, 'Beyond Skills and Doctrine: The Need for Policy Skills and Interdisciplinarity' (2018) 48 *VUWLR* 353.

[15]   Edward Phillips and others, 'Exceeding the Boundaries of Formulaic Assessment: Innovation and Creativity in the Law School' (2010) 44(3) *The Law Teacher* 334.

solely on summative forms of assessment does not necessarily foster life-long learning or encourage active participation in the learning process, which the practice of law requires with its ever-changing content.[16]

Third, the way in which assessment is embedded into the design of the curriculum is important. Didactic methods of teaching predominate in many law schools,[17] where the aim is to deliver a large amount of substantive content through a traditional lecture format. However, research shows that courses designed from the orientation of student-learning – i.e., those which develop and focus on delivering learning outcomes rather than content delivery – create the context for deep learning to occur.[18] Various methods fall under the rubric of OBE.[19] Within a law course, OBE focuses on 'what sort of lawyer will be produced' rather than focusing primarily on content delivery. Outcome-based education is particularly apt for environmental lawyers who are often working within legislative mandates to promote sustainable development. A key characteristic of OBE is switching from a more passive approach to facilitating active learning as a means to increase student engagement and achievement. Some methods of teaching law, such as the Langdellian case-based method and Socratic approaches,[20] do allow for more active student participation and the possibility of assessment based on that participation. However, scholars have noted the limitations of these pedagogies:[21] in particular, they disproportionately disadvantage students from cultural minorities[22] and the millennial generation.[23] Nevertheless, OBE can encompass many different forms of experiential learning other than the Socratic method, as we discuss in part 4 below.

---

[16] K Sita Manikyam and A Lakshminath, 'Legal Education: Ideological and Institutional Perspectives' in BC Nirmal and Rajnish Kumar Singh (eds), *Contemporary Issues in International Law: Environment, International Trade, Information Technology and Legal Education* (Springer and Satyam Law International 2018); David Boud and Nancy Falchikov, 'Aligning Assessment with Long-term Learning' (2006) 31 *Assessment & Evaluation in Higher Education* 399.

[17] Ross (n 14); Áine Hyland and Shane Kilcommins 'Signature Pedagogies and Legal Education in Universities: Epistemological and Pedagogical Concerns with Langdellian Case Method' (2009) 14(1) *Teaching in Higher Education* 29.

[18] Boud (n 2).

[19] Kola (n 8).

[20] Ross (n 14) (noting the dominance of these pedagogies in lower level or core subjects in particular); Hyland and Kilcommins (n 17).

[21] Hyland and Kilcommins (n 17).

[22] Sam Banks, 'Pedagogy and Ideology: Teaching Law as if it Matters' (1999) 19(4) *Legal Studies* 445; Barnes (n 14).

[23] Richard Jochelson and David Ireland, 'Law Students' Responses to Innovation: A Study of Perspectives in Respect of Digital Knowledge Transmission, Flipped Classrooms, Video Capsules and Other Means of Classroom Dissemination' (2018) 41(1) *Manitoba LJ* 131.

In conjunction with an OBE-focus, learning, assessment and the desired outcomes need to be appropriately aligned to best promote students meeting the learning outcomes of the course.[24] For constructive alignment, Norton suggests designing the assessment before the content of the course.[25]

Fourthly, there is increasing evidence supporting the value of 'authentic assessment', particularly in professional degrees such as medicine and law.[26] Authentic assessment focuses on higher order skills such as 'problem solving and critical thinking, through tasks that are more realistic or contextualised to the "real world"'.[27] Such skills are relevant to all law students but ensuring tasks are 'contextualised to the real world' is particularly critical for environmental lawyers. Environmental lawyers do not operate in an artificial world created by law (like say, trusts) rather they are continually constrained by physical realities and, to understand those physical limits, must work with experts from the physical and social sciences. Thus, in *environmental law* pedagogy exposure to multi-disciplinary expertise promotes authenticity. In summarising the growing body of research, Villarroel et al report that authentic assessment positively impacts 'the quality and depth of learning achieved by the student and the development of higher-order cognitive skills ... students' growth in personal confidence ... autonomous practice ... academic engagement ... motivation ... self-regulation ... and metacognition'.[28] There are three core components to authentic assessment: realism; cognitive challenge; and evaluative judgement (i.e., enabling students to make 'decisions about the quality of work of oneself and others').[29] In legal pedagogy, mimicking professional practice through group activities and presentations helps foster professional competencies and constitutes 'realism'.[30] Certainly, employing some form of oral assessment is seen as increasing authenticity because: '[t]he ability to converse on complex legal and related issues with fluency, accuracy

---

[24]   John Biggs, 'Enhancing Teaching Through Constructive Alignment' (1996) 32(3) *Higher Education* 347; Anthony Niedwiecki, 'Teaching for Lifelong Learning: Improving the Metacognitive Skills of Law Students Through More Effective Formative Assessment Techniques' (2012) 40(1) *Capital University Law Review* 149.

[25]   Norton (n 1) 136.

[26]   Verónica Villarroel and others, 'Using Principles of Authentic Assessment to Redesign Written Examinations and Tests' (2019) *Innovations in Education and Teaching International* doi.org/10.1080/14703297.2018.1564882 accessed 20 November 2019.

[27]   Anna McKie, 'Does University Assessment Still Pass Muster?' *Times Higher Education* (London, 23 May 2019).

[28]   Villarroel (n 26) 2.

[29]   Ibid., 3.

[30]   McKie (n 27).

and effectiveness is not only desirable, but virtually mandatory to a successful professional life as a lawyer'.[31]

4. EMERGING FORMS OF ASSESSMENT IN LAW

In response to research that encourages lecturers to design courses that focus on the 'sort of lawyer that will be produced' and the need for authenticity, increasingly novel methods of assessment have been developed. Table 8.1 below summarises various methods discussed in the literature that have particular relevance to environmental law pedagogy.

Each of these methods have been reported as having particular advantages, and sometimes disadvantages, over traditional teaching and assessment methods in law. For example, the advantages of on-line group projects were reported to be that: the students felt less isolated; believed their work was valued; employed more flexible time management and, as a corollary, were able to dig deeper into materials without their workload becoming unmanageable.[32] However, problems arose with collaborative work that included group conflict; organisation, communication and logistical issues; and a student perception of holistic marking which did not reflect their individual input into the project.[33] Other assessment methods reported equally mixed results: for example, while annotated portfolios may include personal opinions and afford the opportunity for reflections to be recorded, this falls short of fully reflexive learning approaches that compel students to reflect upon their social environment and think afresh.[34] However, the fact that these assessment methods have downsides does not mean rejecting their use; rather, academics should be cognisant of the disadvantages and work to address them.

5. OUR EXPERIENCES WITH DESIGNING AND EMBEDDING THE ASSESSMENT IN OUR COURSE

Our new course, 'Interdisciplinary Aspects of Climate Change', offered much scope for innovative approaches to OBE and authentic assessment.

---

[31] Rowena Cantley-Smith, 'Put Down Your Pen: The Role of Oral Assessment in Undergraduate Law Students' (2006) 13 *James Cook University Law Review* 30, 32.

[32] Lisa Bugden, P Redmond, and J Greaney, 'Online Collaboration as a Pedagogical Approach to Learning and Teaching Undergraduate Legal Education' (2018) 52(1) *The Law Teacher* 85.

[33] Ibid.

[34] Helen Walkington, Jennifer Hill, and Pauline Kneale, 'Reciprocal Elucidation: A Student-Led Pedagogy in Multidisciplinary Undergraduate Research Conferences' (2017) 36(2) *Higher Education Research and Development* 416.

Table 8.1   *Emerging forms of assessment in law*

Continuous professional development[a]	Credits are allocated to certain experiential learning activities including: attending court and/or guest lectures; becoming an active member of a law society or environmental lawyers group; obtaining part-time work in a legal firm, law sector of an NGO or volunteering at a law centre. Students submit a written report reflecting upon their experience.
Annotated portfolios[b]	The students select a piece of work or a collection of their best work showing the process from inception to conclusion. Students reflect on their work, explaining the methodological approach they chose, what they value in their work, and what they would do differently in the future. Both substantive work and reflections contribute to final mark.
Utilising online learning platforms[c]	Examples include: a) collaborative group projects: lecturers can post group study projects and tutorials (with the relevant materials that could include webinars, research articles, videos etc.), with the aim of students organising themselves to complete the project; b) forms of 'on-line gaming' that allow students to 'communicate with real or fictitious persons and institutions, and receive feedback on their work in-role';[d] c) web page design:[e] each student designs a website that incorporates a bulletin board, where they post information and updates on current environmental law issues and provide links to appropriate legal resources. Marks are allocated from lecturers, peer assessment, and for providing peer assessment to others; d) United Nations simulation:[f] based on a simulation of the world climate negotiations using the interactive Climate Rapid Overview and Decision Support (C-ROADS) computer program. Students play the roles of negotiators from major nations and then receive immediate feedback on the implications of their proposals for atmospheric greenhouse gas concentrations.
Write a journal article[g]	Students are guided through the process of writing an article. Marks are allocated for: literature search; submitting a proposal to classmates for review; presentation at a mini-conference; submission of a draft for editing; participating in a proofreading and editing workshop (as author and reviewer); and the finished article.
Immersive learning[h]	Participating in a residential course with an explorative rather than prescriptive approach to learning, including: hands on learning of environmental matters (through food gathering and preparation as an example); formal lectures with experts from different fields; and group work.

Simulated problem-based assessment[i]	Examples include: a) a simulated regulatory process concerning the development of a parcel of vacant property, where the student acts for a client embroiled in a planning/environmental law controversy; b) adopting the role of the lawyer, submitting a memorandum on a problem, and making oral submissions to the class; c) analysing an enforcement action against unpermitted land use; d) drafting an environmental impact assessment; e) drafting an ordinance (for habitat regulation of a protected species or similar); f) evaluating the process and presentations made at a hearing (after having attended court); g) developing a semester-long case study on a complex issue – for example, exploring the environmental impacts of a battery hen facility. Students identify the environmental and legal issues (e.g. nuisance, hazardous substances control, solid waste regulation, storm-water run-off, control of particulate emissions, environmental crimes and environmental auditing)[j] and write a case study on it; h) environmental law moots.[k]
Clinical Legal Education[l]	Providing students with real practical experience (via in-house environmental clinics, external internships at firms or community law centres) or through problem-based learning based on real scenarios. Students are assessed on their participation (evaluated by their mentors/supervisors and through site visits by lecturers).

Notes:

a. Edward Phillips and others, 'Exceeding the Boundaries of Formulaic Assessment: Innovation and Creativity in the Law School' (2010) 44(3) *The Law Teacher* 334.

b. Steven Johansen, '"What Were You Thinking?": Using Annotated Portfolios to Improve Student Assessment' (1998) 4 *Legal Writing* 123.

c. Phillips, et al (n a); Lisa Bugden, P Redmond, and J Greaney, 'Online Collaboration as a Pedagogical Approach to Learning and Teaching Undergraduate Legal Education' (2018) 52(1) *The Law Teacher* 85; Terry Hutchinson, 'Critique And Comment: Developing Legal Research Skills: Expanding The Paradigm' (2008) 32 *Melbourne U LR* 1065.

d. Craig Newbery-Jones, 'Ethical Experiments with the D-pad: Exploring the Potential of Video Games as a Phenomenological Tool for Experiential Legal Education' (2016) 50(1) *The Law Teacher* 61, 68.

e. Phillips, et al (n a).

f. Peter Doran, 'Head, Hand and Heart: Immersive Learning for a Demanding New Climate at Queen's University Belfast's School of Law' (2016) 50(3) *The Law Teacher* 341.

g. Phillips, et al (n a).

h. Doran (n f).

i. Keith Hirokawa, 'Teaching from the Dirt: Best Practices and Land Use Law Pedagogy' (2011) 2(1) *Pace Environmental Law Review* 68.

j. Heidi Robertson, 'Methods for Teaching Environmental Law: Some Thoughts on Providing Access to the Environmental Law System' (1998) 23(2) *Columbia Journal of Environmental Law* 237.

k. Ibid.

l. Ibid.; Linden Thomas and others (eds), *Reimagining Clinical Legal Education* (Hart 2018); William Sullivan and others, *Educating Lawyers: Preparation for the Profession of Law* (John Wiley & Sons 2007); Molly George and others, 'Learning by Doing: Experiential Learning in Criminal Justice' (2015) 26(4) *Journal of Criminal Justice Education* 471.

We wanted the assessment programme to facilitate active learning through student engagement, particularly through forms of oral assessment that allow students to communicate effectively and engage in discussions that address complex issues with colleagues from different disciplines. It was also essential that students reflected 'on their own learning in the light of divergent perspectives, questions and frames of reference'.[35]

A pedagogical method discussed in the literature that seemed to fit our multi-layered requirements concerned 'student conferences'.[36] Walkington et al describe multi-disciplinary undergraduate student conferences as a form of 'reciprocal elucidation' in which: 'bidirectional exchange of ideas and insights enabled students to ask and answer questions that transformed each other's thinking, allowing them to arrive at understandings they could not have achieved by themselves'.[37]

The literature reports that group-based student conferences, where students present their own research in either paper or poster form, can help meet key learning objectives of reflection, discussion, debate and help foster professionalism.[38] They may also constitute a form of authentic assessment (depending upon the future profession of the students).[39] Students involved in research conferences are said to have increased confidence in their communication skills and take greater pride in their research.[40] Further, Hill and Walkington

---

[35]   Ibid.

[36]   Ibid; Jennifer Hill and Helen Walkington, 'Developing Graduate Attributes Through Participation in Undergraduate Research Conferences' (2016) 40(2) *Journal of Geography in Higher Education* 222; Meg O'Sullivan, 'Ownership, Community, and Accomplishment in the History Seminar: The Possibilities of Undergraduate Research Conference Presentations' (2018) 43(1) *Teaching History: A Journal of Methods* 36; L DiAnne Borders and James Benshoff, 'The Mini-Conference: Teaching Professionalism Through Student Involvement' (1992) 71(1) *Journal of Counselling & Development* 39; Joellen Coryell and Kayon Murray, 'Adult Learning and Doctoral Student Research Forum Participation: Insights into the Nature of Professional Participatory Experience' (2014) 9 *International Journal of Doctoral Studies* 309; Cara Hersh, Molly Hiro, and Harman Asarnow, 'The Undergraduate Literature Conference: A Report from the Field' (2011) 11(2) *Pedagogy* 395.

[37]   Walkington, Hill, and Kneale (n 34).

[38]   Borders and Benshoff (n 36); Brett Freudenberg and others, 'A Penny for Your Thoughts: Can Participation in a Student-Industry Conference Improve Students' Presentation Self-Efficacy and More?' (2008) 15(5) *The International Journal of Learning* 188.

[39]   Teresa Larkin, 'The Student Conference: A Model of Authentic Assessment' (2014) 4(2) International Journal of Engineering Pedagogy 36; Nick Lund, 'Ten Years of Using Presentations at a Student Conference as a Final Assessment' (2013) 12(2) *Psychology Learning and Teaching* 185.

[40]   Lund (n 39); Mark Caprio and Robert Hackey, 'If you Built it, They Will Come: Strategies for Developing an Undergraduate Research Conference' (2014) 31(3) *The*

report that students: 'demonstrated intellectual autonomy, repurposing their work for presentation to a multidisciplinary audience through conversation with and benchmarking against peers ... consciously balancing the contextual nature of their disciplinary knowledge with intra-personally grounded goals and values'.[41]

Within our course, careful thought was given to how best to embed the student-conference assessment method. To facilitate constructive alignment between learning, assessment and objectives, the teaching programme was organised into seminars that coalesced around particular themes in order to foster engagement in cross-disciplinary discussions and debate as much as possible. For example, we considered various 'bottom-up' approaches to climate-change mitigation that encompassed: local authority actions and relevant regulations, while looking at practical measures for mitigation in the built environment; corporate social responsibility and company law, highlighting innovative commercial practice and carbon accounting; and land use law and developments in agricultural practice.

Tutorials were designed to enable students to form multi-disciplinary working groups and identify a cross-disciplinary problem. Groups comprised three or four students (depending on the class numbers). Group presentations addressed topics that were negotiated by group members in discussion with the course coordinator, who ensured that each topic in the student conference builds upon specific aspects of the course that are of importance and interest to students. Under this approach each group is required to research and prepare a clearly defined topic that aims to extend the learning experiences of the class in ways that are clearly linked to and inform the learning outcomes of the course. Importantly, the internal assessment task is used to provide a framework for thinking about *solutions* to climate change. We embedded that foci by structuring lectures to reinforce a problem-solving mentality, with each lecturer addressing 'past problems', 'present practice' and 'future solutions' to climate change from the perspective of their discipline, and ensuring the student research followed a similar path. By way of illustration, one group of students (consisting of two law students, and two other students studying Geography and Microbiology) considered how technological advances in the dairy industry (in terms of herd, feed and pasture management) could facilitate agriculture's inclusion in the New Zealand emissions trading scheme – an issue that is challenging the legislature at present. Presentations were 20 minutes long with ten minutes set aside for questions and we required a number of additional tasks to be completed (e.g., the groups had to prepare

Journal of Health Administration Education 247.
    [41]   Hill and Walkington (n 36).

a short written summary, bibliography and source visual aids in addition to the oral presentation).

We provide scaffolding for the presentations through a 'Presentation Guidance'.[42] The students were told that the Presentation Guidance aligned with the marking schedule and marks were given for careful reflection on the questions posed in the Guidance. For example, parts of the Guidance direct the students to thinking about research methodology and ask:

- what materials did you use and why did you select and/or find those materials helpful while discounting other sources, or were there obvious gaps in the literature and if so how did you deal with this?
- were there tensions in the discourse concerning your topic, for example did researchers take competing stances, suggest alternate causes or solutions to the problem, if so which did you prefer and why?

To try and avoid some of the disadvantages with group work identified in part 4 above, we advised the students to identify, discuss and draw on their particular strengths in order to allocate required tasks. The Guidance asks 'how did you allocate the work within the group and what was the approach you took to working together?' In all the group presentations bar one, all the members have contributed to the oral presentations. In the group where one student felt unable to make an oral presentation, the group explained how they negotiated amongst themselves to both support the anxious student and ensure the workload was allocated fairly.

Conference presentations are assessed in accordance with the marking schedule by panels of lecturers from different disciplines, thereby emphasing to students the need to communicate ideas clearly to people from many different backgrounds. Both lecturers and student-colleagues asked questions and marks were awarded for the presenters' ability to respond coherently while showing evidence of deeper learning about their topic. The lecturers on the panel discuss and negotiate a final grade for the group, with each student in the group receiving the same grade (reinforcing again the critical importance of teamwork in the climate change sphere). The students receive both oral and written feedback on their presentation.

---

[42] Patricia Ann Mabrouk, 'Survey Study Investigating the Significance of Conference Participation to Undergraduate Research Students' (2009) 86(11) *Journal of Chemical Education* 1335.

6.   EVALUATION

Anonymous, written student surveys, taken in class at the start of the course, revealed some anxiety about the student conference process. In response to an open-ended question – 'what do you feel about the assessment process?' – some students noted that they did not 'like to speak in public', others were concerned about 'group dynamics' or not 'being able to come up with solutions'.[43] In 2018, for example, seven out of 22 students initially expressed some negative thoughts about the student conference whereas eight expressed positive thoughts (e.g., 'presentations are good for building confidence as a lawyer' and were 'good prep for the real world'). Interestingly, none of the original anxieties were repeated and/or confirmed in final on-line evaluations taken at the conclusion of the paper.[44]

Both initial surveys and final evaluations identified that the vast majority of students appreciated the interdisciplinary format of the course, with many stating that was why they originally enrolled. Being exposed to different perspectives and broader understanding of a holistic set of solutions was seen as positive by many students because 'climate change is a complicated issue' that 'requires knowledge from many different fields' and the course enabled them to 'contextualise the climate change challenges within their own disciplines'. Beyond just discussing the negative impacts of climate change, student comments noted their appreciation of the way that the course provided 'a greater understanding of solutions', and was 'informative and positive' rather than dwelling on 'how humanity is doomed'. In response to the question 'what do you feel about the assessment process?', a number of students volunteered that the internal assessment was a good way of understanding and testing different perspectives and possible solutions. For example, in 2018 comments included, 'I think the group work is very important to build community and links'; the group presentations 'allow us to both develop our own ideas but hear others opinions as well', and they are a 'great way to work together and learn from a group'. On one occasion group members were unable to reach an agreed research focus (even with lecturers' help) and one of the students joined another group to help ease group dynamics. Interestingly, a relatively consist-

---

[43]   The initial written surveys were carried out in class over the first four years that the course has been offered at the University of Otago (2016–2019). The survey questions were open-ended, such as 'why did you decide to take this paper?' Quotes in the text are taken directly from the survey responses.

[44]   Final course evaluations ask some open-ended questions (such as 'for me the best aspect of the paper was ...', 'the change I would most like to see in this paper is ...'), in conjunction with more targeted questions (such as 'to what extent did the assessments help you to learn').

ent theme across the years has been the desire for *more* assessment,[45] including short written assignments and opportunities to practise making 'smaller presentations … throughout the semester' before the final student conference.

The lecturers believe that the assessment method has been successful and the student conference has proven to be a highlight of the course, with many students excelling in the task. Positive features of the assessment included the inherently more collaborative format of group (vs. individual) work which requires students to converse on complex issues across disciplines, student ownership of their learning, and the practice they gain in developing oral presentation skills. The academic literature reports that student presentations encourage audience questions[46] so leading to better class engagement.[47] We observed that students in the audience appeared more confident in asking their peers questions and challenging their responses than they did with the lecturers in the course.

At present, we are looking at ways to refine the assessment process. Possibilities for extending the conference methodology in the future may include the 'submission of an abstract, draft for the instructor to review, second draft for formal peer review and copy for publication in the conference pro-ceedings'.[48] However, one aspect of the assessment method that has challenged the teaching team is how to clearly chart students' ability to 'transform … each other's thinking, allowing them to arrive at understandings they could not have achieved by themselves', that is, to better achieve 'reciprocal elucidation'.[49] Persuasion and the ability to adapt one's reasoning is an important part of an environmental (arguably, all) lawyers' toolbox, and accordingly a skill to be developed in law students. Students in the course informally report that this interchange takes place within their groups while they are developing their research presentation but the challenge for the teaching team is how to best observe, guide and (if possible) use this development as part of a formative assessment. One member of our team had experienced considerable success in using personal reflective essays to chart student transformation in a different course covering sustainability. We are considering how best to incorporate this

---

[45]   Perhaps reflecting an anxiety about having a grade based on just two assessments (i.e., the conference and the final exam) which is relatively standard in single semester papers at Otago.

[46]   J M K MacAlpine, 'Improving and Encouraging Peer Assessment of Student Presentations' (1999) 24(1) *Assessment & Evaluation in Higher Education* 15.

[47]   M G Arenas and others, 'Using Student Conferences to Increase Participation in the Classroom: A Case Study' (2012) 55(4) *IEEE Transactions On Education* 580.

[48]   Larkin (n 39).

[49]   Walkington, Hill, and Kneale (n 34).

pedagogy into our course at present and the final part of the chapter discusses this approach.

7.   FUTURE ADAPTATION AND IMPROVEMENT: CHARTING STUDENT TRANSITIONS

A critical starting point for reciprocal elucidation is that students are clear on their own personal position before confronting others' perceptions. Our colleague required students in his paper to complete a personal reflective essay that addresses key climate change discourses and debates. He employed Lester Milbrath's (1984) chapter titled 'Can Modern-day Prophets Redirect Society?' from the book *Environmentalists: Vanguard for a New Society* as a starting point for such a task.[50] The chapter concerns social change, environmental threats and whether science and technology do or do not offer the means for a secure future for humanity and others. Milbrath's writing sets up two competing schools of thought for social change based on contrasting and largely incompatible worldviews or paradigms. In explaining the dominant social paradigm versus the new environmental paradigm, Milbrath introduces the reader to the concepts of 'vanguards' and 'rearguards' of social and economic change, and invites the reader to contemplate and reflect upon the world views that underpin their respective positions. The chapter also addresses different avenues of social change, including evolutionary succession, social learning and scientific/technological development.

Milbrath's chapter provides the background for a personal and reflective essay (as a formative assessment) that challenges students to reflect upon foundational debates that are central to the challenges of climate change. It offers a starting point for reflexive work that requires students to consider where they stand on the issues addressed by Milbrath, and why. Milbrath raises a number of questions for the reader to contemplate on the prospects for a sustainable society, and how it may be best achieved. In identifying the issues raised, considering the discourses and engaging with the debates that are addressed by Milbrath, students are drawn into a dialogue that is confronting. Students are required to engage with debates that draw their own personal lives and lifestyles into question. Students are challenged to consider where they personally stand on one or more of the key questions addressed by Milbrath. Furthermore, the personal and reflective nature of the assignment requires students to reflect

---

[50]   Despite being published in the mid-1980s, climate change features as a central environmental challenge in the chapter. This highlights the passage of precious time and the lack of progress made in addressing the climate challenges, and invites students to consider why so little progress has been achieved over the course of 35 intervening years.

upon their own lived experiences. This may encourage students to reflect upon personal experiences from earlier periods of their lives, as well as contradictions and conflicts between their philosophical position and aspects of their personal lives, and to better understand alternate perspectives presented by their colleagues. Personal and reflective essays can serve as a platform that then may inform the contributions of the student to research, preparation and delivery of the group presentations. This reflective exercise may help students broach any disagreements in their group, think beyond 'their bubbles', and learn to negotiate with others respectfully and with empathy. In future years, we propose to adapt the course structure to incorporate short reflective essays that may help chart students' transition during the course. This is clearly a work in progress but the important point for the present chapter is the need for course designers to keep evaluating and refining the chosen assessment method over time.

8.   CONCLUSION

Focusing on assessment methods provided a useful foundation for building our novel course. From the lecturers' perspectives, the four years (to date) of the Interdisciplinary Aspects of Climate Change-course have demonstrated that an interdisciplinary approach can be utilised and prove successful in the context of climate change pedagogy. Our experience with group-based student conferences demonstrate their value in this context. The novel assessment method has been critical in helping to break down barriers between disciplinary silos and facilitating interdisciplinary problem-solving, which is a critical aspect of advanced environmental law pedagogy and practice. Through this assessment method, our environmental law students have been exposed to a number of the major challenges that environmental law practice demands and started the journey of navigating this tricky professional terrain.

9. Environmental law clinics in Australia and the United States: a comparison of design and operation

Evan Hamman and Jill Witkowski Heaps [1]

INTRODUCTION

Specialist legal clinics are a relatively new edition to the field of clinical legal education (CLE). They encourage students to develop the skills required for specific practice areas including immigration, labor law, domestic violence, human rights and environmental law. Environmental law clinics (ELCs) can be seen as one type of specialist legal clinic. Their focus, as the name implies, is on the teaching and practice of environmental law. The scope of the activities of ELCs is potentially very broad with students conducting or assisting with litigation, law reform, advocacy and other community education initiatives.[2] There are also documented instances of cross-disciplinary work, where the study areas of law, science, media and business can interact to deliver gains to the community and learning opportunities for students.[3]

In this chapter, we consider the establishment and development of ELCs by comparing examples from the United States (US) and Australia. We describe the differing approaches of these jurisdictions and discuss the results with

---

[1] The authors are grateful to Professor Rob Fowler from the University of South Australia for helpful comments on an earlier version of this chapter and to Ms Arianda Fernando for her editorial assistance.

[2] Adrian Evans, 'Greenprint for a Climate Justice Clinic: Law School's Most Significant Access to Justice Challenge' (2018) 25(3) *International Journal of Clinical Legal Education* 7; Evan Hamman, 'Establishing an Environmental Law Clinic in China: A Review of Relevant Factors and Various Models' (2018) 25(2) *International Journal of Clinical Legal Education* 122.

[3] Heidi Gorovitz Robertson, 'Methods for Teaching Environmental Law: Some Thoughts on Providing Access to the Environmental Law System' (1998) 23 *Columbia Journal of Environmental Law* 237, 269.

a view towards highlighting some of the underlying factors that might contribute towards success.[4]

CLINICAL LEGAL EDUCATION (CLE)

Boersig and others define CLE as 'the teaching of law and legal practice, procedures and skills through experiential learning'.[5] The phrase 'experiential learning' can be defined as:

> Learning in which the learner is directly in touch with the realities being studied. It is contrasted with the learner who only reads about, hears about, talks about, or writes about these realities but never comes into contact with them as part of the learning process.[6]

There are various approaches to CLE including on-campus programs overseen by academic staff (often referred to as 'clinicians'). Other models include legal 'externships', or partnerships with government institutions, non-government organisations (NGOs), private attorneys or law firms that provide a structured learning environment for students to gain hands on experience as part of their degree.[7]

Aside from the reported pedagogical benefits of students seeing 'law in action', CLE can also improve the employability and confidence of students in the workplace, as well as help them to establish useful networks for later in life.[8] Importantly, CLE is likely to give students an appreciation of the fact that

---

[4]   The information in this chapter is sourced from the peer-reviewed literature, the 'grey literature', university websites and the experiences of the authors themselves. Published literature on ELCs is very limited, and the contents of this chapter should be read with that in mind. Further research, especially empirical research, is needed to reach firmer conclusions on whether ELCs are truly 'successful' either in terms of pedagogical benefits for students or operationally for universities and their end-users. Finally, given the rapid changes facing the university sector today, some of the programs referred to in this chapter at the time of publication may have evolved or in some cases been discontinued.

[5]   John Boersig, James Marshall and Georgia Seaton, 'Teaching Law and Legal Practice in a Live Client Clinic' (2002) 51(6) *Newcastle Law Review* 51, 52. In the US, the term "CLE" refers to Continuing Legal Education and clinical education is referred to as "Clinics" or "clinical education." In this chapter we refer to CLE as Clinical Legal Education which is widely used in an Australian context.

[6]   David A. Kolb, *Experiential Learning: Experience as the Source of Learning and Development* (FT Press, 2nd ed, 2014) 18.

[7]   See the various models of CLE set out in Jeff Giddings, *Promoting Justice through Clinical Legal Education* (Justice Press, 2013).

[8]   Colin G. James, 'Lawyers' Wellbeing and Professional Legal Education' (2008) 42(1) *The Law Teacher: The International Journal of Legal Education* 85.

law does not operate in 'a vacuum', and that 'law on paper' is not always the same as 'law in practice'.

SPECIALIST LEGAL CLINICS

When the first legal clinics opened their doors in the US in the late nineteenth and early twentieth century, they were largely considered 'generalist' – focusing on serving individuals who could not afford an attorney.[9] Gradually, these models moved to become more specialised – a transition which mirrored the increasing specialisation of the profession in the US. In the 1950s, the US experienced a noticeable shift from the generalist 'country lawyer model' to more specialised legal practices. This was driven, at least in part, by a need for greater professionalism in the law, but was also due to an 'explosive growth in [the] complexity of law, particularly federal law'.[10]

Throughout the 1970s and 1980s, legal clinics in the US and elsewhere tended to focus on either criminal or civil law, with some clinics covering both.[11] Thereafter, a number of specialist clinics emerged, focusing on legal practice areas as diverse as immigration law, human rights, environmental law and family law. In recent times, the American Association of Law School's Clinical Conference has recognised at least 22 clinical specialty areas.[12]

One of the major benefits of specialist clinics is that they offer a focus on a discrete area of law that is increasingly 'in demand' from students, the profession and society. The nature of the clinic is likely to guide what values

---

[9]   The first American law schools to establish general legal aid programs include the University of Pennsylvania, University of Denver, Harvard and University of Minnesota. See J.P. Sandy Ogilvy, 'Celebrating Clepr's 40th Anniversary: The Early Development of Clinical Legal Education and Legal Ethics Instruction in U.S. Law Schools' (2009) 16 *Clinical Law Review* 1, 4. The University of Southern California established an experimental, six-week clinical program in 1928, followed by the first full-fledged in-house clinical program at Duke University. See John S. Bradway, 'The Beginning of the Legal Clinic of the University of Southern California' (1929) 2 *Southern California Law Review* 252. In 1947, the University of Tennessee created an on-going, in-house clinical program, which remains the longest continually established program in the US. See Ogilvy (this note) at 4.

[10]   Michael Ariens, 'Know the Law: A History of Legal Specialization' (1994) 45 *Southern California Law Review* 1003, 1009.

[11]   Antoinette Sedillo Lopez, 'Learning Through Service in a Clinical Setting: The Effect of Specialization on Social Justice and Skills Training' (2001) 7 *Clinical Law Reiew* 307, 308 (observing that when she began clinical teaching in 1986, 'clinicians seemed to teach in either civil or criminal settings, with a few brave souls doing both').

[12]   JoNel Newman, 'Re-Conceptualizing Poverty Law Clinical Curriculum and Legal Services Practice: The Need for Generalists' (2007) 34 *Fordham Urban Law Journal* 1303, 1309.

and skills it will need to teach.[13] For complex areas of law, like environmental law, attorneys may need to specialise in order to meet requirements of competency.[14] Specialist clinics therefore may reflect the reality of practice in complex legal areas. In a legal aid setting, specialisation may also permit 'the highly efficient delivery of discrete services to much larger numbers of clients than could reasonably be served by a general practice model'.[15] Similarly, specialisation enables law schools 'to offer better supervision, because they themselves don't have to spread their knowledge over several fields'.[16] As Schrag remarks, specialisation can promote: 'clinic cohesion and educational sharing by enabling students to comment with some degree of expertise on each other's cases, and by making each student's case work potentially useful to every other student'.[17]

Whilst it is true that some law students may prefer the variety of tasks afforded by a generalist clinical experience,[18] which aims to equip them with skills across a variety of subject areas,[19] other students may benefit from an intense focus on a particular subject area that may have already sparked their interest (human rights, environmental law, access to justice etc.). As Evans and Hyams point out: 'Specialisations [can] "speak" directly to the burgeoning particular interests of individual students and can generate an even greater degree of energy for the specialisation than they experienced in [a] general practice [model].'[20]

That said, students in specialist clinics may be limited by the types of lawyering experiences they are exposed to, and in the context of poverty law, for example, some have argued that specialisation may in fact end up disadvantaging clients.[21]

---

[13]   Paul D. Reingold, 'Why Hard Cases Make Good (Clinical) Law' (1996) 2 *Clinical Law Review* 545, 545–6.

[14]   Ariens (n 10) 1008–9.

[15]   Newman (n 12) 1309.

[16]   Philip G. Schrag, 'Constructing a Clinic' (1996) 3 *Clinical Law Review* 175, 191.

[17]   Ibid.

[18]   Reingold (n 13) 546.

[19]   Jackson Walkden-Brown and Lindsey Stevenson, 'Preparing for Practice: Clinical Legal Education Through the Lens of Legal Education Discourse' (2018) 3(1) *Australian Journal of Clinical Education* 1.

[20]   Adrian Evans and Ross Hyams, 'Specialist Legal Clinics: Their Pedagogy, Risks and Payoffs as Externships' (2015) 22 *International Law Journal of Clinical Legal Education* 1, 13.

[21]   Newman (n 12), 1305.

ENVIRONMENTAL LAW CLINICS (ELCS)

Given the practice and literature on CLE is increasingly dense,[22] it is perhaps surprising there has been little published information on what an ELC actually is. In this chapter, we have defined an ELC as follows: 'A type of specialist legal clinical model whereby law students, under supervision, engage with various aspects of the practice of environmental law in order to meet community needs as well as their own learning goals.'[23]

This definition encapsulates four key components: (1) a specialist model for experiential learning; (2) with academic supervision; (3) which meets defined pedagogical goals; and (4) which provides a service to the community. Such a definition seems consistent with the broader objectives of CLE, discussed above, which ultimately seeks to 'compel students, through a constant reality check, to integrate their learning of substantive law with the justice or otherwise of its practical operation'.[24]

Notwithstanding the lack of academic literature surrounding ELCs, there appear to be many functioning examples of ELC models across the world, including in the US and Australia (discussed below), as well as China,[25] Canada,[26] Puerto Rico,[27] Mexico[28] and Spain.[29] The next section of this chapter

---

[22] In an Australian context, see, e.g., Giddings (n 7); and also Walkden-Brown and Stevenson (n 19).

[23] This is largely the same definition adopted in Hamman (n 2).

[24] Evans and Hyams (n 20) 4.

[25] United Nations Environment Programme, 'First environmental law clinic opens in Wuhan University, China' (Web Page, 12 July 2018) https://www.unenvironment.org/news-and-stories/blogpost/first-environmental-law-clinic-opens-wuhan-university-china accessed 20 May 2020.

[26] Environmental Law Centre, University of Victoria, 'Clinic' (Web Page) http://www.elc.uvic.ca/programs/clinic/ accessed 20 May 2020.

[27] University of Puerto Rico, School of Law, 'Official Guide' (Web Page) https://officialguide.lsac.org/Release/SchoolsABAData/SchoolPage/SchoolPage.aspx?sid=120 accessed 20 May 2020; Vermont Law School, 'Protecting Puerto Rico's Rich Ecosystems from Proposed Via Verde Pipeline' (Web Page) https://www.vermontlaw.edu/academics/clinics-and-externships/ENRLC/cases/protecting-puerto-ricos-rich-biodiversity-from-proposed-via-verde-natural-gas-pipeline accessed 20 May 2020.

[28] Juan Antonio Herrera-Izaguirre, Fernando Hernández-Contreras, José Gerardo Rodríguez-Herrera and Roberto Hinojosa de León, 'Environmental Law Clinic: The FCA and CS Experience in Nuevo Laredo, Tamaulipas' (2010) 4(3) *Clinicas de deerecho Ambiental* 13 http://search.proquest.com/docview/2135187152/ accessed 20 May 2020.

[29] S Borràs et al., 'The Environmental Law Clinic: A New Experience in Legal Education in Spain' (Chapter 5) in Daniela Ikawa, Leah Wortham (eds), *The New Law School, Re-examining Goals, Organization and Methods for a changing world* (Public Interest Law Institute, 2010).

discusses some of these examples focusing on their reported modes of delivery (e.g., casework, advocacy, law reform, advice work, etc.) and perceived pedagogical benefits to students.

ELCS IN THE UNITED STATES

There has been a lively debate in the US about the place of clinical and experiential education alongside traditional lecture-based and doctrinal teaching.[30] The American Bar Association (ABA) requires law students to complete six credits of clinical or experiential classes prior to graduation.[31] Several influential reports analysing legal education, including the Carnegie Report,[32] have recommended that US law schools increase their focus on experiential learning to help law students be better prepared to practice law upon graduation. As a result, many US law schools have now added specialty clinics (like ELCs) to increase options for students to complete the experiential requirement and to better prepare them for practice.

The first wave of ELCs in the US began in the 1980s with clinics opening at the University of Denver, Pace Law School, Tulane Law School, Delaware Law School and the University of Maryland. Other law schools with a focus on environmental law, followed suit, with Lewis & Clark Law School establishing an ELC in 1996, Washington University in 2001 and Vermont Law School in 2003.[33] At the time of writing this chapter, it is believed that there are an estimated 62 ELCs operating throughout the US. Some are operated

---

[30]   Tamara Kuennen, 'Missing the Value of Clinical Education' (2015) 92 *Denver University Law Review* 189; Martin J. Katz, 'Understanding the Costs of Experiential Legal Education' (2014) 1 *Journal Experiential Learning* 28, 28; Robert Kuehn, 'Pricing Clinical Legal Education' (2014) 92 *Denver University Law Review* 1, 5.

[31]   American Bar Association (ABA) Standard 303(a)(3), 'A law school shall offer a curriculum that requires each student to satisfactorily complete at least the following… one or more experiential course(s) totaling at least six credit hours. An experiential course must be a simulation course, a law clinic, or a field placement.' ABA Standards and Rules of Procedure for Approval of Law Schools, 'Program of Legal Education (Chapter 3)' (Web Page) https://www.americanbar.org/content/dam/aba/administrative/legal_education_and_admissions_to_the_bar/standards/2019-2020/2019-2020-aba-standards-chapter3.pdf accessed 20 May 2020.

[32]   William M. Sullivan, Anne Colby, Judith Welch Wegner, Lloyd Bond, Lee S. Shulman, *Educating Lawyers: Preparation for the Profession of Law* (1st ed, Jossey-Bass, 2007) available at http://archive.carnegiefoundation.org/pdfs/elibrary/elibrary_pdf_632.pdf accessed 20 May 2020 (encouraging schools to make better use of second and third years of law school by providing students advanced clinical training).

[33]   Environmental law is considered a specialty subject in the US, with US News and World Report providing separate rankings for law school environmental programs

through a 'partnership model' with NGOs where the clinic director serves as both legal faculty and an attorney for an NGO.[34] In contrast, arrangements where students are supervised by NGO attorneys at the offices of the NGO and work exclusively for that NGO, are considered 'field placements', rather than clinical experiences.[35] Moreover, the ABA requires that all legal clinics be run by a law faculty, and include a classroom component.[36]

Because an undergraduate degree is required for admission to a Juris Doctor (JD) degree in the US, all US law students in ELCs are, in effect, pursuing post-secondary education. Some ELCs, like those at Washington University and Duke University, are interdisciplinary clinics that seek to partner law students with either masters or undergraduate students in fields like environmental science, engineering or public health. Others accept students who are already lawyers and are pursuing Masters of Law (LLM) degrees, while others still have 'LLM Fellows' whereby lawyers pursuing their advanced degree in environmental law also serve as part-time attorneys in the clinic.

Some US-based clinical models are one-semester clinics, while others allow a second semester, or require two semesters. Several ELCs are limited to third year students – in their final year of law school – whilst others accept second year law students. Limitations on when a student may participate in a clinic can be tied to a local 'student practice rule'. In contrast to Australia (see below), this rule allows US law students to appear as attorneys before the court practicing under their supervisor's legal license if they meet certain criteria, which may include successfully completing a certain number of semesters of law

---

and schools offering LLM degrees and Master's degrees in Environmental Law and Policy.

[34] For example, University of Michigan's Environmental Law and Sustainability Clinic directed by a clinical assistant professor who also serves as an attorney at National Wildlife Federation's Great Lakes Center. The Vermont Environmental Advocacy Clinic is similarly led by an attorney who serves as both an assistant professor and Legal Advocacy Director at National Widlife Federation. Students at New York University's environmental law clinic work under the supervision of professors who are also attorneys from the Natural Resources Defense Council.

[35] The ABA defines a 'field placement course' as a course that:

provides substantial lawyering experience that (1) is reasonably similar to the experience of a lawyer advising or representing a client or engaging in other lawyering tasks in a setting outside a law clinic under the supervision of a licensed attorney or an individual otherwise qualified to supervise and that is designed to ensure sufficient student training, feedback, and opportunities for self-evaluation.

See ABA Standard 304(d).

[36] See ABA Standards, Standard 304(b).

school; and taking classwork in specific subjects, such as legal professional responsibility.[37]

Finally, ELCs in the US vary rather significantly in the type of work they do. Some focus on implementing federal environmental law, as well as administrative laws and state-level environmental law. Others can directly represent clients in litigation and students can participate by way of the student practice rules explained above. Some clinics represent clients in administrative processes but do not litigate directly on their behalf. Other clinical models seem to engage at a policy level, for example, preparing advisory 'white papers' on environmental law issues or drafting bills or ordinances and helping clients have them enacted. Students in ELCs in the US are supervised on cases or projects by attorneys licensed to practice law. US ELCs are led by a 'director'; some ELCs may have one or more additional attorneys on staff. Some clinics may have non-lawyers, such as engineers or community outreach staff, others may have several attorneys at their disposal. Some clinics may have non-lawyers such as engineers, paralegals, legal secretaries, or community outreach staff to assist with research and administrative work. Others may have several attorneys at their disposal. Finally, some ELCs in the US may have the entire student cohort work on cases or projects as a team, while other models may split students up and have them work on cases individually.

ELCS IN AUSTRALIA

In recent years, Australia has seen a 'proliferation' in CLE opportunities in law schools.[38] Broadly speaking, CLE in Australia has mostly followed a generalist model, that is, 'where the client and caseload intake is limited primarily by the financial means of the clients rather than by the legal subject matter of their problems'.[39] Giddings confirms this, pointing out that the first generalist legal clinic in Australia was established at Monash in 1975.[40] It was not until the 1990s, however, that specialist clinics, including ELCs, began to emerge, with the first specialist models focusing on community development and social-justice.[41] On occasion, environmental law matters were pursued through a related specialist forum, such as the Victorian Civil and Administrative

---

[37]   Sara B. Lewis, 'Rite of Professional Passage: A Case for the Liberalization of Student Practice Rules' (1998) 82 *Marquette Law Review* 205, 207.

[38]   Walkden-Brown and Stevenson (n 19).

[39]   Susan Campbell and Alan Ray, 'Specialist Clinical Legal Education: An Australian Model' (2003) 3 *International Journal of Clinical Legal Education* 67, 67.

[40]   Jeff Giddings, 'Clinical Legal Education in Australia: A Historical Perspective' (2003) 3 *International Journal of Clinical Legal Education* 7, 11.

[41]   Ibid.

Tribunal (VCAT) clinic that has assisted clients to 'make or defend claims in diverse areas such as planning and environmental, tenancy, consumer, guardianship, mental health, equal opportunity and building and property law'.[42]

Unlike the US, the Australian law school landscape seems to have been limited by the amount of resources it has invested in CLE and experiential learning more generally. This has been an historical concern for law schools in Australia, with often only a handful of faculty staff and specialist 'clinicians' employed directly in experiential courses.[43] Nevertheless, today, most Australian law schools do operate some form of clinical education, commonly as an elective unit for penultimate or final year students.[44] Most of these experiences seem to be generalist in nature and only a handful seem to offer specialist educational experience in environmental law.[45] Unlike the US where many of the clinics seem to be hosted 'in house', Australian ELCs tend to follow an 'externship' or 'placement' model whereby students are hosted by an NGO, government institution or other related organisation under the supervision of legal practitioners. Examples of this kind of model have been reported at Macquarie Law School[46] and the Australian National University (ANU).[47]

Several Queensland-based universities also provide placements with NGOs, including the University of Queensland[48] and Queensland University of Technology (QUT), where students assist with supervised research projects, such as environmental law reform and community education.[49] At Newcastle Law School, students have reportedly been involved in interviewing clients, conducting research and preparing advice for environmental cases advocated through private law firms.[50] As Evans notes, this type of 'partnership model'

---

[42]   Evans and Hyams (n 20) 17.

[43]   For an early discussion, D.C Pearce, E. Campbell and D. Harding, Australian law schools: a discipline assessment for the Commonwealth Tertiary Education Commission. (Australian Government Publishing Service, Canberra, 1987).

[44]   Giddings (n 7).

[45]   Environmental law is considered an elective in Australia, it is increasingly popular with students and most universities seem to offer the course at least once a year.

[46]   Macquarie University, 'Environmental Law Policy Clinic – LAW879' (Web Page, 27 August 2018) http://handbook.mq.edu.au/2019/Units/PGUnit/LAW879 accessed 20 May 2020.

[47]   Australian National University, 'Environmental Law Clinic' (Web Page) https://programsandcourses.anu.edu.au/2019/course/LAWS4281 accessed 20 May 2020.

[48]   The University of Queensland, 'Clinical Legal Education' (Web Page, 29 December 2019) https://law.uq.edu.au/clinical-legal-education accessed 20 May 2020.

[49]   Evan Hamman, Rowena Maguire and Judith McNamara, 'Pro Bono Partnerships in Environmental Law: Enhancing Outcomes for Universities and CLCs' (2014) 39(2) *Alternative Law Journal* 115.

[50]   Michelle Lam, 'Law Students get Hands-on Experience in Public Interest Environment Law' (2011) 49(10) *Law Society Journal* 23.

(with private firms or barristers) can be advantageous in leveraging 'existing private lawyer goodwill and [at the same time], harness[ing] law school alumni beneficence'.[51]

Like the US, there have been examples of interdisciplinary ELCs in Australia, such as the 'sustainability business clinic' in Melbourne, which provided opportunities for students from different disciplines to work on common environmental concerns.[52] More recently, there have been examples of 'US-style' litigation clinics, for example, a climate justice clinic at Monash University.[53] That said, opportunities for Australian law students to directly advocate on a clients' behalf seem limited by the strict rules of practice in Australia surrounding court appearance and the fact that most public interest environmental litigation (PIEL) in Australia is initiated by community groups (Greenpeace, Australian Conservation Foundation, WWF-Australia, etc.), represented by expert lawyers working for specialist NGOs like the Australian Environmental Defenders Office (EDO) or Environmental Justice Australia (EJA).[54]

DISCUSSION

The above gives rise to several points of discussion about the differences between the US and Australian models and what might constitute a functioning and potentially successful ELC. First, at the core of all models of CLE, including specialist ELCs, are its students. Thought needs to be given to the students undertaking the clinical program, including: their needs and capabilities; their age and professional maturity; and their education level. As noted above, all US students are graduate (post-secondary) students having received an undergraduate degree before beginning their legal education. Moreover, a significant portion of law students in the US have had a full- or part-time job for at least a year prior to starting their legal education.

Law students in Australia, on the other hand, are still at the undergraduate level and many may not have encountered office work or practical legal experience prior to undertaking their clinical program. As Wei points out, 'legal

---

[51]   Evans (n 2) 9.

[52]   Brad Jessup and Claire Carroll, 'The Sustainability Business Clinic – Australia Clinical Legal Education for a "New Environmentalism" and New Environmental Law (2017) 34(6) *Environmental and Planning Law Journal* 542.

[53]   Evans (n 2).

[54]   Prior to 2019, EDO was comprised of several different organisations (EDOs) across each state and territory. They have now merged under one umbrella organisation. EJA is a separate organisation which was, until May 2014, known as EDO Victoria.

education is an "advanced" degree in the US',[55] and therefore US students are arguably more likely to have a higher degree of professional maturity and 'business acumen' when it comes to their involvement in ELCs. A complementary issue is the amount of time the students have allocated for clinical work. Students who can dedicate more time in their schedules are better situated to be able to handle time-sensitive issues, while students who can commit to the clinic for more than one semester can better handle longer-term or more complex cases.

A second point to note is that the university oversight of ELCs can vary significantly across and within law schools. For example, while some US law schools have appointed a 'Dean of Clinical Education' to bring consistency to clinical offerings, others let each clinic director develop and run the ELC according to their own preferences. In Australia, whilst many law schools have appointed a 'Dean of Teaching and Learning', it seems clear that CLE does not enjoy the same level of investment as it does in the US and there are few, if any, executive level positions established specifically for clinical programs in Australia.

Moreover, the 'classroom' component of ELCs varies from school to school in the US, but typically seems to involve a combination of lectures about key environmental law issues, as well as content relating to litigation practice, simulation of litigation skills (such as client interviewing, depositions, cross examination, oral argument and settlement discussions) and informal student discussion concerning cases (often referred to as 'case rounds'). In Australia, whilst most students may have been encouraged to study environmental law before undertaking a clinical experience, they may not receive any additional 'content' instruction related to environmental law during their time in the clinic. In short, the CLE experience may be separated from the traditional teaching of environmental law.

Third, and allied to the above point, is the need to closely consider assessment of students in the ELC. Assessment has long been a point of discussion in clinical experiences.[56] Ideally, ELCs, like any other experiential initiative, should involve a form of assessment that is rigorous, authentic and linked to the broader pedagogical and learning goals of the program. For example, if one of the goals of the ELC is that the students deeply understand substantive aspects of environmental law, then some type of substantive content in the assessment task may be appropriate. Alternatively, if the proposed outcomes are that the

---

[55]   Xu Wei, 'A Comparative Study of Environmental Law Clinics in the United States and China' (2010) 19 *Education Law Journal* 75.

[56]   James Carr, 'Grading Clinic Students' (1973) 26 *Journal of Legal Education* 223.

student understands the social context, politics and access to justice challenges surrounding environmental issues, then some form of critical review of their experience may be necessary (e.g., in the form of an essay, reflective account, class presentation, etc.).[57] In the US, allowing students an opportunity for self-evaluation has often become a critical component of assessment whilst in Australia, most CLE-related assessment has involved both practical (i.e., reflective) and academic (i.e. substantive) components.[58]

A fourth consideration for ELC design and operation is supervision – an aspect that is often overlooked.[59] Because US law students are typically older and more experienced than their Australian counterparts, they are likely to be better prepared to be successful in a model whereby students act as an attorney in a case, with licensed attorneys supervising and advising as the case progresses. Australian students, on the other hand, may feel more comfortable with an externship, placement or partnership model, which focuses on 'shadowing' or supporting a licensed attorney or completing discrete research tasks without any client-facing role.[60] Another important point of difference in this regard is that, in the US, there appears to be more opportunity for students to undertake work on 'written briefs' prior to and during a trial. Conversely, in Australia, emphasis in litigation is often placed on oral submissions before the Court (especially by barristers), thereby limiting the ability of law students to contribute directly in environmental cases.[61]

One final matter worth nothing is that ELCs, in whatever form they take, are increasingly likely to be subjected to political interference in their affairs. This

---

[57] In the US, ELCs frequently adopt the casework (i.e., litigation) model of representing clients, but this can make assessment challenging with each student working on a case or project with different skills needed (and therefore making comparison between students challenging). For this reason, many US ELCs conduct assessment based on student improvement or demonstration of competence in legal skills. At times, student self-evaluations are also utilised, as they are in Australian examples. Several US ELCs require students to prepare a portfolio at the end of the semester, showcasing the work they have achieved. This is similar to some Australian models, where students are asked to reflect on their experiences.

[58] Walkden-Brown and Stevenson (n 19).

[59] On supervision, see Jeff Giddings and Michael McNamara, 'Preparing Future Generations of Lawyers for Legal Practice: What's Supervision Got to Do With It?' (2014) 37(3) *University of New South Wales Law Journal* 1226.

[60] See for example the legal externships hosted by external organisations at Monash University, 'Types of Clinics' (Web Page) https://www.monash.edu/law/home/cle/types-of-clinics accessed 20 May 2020.

[61] There is no student practice rule in Australia. A law student would need to seek 'leave of the Court' in order to appear. For a basic overview of 'leave of the Court' for trainee solicitors, see: Rena Solomonidis, Jacqui Caust and Stephanie Rennie, 'Court Disaster and How to Avoid it' (2011) 47 *Young Lawyers Journal* 4.

has proven to be the case in the US in particular, but less so in Australia.[62] The US-based Tulane ELC, for example, faced government and industry backlash in 1999 from its work representing community members opposing a new industrial development.[63] Faced with a well-organised and well-represented community, the developer eventually withdrew a proposed polyvinyl chloride plant. Infuriated by the resulting loss of tax revenues, Louisiana's Governor and Secretary of the Louisiana Department of Economic Development engaged in a series of very public criticisms of Tulane's ELC. It was reported that the Secretary had intended 'to use every legitimate method at [his] command to defeat' the Tulane clinic, including accusing the clinic of merely 'indulging in an "amusing" academic exercise [to stifle economic progress]'.[64] The Louisiana legislature then attempted to destabilise the Tulane ELC by adopting a student practice rule restricting law students to only representing 'indigent clients'.[65]

In another US example, the ELC at the University of Maryland was subjected to threats from the Maryland legislature and Governor. These actions were in response to the ELC's actions in a lawsuit seeking to hold a company responsible for manure pollution from a chicken farm. After losing the case in the federal district court, the Maryland legislature voted to withhold funding for the state-funded law school if the clinic refused to reveal details about its

---

[62]   In Australia, the EDOs which take charge of most public interest environmental litigation have been subject to attack. See Jacqueline Peel, Hari M. Osofsky, *Climate Change Litigation: Regulatory Pathways to Cleaner Energy* (Cambridge University Press, 2015), 307.

[63]   Oliver Houck, 'Shintech: Environmental Justice at Ground Zero' (2019) 31 *Georgetown International Law Review* 455.

[64]   Submission of the Association of American Law Schools to the Supreme Court of the State of Louisiana Concerning the Review of the Supreme Court's Student Practice Rule, 4 *Clinical L. Rev.* 539, 540 (1998), citing Letter from Louisiana Assoc. of Business and Industry to Chief Justice Calogero (Sept. 9, 1997), at 1. The Secretary, Kevin P. Reilly, Jr., was quoted in Vicki Ferstel, Shintech's Opponents Tracked in *The Advocate Online*, at http://www.theadvocate.com/advocate/ 110597/news/1105shin. htm (published Nov. 5, 1997).

[65]   For a detailed summary of the case, the political ramifications and the change to Louisiana's student practice rule, see Robert Kuehn, 'Denying Access to Legal Representation: The Attack on the Tulane Environmental Law Clinic' (2000) 4 *Washington University Journal of Law & Policy* 33.

clients, cases and finances.[66] Clinical professors from across the US weighed in to support the ELC during the ordeal.[67]

Both of these instances reveal that ELCs are likely to be 'opposed not just by individual defendant corporations and various levels of government, but also by entrenched power groups within some industry sectors'.[68] Giddings agrees and notes that some of the most savage attacks on legal clinics have been reserved for ELCs.[69]

CONCLUSION

This chapter has examined the role of CLE in the teaching and practice of environmental law. CLE can have tremendous benefits for students, law schools and the community, and, increasingly, models of specialist ELCs have emerged throughout the world, including in the US and Australia. Whereas US models tend to be litigation-focused and hosted 'in house' under the supervision of licensed attorneys, law students in Australian ELCs tend to experience project-based, externship opportunities working on matters such as law reform, community outreach and the provision of advice. Unlike the US, there are no 'student practice rules' in Australia, and opportunities for law students to directly engage in courtrooms are limited. This chapter has discussed some of the basic differences between US and Australian ELC models. Further empirical research is now needed into the factors of design that are likely to lead to pedagogical and operational success.

---

[66]   The New York Times, 'School law clinics face a backlash' (Web Page, 3 April 2010) https://www.nytimes.com/2010/04/04/us/04lawschool.html accessed 20 May 2020.

[67]   In a third example, the ELC at Rutgers University in Trenton, New Jersey, came under attack when the clinic represented a community opposing a commercial development. The developer filed suit against the ELC under the open-records law seeking copies of internal documents, saying he planned to expose how the clinic used taxpayer money to discourage investment in the state. See ibid.

[68]   Evans (n 2) 21.

[69]   Giddings (n 7) 133. See also Kuehn (n 65).

PART III

The teaching of international environmental law

10. Game on! Game-based learning as an innovative tool for teaching international environmental law[1]

Alexandre Lillo and Thomas Burelli

INTRODUCTION

Advocating the use of games as a teaching method at the university level may seem paradoxical at first glance. Indeed, while games are often described as fun activities, university is usually associated with seriousness.

The use of games could appear even more controversial in the context of legal education where lectures largely remain the dominant teaching strategy. Yet, law schools do have occasional practical experiences through moot courts. Defined as simulations with no gaming aspect,[2] the objective of a moot court is to place the student in an authentic situation which mimics the realities of the courtroom. To reinforce experiential learning,[3] some universities, such as Harvard, have also developed problem-based teaching.[4]

---

[1]   We would like to thank David Macdonald from Teaching and Learning Support Service of the University of Ottawa for reviewing and commenting on this article (before – finally – investing in Zelda Breath of the Wild and consuming his valuable extra time in countless hours of prodigious gameplay). His inputs have greatly improved this contribution.
[2]   Jennifer L. Rosato, 'All I Ever Needed to Know About Teaching Law School I Learned Teaching Kindergarten: Introducing Gaming Techniques into the Law School Classroom' (1995) 45:4 *JLE* 568, 570 [Rosato].
[3]   Some experiential-learning approaches can be observed in the legal education literature, see for example: Justin R. Blount, 'An Experiential Contract Negotiation Exercise for Business Law Students' (2019) 36:1 *JLSE* 103 [Blount]; Timothy L. H. McCormack and Gerry J. Simpson, 'Simulating Multilateral Treaty Making in the Teaching of International Law' (1999) 10 *LER* 61 [McCormack and Simpson]; Rebecca Byrnes and Peter Lawrence, 'Bringing Diplomacy into the Classroom: Stimulating Student Engagement through a Simulated Treaty Negotiation' (2016) 26 *LER* 19 [Byrnes and Lawrence].
[4]   See online: https://casestudies.law.harvard.edu/ accessed 28 April 2021.

In the general context of universities, there is a recent movement in favour of active learning. More and more resources are devoted to such initiatives and incentives are provided to encourage these kinds of teaching methods. For instance, the University of Ottawa, Canada, opened a new building in 2018 focusing on active and experimental learning.[5]

As part of an international environmental law course, we created the Ottawa Conference on Climate Change: an activity where participants negotiate a fictitious treaty in the field of climate change.[6] As we experienced, the use of active learning approaches is not without obstacles. One of the core challenges relates to understanding what a 'game' or a 'simulation' is in the context of higher education and how definitions can affect contribution to the scholarship of teaching and learning. To that extent, defining its characteristics and attributes is a valuable exercise as it allows to demystify the concepts and to identify the role they can hold in the classroom. In particular, achieving this task will help one better define learning outcomes, pedagogical activities and evaluations associated with it.

This chapter intends to answer the following questions: (1) How can the various educational activities based on games be distinguished and what are their characterizing attributes? (2) What type of game-based activity can be created in the field of international environmental law? (3) How can game-based learning benefit the advancement of legal teaching and research?

To do so, this chapter first explores the diverse concepts associated with game-based learning. By confirming the coexistence of conflicting definitions, we will then suggest a set of characteristics for concepts such as games, simulations, gamification, simulation games and serious games. As a second step, we use some of the suggested criteria to illustrate and characterize the nature of the Ottawa Conference on Climate Change. Following this case study, we finally describe some of the key teaching and research benefits of such learning activities.

---

[5] University of Ottawa, 'Sneak peek at CRX, the new Learning Crossroads' online: https://www.uottawa.ca/gazette/en/news/sneak-peek-crx-new-learning-crossroads accessed 28 April 2021.

[6] For more details, visit our website: https://lip-aec.com/fr/ accessed 28 April 2021. We would like to thank The Law Foundation of Ontario for funding the creation of this website, as well as the University of Ottawa Teaching and Learning Support Service for assisting us throughout its development.

1.   EXPLORING MYSTERIOUS LANDS: DEFINING
        AND CHARACTERIZING GAME-BASED
        ACTIVITIES IN HIGHER EDUCATION

Game-based learning derives from both socio-constructivism and active learning theories. Socio-constructivism views learning as a knowledge construction process influenced by social[7] and cooperative[8] interactions as well as material environments.[9] As a teaching strategy, active learning is comprised of two elements. It first requires that students engage with the teaching material so they can be involved in their own learning process. Secondly, it suggests a meta-cognitive dimension by encouraging students to reflect about what they are actually doing within the classroom.[10] The combination of socio-constructivism and active learning can result in many different outcomes. Experiential learning[11] can be interpreted as one of them.[12]

Although game-based learning is gaining scholarly and practical interest as a teaching method, it remains unclear as a concept. Many terms with links to game-based learning are overlapping in the literature.[13] These include simulations, games, gamification, serious games and simulation games. Authors in this field do not always draw a distinction between these variations nor provide

---

[7]   Anastassis Kozanitis, 'Les principaux courants théoriques de l'enseignement et de l'apprentissage: un point de vue historique' (Bureau d'appui pédagogique, École Polytechnique Montréal 2005).

[8]   Erik De Corte, 'Historical Developments in the Understanding of Learning' in Hanna Dumont, David Istance and Francisco Benavides (eds), *The Nature of Learning Using – Research to Inspire Practice* (OCDE 2010), 35.

[9]   Paulo Freire, *Pedagogy of Freedom: Ethics, Democracy, and Civic Courage* (Rowman & Littlefield Publishers 2000) [Freire].

[10]   See Arthur W. Chickering and Zelda F. Gamson, 'Seven Principles for Good Practice in Undergraduate Education' (AAHE Bulletin, 1987) and Michael Prince, 'Does Active Learning Work? A Review of the Research' (2004) 93:3 *JEE* 223.

[11]   David A. Kolb, *Experiential Learning: Experience as the Source of Learning and Development* (Pearson Education Ltd, 2nd ed 2015).

[12]   Lewis H. Linda and Williams J. Carol, 'Experiential Learning: Past and Present' in Lewis Jackson and Rosemary S. Caffarella (eds), *Experiential Learning: A New Approach* (Jossey-Bass 1994), 5.

[13]   Louise Sauvé, Lise Renaud and David Kaufman, 'Les jeux, les simulations et les jeux de simulation pour l'apprentissage' in Louise Sauvé and David Kaufman (eds), *Jeux et simulations éducatifs – Études de cas et leçons apprises* (Presses de l'Université du Québec 2010), 13 [Sauvé, Renaud and Kaufman].

definitions.[14] Yet, it is crucial to delineate a clear and precise meaning as it has an impact on the objectives and design of an adapted activity.[15]

Producing widely accepted definitions is challenging. One alternative avenue, and early contribution to an eventual definition, is to set precise characteristics. Such tools can help scholars create a 'safe zone' within a semantic void. To explore the land of game-related concepts in higher education, we will review some of the proposed definitions and attempt to identify the criteria characterizing each of them.

Games

The notion of game might be the most widespread. It has many definitions within the specialized literature. Sauvé, Renaud and Kaufman provide a useful non-exhaustive review of the various definitions.[16] Based on their work, a game can be generally understood as a fabricated situation in which participants, seeking to achieve an objective or to reach a goal, are subject to rules that influence their actions.

Used in an educational context, 'the interactive, participatory and engaging features of games'[17] can help reinforce general, disciplinary or cognitive abilities[18] as well as preserving a motivational dimension beneficial to learning.[19] Moreover, games are learner-centred activities that foster participation and that can be suitable for most learning preferences. Therefore, games designed for higher education have the following characteristics:

- A fictitious scenario creating conflictive or cooperative interactions;
- At least one participant with specific objectives;
- A set of rules defining controlled environment and actions;
- A specific goal to achieve;

---

[14] Sauvé, Renaud and Kaufman, ibid., 15.

[15] For instance, Lameras et al. incorporated definitions as part of a coding scheme for a research on serious games. They did so stating that identifying the definitions used by one author in a study 'allowed preconceiving the plethora of different ways of usage identified in the literature and understanding disjunctions between espoused theories (ie, conceptions) and theories in use (actions)' (Lameras et al., 'Essential Features of Serious Games Design in Higher Education: Linking Learning Attributes to Game Mechanics' (2017) 48:4 *BJET* 972, 978 [Lameras]).

[16] Sauvé, Renaud and Kaufman, *supra* note 13, 15–21.

[17] Ángel del Blanco et al., 'A Framework for Simplifying Educator Tasks Related to the Integration of Games in the Learning Flow' (2012) 15:4 *ET&S* 305.

[18] Sauvé, Renaud and Kaufman, *supra* note 13, 339.

[19] Monique Boekaerts, 'The Crucial Role of Motivation and Emotion in Classroom Learning', in Hanna Dumont, David Istance and Francisco Benavides (eds), *The Nature of Learning Using – Research to Inspire Practice* (OCDE 2010), 91.

– A pedagogical purpose embodied in the use of educational theories, teaching and learning approaches, assessment and feedback.

These characteristics allow the distinction between games and the act of playing.[20] As has been written, '[w]hile games are usually played, play represents a different and broader category than game'.[21] In fact, Roger Caillois proposed, back in 1958,[22] to discern between paidia and ludus. 'Whereas paidia (or "playing") denotes a more free-form, expressive, improvisational, even "tumultuous" recombination of behaviors and meanings, ludus (or "gaming") captures playing structured by rules and competitive strife toward goals.'[23]

Simulations

If the concept of games is broad and open to interpretation, simulations define a more structured idea. Even if it lacks consistency within the specialized literature,[24] educational simulation, in the vast field of social sciences,[25] can be defined as '[p]edagogically mediated activities used to reflect the dynamism of real life events, processes, or phenomena, in which students participate as active agents whose actions are consequential to the outcome of the activity'.[26] They provide many benefits revolving around active experimentation, problem interpretation, abstraction or conceptualization and reflection.[27]

---

[20]   Some authors also refer to the distinction between gameful and playful. See: Jane McGonigal, 'We don't need no stinkin' badges: How to re-invent reality without gamification', Presentation at GDC 2011, online: https://www.gdcvault.com/play/1014576/We-Don-t-Need-No accessed 28 April 2021 [McGonigal].

[21]   Sebastian Detering et al., 'Gamification: Toward a Definition' (CHI, May 2011) [Detering, May 2011].

[22]   Roger Caillois, *Les jeux et les hommes* (Gallimard 1958).

[23]   Sebastian Detering et al., 'From Game Design Elements to Gamefulness: Defining Gamification' (MindTrek'11, September 2011) [Detering, September 2011].

[24]   See Cory Wright-Maley, 'Beyond the "Babel problem": Defining Simulations for the Social Studies' (2015) 39 *JSSR* 63 [Wright-Maley] and Sauvé, Renaud and Kaufman, *supra* note 13, 21.

[25]   Simulations in the field of social sciences can be quite different from the ones developed for natural (or hard) sciences. In the latter, simulations are usually used to replicate a complex or critical situation without real risks (e.g., surgery or flight simulators).

[26]   Wright-Maley, *supra* note 24, 70.

[27]   Marcelo Milrad, 'Using Construction Kits, Modeling Tools and System Dynamics Simulations to Support Collaborative Discovery Learning' (2002) 5:4 *JETS* 76, 80.

As such, simulations designed for higher education can be portrayed by the following attributes:[28]

- An accurate, simplified and structured representation of a real-life situation;
- A group of participants acting as agents having control over the scenario;
- A dynamic scenario creating multiple alternatives and unpredictable outcomes;
- A pedagogical purpose embodied in the use of educational theories, teaching and learning approaches, assessment and feedback.

Gamification

Gamification is a more recent concept. It started to be employed within the specialized literature as of 2010.[29] In addition to its educational and pedagogical relevance, it is also extensively used in many fields such as business or social networks.[30] Gamification can be defined as 'the use of game design elements in non-game contexts'.[31] Many experts agree that the process of gamifying is not a matter of simply using points, creating leaderboards or inserting badges and accomplishments.[32] In fact, gamification is about reproducing a gameful experience in a real-world situation with the purpose of creating a motivational response.[33] In the context of higher education, gamification is structured around five additional attributes:[34]

- Gamefulness;

---

[28] Wright-Maley, *supra* note 24, 67–70 and Sauvé, Renaud and Kaufman, *supra* note 13, 21–6.

[29] Detering, May 2011, *supra* note 21, 1.

[30] For series of great examples, see: https://yukaichou.com/gamification-examples accessed 28 April 2021.

[31] Detering, September 2011, *supra* note 23, 2.

[32] Although, we argue that some learning outcomes can justify the mere use of such game elements. Once again, the process of defining clear and precise educational objectives can lead, although it is unlikely, to basic gameful design (Rosato, *supra* note 2, 573).

[33] Many authors discuss this nuance. See: Detering, September 2011, *supra* note 23; McGonigal, *supra* note 20; Sebastian Detering, 'Pawned. Gamification and Its Discontents' (Presentation at Playful 2010), Yu-kai Chou, 'Gamification to improve our world' (TED Talk 2014).

[34] Detering, September 2011, *supra* note 23, 2–4. The four first attributes were proposed by Detering et al., to which we suggest adding a pedagogical purpose to fit the use of gamification in higher education. Also, it is an intentional choice not to dwell into the details of each component. Although the literature on this topic is flourishing, a technical and open discussion is still ongoing regarding those four elements.

- Game elements;
- Gameful design;
- Non-game context;
- A pedagogical purpose embodied in the use of educational theories, teaching and learning approaches, assessment and feedback.

Simulation Games

Simulation games are hybrids comprised of game mechanics in a simulated context.[35] They can be described as activities staging a simplified, accurate and dynamic real-life situation structured by components of games such as rules, competition, cooperation, etc.[36] Simulation games are thus built with both games and simulations attributes. In the context of higher education, they combine the following characteristics:

- Reproduce a realistic situation;
- Convene at least one participant;
- Integrate gameful design and interactions;
- A pedagogical purpose embodied in the use of educational theories, teaching and learning approaches, assessment and feedback.

Based on these characteristics, one could argue that simulation games are analogous to gamified simulations. In other words, we suggest that simulation games can be described as simulations that went through the process of gamification.

Serious Games

Similarly to the other variations of game-based learning strategies, serious games do not have a widely accepted definition.[37] The dominant conception presents serious games as a game with 'an explicit and carefully thought-out [...] purpose and [...] not intended to be played primarily for amusement. This does not mean that serious games are not, or should not be, entertaining'.[38]

---

[35]   Sauvé, Renaud and Kaufman, *supra* note 13, 27.

[36]   Simulation games can be a source of confusion as some authors support that they are equivalent to serious games (Sauvé, Renaud and Kaufman, ibid., 27–8).

[37]   See Lameras, *supra* note 15, Ralf Dörner et al., 'Introduction' in Ralf Dörner et al. (eds), *Serious Games* (Springer 2016), 1, 8 [Dörner] and Tim Marsh, 'Serious Games Continuum: Between Games for Purpose and Experiential Environments for Purpose' (2011) 2 *EC* 61 [Marsh].

[38]   Clark C. Abt, *Serious Games* (Viking Press 1970), 9 [Abt].

Other more recent definitions embrace this direction and present serious games as games that do 'not have entertainment, enjoyment, or fun as their primary purpose'.[39] Still, some authors follow a broader avenue by presenting serious games as a game 'created with the intention to entertain and to achieve at least one additional goal (e.g., learning or health) [which can be qualified as] characterizing goals'.[40] In the absence of a common understanding of what serious games are, there is an ongoing debate as per what key attributes define the scope of this concept. For instance, some authors support that *serious games* are digital, virtual or computer-based[41] whereas others do not provide details, therefore leaving the door open to various interpretations, including physical models and in-class activities.[42] If a consensus seems to exist regarding the fact that entertainment should not be the (sole) purpose of *serious games*, characterization of what should be their primary purpose varies largely. Some authors support that the meaning is implicitly designed by either the creators or the players,[43] while others argue that the dominant function is experiential[44] or educational.[45] Based on these observations, we argue that *serious games* designed for higher education can be illustrated by the following attributes:

- A gameful dimension;
- A primary purpose surpassing pure entertainment;
- At least one participant;
- A pedagogical purpose embodied in the use of educational theories, teaching and learning approaches, assessment and feedback.

This theoretical analysis comes to show that literature surrounding game-based learning is intertwined. Definitions overlap and characteristics are entangled, especially when it comes to the more specific (and recent) concepts such as simulation games, serious games and gamification. This precarious research environment creates an even more complex task for scholars. In fact, as we mentioned earlier in this chapter, the use of such disconnected definitions creates obstacles to the fulfilment of research needs in this field. If the object of the research is biased, producing relevant results and creating useful material becomes a wobbly target. The potential contributions to a growing discipline

---

[39] David Michael and Sande Chen, *Serious Games: Games That Educate, Train and Inform* (Thompson 2006), 21 [Michael and Chen].
[40] Dörner, *supra* note 37, 3.
[41] See Marsh, *supra* note 37, Dörner, *supra* note 37.
[42] See Lameras, *supra* note 15, Michael and Chen, *supra* note 39 and Abt, *supra* note 38.
[43] Dörner, *supra* note 37.
[44] Marsh, *supra* note 37.
[45] Lameras, *supra* note 15.

are therefore compromised as the building blocks do not properly fit together. In the absence of a strictly accepted definition for each concept, we suggest that creating a set of shared characteristics is a preliminary, and probably simpler way for researchers to move forward on a common basis. In fact, outlining specific attributes characterizing a concept seems equally beneficial to the advancement of research in this field.

Where does the Ottawa Conference on Climate Change stand on the spectrum of game-based learning? This activity we started developing back in 2017 is an appropriate case study to apply the previously set distinctions. In the following section, we will attempt to characterize this learning activity based on its constitutive attributes.

2.   PUTTING THE LOOT[46] TO USE: DESCRIBING AND CHARACTERIZING THE OTTAWA CONFERENCE ON CLIMATE CHANGE

Beyond our personal love for games, the decision to create and use a simulation to teach international law was based first and foremost on pedagogical considerations. Our goal was to create an activity that allows students to experience situations and aspects authentic to international environmental law. To do so, we choose to focus on one of the most practical dimensions of international law: the negotiation of treaties.

The Ottawa Conference on Climate Change is structured around four pillars: a realistic experience, a gameful design, a dynamic environment and a simplified representation. Each of these pillars can be described through a distinctive component of this activity.

The Creation of a Fake Treaty – Mirroring a Realistic Situation

The activity requires the negotiation of a fictive treaty on climate change[47]. The main focus during the creation of this treaty, as well as the material used for the activity, was to be as close to reality as possible.

---

[46]   In the video games universe, *loots* are any kind of rewards (items, virtual currency, experience, etc.) a player gains after completing a quest or defeating an enemy – such rewards are sometimes called 'drops'. For more information, see: Nathan Lawrence, 'The Science Behind Why We Love Loot' (2015) 68 *Game Informer*.

[47]   The topic of the treaty can be adapted. We have created other versions on biodiversity, water, and forests.

Figure 10.1   Logo created for the diplomatic conference on climate change

The draft treaty provided to the students is presented as a working document in which some articles are not opened to negotiation, while others, in brackets, can be negotiated.[48] Compared to the real negotiation process, the use of the brackets is simplified.[49] During negotiations, the provisions that participants must discuss are divided into several distinct options. They are usually not allowed to modify the suggested options and must agree to vote one of them.

> **BOX 10.1   EXAMPLE OF A PROVISION OPENED TO NEGOTIATION**
>
> This Convention aims to strengthen the global response to the threat of climate change, in the context of sustainable development and efforts to eradicate poverty, including by:
>
> **[Option 1]**
>
> • Holding the increase in the global average temperature to well below 2°C above pre-industrial levels and pursuing efforts to limit the tem-

---

[48]   To download the fictitious treaty: https://lip-aec.com/wp-content/uploads/2020/08/Projet-de-Convention-dOttawa-eng-Master-version.docx accessed 28 April 2021.

[49]   Here is a definition of the use of brackets in a draft document of the Paris Agreement: 'The brackets mean that the States participating to the negotiation do not agree on these elements in brackets.' See online: http://unfccc.int/resource/docs/2015/adp2/eng/11infnot.pdf accessed 28 April 2021.

perature increase to 1.5°C above pre-industrial levels, recognizing that this would significantly reduce the risks and impacts of climate change.

[Option 2]

- Holding the increase in the global average temperature below 2°C above pre-industrial levels.

[Option 3]

- Holding the increase in the global average temperature below 1.5°C above pre-industrial levels.

[Option 4]

- Systematically adopting the recommendations published by the Intergovernmental Panel on Climate Change (IPCC).

[Option 5]

- Undertaking to limit as much as possible, and to the best of their ability, the rise in the average temperature of the planet.

The treaty is composed of 19 articles among which 13 articles are opened to negotiation. Eight articles are specific to the topic of climate change and five are classic provisions of public international law.

BOX 10.2   LIST OF THE TOPICS OPENED TO NEGOTIATION

- Temperature rise objective
- Greenhouse gas emissions target
- Calculation of GHG emissions
- Emission peak target
- Differentiated obligations
- Principle of non-regression
- Funding measures
- Market-based tools
- Reservations

- Compliance
- Right to vote
- Withdrawal from the treaty
- Entry into force

Initially, the options were solely based on existing provisions of international law, including past provisions (such as the Kyoto Protocol), current provisions (such as in the Paris Agreement) or provisions discussed during past negotiations (such as during the COP 21 in Paris). In some cases, these provisions allowed us to offer a variety of options to students. However, the reality of international negotiation did not allow us to highlight some important topics or ideas that we wanted the students to explore. This is why we decided to create certain articles from scratch. These provisions are nevertheless relevant in the broad field of international environmental law, which can be elements that are discussed by the civil society, provisions only adopted at a national level or suggestions arising from the literature.

The choice and number of the topics opened to negotiation rest on the organizer. It can be adapted according to the learning outcomes of the activity. Our experience shows that twelve articles are enough to conduct an activity during approximately two hours. The duration does not include the debriefing which can be organized right after the activity or at the beginning of another class/meeting.

The Role-playing Component – A Gameful Design Allowing for Competition and/or Cooperation

Participants are divided into six teams and are asked to play a specific role during the negotiation.[50] Each team represents a specific geographical region based on the information provided by the United Nations Program for the Environment (UNEP).[51] The UNEP periodically publishes regional reports on the state of the environment. Regional summaries are given to participants.

---

[50] For more details, visit our website: https://lip-aec.com/fr/changements -climatiques/#tab8 accessed 28 April 2021.

[51] The regional reports published by the UNEP are available online : https://www .unenvironment.org/global-environment-outlook/why-global-environment-outlook -matters/regional accessed 28 April 2021.

Figure 10.2   The accreditation used to identify the delegations

The objective is to provide participants with real and up-to-date data that they have to read, to understand and to work with. The participants can also look for more specific information. The reason why specific roles and profiles are assigned is to create a diversity of perspectives which lead to fruitful debates and confront students to various arguments.

The roles given to the participants are important to relate to real data and issues but also to increase their engagement during the simulation. The fictive treaty and the roles assigned to the students are part of the narrative;[52] they contribute to create a realistic learning experience structured around the gameful mechanic of role-playing.

Phases and Rules – Creating a Dynamic and Controlled Environment

The course of the activity is composed of several phases:[53] the preparation before negotiation (1); the actual negotiation in class (2); and the debriefing taking place after the activity (3).

During the first phase, each delegation is asked to prepare a document in which they need to select and prioritize the options for each provision opened for negotiation. The delegations only have to justify their top choice. This phase is crucial to ensure that the participants read the documents provided and that they think of a negotiation strategy. This step also allows the organizer to

---

[52]   Michael Sailer, Jan Ulrich Hense, Sarah Katharina Mayr, Heinz Mandl, 'How Gamification Motivates: An Experimental Study of the Effects of Specific Game Design Elements on Psychological Need Satisfaction' (2017) 69 *Computers in Human Behavior* 371, 373.

[53]   For more details, visit: https://lip-aec.com/climate-change/#tab4 accessed 28 April 2021.

control the diversity of pre-negotiation positions and, if necessary, to rebalance them.[54]

The simulation in class is the second phase of the activity. After getting ready with their respective delegations, the participants are gathered in a physical environment with the only objective to reach a common agreement. Three principles guide this second phase: the simplicity of the rules, a great deal of freedom for participants and the playful aspect of the activity.

Rules are deliberately simple and minimal to allow participants to understand quickly how the activity works. They are given the following rules:[55]

– The final adoption of a treaty requires each delegation to agree on one option for each provision open to negotiation;
– At any moment all delegations can close the negotiation of a provision by agreeing on a specific option;
– If all the delegations express their agreement by signing the form,[56] the article is adopted;
– A signed provision cannot be negotiated again during the activity.

Complete freedom is granted to the participants for the organization of space and debates during the simulation. They can decide, for instance, to create sub-groups to discuss specific provisions. This autonomy can be a little confusing for some participants. However, they generally adapt quickly.

Figure 10.3   The powers that can be used by the participants

---

[54]   It is to be noted that after running the simulation more than ten times times, we never had to rebalance the positions 28 April 2021.
[55]   For more details, visit: https://lip-aec.com/climate-change/#tab5.
[56]   The form can be downloaded here: https://lip-aec.com/wp-content/uploads/2020/11/Choices_DelegationsENG.xlsx.

In order to make the activity more dynamic, to make sure that each delegation remains on guard, but also to mimic some aspects of international negotiation, we have introduced two additional elements. The first element is the existence of special powers held by each delegation. These powers make it possible to influence the voting rules or the negotiation process.[57] We have also planned special events during the simulation to introduce specific aspects of international negotiation such as the lack of time or the disruption of the debates for unforeseen reasons.[58]

The debriefing is the last phase of the activity. The result of the negotiations and, in particular, the treaty adopted by the participants, are discussed in the light of international law. At this point, the students are also asked to discuss how they experienced the simulation. Both this cognitive and meta-cognitive dimension appeared essential to meet the pedagogical objectives of the activity.

An Immersive Context – Designing an Accurate yet Simplified Scenario

In order to make the activity more immersive for the participants and to stimulate their engagement, we created a set of elements to stage a formal environment: a logo defining a visual identity, banners displayed in the room, badges to identify each delegation, but also roles played by the organizers (for instance, one of the organizers acts as the president of the negotiations[59]). These elements seem to help participants taking the activity (more) seriously and to respect the limits and orientations related to their roles.

A fake Twitter feed was also created to share some important data and facts with the participants during the activity. This visual tool is also used to trigger special events that disturb the negotiations and introduce uncertainty.[60]

Based on these four pillars, the Ottawa Conference on Climate Change can be characterized as a model of simulation game (or a gamified simulation) for higher education. It intends to recreate a realistic situation so participants can engage in a real-life experience. Yet, it is also concerned with being a simplified application; for instance, it excludes most of the formal procedures that law usually requires. The in-class activity is also structured around rules and gameful design allowing for a dynamic, engaging and uncertain environment.

---

[57]   For a detailed description of the powers included in the activity, visit: https://lip-aec.com/climate-change/#tab9 accessed 28 April 2021.

[58]   For a detailed description of the events, visit: https://lip-aec.com/climate-change/#tab10 accessed 28 April 2021.

[59]   For more information, visit: https://lip-aec.com/climate-change/#tab6 accessed 28 April 2021.

[60]   https://lip-aec.com/wp-content/uploads/2020/11/Twitter-Feed_2020-ENG.pptx accessed 28 April 2021.

In the following section, we will see that this process of characterization allows us to 'unlock' the full potential of game-based learning strategies.

#BreakingNews NGOs have entered by force to make their voices heard! The session has been interrupted for 5 minutes. #OCC2020 Precious time is lost #NotHappy

Figure 10.4   Example of a fake tweet used during the simulation

3.   WHY TO JOIN THE CAMPAIGN? THE HIDDEN TREASURES OF GAME-BASED LEARNING IN HIGHER EDUCATION

When this activity was first implemented, learning outcomes were essentially focusing on creating a different learning environment and familiarizing students to the work of international negotiators. As organizers, we did not anticipate the extended potential and effects of this teaching strategy from an educational and a research point of view. To this day, we are still discovering and exploring new perspectives. Here are a few of our key learnings.

Game-based Learning is an Approach that Enriches in-Class Teaching

The Ottawa Conference on Climate Change generates a sandbox in which participants are free to evolve and create. There is no certainty with respect to the final result and how participants will get there. The negotiations could be a success or a failure.[61] Yet, this is its intrinsic value. Such an activity offers the opportunity to observe how participants tackle legal problems and the dynamics they spontaneously develop to resolve them.

Several elements can be observed. First, the strategies used by delegations to reach an agreement can be examined. In some cases, participants gather in smaller groups to negotiate specific provisions. In other cases, participants decide to discuss all together. Some groups of participants validate the provisions one by one, while others wait for the final moments to vote the whole text. These strategies are very interesting to record because they can be associated with real negotiation processes during the debriefing.[62] Secondly, arguments used by the participants to support their standpoint can be observed. They also provide great pedagogical material to support the feedback phase. Thirdly, understanding and interpretation of the various options within the treaty can be monitored. They create examples to be discussed in class. Every time this activity was held,[63] a vast diversity of strategies and arguments were observed. Virtually each of them can become a topic of discussion with students and lead to learning in the field of international environmental law.

Following the activity, additional material can be discussed in class. It is possible to analyse how close each delegation was from the priorities established prior to the negotiations and to review what compromises were made. Beyond what can be called a 'delegation score', it is also useful to examine the final agreement and to evaluate its actual capacity to protect the environment. It allows students to question and discuss the tensions between the respective objectives of each delegation and the global issues that they are collectively trying to deal with.[64]

The data collected during the simulation and the results of the negotiations are used to design the next few classes. By then, students have knowledge

---

[61]   For instance, participants could fail to adopt a treaty at the end of the activity. Although it is presented as one of their objectives within the rules, it would be a limited failure because delegations would have negotiated and discussed the treaty and would have created a common understanding. In a way, at the end of the simulation, there is always an outcome which is likely to be another version of the treaty than the initial draft. Such a scenario, as we will discuss, still creates a 'pedagogical win'.

[62]   During the Conference of the Parties to the Convention on Biological Diversity the plenary session was extended until 2:59 am on Saturday, 30 October 2010 to secure the adoption of the Nagoya Protocol. See online the report of the session established in the Earth Negotiations Bulletin: https://enb.iisd.org/download/pdf/enb09544e.pdf.

[63]   The simulation has been organized more than ten times in different contexts. It was held at the University of Ottawa and at the University of French Polynesia.

[64]   For details about the delegation score and environmental protection score, visit: https://lip-aec.com/climate-change/#tab11 accessed 28 April 2021.

about the discussed topic and the legal tools that go along with it. It creates links between the student experience and the material used in class. Because students participated to the production of knowledge and are connected to the elements discussed in class, the following lectures appear to be more relevant and engaging for them.

Game-based Learning Leads to Significant Research Opportunities

At first, we did not expect that the organization of a simulation in class would have research potential. Our desire to create a simulation has brought us to delve into the scholarship of teaching and learning. To this date, we mainly explored two elements:

– Theories and tools relating to the creation and implementation of game-based learning strategies in class; and

– Research carried out on the evaluation of such activities, especially with respect to measuring the impact on student learning.

While we can find a lot of examples of very specific activities created for different purposes, there are not many sources about the methodology to create such activities,[65] particularly in the field of legal education.[66] We believe it would be possible to create models of activities involving specific learning skills that could be shared and adapted to several disciplines.[67] Various attempts to build such taxonomies have been made and reported in the literature.[68] However, the

---

[65]   Some researchers observed that one of the main barriers to the use of games and simulations in higher education was actually the limited access to tools and methodology strategies. See: Jonathan Lean et al., 'Simulations and Games – Use and Barriers in Higher Education' (2006) 7:3 *Active Learning in Higher Education* 227 [Lean et al.].

[66]   See, e.g.: Blount, *supra* note 3; McCormack and Simpson, *supra* note 3; Byrnes and Lawrence, *supra* note 3.

[67]   Some efforts have been made to link types of games or game mechanisms to learning outcomes. See for instance: Barbi Honeycutt, 'Applying Bloom's Taxonomy to Game Design', online: https://people.ok.ubc.ca/bowenhui/game/readings/BloomsIdeas .pdf; L. Buchanan, F. Wolanczyk and F. Zinghini, 'Blending Bloom's Taxonomy and Serious Game Design', online: http://citeseerx.ist.psu.edu/viewdoc/download?doi= 10.1.1.218.376&rep=rep1&type=pdf accessed 28 April 2021; Thomas C. Carton, 'Applying Bloom's Revised Taxonomy In Business Games' (2008) 35 *Developments in Business Simulation and Experiential Learning* 265.

[68]   David Robinson and Victoria Bellotti, 'A preliminary taxonomy of gamification elements for varying anticipated commitment' (IACM CHI 2013), online: http://gamification-research.org/wp-content/uploads/2013/03/Robinson_Bellotti.pdf accessed 28 April 2021; Robin Hunicke et al., 'A formal approach to game design and

classification offered is still contested[69] and, in many cases, the relationship with learning outcomes is not discussed.[70]

Beside the systematization of tools to create activities, one other significant research need relates to measuring the impact of such teaching methods on student learning. While there is an existing debate with regard to the actual learning outcomes that can be met using game-based learning,[71] several authors point out a need for further research on assessing the impact on student learning.[72] Whether it concerns learning outcomes, learning preferences or skill acquisition, there is a 'lack of empirical evidence in support of [game-based teaching] efficacy'.[73]

CONCLUSION

Game-based learning offers new perspectives in the context of higher education. This teaching strategy provides interesting avenues for the development of positive, immersive and interactive environments. As well, there is ample opportunity to develop more tools and resources to support such initiatives. However, as an emerging scholarly field, game-based learning suffers from a severe lack of research. There is an increasing need for:

– Common definitions and shared criteria so researchers can build on the same basis;
– The creation of 'ready to go' tools to facilitate construction and reproduction of such activities;

---

game research' (AAAI Workshop 2004); Detering, September 2011, *supra* note 23; Rita Orji et al., 'Modeling the Efficacy of Persuasive Strategies for Different Gamer Types in Serious Games for Health' (2014) 24:5 *User Modeling and User-Adapted Interaction* 453; Wendy L. Bedwell et al., 'Toward a Taxonomy Linking Game Attributes to Learning: An Empirical Study' (2012) 43:6 *Simulation & Gaming* 729 [Bedwell et al.]; Manuel Schmidt-Kraepelin et al., 'What's in the Game? Developing a Taxonomy of Gamification Concepts for Health Apps' (51st Hawaii International Conference on System Sciences 2018). Online: https://pdfs.semanticscholar.org/79ae/4cf99f5c51d1eaafbb0fb9b52f1e10fa7aa4.pdf accessed 28 April 2021.

[69] Sofia Schöbel and Andreas Janson, 'Is it all about having fun? Developing a taxonomy to gamify information systems' (ECIS 2018).

[70] Alessandra Antonaci et al., 'A Gamified Collaborative Course in Entrepreneurship: Focus on Objectives and Tools' (2015) 51 *Computers in Human Behavior* 1276; Bedwell et al., *supra* note 67.

[71] Lean et al., *supra* note 64.

[72] See Chad Raymond and Simon Usherwood, 'Assessment in Simulations' (2013) 9:2 *JPSE* 157 and Sylvester Arnad et al., 'Mapping Learning and Game Mechanics for Serious Games Analysis' (2015) 46:2 *BJRET* 391.

[73] Lameras, *supra* note 15.

- Interdisciplinary collaboration to better use modern campus' resources;
- The development of strategies and tools to measure what learning outcomes are actually met using game-based teaching as well as the impact on student learning.

However, additional research is not an end point per se. We strongly believe that newly created results and material should be openly shared within academic, public and private communities. If a snowball effect is to be created in the field of game-based learning, there is a greater need for shared and open-access resources.

Although gaps exist within research, game-based learning creates endless possibilities. Activities such as the Ottawa Conference on Climate Change are created to offer students a chance to learn international environmental law differently. Built as a simulation game and adaptable to many topics, this teaching strategy offers a transformative learning and teaching experience for those involved. Moreover, the use of game mechanics to teach law is an attempt to create a disruptive learning environment.

Student feedback is widely positive, universities are beginning to support such initiatives and research funding is becoming more available. All lights are green, it is time to move forward and use games within the university context. Additionally, game-based learning is to be perceived as a transformative strategy for learning (i.e., one that gives students agency in their learning) rather than a tool used to frame students toward a specific result.[74] We strongly believe that it is a great opportunity to help tomorrow's citizen gain the necessary skills to tackle the fundamentally important socio-environmental challenges they will face, rather than to train them to fit a scheme that desperately needs to evolve.

---

[74] This teaching strategy contributes to what Paulo Freire called, two decades ago, a need to move from an educational system for training to an educational environment for formation. See: Freire, *supra* note 9.

11. Teaching international environmental law as a story

Chris McGrath[1]

INTRODUCTION

Teaching environmental law cries out like a wolf on a winter night for stories, especially when illustrated with colourful maps and pictures to bring the stories to life. Many teachers do just this throughout their lessons and writing seeking to inform, inspire and transform. For instance, Peter Christoff provided a masterclass in storytelling to bring international environmental law to life in a critique of the Paris Agreement. He drew readers into his analysis by setting the scene and introducing the characters with a sense of foreboding and tension painted with beautiful word pictures and metaphors as follows:[2]

> The 2015 UN climate talks (COP 21) were held in the sprawling aerospace complex at Le Bourget, a northern suburb of Paris.... Two shadows hung over the negotiations. France was in a state of emergency following the terrorist attacks in Paris a fortnight earlier. ... The other shadow was that of the 2009 Copenhagen COP. Negotiators recognised that a repetition of that experience would fatally undermine the legitimacy of the United Nations Framework Convention on Climate Change (UNFCCC). The lessons of Copenhagen would discipline diplomatic behaviour before and during the Paris talks. COP 21 was carefully and sometimes theatrically managed – down to COP President Laurent Fabius' diminutive green gavel, the shape and colour of the Paris COP's leaf-like logo – to lower expectations but maximise the chances of success.
>
> At its conclusion, COP 21 was more rock concert than international negotiation. When Fabius gavelled through the Paris Agreement, the thousands of delegates crammed into two vast plenary rooms cheered, applauded and took photos and selfies. On stage, a phalanx of dignitaries – Fabius, Hollande, Tubiana, Figueras, and Ban Ki-Moon – raised their joined hands in triumph. The party-like atmosphere reflected relief that the deal had been sealed. ...

---

[1] Thanks to Declan Norrie for valuable research assistance.
[2] Peter Christoff, 'The Promissory Note: COP 21 and the Paris Climate Agreement' (2016) 25 (5) *Environmental Politics* 765–6.

Even if they do not have Christoff's mastery of storytelling, good teachers use stories throughout their teaching, both consciously and unconsciously.

This chapter begins by diving into the ocean of literature viewing storytelling as a foundational and valuable pedagogical tool in education. Based on the wider literature and reflective learning from teaching using storytelling as a pedagogical tool,[3] this chapter then describes two ways of structuring the teaching of international environmental law to align with storytelling naturally.

First, this chapter describes a simple structure for explaining international treaties as a natural story built on – and embedded in – the normal process for creating and administering international treaties. We can call it a 'coat hanger' structure on which to hang lectures explaining any treaty. A major advantage of using this approach is that it embeds the normal process for creating and administering international treaties into any lesson, thereby reinforcing this fundamentally important process for students.

Second, this chapter describes how a course on international environmental law can be structured in a story set in the historical and political context of the development of the major international environmental treaties since 1945. This moves beyond simply explaining the history and political context of an individual treaty in the basic storytelling structure – the 'coat hanger' structure – for any individual treaty. Embedding a whole course covering multiple treaties within this frame of reference provides a meta-narrative linking the course and a framework to analyse critically the many realpolitik factors that affect treaty creation and implementation. This can also be woven into a wider discussion of contemporary analytical paradigms such as the Anthropocene.[4] This is valuable for helping both teachers and students to engage with each other and create a more profound and lasting understanding of the complex reality of international environmental law, its implementation by nations around the world in their legal systems and contemporary analytical paradigms. This reflects the general benefits of using storytelling as a pedagogy (a teaching strategy).[5]

---

[3]   I taught a course on international environmental law and policy at the University of Queensland (UQ), Australia, from 2010–19 to (cumulatively) around 1000 undergraduate and postgraduate tertiary students using the approaches to storytelling described here. A website describing the course and providing links to lectures and student feedback on it is available at Environmental Law Australia, 'International Regulatory Frameworks for Climate Change and Environmental Management (ENVM3104 & ENVM7124)' http://envlaw.com.au/envm7124/ accessed 25 May 2019.

[4]   See, e.g., Jeremy Baskin, 'Paradigm Dressed as Epoch: The Ideology of the Anthropocene' (2015) 24 *Environmental Values* 9–29.

[5]   See, especially, Craig Abrahamson, 'Storytelling as a Pedagogical Tool in Higher Education' (1998) 118 (3) *Education* 440; Jennifer Moon, *Using Story in Higher Education and Professional Development* (Routledge 2010); and Kieran Egan

STORYTELLING PEDAGOGY

The ocean of literature on storytelling pedagogy is wide and deep.

Even so, the idea of storytelling as a pedagogy can 'meet a solid block of prejudice' with derisive comments that it is 'only a story' or 'mere entertainment'.[6] We should set those prejudices aside as mistaken. Storytelling is not merely for children or entertainment; it can and should be central to pedagogy even in higher education and adult learning.[7]

In Kieran Egan's influential work on imaginative education, storytelling is a core cognitive tool used for successful education and learning from young children to adults.[8] He writes with colleague Gillian Judson that stories:

> ... are forms of language that tell us how to *feel* about their content. What stories do for us—and, indeed, how they can powerfully contribute to learning—is that they engage human minds by tying up our emotions and imaginations with their content.

Storytelling is a universal teaching technique used to engage students and link information in memorable ways.[9] Egan and Judson point out:[10]

> The story form is a cultural universal – everyone, everywhere has told and used stories. ... Given [its] importance as is evident in cultures around the world and throughout history, we would surely be remiss to ignore a story's possibilities in education.

Stories are integral to how we remember and understand complex information about the world around us.[11] Storytelling is a foundational pedagogy in virtually all teaching, whether it is recognised or not.

Stories take many forms and have many purposes.[12] They may be based on reality, fiction or a mixture of both. The words: 'story' and 'narrative' are often used interchangeably and have various meanings;[13] but, as a simple rule of thumb, whenever we link information with scenes, characters and a sequence of events (a plot), we are storytelling.

---

and Gillian Judson, *Imagination and the Engaged Learner: Cognitive Tools for the Classroom* (Teachers College Press 2016).
  [6]   Moon n 5, at 3.
  [7]   Abrahamson n 5; Moon n 5.
  [8]   See Egan and Judson n 5, ch 3.
  [9]   See, Abrahamson n 5; Moon n 5; Egan and Judson n 5, 13.
  [10]   Egan and Judson n 5, 13.
  [11]   Abrahamson n 5; Moon n 5.
  [12]   See the discussion in Moon n 5, chs 2, 5 and 6.
  [13]   Ibid.

Storytelling as a pedagogy includes incidental use of anecdotes and other short stories to supplement and enrich other teaching strategies in an infinite variety of ways.[14] For instance, case study material and scenarios used in teaching that may be constructed from someone's real experience or fiction are often stories.[15] Storytelling as a pedagogy may also be much more than incidental. In narrative inquiry, storytelling is *the* method for education and research.[16]

What makes a *good* story depends on the purpose and context of telling it. A common storytelling method is to set the scene, introduce the main character or characters and explain how events unfolded.[17] For instance, in a lesson on the World Heritage Convention (Box 11.1 below) (the Convention) the international cooperation to relocate the Abu Simbel temples in Egypt makes a good story. A story about it might begin like this:

> The Abu Simbel temples were a treasure of ancient Egyptian civilization. They were to be flooded by the construction of the Aswan High Dam on the Nile River by the Egyptian Government in the 1950s. The international cooperation to save them was one of the catalysts for the *World Heritage Convention. ...*

Telling a story in a lesson on the Convention about saving the Abu Simbel temples fulfils multiple purposes at once. A good story like this – told in vivid detail with maps and pictures – captures students' interest but it does much, much more. It can inspire them as a success story and help them understand the value of the Convention, thereby engaging their emotions and imaginations. It also helps them remember and gain critical insight into why the Convention was created, including the national and international tensions that both drove it and limit it. This leads naturally into an examination of the framework of the Convention and its operation along a path that is concrete and real rather than abstract. In this way, a good story is multidimensional and serves multiple purposes. It not only captures students' interest and helps them remember information; it can also lay the foundation for critical thinking.

---

[14]   See ibid., ch 2.

[15]   Ibid., 13.

[16]   Janice Huber, Vera Caine, Marilyn Huber and Pam Steeves, 'Narrative Inquiry as Pedagogy in Education: The Extraordinary Potential of Living, Telling, Retelling, and Reliving Stories of Experience' (2013) 37 *Review of Research in Education* 212, 226–7.

[17]   Moon n 5 gives both a solid theoretical framework for storytelling in higher education and practical guidance, for instance, on the deployment of meaning and framing in story (ch 4). Her work is multi-layered and thought-provoking for both new and experienced storytellers.

Storytelling, then, can play many roles in education and learning, including for international environmental law. In this context, we can turn to exploring two ways of structuring the teaching of international environmental law to naturally align with storytelling.

A BASIC STORYTELLING STRUCTURE FOR ANY TREATY

The normal process for creating and administering international law provides an excellent structure for teaching lessons on any international environmental treaty. It allows lessons to naturally adopt a narrative, storytelling style. Figure 11.1 below provides a simple flowchart of this process.[18] It can be used as a handout in an early lesson in any course or individual lesson on international environmental law to help students grasp this fundamentally important process and key terms such as 'ratification', 'entry into force' and 'conference of the parties' (COP).

Using this structure, a lesson can begin by setting the scene through discussing the international problem that generated the need for the treaty (this is helpfully summarised in the preamble to each treaty), then when it was negotiated and agreed. The characters are naturally introduced by discussing the number of parties that have signed and ratified it (including notable exceptions such as the failure of the United States of America (USA) to ratify the United Nations Convention on the Law of the Sea 1982 or the Kyoto Protocol), and when it entered into force. The major obligations and mechanisms created by the treaty can be explained, then its implementation over time through COPs, or other meeting of the parties, becomes the plot. If desired, the lesson can progress naturally to critical analysis, for example, by discussing how well or how poorly the treaty is being implemented.

---

[18] For more detail, see the United Nations, *Treaty Handbook* (Revised edn, UN 2012).

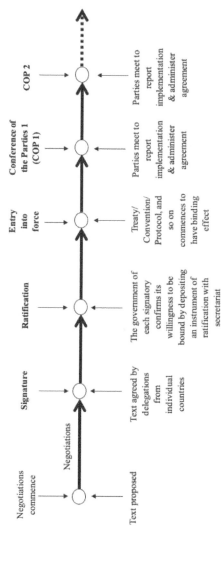

Note: This is a typical process only. Not all treaties/conventions/agreements follow this process or use these terms.

Figure 11.1   Typical process of international agreements being created and administered

Box 11.1 provides a case study of the possible structure and content for a lesson on the World Heritage Convention 1972.

BOX 11.1: CASE STUDY OF A STORYTELLING LESSON ON THE WORLD HERITAGE CONVENTION 1972[a]

- A lesson using storytelling on the World Heritage Convention might begin with a brief introductory overview to set the scene for this famous and widely adopted treaty, explaining when it was signed, when it entered into force and how many parties have now ratified it (thereby introducing the crowd of characters in the story and making the treaty relevant, particularly to international students).
- The lesson might then identify the problem the Convention was designed to address, as set out in the Convention's preamble: recognition by the global community of the need for international cooperation to avoid the loss of the world's natural and cultural heritage.
- To bring the need for the Convention to life, a good story to weave in at this point (replete with colourful maps and pictures) is one of the catalysts for the Convention – the decision by the Egyptian Government in the 1950s to build the Aswan High Dam on the Nile River, thereby flooding the valley containing the Abu Simbel temples, a treasure of ancient Egyptian civilization. The World Heritage Convention website has maps, pictures and a great film with historic footage of this to easily incorporate multi-media.[b]
- More strands can be woven into the story by giving brief (and colour filled) examples or case studies of famous World Heritage properties around the world with plenty of maps and pictures to engage students, such as:
  - the Pyramids of Giza in Egypt;
  - the Great Wall of China in China;
  - Ha Long Bay in Vietnam;
  - Machu Picchu in Peru; and
  - the Great Barrier Reef in Australia.
- Once the Convention has been brought to life and (hopefully) everyone is engaged, the lesson might turn to the text of the Convention to show the mechanics of how it works: the key definitions (arts 1 and 2); the main obligations (arts 4–6); governance by the World Heritage Committee (art 8); and the World Heritage List (art 11). This is a good opportunity to reinforce the principles for treaty interpretation in art 31

of the Vienna Convention of the Law of Treaties 1969 if these have been covered in an earlier lesson.

- This Convention is a good opportunity to explain the role and importance of manuals agreed at COPs that flesh out the detailed operation of some treaties in practice, so link in the Operational Guidelines for the Implementation of the World Heritage Convention[c] to, for instance, explain the criteria for listing World Heritage properties.
- The lesson can conclude with some critical discussion of the immense challenges facing the protection of many World Heritage properties at present and into the future due to climate change and how the World Heritage Committee has, until recently, largely ignored that threat. As alluded to earlier, this can be woven into a discussion of contemporary analytical paradigms such as the Anthropocene.

Notes:

a. As a practical example of the delivery of such a lecture, a recording of my own 2017 lecture on 'Ramsar, World Heritage and CITES' is available at Chris McGrath, 'Ramsar, World Heritage and CITES' (Environmental Law Australia, 28 November 2017) http://envlaw.com.au/envm7124/ accessed 25 May 2019.

b. UNESCO World Heritage, 'Nubian Monuments from Abu Simbel to Philae' http://whc.unesco.org/en/list/88/ accessed 25 May 2019.

c. UNESCO, 'Operational Guidelines for the Implementation of the World Heritage Convention' (UNESCO World Heritage Centre, 2017), https://whc.unesco.org/en/guidelines/ accessed 25 May 2019.

CONTRAST WITH TYPICAL COURSE STRUCTURE

How the basic storytelling structure for any international treaty can be linked for an entire course teaching international environmental law is discussed below. The course structure discussed examines the major international environmental treaties in chronological order set in their historical and political context. However, such a structure does not reflect the typical course structure for teaching international environmental law.

International environmental law is typically taught, after considering introductory concepts, as a series of inter-related topics in categories such as 'World Heritage', 'Biodiversity', 'Fisheries' and 'Climate Change'. This approach is clear in the structure of textbooks commonly used for teaching international environmental law. For example, Philippe Sands and Jacqueline Peel's text, *Principles of International Environmental Law*, has the following structure:[19]

Part I. The Legal and Institutional Framework
   1. The Environment and International Society: Issues, Concepts and Definitions
   2. History
   3. Governance: States, International Organisations and Non-State Actors
   4. International Law-Making and Regulation
   5. Compliance: Implementation, Enforcement, Dispute Settlement
Part II. Principles and Rules Establishing Standards
   1. General Principles and Rules
   2. Atmospheric Protection
   3. Climate Change
   4. Freshwater Resources
   5. Biological Diversity
   6. Oceans, Seas and Marine Living Resources
   7. Hazardous Substances and Activities, and Waste
   8. The Polar Regions: Antarctica and the Arctic
Part III. Techniques for Implementing International Principles and Rules
   1. Environmental Impact Assessment
   2. Environmental Information and Technology Transfer
   3. Liability for Environmental Damage
Part IV. Linkage of International Environmental Law and Other Areas of International Law
   1. Human Rights and International Humanitarian Law
   2. International Economic Law: Trade, Investment and Intellectual Property
   3. Future Developments

Similarly, Pierre-Marie Dupuy and Jorge Viñuales' text, *International Environmental Law*, structures substantive regulation in categories or sectors such as 'Oceans, Seas and Freshwater', 'Protection of the Atmosphere', and 'Species, Ecosystems and Biodiversity'.[20]

---

[19] Philippe Sands and Jacqueline Peel (with Adriana Fabra and Ruth MacKenzie), *Principles of International Environmental Law* (4th edn, Cambridge University Press 2018).

[20] Pierre-Marie Dupuy and Jorge E Viñuales, *International Environmental Law* (2nd edn, Cambridge University Press 2018).

The United Nation's online courses on multilateral environmental agreements also adopt a similar, overall structure, grouping courses in five categories for:[21]

1. Biological diversity (10 courses)
2. Chemicals and waste (4 courses)
3. Climate, atmosphere and land (4 courses)
4. International environmental governance (9 courses)
5. Oceans and freshwater (3 courses)

This general approach of using descriptive categories such as 'Biological Diversity' and 'Climate Change' to structure the teaching of international environmental law clearly has a number of advantages.[22] Such categories are widely known and understood. While there is considerable variation in the use of terms, there is at least a basic level of common understanding if, for instance, parts of a course address 'Climate Change' and other parts consider 'Fisheries'. These broad categories also reflect the titles and focus of major treaties such as the Convention on Biological Diversity 1992 and the United Nations Framework Convention on Climate Change 1992 (UNFCCC).

There are, however, disadvantages to this structure. The main problem with using these descriptive categories is that many modern environmental problems do not fit into neat categories; they are inter-related and overlap. For example, biodiversity and World Heritage properties such as Australia's iconic Great Barrier Reef will be enormously impacted by climate change even if the 2°C or 1.5°C goals of the Paris Agreement are met.[23] The IPCC's recent Special Report on Global Warming of 1.5°C found: 'If global temperatures rise to 1.5°C above pre-industrial levels, most coral reefs are expected to be lost around the globe, while at 2°C virtually all coral reefs are expected to be lost.'[24]

---

[21] See InforMEA 'United Nations Informal Portal on Multilateral Environmental Agreements' https://elearning.informea.org/ accessed 25 May 2019.

[22] Discussed in Chris McGrath, *Does Environmental Law Work? How to Evaluate the Effectiveness of an Environmental Legal System* (Lambert Academic Publishing 2010) 61.

[23] Intergovernmental Panel on Climate Change (IPCC), *Global Warming of 1.5°C: An IPCC Special Report on the Impacts of Global Warming of 1.5°C above Pre-industrial Levels and Related Global Greenhouse Gas Emission Pathways, in the Context of Strengthening the Global Response to the Threat of Climate Change, Sustainable Development, and Efforts to Eradicate Poverty* (World Meteorological Organization 2018) 10, 226, 229–30, 235 and 254, http://www.ipcc.ch/report/sr15/ accessed 25 May 2019.

[24] Ibid., 10.

Given the enormous impacts of climate change on biodiversity and World Heritage properties, treating them as separate topics would be profoundly wrong. In practice, a course structured around these topics can largely overcome this problem by recognising the inter-related nature of the environmental issues and international regimes designed to address them. This is how the parties to the treaties themselves generally address these overlaps.

There is, therefore, nothing fundamentally wrong with using the typical course structure built around topics such as 'Biological Diversity' and 'Climate Change', while recognising the overlapping and inter-connected nature of the international regimes.

The proposal presented in the next section of structuring a course on international environmental law as a story, dealing with each of the major international environmental treaties in chronological order and set in their historic and political context, rather than categories such as 'Biological Diversity' and 'Climate Change' is a potentially better pedagogical structure. It is a potentially better structure simply because it builds on the premise that storytelling helps to engage students and link complex information in memorable ways.[25] Whether this structure suits an individual teacher's style and pedagogy depends, of course, on the individual.

A NEW COURSE STRUCTURE: A STORY SET IN ITS HISTORICAL AND POLITICAL CONTEXT

This section explains in a broad, narrative style how an entire international environmental law course can be structured as a story examining all of the major international environmental treaties since 1945 in chronological order set in their historical and political context. The intention is not to set out a 'perfect' course and detailed syllabus to be copied but, rather, to set out a broad approach that other teachers might adapt to suit their own style.[26]

The evolution of international environmental law set within its historic and political context can be summarised in many ways. I use four, broad periods in my courses: 1945–60; 1960–80; 1980–90; and 1990–present. I say to students clearly this is my own summary simply for the purpose of our course, not periods that are found in a modern history book. I discuss the summaries with my students and seek their perspectives, particularly international students, to engage them in critical analysis and reflective learning. Using these periods

---

[25]   Abrahamson n 5; Moon n 5; Egan and Judson n 5.
[26]   Given the purpose of this section and that references for the points made are easily found, references are kept to a minimum to avoid bogging down the broad narrative.

for the historic and political backdrop, I examine the major treaties negotiated in each period in chronological order, starting with the context in which they were agreed and jumping forward to their current operation for each.

1945–60

The period from 1945–60 was a post-World War II (WWII) period of rebuilding with rapid industrial growth in the USA, Europe and many parts of the world driven by major technological advances. In the immediate aftermath of WWII, government and public concern for the environment was low and few environmental treaties were negotiated. It was also a period of ongoing conflict with the Chinese Revolution in 1946–50 and the Cold War between USA and Russia commencing, giving the threat of nuclear war. Black and white images of European cities in rubble and an atomic blast can be used to paint the picture of this period.

The Charter of the United Nations 1945 provides not only a logical starting point but an opportunity to introduce key international actors, such as the United Nations (UN), and key concepts, such as sovereignty. Common misconceptions about the UN can be addressed, such as the limits on its ability to compel individual states to take any action.

The International Whaling Convention 1946 is a short treaty where students can be introduced to the typical process for creating and administering treaties (Figure 11.1 above), the normal treaty structure and the highly political nature of many treaties. It also provides an opportunity to explain the principles for treaty interpretation set out in articles 31 and 32 of the Vienna Convention on the Law of Treaties 1969, which lays the foundation for students to apply these principles to interpret provisions of other treaties. The recent litigation between Australia and Japan over whaling in the Antarctic provides a good case study to examine international dispute resolution in the International Court of Justice (ICJ), again with lots of pictures and maps to bring the story to life.[27]

The General Agreement on Tariffs and Trade 1947 (GATT) negotiated in this period, updated with reference to later trade agreements such as the World Trade Organisation agreements that resulted from the 1986–94 Uruguay Round negotiations, provides a good opportunity to explore the importance of international trade laws for environmental protection. I start lectures on GATT by handing out packets of chips and biscuits containing palm oil (which most confectionery does) before telling the story of the destruction of rainforests in Borneo for palm oil production (as always, with many colour pictures and

---

[27]   Whaling *in the* Antarctic (Australia v Japan*: New Zealand intervening*) [2014] ICJ Reports 226.

maps). After explaining what palm oil is and its widespread use in confectionery, I ask students to read the list of ingredients on the packets of the chips and
biscuits they have just eaten. At this point they realise they have just eaten palm
oil and have possibly contributed to the destruction of rainforests in Borneo.
This brings home a key teaching point: that international environmental law
touches them directly in their daily lives whether they are aware of it or not.

The next major international environmental treaty in this period, the
Antarctic Treaty 1959, provides a good illustration of the importance of
understanding the historic and political context of a treaty. Articles 1(1) and
5(1) provide:

> Antarctica shall be used for peaceful purposes only. There shall be prohibited, inter
> alia, any measures of a military nature, such as the establishment of military bases
> and fortifications, the carrying out of military maneuvers, as well as the testing of
> any type of weapons. ...
> Any nuclear explosions in Antarctica and the disposal there of radioactive waste
> material shall be prohibited.

It seems truly bizarre in the modern world to even contemplate nuclear testing
in Antarctica, yet at the height of the Cold War when the Antarctic Treaty was
negotiated, this was a major international concern and the treaty represented
a massive international achievement.

1960–80

The 1960s to 1980s was a period when government and public concern about
the environment emerged and there were ground-breaking environmental
treaties negotiated that laid the cornerstones for the modern international environmental legal system. It was still an ongoing period of rapid industrial and
population growth in many parts of the world driven by major technological
advances. The Cold War between USA and Russia continued; the USA was
defeated in the Vietnam War; and there was an ongoing threat of nuclear war.

The burst of environmental treaties in the early 1970s reflected this changing
political context: The Ramsar Convention 1971, World Heritage Convention
1972 and the Convention on International Trade in Endangered Species of
Wild Fauna and Flora 1973 (CITES). Each of these treaties – and all of the
major treaties – have excellent websites that provide smorgasbords of pictures
and case studies to bring them to life.[28] The Ramsar Convention and the World

---

[28]   See 'Ramsar' https://www.ramsar.org/; UNESCO 'World Heritage Convention'
https://whc.unesco.org/; and CITIES 'CITIES at Work' https://cites.org/ accessed 25
May 2019.

Heritage Convention provide good opportunities to illustrate that short treaties establishing broad frameworks are fleshed out through later technical agreements in COPs. Each has important manuals agreed at their respective COPs that flesh out their detailed operation: respectively, the Ramsar Convention Manual[29] and the Operational Guidelines for the Implementation of the World Heritage Convention.[30]

The International Convention for the Prevention of Pollution from Ships, 1973 as modified by the Protocol of 1978 (MARPOL 73/78) is another major international regime established in this period. Stories of the *Torre Canyon* oil spill disaster in 1967 and the *Amaco Cadiz* disaster in 1978 provide graphic historic context to explain how some treaties are created in response to major disasters. These 'disaster-driven' treaties can be contrasted with more pro-active treaties. They also lay a useful foundation for later discussion of the possible future of the international climate regime: will it evolve rapidly and in ways that, at present, seem politically impossible in response to disasters as MARPOL 73/78 did?

1980–90

The 1980s was still a period of ongoing growth and expansion in many parts of the world but government and public concern for the environment was dramatically heightened by emerging global threats such as scientific discovery of the hole in the ozone layer and the Chernobyl nuclear disaster in 1986. The Brundtland Report in 1987 established 'sustainable development' as a key international principle.[31] This was also a period of major geo-political shift as the Soviet Union disintegrated and the Berlin Wall fell.

The negotiations for the seminal United Nations Convention on the Law of the Sea 1982 (UNCLOS) were concluded during this period reflecting Gillian Triggs' comment that the 'international law of the sea ebbs and flows with the evolving geo-political priorities of the age'.[32] The story of the Bering Sea Fur Seals Arbitration[33] lays a good foundation for exploring maritime zones

---

[29]   Ramsar Convention Secretariat, *The Ramsar Convention Manual: a Guide to the Convention on Wetlands (Ramsar, Iran, 1971)*, (6th edn, Ramsar Convention Secretariat 2013), https://www.ramsar.org/document/the-ramsar-convention-manual -6th-edition accessed 25 May 2019.

[30]   UNESCO n 28.

[31]   World Commission on Environment and Development, *Our Common Future* (UN 1987).

[32]   Gillian Triggs, *International Law: Contemporary Principles and Practices* (LexisNexis 2006) 268.

[33]   *Award between the United States and the United Kingdom relating to the rights of jurisdiction of United States in the Bering's sea and the preservation of fur seals,*

in UNCLOS and modern fisheries management regimes. The current dispute over the South China Sea provides an excellent story of ongoing challenges for delineating maritime boundaries that control access to fisheries and other resources. UNCLOS provides a strong regime for managing fisheries within national maritime zones but is weak outside those areas on the High Seas. Any of the multilateral treaties managing fisheries on the High Seas, such as the Convention on the Conservation of Southern Bluefin Tuna 1994, can be used as examples of the international regimes that attempt to plug this hole in UNCLOS.

The Vienna Convention for the Protection of the Ozone Layer 1985 and Montreal Protocol on Substances that Deplete the Ozone Layer 1987 undoubtedly provide the most outstanding success story in international environmental law and can be used to inspire students. They also provide a great story of the role that science can play in driving international law and policy. The Convention and Protocol's rapid adoption following the discovery of the hole in the ozone layer, the research for which was published in *Nature* in 1985,[34] is truly remarkable when compared with the glacial pace and ongoing difficulties of the response to climate change. Recent evidence of breaches of the Convention and Protocol in China[35] also show that the story does not end: ongoing implementation and monitoring of international regimes is essential.

1990–present

The period after 1990 can be called the 'modern period' when all of the major international environmental treaties were in place after the Rio Summit in 1992. It is, undoubtedly, a complex period with many conflicting and confounding international pressures variously driving and inhibiting international cooperation such as global terrorism, numerous wars and financial crises. In it, China has risen as a global superpower. The overarching policy rubric of sustainable development came to be embodied in the UN Sustainable Development Goals.[36] Climate change became a dominating concern but international progress gradually stalled after the Kyoto Protocol was negotiated

---

Reports of International Arbitrational Awards Vol XXVIII 263 (15 August 1893).

[34] J C Farman, B G Gardiner and J D Shanklin, 'Large Losses of Total Ozone in Antarctica Reveal Seasonal ClO_x/NO_x Interaction' (1985) 315 *Nature* 207.

[35] Stephen Montzka et al, 'An Unexpected and Persistent Increase in Global Emissions of Ozone-depleting CFC-11' (2018) 557 *Nature* 413; and M Rigby, et al, 'Increase in CFC-11 Emissions from Eastern China Based on Atmospheric Observations' (2019) 569 *Nature* 546.

[36] See United Nations Sustainable Development Goals '17 Goals to Transform Our World' https://www.un.org/sustainabledevelopment/ accessed 25 May 2019.

in 1997. Momentum for global action on climate change was re-kindled in the lead-up to the Paris Agreement in 2015, led by the USA under President Obama and China. After the Paris Agreement, global momentum for multilateral cooperation has again been damaged by Brexit in 2016 and the election of the Trump administration in the USA. Under Trump, the USA has indicated its intention to withdraw from the Paris Agreement, hampering (but not stopping) the global momentum to respond to climate change.

The Convention on Biological Diversity 1992 provides a wonderful opportunity for stories and colourful pictures of biodiversity around the world. It can also be used to explore important measures for biodiversity conservation such as the IUCN Red List of Threatened Species[37] and protected areas. This can be used to draw together and emphasise the overlapping and interlinked nature of many other international regimes that conserve biodiversity.

The ebb and flow of climate policy under the UNFCCC, Kyoto Protocol 1997 and Paris Agreement 2015, together with related measures such as REDD+, provide enormous scope for storytelling to explain and link their complex concepts and international politics. Linking the past and present of climate policy with current science also provides an important platform for exploring what the future looks like and how the story may continue from this point. This is a tremendous opportunity for critical analysis and reflection drawing together many threads at the end of a course. For instance, this analysis and reflection may conclude that the Paris Agreement's goals are a paradox: even if we succeed in achieving them, we fail to protect iconic ecosystems such as coral reefs.[38]

CONCLUSION

Storytelling is a universal teaching technique that can be used in a myriad of ways to engage students, link information in memorable ways and lay the foundation for critical thinking. Good stories capture students' interest and engage their emotions and imaginations. Good stories are multidimensional and serve multiple purposes.

This chapter described two ways of structuring the teaching of international environmental law to naturally align with storytelling that is multidimensional

---

[37] See IUCN Red List 'The IUCN Red List of Threatened Species' https://www .iucnredlist.org/ accessed 25 May 2019.

[38] Chris McGrath, 'Paris Agreement Goals Slipping Away and with them Australia's Chance to save the Great Barrier Reef' (2019) 36 Environmental and Planning Law Journal 3; and Chris McGrath, 'Paris Agreement Paradox: If We Succeed, We Fail' (Environmental Law Australia 2019), http://envlaw.com.au/paris-agreement-paradox/ accessed 25 May 2019.

and serves multiple purposes. The first was a 'coat hanger' structure on which to hang lessons explaining any treaty: a simple structure for explaining international treaties as a natural story built on – and embedded in – the normal process for creating and administering international treaties. Second, this chapter described how a course on international environmental law can be structured in a story set in the historical and political context of the development of the major international environmental treaties since 1945. This is valuable for helping both teachers and students to engage with each other and create a more profound and lasting understanding of the complex reality of international environmental law. It should make teaching and learning about international environmental law more multidimensional and can be used as a frame within which to discuss contemporary analytical approaches such as the Anthropocene. It should also be more fun, which is an infectious ingredient for good teaching and learning.

PART IV

Environmental law at the postgraduate level

12. The emergence of specialist postgraduate coursework programs in environmental law

Heather McLeod-Kilmurray[1]

INTRODUCTION

'[B]ringing graduate legal education into the discussion [on the future of the law faculty] provides valuable lessons about a faculty's mission, pedagogy, and culture.'[2] Postgraduate programs in environmental law are relatively new. In fact, there were few courses in environmental law[3] even at the undergraduate level until about 50 years ago, and in most countries it is still not a mandatory course. Similarly, graduate studies in any area of law were rare in common law jurisdictions.[4] Most lawyers in North America do not have graduate law degrees. Why do some law students or practitioners pursue further studies, in particular through specialist postgraduate coursework programs in environmental law?

---

[1] Thanks to Angela Lee and Krystal-Anne Barber for their excellent research assistance, and Prof. Lynda Collins for her comments.
[2] Rosalie Jukier and Kate Glover 'Forgotten? The Role of Graduate Legal Education in the Future of the Law Faculty' (2014) 51(4) *Alberta L Rev* 761 at 762.
[3] Some argue that the term 'environmental law' should be replaced by a broader vision such as 'sustainability law' or 'ecological law' (e.g., Geoffrey Garver 'The Rule of Ecological Law: The Legal Complement to Degrowth Economics' (2013) 5(1) Sustainability 316) or 'wild law' (e.g., Cormac Cullinan, *Wild Law: A Manifesto for Earth Justice* (2d ed., Chelsea Green Publishing, 2011)). See also D Tarlock 'Is there Any There There in Environmental Law' (2004) 19 *J of Land Use and Envir L* 213; Stepan Woof, Georgia Tanner, Benjamin J Richardson 'Whatever Happened to Canadian Environmental Law?' (2010) 37 *Ecology L Q* 981. A detailed investigation of this debate is beyond the scope of this chapter, but it could be relevant to new and innovative programs.
[4] Sanjeev S Anand 'Canadian Graduate Legal Education: Past, Present and Future' (2004) 27 *Dalhousie L J* 55 at 110.

What are 'specialist postgraduate coursework programs in environmental law' (SPCELs)? The first thing that comes to mind are non-thesis environmental law LLMs, yet a broader view could include multidisciplinary masters programs with some legal component, such as the Master of Science in Environmental Sustainability at the University of Ottawa,[5] or the MSc in Environmental Management and Policy at Lund University.[6] Many schools offer diplomas or certificates in environmental law, which have fewer requirements and are easier to obtain in terms of time and cost.[7] The recent growth in these programs presents an excellent opportunity to examine what we have been doing in graduate environmental law education, and what new programs, pedagogies and other innovations we could invent to maximize their potential.

This chapter assesses the 'mission, pedagogy and culture' of SPCELs. It highlights their key elements, then explores what specialist environmental law LLM programs *could* be. To improve environmental law scholarship, Fisher et al. argue that 'an extensive, inclusive and critical discourse' about what environmental law scholars are doing is needed.[8] This chapter contributes

---

[5]   https://www.uottawa.ca/environment/grad-programs/masters, accessed 28 April 2021. McGill University's LLM in Environment is offered by the 'Faculty of Law, in conjunction with the School of Environment' https://www.mcgill.ca/law/grad-studies/masters-programs/llm-environment, accessed 28 April 2021 (including a non-thesis option). See also the MSc in Sustainable Energy Development at the Faculty of Law, University of Calgary: https://www.ucalgary.ca/future-students/graduate/explore-programs/sustainable-energy-development-master-science-course-based, accessed 28 April 2021. The University of Westminster's MA in Energy and Environmental Change includes some law courses https://www.westminster.ac.uk/law-planning-housing-and-urban-design-politics-and-international-relations-courses/2019-20/january/full-time/energy-and-environmental-change-ma, accessed 28 April 2021.

[6]   https://www.lunduniversity.lu.se/lubas/i-uoh-lu-XAMIS, accessed 28 April 2021.

[7]   E.g., the University of Calgary's Natural Resources, Energy and Environmental Law Certificate is aimed at practicing lawyers and requires 4 courses for completion: 'https://www.ucalgary.ca/future-students/graduate/explore-programs/natural-resources-energy-environmental-law-certificate-course-based, accessed 28 April 2021; the University of Sydney's Postgraduate Certificate in Environmental Law, aimed at practitioners, also requires four courses, and six months to complete full-time or 12 months part-time: https://sydney.edu.au/courses/courses/pc/graduate-diploma-in-environmental-law.html, accessed 28 April 2021; the National Law School of India University's Postgraduate Diploma in Environmental Law's 12-month program requires four courses and a dissertation: https://www.nls.ac.in/index.php?option=com_content&view=article&id=55:overview&catid=6:academic-programmes&Itemid=71, accessed 28 April 2021.

[8]   Elizabeth Fisher, Bettina Lange, Eloise Scotford and Cinnamon Carlarne 'Maturity and Methodology: Starting a Debate about Environmental Law Scholarship' (2009) 21(2) *J Envir L* 213 at 243.

to the discourse about how to train specialists in environmental law. How can we make these programs engaging, effective and rewarding for students and faculty? Most importantly, how can they provide the best training and experience so that graduates can improve law and policy for environmental sustainability and justice?

I.   MISSION

Anand argues that there are 'three different constituencies for graduate legal education: the lawyer who aspires to become a specialist, the foreign student … who seeks legal education [in a new jurisdiction] and the student who plans on entering the academy'.[9] Students may have several reasons for enrolling in a SPCEL, and this can vary between domestic and international students. The general perception is that those pursuing coursework-based LLMs are interested in gaining environmental specialization,[10] either because they lacked the interest or option to take environmental law in their first degree or because they want to study the issue from a different perspective abroad.[11]

Law faculties also have various goals when creating these programs. Some see coursework graduate programs in law as 'cash-cows' whose considerable tuition fees primarily fund the undergraduate law program.[12] If 'fund-raising' is a main goal, these programs will (i) be largely aimed at international students, who pay much higher fees,[13] and (ii) seek to attract large cohorts.[14] Devonshire acknowledges this reality,[15] but insists that 'any initiatives will be counterproductive if they compromise academic standards',[16] a crucial point for faculty reputation (and self-respect). One advantage of these 'fundraiser' programs is that they can often afford to offer many graduate level courses

---

[9]   Anand *supra* note 4 at 145.

[10]   Ibid., at 65.

[11]   Some note that enrollment in LLMs increases when the market for law practitioners declines: Matt Powell 'LLMs: What are They Good For?' (2010) *Canadian Lawyer Magazine* 1.

[12]   Jukier and Glover *supra* note 2 at 766. See also Anand *supra* note 4 at 66.

[13]   For example, the Dalhousie coursework LLM costs $9,400 for domestic and $19,650 for international students.

[14]   For example, the University of Cambridge has a nine-month coursework-based LLM with 160–180 students, from 40–50 countries: https://www.llm.law.cam.ac.uk/why-an-llm/intellectual-life-in-the-cambridge-law-faculty.html./, accessed 28 April 2021.

[15]   Peter Devonshire 'Law Schools and the Market for International Postgraduate Students' (2015) 25 *Legal Educ. Rev.* 271 at 271.

[16]   Ibid., at 273.

designed for the program.[17] The large international cohort they tend to attract, sometimes including students and practitioners from other fields of expertise, enriches the learning environment for both students and faculty.[18]

However, faculties have other motivations. Anand claims that offering graduate degrees in law achieves prestige for the faculty.[19] Undergraduate students benefit from the internationalization, multiculturalism, comparative learning and legal pluralism brought by an international cohort,[20] and the specialization that advanced environmental law courses allow.[21] Environmental faculty members also benefit from the opportunity to create these courses and to engage with an experienced and international, interdisciplinary cohort.[22] Ideally some schools are motivated by the goal of capacity building to resolve environmental issues both domestically and internationally.

If these are some reasons *why* we create these programs, the question of *how* to build them depends on what specialist environmental lawyers actually do. Environmental law careers can involve issues from climate change, species at risk and environmental health concerns to legislative drafting and policy making for sustainability. They are multidisciplinary, often multijurisdictional, and cover a broad spectrum of the law (public law, private law, litigation, legislative drafting, policy making, corporate compliance, etc.). This suggests that faculties have two main options: (i) create broadly based graduate programs with many options for courses, training and practice experiences that enable graduates to pursue any of these options, or (ii) create highly specialized programs at different schools among which students can choose.

Devonshire believes that 'non-brand' law schools compete with larger, more established schools through 'interdisciplinary and interjurisdictional Masters' or 'niche LLM programs' such as online degrees[23] or specializations specific to the location. We will turn to the issues of interdisciplinarity and

---

[17]   Pace Law states that it offers over 40 environmental law courses for LLM students: https://law.pace.edu/graduate/llm-environmental-law, accessed 28 April 2021.

[18]   Other than a mandatory 'Theory and Methodology' course for both coursework and thesis-based LLM (and sometimes even PhD) students, as discussed below.

[19]   'When a law school claims that it is one of the leading producers of law faculty or practitioner specialists at home or abroad, it enhances [its] reputation and influence.' Anand *supra* note 4 at 66–7.

[20]   Devonshire *supra* note 15 at 274 and 275.

[21]   See Devonshire ibid., at 274. See also Jukier and Glover *supra* note 2.

[22]   Jukier and Glover ibid., and Anand *supra* note 4. This can encourage increased faculty involvement in, and commitment to, the graduate program more generally.

[23]   Anand *supra* note 4 at 284. Lewis & Clark launched an entirely online version of its highly-ranked LLM in Environmental, Natural Resources and Energy Law in Fall, 2019: https://law.lclark.edu/programs/environmental_and_natural_resources_law/llm-via-distance-learning//, accessed 28 April 2021.

internationalization below. In terms of specialization, some schools play to their strengths, whether geographic location (e.g., the University of Calgary's specialized Certificate in Natural Resources, Energy and Environmental Law,[24] or Dundee's Centre for Energy, Petroleum and Mineral Law and Policy's three separate LLMs[25]). Others focus on the specializations of faculty members (e.g., Université Laval's LLM in Sustainable Development and Food Security,[26] or Charles University's degree in environmental law and international human rights).[27]

Some target practitioners by focusing on advanced skills training (discussed further below). There are also joint programs: for example, JD/LLM programs connecting two law schools, where students engage directly in globalization and comparative learning.[28] Another approach is the 'Professional Stream LLM'. Osgoode Hall's program is open to lawyers, paralegals and '[a]pplicants without a law degree, but with relevant work experience [who] bring a wealth of industry knowledge to the classroom'.[29] However tuition for a Canadian student is over $25,000 per year, and $40,000 for international students.[30] In these programs, many courses are mandatory and this ensures a sufficient number of students which, combined with the high tuition, makes a range of specialized graduate courses feasible.

---

[24]   https://www.ucalgary.ca/future-students/graduate/explore-programs/natural-resources-energy-environmental-law-certificate-course-based,   accessed   28   April 2021.

[25]   The three LLMs are in International Energy Dispute Resolution and Avoidance; International and European Union Electricity Markets; and The Law Carbon Economy: https://www.dundee.ac.uk/study/pg/energy-law-and-policy/, accessed 28 April 2021.

[26]   https://www.fd.ulaval.ca/etudes/maitrise-droit-environnement-developpement-durable-securite-alimentaire, accessed 28 April 2021.

[27]   Charles University, Czech Republic: https://www.prf.cuni.cz/en/specialisation-ii-1404044584.html, accessed 28 April 2021.

[28]   Devonshire *supra* note 15 at 277–279: 'this has aptly been described as an immersion model that reflects the aspirations of global legal education', in an experiential way. He also lists the 'financial advantages' of this approach. Some environmental organizations work with law faculties to provide similar programs: e.g., WWF and the National Law University, Delhi: https://d2391rlyg4hwoh.cloudfront.net/downloads/pgdelp_prospectus_sep_19.pdf, accessed 28 April 2021. This program is offered *only* in distance or online modes, and all courses are compulsory.

[29]   https://www.osgoodepd.ca/graduate-programs-and-courses/specializations/, accessed 28 April 2021.

[30]   https://www.osgoodepd.ca/graduate-programs-and-courses/tuition-fees-awards, accessed 28 April 2021. The thesis-based LLM is about $5,500 for domestic and $19,500 for international students.

II.   PEDAGOGY

Curriculum Design

It is important to address a key debate. It is generally assumed that the distinction between 'practical' and 'academic' graduate degrees is the difference between coursework and thesis-based degrees. However, as Jukier and Glover argue:

> [I]t is much too simplistic to draw stark, mutually exclusive distinctions between the legal academy and the practicing bar or between theory and practice. Moreover, it generates the impressions that (1) legal education programs can, or should be, categorized according to the career aspirations of their students; and (2) graduate and undergraduate education are, or should be, in separate silos within a law faculty, such that the future of one is not meaningfully connected to the future of the other.[31]

Indeed, while many lawyers do pursue an LLM with the goal of returning to practice, their experience may inspire them to change course toward a doctorate and academia.[32] It is also inaccurate to suggest that practicing lawyers have no use for theory, and that academics have no grasp of, or connection to, the practice of law.[33] Therefore legal education at any level should not make this absolute distinction. Most coursework graduate programs therefore require some form of research project, and arguably even the most 'academic' masters or doctoral student in law should have the opportunity to engage in experiential learning.[34] This more nuanced view should guide program development.

Many SPCELs do require students to complete some type of Legal Theory and Methodology course. Some of these include thesis-stream LLM students, allowing for collegiality and cross-pollination between environmental specialists with differing approaches, questions and insights. More than one course on methodology could be offered – one for research and others for more practice-oriented skills. The latter could be designed and taught by legal practitioners and/or experts from other faculties such as environmental sciences.

---

[31]   Jukier and Glover *supra* note 2 at 768.

[32]   Ibid., at 769.

[33]   As Rod MacDonald has said, 'law remains for many professors a mere technology (nicely captured by the idiotic ambition to teach students to 'think like lawyers' (as if the 'like a lawyer' part of the phrase were more important than the 'thinking' part))': 'Still "Law" and Still "Learning"? (2003) 18(1) *Cdn J of Law and Soc* 5 at 14.

[34]   E.g., Vermont's Masters of Environmental Law and Policy allows experiential learning, including through its environmental law clinic: https://www.vermontlaw.edu/academics/degrees/masters, accessed 28 April 2021.

Many programs also mandate a core substantive environmental law or sustainability course designed to (a) establish a cohort of colleagues and (b) ensure all students have a baseline knowledge of environmental law.[35] This is almost always a graduate level course. Indeed, most law faculties outside North America offer almost exclusively graduate-level courses in these programs, while in North America most students choose most of their optional courses from the list of upper year JD courses.[36]

Professional Skills Training

Many of the coursework environmental graduate programs designed for practitioners distinguish themselves through focusing on professional and practical skills training. For example, the University of Aberdeen offers two Oil and Gas Law LLMs: one with dissertation and the other 'with Professional Skills' which:

> will help you build your practical expertise and gain valuable contacts that will help advance your legal career.... The flagship feature ... is the professional skills modules.... You will undertake additional classes based on simulated practical exercises and submit a portfolio of works, bringing general principles into direct and immediate application.[37]

Pace Law's LLM students can participate in its 'UN Diplomacy Practicum at the United Nations'.[38] Professional skills can be obtained through in class

---

[35]   E.g., the 'Sustainability and Law' course at the University of Ottawa: https://catalogue.uottawa.ca/en/graduate/master-laws-llm-concentration-global-sustainability-environmental-law/#Requirementstext, accessed 28 April 2021.

[36]   There is often a 'chicken and egg' problem in North American common law graduate programs. While provincial regulators require that graduate students take primarily graduate level courses (e.g., the Ontario Universities Council on Quality Assurance Framework: https://oucqa.ca/resources-publications/quality-assurance-framework/, accessed 28 April 2021), faculties require that courses have a minimum enrolment to make them financially feasible and intellectually stimulating. Some address this by (a) allowing JD or PhD students (or graduate students from other faculties) to attend graduate level courses or (b) adding additional requirements for graduate students in JD courses: Anand *supra* note 4 at 108. Another option is to make all graduate program courses mandatory (yet this restricts student flexibility) or allow students to take directed research courses with one professor (Anand *supra* note 4 at 103), however these require much individual faculty time and are essentially research, not coursework.

[37]   https://www.abdn.ac.uk/study/postgraduate-taught/degree-programmes/218/oil-and-gas-law-with-professional-skills//, accessed 28 April 2021.

[38]   '[S]tudents work two days a week at the United Nations with delegations and/or member nations, providing legal and policy support on climate change and sustainability issues': Pace *supra* note 17.

exercises, work placements, internships and many other means. They are a key element distinguishing many postgraduate environmental law programs.

Interdisciplinarity

One thing that makes environmental law complex is its inherent interdisciplinarity,[39] and 'environmental law scholars need to understand what it actually means to be interdisciplinary'.[40] Environmental law teachers must do the same, and impart this to specialized graduate students. Fisher et al. point out that environmental law is interdisciplinary in many ways. It requires us to be experts in many legal fields[41] and be able to share this expertise with non-lawyers to solve complex problems ('contributory expertise'). We also need 'interactional expertise'[42] so we can work with scientists, economists and other experts. Environmental litigators work with expert witnesses,[43] and environmental law specialists may appear before, or be appointed to, specialized environmental courts and tribunals, which often include lawyers and experts in urban planning, hydrogeology, etc.[44] Specialized environmental law programs should therefore teach students how to (i) unpack a multidisciplinary environmental problem, (ii) identify which specializations would contribute to its resolution, and (iii) be capable of productive communication with such experts (which involves both asking the right questions and understanding the answers).

---

[39]   Fisher et al *supra* note 8 at 215. Others questions the merits of, or capacity to truly do, interdisciplinarity in environmental law: see, e.g., Ole W Pedersen 'The Limits of Interdisciplinarity and the Practice of Environmental Scholarship' (2014) 26 *J of Envir L* 423.

[40]   Fisher et al *supra* note 8 at 247. This requires understanding the difference between interdisciplinarity, multidisciplinarity and transdisciplinarity (at 234), and which one or more of these a program seeks to explore.

[41]   These include torts, property, administrative, criminal, international, comparative, trade and human rights law, among many others. It also includes legal pluralism in terms of understanding social dynamics and pressure points for decision making and behavioural change – see Fisher *supra* note 8 at 235–7, and 241.

[42]   Ibid., at 232.

[43]   Fisher et al argue that we need to be 'dynamic … and … agile', and 'more critical about the "empirical and theoretical claims from other disciplines"', ibid., at 232 and at 248, citing L Heinzerling 'The Environment' in P Cane and M Tushnet, eds, *The Oxford Handbook of Legal Studies* (Oxford: OUP, 2003) at 703.

[44]   See, e.g., Ontario Environmental Review Tribunal: https://elto.gov.on.ca/tribunals/ert/about-the-ert/, accessed 28 April 2021; the New South Wales Land and Environment Court: http://www.lec.justice.nsw.gov.au/Documents/Annual%20Reviews/2018%20Annual%20Review.pdf, accessed 28 April 2021.

Many options exist to enhance these skills. If students are limited to courses within the law faculty, these courses could include readings, guest lecturers and practical exercises relating to science, economics etc. For example, our Sustainability and the Law syllabus invites guest speakers such as a biologist, an international climate negotiator, a classical economist and an ecological economics critic, an expert in Indigenous law and legal orders, and an environmental engineer and corporate consultant. In addition to doing readings from within these disciplines, students engage in discussions with these experts who speak different 'languages' and answer questions from within their particular perspectives.[45] Similarly, Pace's environmental LLM mandates the 'Science for Environmental Lawyers' course 'to help future environmental lawyers achieve the level of scientific literacy required to assess the quality of scientific evidence and think critically about environmental issues'.[46] Another program design could allow students to take relevant optional courses in other faculties.

Some programs are entirely designed and presented by two or more faculties, such as the MSc in Environmental Sustainability, offered by Ottawa's Institute of the Environment.[47] The program includes eight compulsory courses, including Applied Environmental Sustainability, a capstone Seminar in Environmental Sustainability, and foundational courses in environmental policy, environmental science, environmental economics and environmental law. Also required are Professional Skills for Environmental Sustainability and Evidence Synthesis and Evaluation.[48] However, these interdisciplinary programs require far more planning, institutional support and collective engagement.

The cohort of graduate students can also be multidisciplinary, to ensure that faculty and students are constantly engaged in interdisciplinary learning but gaining interactional expertise.[49] This may require adjusting admissions policies. Some postgraduate programs explicitly invite non-lawyers to apply,

---

[45] Syllabus on file with author.

[46] https://law.pace.edu/courses/science-environmental-lawyers, accessed 28 April 2021.

[47] https://catalogue.uottawa.ca/en/graduate/master-science-environmental -sustainability/. The Institute of the Environment is multidisciplinary: https://www .uottawa.ca/environment/about; the program was designed largely by Prof. Nathalie Chalifour of the Law Faculty.

[48] Alternatively, double degree programs exist, such as the JD-Master of Environmental Studies at York University, a collaboration of the Law and the Environmental Studies faculties: https://www.osgoode.yorku.ca/programs/juris-doctor/ jd-admissions/joint-combined-programs/jd-mes/, accessed 28 April 2021.

[49] Where advanced interdisciplinarity is not available, there are creative ways to enhance this element. For example, PhD students at UC Berkley engage in 'interdisciplinary dissertation workshops':

others have a discretionary policy on admitting non-lawyers, while others require a law degree. Setting or revising admissions policies can be controversial, however the faculties who do it must find that the benefits outweigh the challenges.[50]

Internationalization, Multiculturalism and Diversity

Just as it is inherently interdisciplinary, environmental law and practice is frequently transboundary, involving 'jurisdictional plurality' and multijurisdictional frameworks.[51] Experts benefit from being able to spot 'intellectual blind spots' and develop the ability to do 'co-ordinated analysis' of complex problems.[52] It can also be useful to look to other jurisdictions for best practices (or approaches to avoid), so comparative environmental law is valuable. This includes comparing perspectives that may vary based on cultural, gender, economic and other vectors of diversity.[53]

Anand cites several reasons why a coursework intensive LLM would be attractive to international graduate students in particular: (1) coursework is more achievable than a thesis/dissertation if their undergraduate law degree was not in the language or the legal system of the faculty at which they are taking their LLM; (2) the degree is done within one year, rather than being subject to time variations that satisfactory completion of a thesis can cause; and (3) students obtain more exposure to host laws and legal culture(s) through courses than they would from focusing on a thesis with just one supervisor.[54]

---

three day, off campus workshops [which] bring together students … working on similar themes … in different departments …. They help break the sense of isolation …, [and] precipitate the formation of a cross-disciplinary intellectual community that endures beyond the workshop …

Anand *supra* note 4 at 158.

[50]   Some see this as partly 'an initiative to widen market appeal'; Devonshire specifically lists environmental law as one of the options often offered: *supra* note 15 at 283.

[51]   Fisher et al *supra* note 8 at 239.

[52]   Ibid., at 240.

[53]   Lund's International Master's Programme in Environmental Management and Policy states that 'Our teaching approach is characterized by a multidisciplinary and multicultural classroom - features that apply to both teachers and students – contributing to a creative atmosphere that pervades the whole of the institute.' https://www.lunduniversity.lu.se/lubas/i-uoh-lu-XAMIS, accessed 28 April 2021.

[54]   Anand *supra* note 4 at 18.

Vai Io Lo has suggested four models for internationalizing[55] graduate programs in law: 'inclusive, integrative, experiential and preferential'.[56] Admitting international students inherently adds international and comparative learning through interaction. Programs could make one international environmental law course mandatory as part of the degree. Other ideas include creating optional or mandatory placements in international organizations or in other jurisdictions. Multi-jurisdictional joint JD-LLMs[57] allow a lived international/comparative law experience, provide students with greater course selection and the possibility of internships or work experience abroad.

Yet inviting international students requires adequately supporting them. Some may not have the language capacities or familiarity with the host legal system to fully benefit from the program. Some faculties include courses to assist in this process; for example, the University of Toronto's coursework LLM offers a course in Canadian Legal Methods and Writing: 'Students also participate in the Comparative Legal Systems Seminar, where international LLM students present research about the legal systems in their home countries.'[58] Pace requires international LLM students to complete two courses: 'Introduction to American Legal Systems' and 'Introduction to US Legal Research'.[59] Others provide an orientation course prior to the semester,[60] and other accommodations or approaches could be considered[61] or invented.

---

[55]   More ambitious possibilities include creating wholly transnational programs, to match the globalisation of both legal education (Devonshire *supra* note 15 at 276) and environmental law itself.

[56]   Inclusive means adding international law materials into the program; integrative involves weaving this material into domestic law; experiential involves experiencing the law of other jurisdictions in person (such as through summer or exchange programs or joint degrees); and preferential 'allows students to study abroad and engage more fully in the ethos of foreign legal systems': Vai Io Lo 'Before Competition and Beyond Complacency: The Internationalisation of Legal Education in Australia' (2012) 22 *Leg Educ Rev* 3, at 7–10, as cited in Devonshire *supra* note 15 at 275.

[57]   Devonshire *supra* note 15 at 277 mentions the LLB-LLM at National University Singapore and New York University: https://www.law.nyu.edu/llmjsd/jointdegrees/llbllmprogramwithnus, accessed 28 April 2021.

[58]   https://www.law.utoronto.ca/academic-programs/graduate-programs/llm-program-master-laws/coursework-intensive-llm, accessed 28 April 2021.

[59]   Pace *supra* note 17.

[60]   Julia E Hanigsberg 'Swimming Lessons: An Orientation Course for Foreign Graduate Students' (1994) 44 *J Legal Educ* 588, as cited in Anand *supra* note 4 at 68. See also Devonshire *supra* note 15 at 279.

[61]   Osgoode Hall allows international LLM students to enrol in its university's English Language Institute's 'Intensive Advanced Legal English Program'. It also offers a 'Certificate in Foundations for Graduate Legal Studies': https://www.osgoodepd.ca/graduate-programs-and-courses/non-degree-offerings/. Students can also enrol for just one LLM course rather than completing the entire degree.

Again, admissions policies are important to ensure international diversity (in addition to many other kinds of diversity, which are essential to discussing many environmental topics such as environmental justice and climate justice). Devonshire argues that an admissions policy 'that promotes student diversity is beneficial not only from a marketing perspective but also to enhance the learning environment.... A diverse cohort of international students is the catalyst for a transformative educational experience'.[62] Faculties must also address financial realities and seek to provide as many scholarships and bursaries as possible to make the goals of internationalization and diversity attainable.

Format

If the program is primarily seeking to attract practitioners, it could consider offering graduate programs in a format that suits their schedules and requirements, to the extent possible. For example, should the program be offered in both full- and part-time options? Should some or all courses be offered on lunch-hours, evenings or weekends, or as intensive courses completed within short timeframes? Should distance learning or online options be offered?

The Osgoode Professional LLM includes a distance education option,[63] and 'most of the courses ... are taught in three-hour blocks one evening a week'.[64] Similarly, most subjects in the University of Melbourne's Environmental LLM 'are taught intensively, ... typically ... over five days, ... semester-length subjects are generally taught for two hours in the evening each week'.[65] Vermont Law's Environmental Masters offers a 'summers only' option.[66] Online and distance learning options require careful design and management to enhance advantages such as accessibility and flexibility, while overcoming potential disadvantages such as reduced interaction and student isolation. Improvements in technology will likely increase the viability and quality of these approaches.

The size of the cohort is a significant practical consideration. While large cohorts, and the income they produce, make a larger number and variety of courses possible, they can also reduce collegiality, cohesiveness and interaction. Each school must carefully consider where it wants to strike this balance,

---

[62]   Devonshire *supra* note 15 at 289.
[63]   Anand *supra* note 4 at 127.
[64]   Ibid., at 128. See also https://www.osgoodepd.ca/graduate-programs-and-courses/specializations/, accessed 28 April 2021.
[65]   https://study.unimelb.edu.au/find/courses/graduate/master-of-laws/what-will-i-study/, accessed 28 April 2021.
[66]   https://www.vermontlaw.edu/academics/degrees/masters, accessed 28 April 2021.

and students can choose the program that best suits their career goals, personalities and budgets.

Pedagogical Approaches

The variety of class sizes, the international and interdisciplinary character of specialized graduate environmental programs and students also allows professors to experiment with varying pedagogical approaches, such as problem-based learning, placements with environmental NGOs, law clinics, community service learning, etc. Indeed, a well-designed program will consider the size and constitution of the desired cohort in relation to pedagogical approaches it can and wants to adopt. Some argue that graduate students in law should have the option of studying and practicing pedagogy as part of their education. Perhaps those in environmental law should learn not only legal pedagogy but environmental or ecological pedagogy,[67] in order to create new and innovative ways to enhance teaching and learning in environmental law.

For example, we can imagine being much bolder in making environmental pedagogy as unique as its subject matter. Very ambitious approaches include place-based learning, such as field courses in environmental law. Professor Deborah Curran at the University of Victoria Law School is a leader in this area, taking small classes of students (approximately 20) on two-week intensive field courses.[68] The Institute for the Environment's interdisciplinary Masters introduces the programme and the students through a weekend in nature. While these may not be options for all faculties, short field-trips or other similar experiences can be more feasible yet highly meaningful alternatives.

III.   CULTURE

Like any graduate program, it is important to ensure that the full student experience for postgraduate coursework environmental specialists is positive. Two crucial elements are the collegiality and social experience of students, and their incorporation into the broader life of the faculty. A course-based program naturally achieves these more easily than thesis-based programs, since courses ensure students are physically together often and share learning. If courses blend graduate and undergraduate law students, and students from other facul-

---

[67]   See, e.g., Alan K. Knapp, Charlene D'Avanzo 'Teaching with Principles: Toward More Effective Pedagogy in Ecology' (2010) 1(6) *Ecosphere* 1.

[68]   See further details: https://www.uvic.ca/law/assets/docs/pcissummer2019/201905-384-field-course-in-environmental-law.pdf; http://www.bamfieldmsc.com/education/prospective-students/courses/detail/environmental-law-and-sustainability, accessed 28 April 2021.

ties, this encourages collegiality, diversity of views and sharing of law school life. However, special efforts can still enhance the experience. For example, the University of Toronto's 'Comparative Legal Systems Series' mentioned above allows international students to be seen and to make positive contributions to the faculty. Environmental law professors and students can collaborate to offer special events such as research in progress sessions, environmental law career evenings, film nights, or other activities that combine learning, skill building and camaraderie. The faculty should ensure that graduate law student associations are active and well-supported, and can create or encourage a specialized environmental law graduate association, reading groups or similar activities, and provide a space for environmental students to study together and congregate socially. Finally, if course-based graduate programs are mainly designed to produce specialist environmental practitioners, it is essential that students benefit from specialized career-placement services.

More boldly, faculties could consider embodying sustainability within the faculty and the program. For example, Vermont Law School has composting toilets, hammocks in its beautiful green courtyard, and otherwise creates a mood of lived sustainability.[69] The University of Saskatchewan's Law Faculty boasts a living green roof of native grasses.[70] Again, faculty resources vary, but even small efforts can make a big difference. If environmental law and education are place-based endeavours, these physical and atmospheric inspirations can enhance learning, skill-building and engagement. This is part of the 'invisible curriculum'.[71]

CONCLUSION – ADAPTIVE MANAGEMENT

The challenges of environmental sustainability are growing, so it makes sense that SPCELs are in greater demand. If the goal of these programmes is to educate specialists who can create a more sustainable world, we must continue to innovate and make sure they achieve this. There is no single approach to creating an excellent postgraduate coursework environmental law program; instead, we need an ecosystem of options to meet the diverse goals and needs of faculties and students. However, we should also learn from the ecosystem by ensuring that we apply adaptive management. We can monitor the experiences of recent graduates through program evaluations. We can follow with interest the career paths of graduates, and retain them as valuable program resources

---

[69] https://www.facebook.com/vlslibrary/, accessed 28 April 2021.
[70] https://sustainability.usask.ca/footprint/buildings.php#GreenBuildings, accessed 28 April 2021.
[71] Jukier and Glover *supra* note 2 at 784.

for future students. We could ask those who hire them how their knowledge and skills could be improved. We can research and share pedagogical innovations, program structures, syllabi and other tools through academic research, writing, workshops and conferences. These feedback loops can help us to build programs that most fully empower the next generation of environmental law specialists to advance environmental justice and sustainability.

13. Enriching the postgraduate environmental law classroom: combining mixed cohorts and intensive mode teaching

Erika Techera

INTRODUCTION

There is increasing pressure on academics to improve the quality of teaching, to enhance learning outcomes for students and to achieve broader university goals. Yet, public funding in tertiary institutions remains steady, or in relative terms is reducing, resulting in requirements to teach in more economically efficient ways and to reduce unnecessary costs.[1] This has led in part, along with the development and availability of new technologies and student demand, to a trend towards online teaching and/or blended learning.[2] At the same time, university rankings have grown in importance in Australia, placing pressure on academics to enhance the quality and quantity of research outputs, which affects the amount of time that can be devoted to the development of teaching methods and materials, which in turn 'can have a negative impact on teaching quality'.[3] Additionally, as universities expand student recruitment activities,

[1] Universities Australia, (2016) *Higher Education and Research Facts and Figures November 2015*. <https://www.universitiesaustralia.edu.au/ArticleDocuments/169/UA%20Higher%20Education%20and%20Research%20Facts%20and%20Figures%20November%202015.PDF.aspx> accessed 14 June 2019.
[2] Petrea Redmond, (2011) 'From face-to-face teaching to online teaching: Pedagogical transitions'. Paper presented at Ascilite2011 Changing demands, changing directions. <http://www.ascilite.org/conferences/hobart11/downloads/papers/Redmond-full.pdf> accessed 14 June 2019. Blended learning is used here to refer to education in which students are taught through a mix of face-to-face classes and online media.
[3] John Beath, Joanna Poyago-Theotoky, and David Ulph, 'University funding systems: Impact on research and teaching' (2012) 6(2) *Economics: The Open-Access, Open-Assessment E-Journal* 1–24, 2.

teaching must meet the needs of a diverse group of students that include international and domestic, full time and part time, as well as multi-disciplinary learners. These trends mean that teachers are being asked to enhance their teaching methods and materials, improve the learning environment and experience of increasingly mixed cohorts, and work in economically efficient and educationally effective ways to meet both student and university goals. This is no easy task, and identifying best practice options is a valuable exercise, and perhaps an imperative.

This chapter explores these issues and possibilities through the lens of postgraduate university-based courses in environmental law. The pedagogical literature on teaching mixed cohorts and in intensive modes is examined in the next section, followed by a case study drawn from teaching experiences in Australia. The final part of this chapter analyses the lessons learnt for best practice environmental law teaching.

TEACHING ENVIRONMENTAL LAW

Environmental law first emerged as a subject in Australian law schools in the 1970s, around the same time as environmental laws were being adopted. At that stage, and to a great extent even today, the subject was taught as an elective in the qualifying law degree. Over time, some institutions have introduced more than one subject; for example, domestic environmental law is sometimes offered as a separate unit from international environmental law. Although environmental law touches on almost all fundamental areas of law – administrative, constitutional, contract, criminal and tort law for example – it remains almost entirely taught as a standalone subject. Nevertheless, it has been suggested that an environmental sustainability agenda could be embedded in all core units,[4] in similar ways to internationalisation and indigenisation of law curricula.[5] Frequently, environmental law is also offered at the postgraduate level, either as a discrete subject in a general Masters degree, or as part of a specialised Masters degree in environmental law that may include multiple units on various aspects of the field.

---

[4]   David Mohan Ong, 'Prospects for integrating an environmental sustainability perspective within the university law curriculum in England' (2016) 50(3) *The Law Teacher* 276.

[5]   In Australia, the Office of Learning and Teaching has funded projects in both these areas: see Duncan Bentley, *Internationalising the Australian Law Curriculum for Enhanced Global Legal Practice* https://www.academia.edu/29160244/Internationalising_the_Australian_Law_Curriculum_for_Enhanced_Global_Legal_Practice; and the *Indigenous Cultural Competency for Legal Academics Program (ICCLAP)* http://www.icclap.edu.au accessed 14 June 2019.

Since its first introduction, the teaching of environmental law has become much more complex, in keeping with the expansion of this area of the law itself. Relevant literature has highlighted the value of environmental law in teaching critical thinking skills, given the number of environmental controversies and the rapidly developing nature of the field.[6] This remains true today, but the range of issues and legal responses has grown in number and complexity requiring teachers, researchers and learners to have knowledge of a broad range of environmental topics such as pollution, planning, conservation, natural resources management, climate change and energy, combined with an awareness of associated scientific, technological and social science areas. Furthermore, changes in approaches to environmental governance – including increased monitoring and reporting requirements, for example – have been accompanied by a rapid growth in scientific knowledge and data, and innovative uses of technology, expanding further the topics that must be explored in an environmental law course.

Therefore, teaching and learning in environmental law is complex enough even where learners are limited to law students. Yet it is often the case that, in Australian postgraduate programs, this subject is taught to mixed cohorts, involving both law and non-law participants from different backgrounds. The classroom may include domestic as well as international students taking advantage of student mobility program and seeking higher education experiences overseas. Non-law students are drawn from science or engineering backgrounds, where there is an inherent link to the subject matter being studied, as well as business, humanities and other social sciences. Furthermore, mature-age postgraduate students, with industry experience, are also attracted to environmental law, including law graduates who now find themselves advising clients on environmental issues, or non-lawyers needing to understand the basics of environmental regulation. The mixed cohort presents unique opportunities to harness the diversity in the classroom in an area of law that is inherently multi-disciplinary.[7] Yet it also brings challenges where each student has disparate levels of legal knowledge and environmental awareness.

A further feature of contemporary environmental law Masters-level teaching is that it is frequently undertaken in intensive block mode, in order to attract mature-age and part-time students. Again, this cohort is valuable as those students in the workforce bring their skills and expertise and enhance the learning environment. Intensive mode teaching may involve full-time study over

---

[6] Nancy K Kubasek, 'A critical thinking approach to teaching environmental law' (1998) 16(1) *Journal of Legal Studies Education* 19.

[7] Kanchana Kariyawasam and Hang Yen Low, 'Teaching business law to non-law students, culturally and linguistically diverse ("CaLD") students, and large classes' (2014) 11(2) *Journal of University Teaching & Learning Practice* 1.

a short period, rather than weekly across a whole semester. The on-campus session is usually unstructured by the university, with individual teachers left to arrange the time as they wish. This also has advantages, including the availability of large face-to-face time periods for more complex learning exercises. Nonetheless, this mode can be demanding in terms of retaining student interest across these periods of time, and the true benefits can only be gained where students are well-prepared in advance and engaged throughout.

Before identifying ways in which the cohort and delivery mode challenges can be addressed and the benefits harnessed, it is worth reflecting on the goals of environmental law study. For all cohorts, it is important to understand key areas of substantive environmental law, as well as the underlying principles and concepts. But teaching just the substance of the laws may only lead to surface learning. If critical thinking and legal analytical skills are to be built, it is essential to design curricula, materials, activities and assessments with these higher level learning outcomes in mind. Furthermore, students must be taught not only the environmental laws, but also how they can be used. Both law and non-law students must be given chances to apply the law themselves, develop legal arguments, resolve disputes and assess future areas for law reform. This is one area where the mixed cohort classroom and intensive teaching periods can be particularly beneficial. Prior to exploring the specific context of environmental law learning, the pedagogical literature related to teaching mixed cohorts, and in intensive modes, will be analysed.

LITERATURE ON MIXED COHORTS AND INTENSIVE MODE TEACHING

Mixed cohorts come in several different varieties: blended classes of domestic and international students, as well as diverse cohorts encompassing different disciplines. The majority of the literature on teaching mixed cohorts focuses on the combination of domestic and international students and issues around recognising and adjusting to the resulting cultural and ethnic diversity. Kraal for example, questions whether 'the normative legal teaching methods changed due to diversity within the classroom, and if so, to what extent'.[8] She argues that overcoming cultural challenges in higher education often comes down to encouraging active engagement from students from countries unaccustomed to Socratic and interactive teaching methods.[9] This is confirmed by other authors

---

[8]   Diane Kraal, 'Legal teaching methods to diverse student cohorts: a comparison between the United Kingdom, the United States, Australia and New Zealand' (2017) 47(3) *Cambridge Journal of Education* 389, 390.
[9]   Ibid., 396.

who recognise the real challenge is overcoming differences in the styles of learning.[10] It has also been identified that much can be gained from a multi-cultural classroom, where students can learn greater understanding of other cultural perspectives.[11]

Clearly some small changes can be adopted to enhance experiences for learners where English is not the first language. Removing colloquialisms and unnecessarily technical language is one such intervention, yet the latter is not always possible in teaching law. Another adjustment, for example, involves the provision of PowerPoint slides after, rather than before, the lecture, which has been shown to encourage listening skills.[12] Material can be provided in other formats including flowcharts to explain legal concepts and processes such as law-making.[13] Group presentations can be a good option for mixed cohorts,[14] but can also frustrate domestic law students who are less challenged by oral communication and the local teaching style. Use of topical case studies and current affairs, such as issues around globally relevant environmental challenges, can also stimulate interest.[15]

The above observations have to be borne in mind in teaching environmental law, particularly in the context of contemporary trends towards blended and intensive mode teaching where the focus of face-to-face time in the classroom is interactivity, rather than passive learning. Although it is clear that doctrinal legal approaches and the Socratic method are traditional legal educational approaches, they may not be suited to international, or indeed non-law, students.[16] Furthermore, problems may be exacerbated where full-time students are combined with professional mature-age graduates who are more used to, and better equipped to, participate in class.[17] Even within entirely law cohorts, some students may not be willing to participate.[18] As will be discussed below, appropriate learning exercises must be designed with the understanding that participation is a cultural challenge to some students, but not to others. It is clear that 'students from diverse backgrounds must be initiated into the context in which they will be expected to learn'.[19] How this is to be done is the

---

[10] Kariyawasam (n 7) 8.

[11] Ibid.

[12] Kraal (n 8) 399.

[13] Kariyawasam (n 7) 3.

[14] Kraal (n 8) 400.

[15] Also highlighted by Susan Fitzpatrick, 'The challenge of teaching law subjects with large and diverse student cohorts' (2009) 2 *Journal of the Australasian Law Teachers Association* 113.

[16] Kariyawasam (n 7) 3.

[17] Kraal (n 8) 396.

[18] Ibid., 398.

[19] Kariyawasam (n 7) 1.

problem, given the often different expectations of the teacher and the student. This is not, however, limited to cultural and linguistic diversity, as students from different disciplinary backgrounds may well have various experiences and expectations about what may happen in the classroom, as well as different terminological understanding, phraseology and methodological approaches. It has been said that 'non-legal students require a different legal curriculum, a variety of integrated formative assessment methods and different pedagogy from that offered to pure law students'.[20] Yet, increasing face-to-face class time is not really an option; and neither is raising the overall workload for students.

Teaching non-law students has been addressed in the literature, most often with respect to business and commerce students.[21] Little attention has been given to science students in law classes, a common phenomenon in environmental law. If maximum advantage is to be taken of the intensive class time, then the 'playing field' needs to be levelled early. Of course this can be done by requiring students to undertake preliminary, 'bridging' style courses.[22] However, this is often unattractive to students for financial and temporal reasons. If the different disciplines are known in advance, then materials can be designed to meet specific needs, but mostly this is not the case.[23] More generally, experience has shown that levelling the playing field is best facilitated by the use of technology. For example, overcoming terminological issues can be achieved when online materials are provided in advance, and which can be tailored to known areas where disciplines are misaligned.

Early formative assessment is also important. If it is critical for students to understand key principles and basic legal provisions, then online multiple-choice tests can be utilised. These may take staff time to design, but savings can also be made where marking can be automated.[24] It is important to bear in mind that multi-disciplinarity in the classroom is not simply a challenge to be overcome. It can be a considerable advantage as other disciplines bring new knowledge and insights of incredible value to understanding the

---

[20]   Ibid.

[21]   See generally, Fitzpatrick (n 15) and Kariyawasam (n 7).

[22]   Kraal (n 8) 395.

[23]   Some scholars have gone further by suggesting that assessments could be tailored to specific cohorts. For example, if school teachers are enrolled they could be asked to design a series of materials and activities for their classroom: Paulette L. Stenzel, 'Teaching environmental law and sustainability for business: from local to global' 30(2) *Journal of Legal Studies Education* 249, 277.

[24]   Fitzpatrick (n 15) 115.

environment, and also to overcoming weaknesses in law that may prevent the achievement of goals.[25]

Teaching in intensive mode has also been the subject of literature,[26] including on legal education.[27] Intensive mode teaching has not been consistently, nor formally, defined. Davies has said it encompasses four different non-traditional teaching modes: block; mixed; sporadic; and sandwich modes.[28] The focus in this chapter is upon block mode teaching where students are on campus engaged in face-to-face classes for whole days across one week. In most Australian institutions, it has been postgraduate law subjects that are taught in this mode. But, as universities seek to make better use of their infrastructure and expand summer and winter schools, undergraduate options are also being taught via block teaching.

Ramsay analysed the extent to which intensive teaching was used in Masters level courses in Australian law schools and demonstrated that this mode was more popular than semester-based classes.[29] The reasons for this growth are four-fold: the students in coursework Masters programs are often working full time and unable to attend weekly classes; interstate students can be attracted to intensive mode subjects; this teaching may appeal to the profession or interstate/overseas teachers; and employers may be willing to pay some of the cost.[30] Ramsay also analysed the literature on this teaching mode and concluded that criticisms were based on the lack of time for coverage of material, analysis and reflection, as well as student fatigue; often it was seen as simply convenient for students, rather than meeting substantive learning outcomes.[31] On the other hand, time in the classroom does not ensure engagement, reflection and analysis, which may be influenced by teacher enthusiasm

---

[25] Scientists and philosophers, e.g., may help to overcome the legal classification of much of the environment as 'things' to be traded or improved, harvested, utilised or wasted. See Nicole Graham, 'This is not a thing: land, sustainability and legal education' (2014) 26 *Journal of Environmental Law* 395.

[26] W Martin Davies, 'Intensive teaching formats: a review' (2006) 16 *Issues in Educational Research* 1, 4–5; and John V Kucsera and Dawn M Zimmaro, 'Comparing the effectiveness of intensive and traditional courses' (2010) 58(2) *College Teaching* 62.

[27] Maree Sainsbury, 'Intensive teaching of graduate law subjects: McEducation or good preparation for the demands of legal practice?' (2008) *Journal of the Australasian Law Teachers Association* 247; and Ian Ramsay, 'Intensive teaching in law subjects' (2011) 45(1) *The Law Teacher* 87.

[28] Davies (n 26) 4–5.

[29] In 2010, across five Go8 law schools, the number of subjects taught intensively varied. At the lower end of the range, one institution taught 49 subjects in this mode, and at the upper end 128 subjects were taught intensively: Ramsay (n 27) 89.

[30] Ibid., 90.

[31] Ibid., 92.

and expertise, as well as active learning techniques.[32] Importantly, advantages of this mode of teaching can include 'enhanced discussion, and the use of creative teaching techniques' where the teacher has 'good planning, structured activities, and a range of teaching strategies'.[33]

Essentially this comes down to providing an 'active learning environment, good subject organisation, and diversity of teaching methods'.[34] Invariably, even teaching in an intensive mode requires some element of blended learning; face-to-face teaching and learning combined with online use of technology. Blended learning, at its simplest, can involve merely providing teaching materials online to be pre-read prior to class. Yet much more can be achieved, as noted above, particularly in terms of ensuring students from multiple backgrounds have built an understanding of foundational legal terminology, principles and approaches. Where students have been pre-prepared and supported in building knowledge and skills to a common level via online learning, the block teaching period can be made more effective.

Best practice environmental education has generally been noted as involving '*issue-based, project-based,* and *investigation-focused* programs in *real-world nature* settings'.[35] Almost no published research examines the combination of mixed cohorts and intensive modes in environmental law education, and yet this combination would appear to provide ample opportunities to meet these three goals. Other scholars note a successful environmental law course involves critical features of '(1) a relational integration of the topics in the course; (2) immersion experiences; (3) being in the places shaped by and shaping law; and (4) interacting with participants and decision-makers and understanding the complexity of the issues they face'.[36] Again these features can be accommodated and the section that follows highlights the author's experience of building them into an international environmental law course.

---

[32]　Ibid.

[33]　Ibid., 93, referring to Eileen Daniel, 'A review of time-shortened courses across Disciplines' (2000) 34 *College Student Journal* 298. See also Howard Martin and Kathleen Bartzen Culver, 'Concentrate, intensify, or shorten? Short intensive courses in summer sessions' (2007) 71 *Continuing Higher Education Review* 59; and Kucsera and Zimmaro (n 26).

[34]　Ramsay (n 27) 97.

[35]　Marc J Stern, Robert B Powell and Dawn Hill, 'Environmental education program evaluation in the new millennium: what do we measure and what have we learned?' (2014) 20 *Environmental Education Research* 581, 600–601.

[36]　Estair Van Wagner, '"Seeing the place makes it real": place-based teaching in the environmental and planning law classroom' (2017) 34 *EPLJ* 522, quoting from Deborah Curran, 'Putting place in law: field school explorations of indigenous and colonial legal geographies' in Deborah Curran et al (eds), *Out There Learning: Critical Approaches to Off-campus Study Programs* (University of Toronto Press 2018).

This case study adds to the environmental law teaching literature and provides an example of teaching in intensive mode with a mixed cohort.

A CASE STUDY OF MIXED COHORTS PLUS INTENSIVE MODE

The observations presented below draw upon the author's experience of teaching international environmental law to mixed cohorts of postgraduate students, in intensive mode, in Australian universities over ten years. This time period has allowed for much experimentation and incremental improvement in materials, exercises and assessments. The course is taught over five full days in Summer School, with an online Learning Management System (LMS) website available six weeks in advance. The students in the classroom are all postgraduates, and are a mix of domestic and international students, with the former group tending to dominate. The cohort may be drawn from the qualifying law degree program (Juris Doctor), the Master of Laws (LLM) or another specialist Masters program which allows law and non-law enrolments. In addition, the course is open to legal practitioners to participate as part of their Continuing Professional Development (CPD).[37] Enrolments have tended to vary from year to year, but average between 15 and 40 students.

The reading materials have been selected to build both substantive understanding of the topics explored and to showcase different styles which may suit one learner over another. There is no set textbook, and instead the reading materials have been drawn from different sources – principally book chapters and journal articles. These are supplemented with online materials including websites, maps, YouTube clips and videos. This spread of materials exposes students to different key scholars in the field, various text and reference books and other materials that may be useful for later research. A list of further readings is also provided, and students are asked at the end of the course to identify a book, article, website or video that would be a useful resource in the future.

The LMS website contains the subject outline and reading list, as well as basic details about the in-class exercises. There is a discussion board and students are encouraged to introduce themselves and share any experiences, insights or materials that may be relevant to others. In some years, part of the assessment has involved compulsory contributions to the discussion board, but that did not seem to enhance engagement in the classroom and can become a burden for the teacher in terms of reviewing responses. The LMS website also has foundational materials (notes, PowerPoint slides with embedded links

---

[37] These participants do not complete assessments but actively participate across the five days.

to other video materials and online information, and a list of further readings) for non-lawyers introducing them to the legal system, key legal terminology, legal research and writing. In addition, some materials on global environmental challenges and international law are provided for law and non-law participants, who may not have studied in these areas before.

The PowerPoint slides for each module of the course are uploaded onto the LMS site in advance of the on-campus session. These slides include hyperlinks to primary materials (such as environmental conventions), as well as to additional materials such as newspaper articles and other grey literature. Students are encouraged to read through the slides in advance of the on-campus session. Experience has shown that the 'summary' that the slides provide, as well as the links to shorter, online materials, encourage engagement with the subject matter early. Whilst students are formally required to have fully completed all the readings in advance, it is clear that they do not always do so. Engagement with the PowerPoint slides, therefore, provides an introduction to each module.

The structure of the on-campus session includes three broad areas. Day one explores foundational principles and approaches, an overview of actors and law-making processes, and the history of international environmental law development. This ensures that all students have a firm grip on the basics. During days two and three, a series of modules focus on a different element of environmental law – biodiversity, marine pollution, atmospheric issues, waste and so on. The last two days are devoted to cross-cutting issues and bringing the whole unit learnings together. There are three assessments for the course, including class participation during the on-campus session. A formative assessment is given in the form of a set question(s) which is included in the subject outline. This assignment is submitted just a few days after the on-campus session. In essence, this requires students to have a draft completed before the intensive block, but provides a short opportunity for enhancements to be made after the face-to-face teaching, and any concerns to be addressed. The final assessment is a research paper with the option of choosing one of two set questions, or a free choice of topics. This is designed to accommodate more junior students who have less experience with designing research papers, as well as mature-age, international and professional students who may have particular topics they wish to explore.

During the intensive session on campus, short mini-lectures are conducted utilising the PowerPoint slides on the LMS site. Guest lecturers participate in some of these, and they often take a more Socratic approach. Students are encouraged to be interactive and specific questions are built into these slides which the students have in advance. In addition to these mini-lectures, there is a series of scaffolded learning activities conducted each day. This keeps the class engaged by enhancing the learning environment, and also provides a different way of applying the law. On the first couple of days these exercises may involve team work, but by the end of the week students are working alone. Initial exercises include 'briefing' the rest of the class on a specific treaty Resolution and its importance, critiquing one of the journal article readings, and highlighting a key environmental challenge currently in the news and what the legal issues might be. These activities build oral communication and critical thinking skills, and help to maintain a real-world focus.

Mid-week, students are asked to work in teams to analyse all the primary treaties and draw up a matrix that identifies which ones embed key principles, have a financial mechanism, include substantive reporting obligations and so on. This encourages students to think about the specific sub-fields of environmental law in a cross-cutting way, rather than just in siloes. Towards the end of that day, students are asked to rank the quality of the different provisions. These two exercises assist students to think about best practice treaty provisions, and to build a resource for use in later activities.

Towards the end of the week, two specific role plays are conducted. The first involves a real-world problem-solving exercise of a dispute between two States over a transboundary environmental issue. Students work in teams, continuing to build the classroom 'community', with roles assigned to expose students to different perspectives – real-life legal advisers are given roles as experts, and vice versa. The final role play involves the negotiation of a new treaty, with each student representing a different country. Students are given background briefings on their given country, and issues that it might wish to pursue. Students must draw on their knowledge of the best practice provisions, and combine that with the particular interests of the nation being represented. Not only does this build communication and negotiation skills, it also cements learnings about each treaty regime and provides an opportunity for students to apply the law. It also assists in developing an awareness of how hard it is to negotiate new treaties.

The teaching therefore combines elements of traditional legal teaching methods – lectures and the case method – with other approaches, such as problem-solving, lab-style activities and role plays. The combination of the mixed cohort and intensive mode teaching allows for this broader range of exercises. In particular, role plays can be conducted because of the longer blocks of time available. At the end of each day of the intensive session, a one page feedback sheet is given to students. It asks them what the top three learnings were, and also whether any material remains unclear. The latter questions allow any misunderstandings to be cleared up at the end of the day.

LESSONS LEARNT

Four key lessons can be drawn from the literature review and the case study that can be used to specifically enhance environmental law teaching and learning for mixed cohorts and in intensive mode: (1) be well-prepared; (2) build a classroom community; (3) design the course materials and assessments specifically to address the mixed cohort and the intensive mode; and (4) keep the classroom exciting, to ensure the students remain fully engaged through innovative learning activities.

Being well-prepared involves not only understanding the subject matter, but also the cohort. Equipping the cohort to do well takes time, but is likely to pay off in terms of a better teaching experience and the benefit of seeing students succeed. Preparing materials designed to level the playing field may be time consuming, but they can be used again in future years.

Building a classroom community is critical and can be advanced online, by encouraging or requiring students to introduce themselves and share insights ahead of the intensive block.[38] Teachers must lead by example, engaging early online themselves, and then maintaining a safe and inclusive classroom environment. Critical thinking skills can be built, whilst also strengthening the community, through a wide range of engaging activities familiar to different sub-groups, such as legal briefings, explanatory notes, journal article critiques and newspaper article analyses.

Well-structured materials are essential.[39] Mixed cohorts require a broader range of resources than those that would be selected or developed for law students. It has been said that 'a law teacher who is delivering a legal education to business students should never assume that the required learning outcomes can be achieved by using the same course model, teaching styles and strategies'.[40] This extends to reading materials and resources which must be selected to meet the learning needs of the non-law student. For example, course materials cannot simply involve traditional academic texts, instruments and cases; the mixed cohort requires a combination of different materials that extends to grey literature drawn, for example, from government, business and non-governmental organisations.[41] Teachers must design teaching materials and exercises that harness and build upon classroom expertise and diversity.[42]

Similarly, it has been noted that 'tailored evaluative methods that departed from objective exams' are needed.[43] Assessments must be designed to align with learning outcomes, but can extend beyond essays to include, for example,

---

[38] Ramsay (n 27) 98.

[39] Ibid., 99.

[40] Kariyawasam (n 7) 2.

[41] Grey literature refers to documents that are not traditional academic or commercial publications. Examples include working papers, government reports, unpublished dissertations, annual reports, newsletters and pamphlets.

[42] Ramsay (n 27) 98.

[43] Martin and Culver (n 33) 65.

journal and newspaper article critique, posters and online blog-based case studies.[44] In addition, multi-mode options could be included for answering a set question. Law students might choose a traditional legal essay style, but more creative possibilities could be provided for those from other disciplines: for example, designing a website, an NGO community pamphlet, or a corporate Board briefing memo.[45]

Keeping the classroom exciting is one of the critical issues in block teaching, noted in the literature above. There are conventional ways to do this – through, for example, experiential opportunities offered by guest lecturers and field trips where appropriate. As well, there are exciting learning activities such as labs, problem-solving exercises and role plays.[46]

CONCLUSION

Teaching environmental law to mixed cohorts in block intensive mode offers some difficulties, but also creates many more opportunities to make learning engaging and innovative. This chapter has demonstrated that by utilising blended learning techniques, many of the problems faced in teaching mixed cohorts can be overcome, and that the environmental law classroom can benefit from having multiple disciplines in the room to enhance the student experience and learning outcomes.

It has been said that best practice requires the teacher to 'abandon old habits and think creatively about methods appropriate for their classroom environment'.[47] This translates into combining doctrinal and experiential opportunities to build legal knowledge and skills, and designing materials and activities that take into account the variety of backgrounds and disciplines of the cohort. As with all teaching and learning, enthusiasm and commitment on the part of the teacher are likely to be significant factors in achieving success.

---

[44] See generally, Wagner (n 36).

[45] Wagner (n 36) 534.

[46] Karl S Coplan, 'Teaching Substantive Environmental Law and Practice Skills Through Interest Group Role-Playing' (2016) 18 *Vt. J. Envtl. L.*194.

[47] Kraal (n 8) 406.

14. Doctoral research in environmental law (Part 1): rationale and some supervision challenges

Willemien du Plessis[1] and Anél du Plessis[2]

INTRODUCTION

Doctoral research is crucial for the continuing development of environmental law as a knowledge field and to produce the next generation of environmental law scholars and thinkers. The conceptualisation, writing and finalisation of any doctoral study involves several stages and role players. It is a complex process of knowledge acquisition, generation and sharing, relationship building, scientific engagement, as well as professional and personal growth.

One of our points of departure is that the supervision of doctoral studies requires a supervisor to be a combination of a guide, mentor, information-source, coach and inspiration. The relationship between the doctoral candidate[3] and supervisor should be a space conducive for the candidate to grow into a competent environmental law researcher and to develop as an individual. The truth remains that supervisors (and examiners) face several challenges; for example, when supervising and assessing second- or third-language English speakers or working with students with problematic socio-economic backgrounds. The challenges experienced by doctoral candidates, globally, range from matters personal (e.g., financial) and cultural (e.g., international study) to institutional barriers and the mastering of the skill and acumen needed at the doctoral level.

[1] The contribution of Willemien du Plessis was supported by a National Research Foundation of South Africa Grant (No. 111762).

[2] The contribution of Anél du Plessis was supported by a National Research Foundation of South Africa Grant (No. 115581). All viewpoints and errors are the authors' own.

[3] In Parts 1 and 2 of this chapter, the concepts of doctoral student, doctoral researcher and doctoral candidate are used interchangeably and refer to a student enrolled for a doctoral qualification.

Canvassed against the above, the two chapters on doctoral research in environmental law (Parts 1 and 2) aim to explore (a) the need for doctoral studies and specialised research in environmental law; (b) the challenges posed by doctoral supervision in the field; and (c) the dynamics of the student-supervisor relationship. The chapters draw on a combination of available literature in social and natural sciences concerning doctoral study supervision, and the more anecdotal and lived experience of the two authors who could relate the findings of these studies to their experience as supervisor of postgraduate studies in the field of environmental law (and who worked together as supervisor and doctoral candidate at an earlier time).[4] While keeping to a message general enough to be of relevance and meaning to a broad audience of environmental law academics, for illustrative purposes the chapters in some instances reflect on the South African situation.

We acknowledge that a doctorate can take many forms, usually a full thesis that may or may not be supported by an oral examination (or external review of the proposal), or a defence of the thesis.[5] At some universities the doctorate is supported by coursework and examination in different formats.[6] Increasingly universities nationally and internationally present joint or double doctoral degrees, or international colleagues agree to jointly supervise a student registered at one of the universities. Our understanding is that in the field of law the role of the supervisor and the supervision task do not differ much from one type of doctoral programme to the next. For present purposes, our discussion is thus of a general nature and we do not distinguish between specific doctoral programme designs.

This chapter (Part 1), firstly contemplates the need for postgraduate studies in the field of environmental law and the relevance of doctoral-level specialisation. Secondly it ventures into some of the challenges associated with doctoral supervision, from the viewpoints of the supervisor and student. The next chapter (Part 2) addresses the supervisor-student relationship in order to arrive at a conclusion and to make some recommendations.

---

[4]   The two authors jointly have 46 years of experience in postgraduate supervision (masters and doctoral programmes). As of 2019, 36 doctoral students and 89 master students have completed their studies or are in the process of completing their postgraduate studies under their supervision.

[5]   Also see Terence Lovat and Allyson Holbrook, 'Ways of Knowing in Doctoral Examination: How Well is the Doctoral Regime' (2008) 3 *Educational Research Review* 66.

[6]   Onati International Institute for the Sociology of Law, 'How do PhDs in different countries differ' http://www.iisj.net/en/socio-legal-master/doctoral-studies/how-do-phds-different-countries-differ accessed 9 July 2019.

NEED FOR POSTGRADUATE STUDIES AND SPECIALISED DOCTORAL RESEARCH IN ENVIRONMENTAL LAW

It goes without saying that knowledge needs to exist to have an impact; and that as a first step, knowledge must be generated. The generators of knowledge in the field of environmental law comprise of established academics, researchers in the non-governmental and judicial sectors, and postgraduate students, especially doctoral candidates. Doctoral candidates specifically find themselves in an 'intermediate position', in which they need to acquire new skills and knowledge but also have to contribute to the advancement of knowledge in the scientific discipline of environmental law.[7] The impetus behind a doctoral study is often of a personal rather than an altruistic nature. The reasons behind enrolling for a doctoral study vary from its being a requirement for professional growth and promotion to a deeply personal desire to achieve the highest possible scholarly qualification.[8] Van Rensburg, Mayers and Roets note in this regard that '(m)any students are far more concerned about completing their research projects and obtaining a degree than about the scientific value of what they are working on'.[9] This said, doctoral candidates in the field of environmental law have the potential to make an invaluable contribution to the development and unravelling of the complexities of this ever-evolving field of law and legal practice.

Pedersen observes with reference to Fisher that 'understanding the legal substance of environmental law requires an understanding of the place of law and the environment in the world' and that, similarly, understanding environmental law scholarship requires an understanding of the place of scholarship and the role it plays in environmental law more widely.[10] In the era of the

---

[7]   See Vincent Larivière, 'On the Shoulders of Students? The Contribution of PhD Students to the Advancement of Knowledge' https://arxiv.org/ftp/arxiv/papers/1108/1108.5648.pdf accessed 1 August 2019, 3.

[8]   Heather J Shotton, 'Reciprocity and Nation Building in Native Women's Doctoral Education' (2018) 42 *American Indian Quarterly* 488, 490, however, indicates that women who have participated in her study 'reflected notions of reciprocity, as they saw a doctorate as a means for bettering their tribe/community or forwarding a research agenda that would benefit Native people in general'.

[9]   G H Van Rensburg, P Mayers and L Roets, 'Supervision of Post-Graduate Students in Higher Education' (2016) 3 *Trends in Nursing* 4.

[10]   Ole W Pederson, 'The Culture of Environmental Law and the Practices of Environmental Law Scholarship' in Ole W Pederson (ed), *Perspectives on Environmental Law Scholarship: Essays on Purpose, Shape and Direction* (Cambridge University Press 2019) 13 (SSRN version) https://papers.ssrn.com/sol3/papers.cfm?abstract_id=3179422.

Anthropocene and its implications for the state of the global natural resource base and sustainability, the function and impact of international and domestic environmental law frameworks are more important than ever. Kotzé explains that:

> The Anthropocene is therefore not only a possible new geological epoch; for law and environmental law scholars specifically, the Anthropocene, acting as a current cognitive framework, is providing a unique opportunity to question and re-imagine the juristic interventions that must ultimately be better able to respond to the current global socio-ecological crisis.[11]

Today, multidisciplinary and interdisciplinary research and the development of conceptual frameworks based on theory and practice are necessary in specialist branches of environmental law such as environmental rights law, climate change law, energy law, water law, waste law, marine and oceans law, mineral extraction law, biodiversity law, agricultural law, spatial planning law and environmental taxation. Environmental law researchers busy with a doctoral degree typically seek to advance the state of knowledge in a specific domain or a combination of domains of environmental law by gathering data and information, evaluating theory and generating original arguments regarding a significant public management/policy, development or governance issue, for example. As with other disciplines, a doctoral thesis in environmental law requires a candidate to develop a sophisticated conceptual framework, undertake independent research at the most advanced academic level, read and interpret published discourses in the field (as well as in other related fields such as natural and social science) and produce a thesis that makes a novel contribution to knowledge. A student in the process of writing up a doctoral study thus busies himself or herself with the exploration and creation of knowledge, the mining of ideas and phenomena that ultimately leads to new insights, individual development, social and environmental justice, the expansion and sharing of knowledge and the improved understanding of the form and function of environmental law. It follows that doctoral candidates contribute to the 're-imagining of the juristic interventions' demanded by the global state of the environment and the role of humankind therein.

As is further discussed below, increasing cultural diversity is a feature of postgraduate student expansion, and 'knowledge sharing and growth are fuelled by the welcoming, and empowering of culturally different perspec-

---

[11]   Louis J Kotzé, *Global Environmental Constitutionalism in the Anthropocene* (Hart Publishing 2016) 7.

tives and voices'.[12] Some of the major environmental challenges the world faces are dominated by scholarly voices from specific geographical regions. International and indigenous doctoral students who often opt to investigate troublesome and difficult research questions can therefore make a meaningful and creative contribution to both 'research cultures'[13] and environmental law knowledge generation itself. In this vein, Samuel and Vithal argue in favour of 'inter-, multi- and juxtadisciplinary ways of research and design of new knowledge systems' and state that 'interconnected realities of different valuing systems, their impact and influence on each other' provide opportunities for new insights and contributions to major disciplinary debates.[14] This view is also relevant in relation to environmental law, where the voices of developing countries and marginalised groups are often inaudible in global discourses around environmental justice, fairness in the global response to climate change, and matters of resource extraction for socio-economic development, to name but a few fields of interest. There seems to be agreement that there is 'real potential (as well as desire)' for environmental law doctoral candidates from different backgrounds and countries 'to shape societal debates and to impact on decisions made beyond the academy'.[15]

The wickedness of the problems experienced in the practice of environmental law and governance requires an understanding of many pull and push factors (e.g., economics, geo-politics, foreign relations, histories, heritage and political legacies), the role of technology and innovation and different kinds of new and established relationships between people, places, institutions (international, national and local, spanning private and public spheres) and, of course, the natural environment. While for a doctoral candidate in environmental law, the latter may be his or her 'home discipline', it is inevitable and important to the solution of today's problems and the generation of knowledge to apply to this base the ideas and theories of (an)other discipline(s).[16] As Pederson indicates, interdisciplinary work in the field of environmental law is not easy. Interdisciplinary scholarship poses real challenges for those scholars (doctoral candidates included) who are 'brave enough to expressly pursue scholarship

---

[12]   Gina Wisker and Gillian Robinson, 'Examiner Practices and Culturally Inflected Doctoral Theses' (2014) 35 *Discourse: Studies in the Cultural Politics of Education* 190.

[13]   See ibid., 191.

[14]   Michael Samuel and Renuka Vithal, 'Emergent Frameworks of Research Teaching and Learning in a Cohort-Based Doctoral Programme' (2011) 29 *Perspectives in Education* 76, 84.

[15]   Pederson (n 10), 12.

[16]   See Susan Carter, 'Examining the Doctoral Thesis: A Discussion' (2008) 45 *Innovations in Education and Teaching International* 365, 370.

through an interdisciplinary project'.[17] But it also highlights the importance of doctoral researchers and supervisors' ability to rely on considerations and frameworks 'ordinarily thought to be external to legal scholarship'.[18]

It follows that postgraduate studies and specialised doctoral research in environmental law are needed to critically question and evaluate, generate, communicate and apply knowledge for an improved understanding of the law and the way in which it can address the exigencies of the Anthropocene as they manifest in the relationship between people and the environment. The knowledge so created must be representative and should have its basis as much in (environmental) law as in other disciplines characterising the socio-ecological crises of our time. Once they have graduated, it is also expected that doctorandi will at some point plough their knowledge and expertise back into the minds of other scholars, a next generation of environmental law researchers, to help ensure the future of this field. Doctorandi should also actively contribute to effecting the recommendations emanating from years of in-depth research. Inter-generational mentoring and research capacity-building can happen within or outside the typical academic environment, especially in environmental law where, as mentioned earlier, there are many actors involved in research and critical enquiries.

CHALLENGES ASSOCIATED WITH POST-DOCTORAL SUPERVISION

Doctoral supervision can be an enriching experience for both the student and the supervisor. The opportunity to study towards a doctoral qualification is one to be seized in every way, especially if one can do so on a full-time basis. Some students are able to study full-time, have a fulfilled personal life, the necessary language ability, the required writing and research skills, as well as enough funding to sustain them during their studies. However, not all students are so fortunate, and some experience many challenges that may hamper their progress towards the finalisation of their doctoral studies. This is even truer of students in developing countries such as South Africa. These challenges are not unique to supervisors of or students enrolled in a doctorate in (environmental) law but they need to be acknowledged.

There is a dearth of literature based on empirical and theoretical research indicating the challenges experienced by supervisors and students in environmental law postgraduate programmes. We know however that some of these challenges are institutional, arising from rules devised by government

---

[17]   Pederson (n 10), 2.
[18]   Ibid.

and universities themselves (e.g., subsidies, the duration of the study and ethics-related matters). Others may relate to the nature of environmental law (e.g., its interdisciplinary nature and the need for prior knowledge of the subject, or an understanding of research methodology), the requirements of the different steps in the research process,[19] or the supervisor's understanding of his or her role as well as his or her relationship with the student. The personal circumstances of the student (e.g., matters of nationality, family demands, a lack of funding, being a part-time student, work-related issues or physical and emotional challenges) or cultural particularities and language deficiencies could also function as barriers to doctoral study or the finalisation of a thesis.[20]

A.   Institutional Challenges

The institutional issues are many. In South Africa (as in other countries) government funds universities based on the enrolment of postgraduate students as well as their subsequent completion rate, amongst other criteria. The subsidy-concept is premised, however, on the average completion rate of students in the natural sciences, not taking into account the fact that students in the humanities and social sciences may not be able to complete their studies in two years (the minimum period prescribed for a doctoral study).[21] A study by Mouton indicates that students in the humanities and social sciences (including law), complete their studies in a period of four years plus[22] – thus severely impacting on the income of the university.[23] Pressure is mounting to deliver

---

[19]   Shosh Leshem and Vernon Trafford, 'Overlooking the Conceptual Framework' (2007) 44 *Innovations in Education and Teaching International* 93, 101.

[20]   Also see Singhanat Nomnian, 'Thai PhD Students and Their Supervisors at an Australian University: Working Relationship, Communication, and Agency' (2017) 53 *PASAA: Journal of Language Teaching and Learning in Thailand* 26; S Loots, L Ts'ephe and M Walker, 'Evaluating Black Women's Participation, Development and Success in Doctoral Studies: A Capabilities Perspective' (2016) 30 *South African Journal of Higher Education* 110.

[21]   Also see Jitka Linden, 'The Contribution of Narrative to the Process of Supervising PhD Students' (1999) 24 *Studies in Higher Education* 351, 352.

[22]   J Mouton, 'Post-Graduate Studies in South Africa: Myths, Misconceptions and Challenges' (2007) 21 *South African Journal of Higher Education* 1078, 1086 indicated that in the period 2000–2005 the average completion rate for a doctorate was 4.7 years, and that most students completed their degrees in under five years. This correlates with international completion rates – see 1087–8.

[23]   Academy of Science of South Africa, 'The PhD study: an evidence-based study on how to meet the demands for high-level skills in an emerging economy' (2010) http://dx.doi.org/10.17159/assaf.2016/0026 accessed 9 July 2019; Chaya Herman, 'Expanding Doctoral Education in South Africa: Pipeline or Pipedream?' (2011) 30 *Higher Education Research & Development* 505.

degrees faster, as universities' income is declining. Universities in developing countries cannot set excessive enrolment fees[24] and bursaries are limited for law studies. Only a limited number of international students can access South African National Research Foundation (NRF) funding.[25] Universities provide bursaries but those are mostly limited to registration costs, often do not cover living expenses, and are awarded for a limited number of years of study.[26]

The number of available and suitably qualified supervisors also raises concern. Mouton[27] indicates that 'the most productive scientists often also assume disproportionate supervisory loads' and that the most productive researchers are nearing retirement age.[28] He also indicates that 'internationalisation and even institutionalisation of corporatism and managerialism in South African universities, has brought with it a concomitant shift in attention from concerns of quality and effectiveness to concerns about efficiency and throughput'. His argument is that government and university managers have perceived ideas about quality, which they link to the number of enrolled doctoral students vis-à-vis undergraduate students, the duration of a doctoral study and the number of masters students who convert their masters dissertations into doctoral theses.[29] Law Faculties may in future have to seriously rethink the concept of doctorates based on the number of credits and the pressure from government in relation to completion rates that is linked to the university financing model. From our experience, it is already noticeable that some uni-

---

[24] Due to the #Fees Must Fall Campaign in South Africa, universities can no longer rely on fees from lower- to middle-income students, who make up the majority of students. Universities receive subsidies based on student enrolment, student completion rate, research articles and books (or contributions in books), as well as so-called third-stream funding, i.e., funding from outside the university for contract work, etc.

[25] Also see Mouton (n 22), 1090. Some international student bursary schemes in South Africa also require South African citizenship or permanent residency.

[26] Supervisors have to apply for additional research funding in the hope that they will also be able to obtain bursaries for their students, but most of these funds also have restrictions as to the recipient of the bursary.

[27] Mouton (n 22), 1079–82. He and his Centre for Research on Science and Technology at the University of Stellenbosch have conducted numerous empirical studies on the research and postgraduate landscape in South Africa, and they are regarded as the experts in this field. Also see Van Rensburg, Mayers and Roets (n 9).

[28] On the importance of scholarly expertise, deep substantive knowledge of a subject field and specialisation for the work of doctoral supervision, see Christine Halse and Janne Malfroy, 'Retheorizing Doctoral Supervision as Professional Work' (2010) 35 *Studies in Higher Education* 79, 86.

[29] Mouton (n 22), 1082 indicates that the perception rests on the faulty premise that 500 000 undergraduate students produce one doctorate (taking into account the professional graduates that rarely register for doctorates), but correctly calculated 22 general bachelor students produced one doctorate in 2004.

versities curb the length of doctoral theses, thereby impacting on the quality and contribution of doctoral research.[30]

In South Africa, the Council for Higher Education sets the outcomes for a doctorate in the Higher Education Qualification Framework (360 credits),[31] which have to be achieved before a doctorate can be awarded.[32] Although these outcomes do not materially differ from what is expected of a doctorate all over the world, they set the bar high, and most doctoral candidates find it difficult to achieve them within two years of commencing with their studies. Students must first prepare a proper research proposal that has to be approved by several critical readers and university committees.[33] In the case of less experienced students, this may take up to a year, given the time needed for a doctoral researcher to become well-versed in his or her field of study.

Although pure doctrinal study is allowed for a legal thesis, there is increasing pressure on doctoral candidates to ensure the relevance of their studies by including empirical research and thus adopting alternative legal research methods. Students must obtain ethical clearance before they can embark on any form of empirical research. University procedures are usually cumbersome and in some South African universities it may take up to two years to obtain ethical clearance to proceed with a study.[34] Students then also have to

---

[30]   As one colleague at the University of the Witwatersrand noticed, the line between masters and doctoral studies seems to be becoming vaguer. This also has an impact on students deciding to do a proper comparative law study to inform their research themes. Being aware of constraints of time and finance, they will then opt to do an in-country study only. Also see Claire Aitchison, 'Writing the Practice/Practise the Writing: Writing Challenges and Pedagogies for Creative Practice Supervisors and Researchers' (2015) 47 *Educational Philosophy and Theory* 1291, 1293.

[31]   If a credit translates into ten notional hours, this means that students (full-time and part-time) are supposed to spend 450 eight-hour working days on their theses, which would include proposal writing, oral defence, research, reading, writing and finalising the technical requirements of a thesis. This proves to be impossible in legal studies; especially where students study part-time.

[32]   The Council for Higher Education (CHE) embarked on a country-wide quality assessment of all doctoral studies provided at South African universities. The assessment does not focus on the quality of the doctorates themselves, but determines whether procedures are in place to oversee the quality of doctorates. The CHE tends to focus on soft issues too, such as access to universities, the number of previously disadvantaged students in the system and their experience, and whether the doctorates contribute to the country's development and equity plans. Also see Mouton (n 22), 1078–90.

[33]   Charmaine Williamson, '"Views from the Nano Edge": Women on Doctoral Preparation Programmes in Selected African Contexts' (2016) 41 *Studies in Higher Education* 859, 860 indicates that the proposal stage is 'the stage where the risk of "drop outs" is at its greatest'.

[34]   Montserrat Castelló and others, 'Why Do Students Consider Dropping out of Doctoral Degrees? Institutional and Personal Factors' (2017) 74 *Higher Education*

get permission from the so-called 'gate keepers' in the field (who could be the relevant director of a government department or a designated employee in a company, a local government official, etc.) which may also prolong the study, especially in a developing world context. In future, universities may have to question their potentially excessive bureaucratic procedures in relation to ethical clearance, where a proposed empirical study is not a medical study or to be undertaken in relation to vulnerable individuals or societies (not that the rationale for ethical clearance is not important). The methodologies of empirical research may also need adjustment in a developing world or decolonised context[35] – where alternative empirical methods may provide the same results, but may not (yet) be specifically recognised by the broader academic world. In this regard, Latib[36] stresses the 'need for embeddedness in African realities and the contending knowledge perspectives on research content and methodology'. Students should be allowed to explore new methodologies, should they be able to provide sufficient evidence of their research abilities and success. The need to fall back on the 'known' as opposed to the 'unknown' in research design and methodology should be avoided if we want to progress in a changing knowledge society that embraces a new generation of environmental law researchers.

B.   Nature of Environmental Law

The need for in-depth specialised studies in environmental law was emphasised in the second section of this chapter. A doctoral study can have a purely legal focus – it can analyse legal rules and doctrines, case law and theory – but in environmental law, a doctoral candidate also needs to understand the relevant science and the methodology that may underpin his or her specific theme of study (whether governance, environmental management, natural, economic or social sciences, to name a few). A cohort of students who enter a doctoral programme also does not have a uniform level of undergraduate and postgraduate training, and supervision may in one instance be straightforward while in other instances the supervisor may need to individualise his or her style of supervision to address the unique needs of the student.

In South Africa (as well as elsewhere in the world) students enrol directly for a law degree (four years), followed by a masters degree (one to two years) which gives them access to doctoral studies (on the condition that they

---

1053, 1065 indicates that sometimes burdensome bureaucratic measures may impact on student success.

[35]   Also see Salim Latib, 'Decolonisation and Scholarship Through Evidence-based Research Supervision in Public Administration' (2017) 52 *Journal of Public Administration* 199.

[36]   Ibid., 205.

comply with certain requirements).[37] They usually do not have a first degree in another science, as is required in the United States of America (USA), for example. A doctoral student in environmental law therefore has to read far more than a student that merely undertakes doctrinal legal research – however, as indicated above, the time-line set by the Department of Higher Education and Training (DHE) in South Africa does not acknowledge this. World-wide, as indicated above, there are also more and more calls for inter-disciplinary and multidisciplinary research – a move away from the traditional discipline-focused research.[38]

The pool of doctoral candidates in law is small, and those that enrol for doctoral study are often foreign students. Law students tend to enter legal practice after their first or second degrees, due to their having financial constraints and having to provide for their families. In South Africa, where it is important to have more South African doctoral students from former disadvantaged back-grounds to enter academia and other professions, many challenges remain. These challenges may be personal or cultural, amongst others.[39] Many students are expected after completion of an undergraduate degree to enter the job market and start providing for the family that has supported them financially during the period of their study. The available bursaries may be able to support the student for the period of his or her doctoral study, but would not be enough to contribute to the family's expenses, needs and requests.[40] In South Africa this is in some circles referred to as the so-called 'black tax'.[41] Students that

---

[37]   Some students complete a Bachelor's degree in Arts or a Bachelor's degree in Commerce before embarking on law studies. It is rare to have students from other sciences undertaking a law degree and if it happens, it is usually much later in life, after disillusion with their initial choice of study or career.

[38]   We do acknowledge the difficulties of interdisciplinary research and the fact that each researcher tries to defend his or her own turf – frowning upon those who dare to venture beyond their initial training. Publications in Nature/Science indicate the many authors that have delivered profound studies – as well as the IPCC reports, where numerous scientists from various disciplines indicate the impacts of climate change. Also see Irma J Kroeze, 'Legal Research Methodology and the Dream of Interdisciplinarity' (2013) 16 *PELJ* 35.

[39]   Also see Chaya Herman, 'Obstacles to Success - Doctoral Student Attrition in South Africa' (2011) 29 *Perspectives in Education* 40, 44–9.

[40]   Ibid., 44.

[41]   In this regard see Mosibudi Ratlebjane, 'How "black tax" cripples our youth's aspirations' (*Mail & Guardian,* 2015) https://mg.co.za/article/2015-10-29-how-black-tax-cripples-our-youths-aspirations accessed 9 July 2019. Also see Castelló and others (n 34), 1053–68 who completed a study on Spanish students, indicating that young, female and part-time students have the highest dropout rate, citing as reasons the need for a balance between work and personal life and the impact of a doctorate on their social interaction with others.

therefore commence full-time doctoral studies are under constant personal pressure, impacting on their stress levels, progress and consequently on their completion rates. Some students may even drop out of the programme. It is therefore necessary for the government, funding institutions, universities and supervisors to take this into account. Supervisors face and have to recognise the challenges of students from disadvantaged backgrounds.[42] Notably, the lure of an academic career is low, as these students are in principle able to obtain high salaries in government and the private sector. Academic salaries are not competitive. There is no need for these students to obtain additional degrees in the private sector as government and industry compete to retain and promote their employees in order to comply with their statutory employment equity obligations.[43] Students who do in fact acquire doctoral degrees tend to subsequently find lucrative employment outside the university sector, resulting in a lack of South African academic role models.

C.   The Doctoral Process

Prospective doctoral students are, furthermore, not always aware of the total-ity of the demands of a doctoral programme.[44] Once accepted for doctoral study, they may be disillusioned or find it a lonely process and may tend to be depressed, lose track of or interest in their studies, neglect their health and well-being and feel that they are alone in the world, that no one understands what they are going through.[45] This is even more the case with a new gen-eration of students, which tend to oppose the lifestyle of their parents, who may have worked tirelessly to give them a better life. There are exceptions of course, but many doctoral students want to maintain their lifestyle and working hours, and are not necessarily prepared to put in the required work or to make personal sacrifices to produce high-quality work and to finalise their studies in time.[46] They often seem to need instant reward, gratification and commen-

---

[42]   Castelló and others, ibid., 1056 also indicates that a lack of resources results in a higher dropout rate.

[43]   See for instance the South African Employment Equity Act 55 of 1998 and the Broad-based Black Economic Empowerment Act 53 of 2003.

[44]   Mouton (n 22), 1090 refers to a lack of research preparation.

[45]   Castelló and others (n 34), 1055. Herman (n 39), 40–52 also identifies 'personal factors, such as time constraints, financial constraints, family responsibilities, lack of a support system' (41), 'child-bearing, health and HIV/Aids' (43). Ibid., 49–50 refers to additional challenges in the South African context, where students indicate that their computers and equipment have been stolen, or where international students indicate that they are home-sick or are experiencing xenophobic challenges.

[46]   There is a difference between part-time and full-time students, as well as national and international students. Our experience, however, is that mothers who need to

dation while the long and arduous route of academic writing and re-writing and more in-depth scholarly reading does not seem to fit well into their world view.[47] In our experience, the new generation of doctoral students often does not appreciate critique of their work, however well intended and despite the fact that it is a key part of scholarly growth and advancement.[48]

Students may enter into doctoral programmes later in life – often doing it part-time with added pressure from work and family. Under circumstances like this, doctoral studies cannot reasonably be expected to be completed in two years, and students may take up to four or five years to complete their doctorates. The South African government subsidy scheme does not differentiate between full-time and part-time students in terms of expected completion rates – it also does not take gender roles or students with different learning needs or disabilities into account.[49] Instead, government is pressuring universities to deliver more doctoral students to raise the national skills level – this despite the fact that the Constitution of the Republic of South Africa, 1996, for example, emphasises non-discrimination and the possibility of differentiation.[50]

D.   Language

Students' ability to write academically and other language-related barriers also hamper the progress of their studies.[51] Students with different cultural backgrounds may have different learning styles, and some students may need more encouragement than others.[52] The supervisor has to be culturally

---

balance a life with children and high-profile jobs actually complete their studies in a record time, vis-à-vis members of the younger generation, who feel that the world owes them a degree. International students face study permit conditions, have limited time and financial constraints, and therefore often show more commitment to complete their studies in time. Also see Newman Wadesango and Severino Machingambi, 'Post Graduate Students' Experiences with Research Supervisors' (2011) 2 *Journal of Sociology and Social Anthropology* 31, 36.

[47]   Also see Castelló and others (n 34), 1055.

[48]   Also see Sara Davis and others, 'Fielding Challenges, Finding Strengths: Supervisors and Students Voice their View on Giving and Taking Supervision' (2010) *The New Social Worker* 6–7, 19.

[49]   Also see Carter (n 16); Williamson (n 33), 339; Bethan Collins, 'Reflections on Doctoral Supervision: Drawing from the Experiences of Students with Additional Learning Needs in Two Universities' (2015) 20 *Teaching in Higher Education* 587.

[50]   Section 9.

[51]   Also see Van Rensburg, Mayers and Roets (n 9).

[52]   See in this regard ibid.; Nomnian (n 20), 26–54; Viviene E Cree, '"I'd Like to Call You My Mother." Reflections on Supervising International PhD Students in Social Work' (2012) 31 *Social Work Education* 451. The topic is further extensively discussed by Wisker and Robinson (n 12).

sensitive and attempt to understand why a student reacts in a certain manner. It may in fact be necessary to explain and discuss relevant cultural differences – a supervisor may typically have a different approach to academic life than what his or her student is used to.[53] Students should be encouraged to explain their culture and to indicate when the actions of the supervisor may offend them.[54] In this vein it should be noted that people whose first language is not English may in writing up their research experience difficulties in expressing themselves differently from the expression in an original author's text or in formulating an idea as eloquently as an English speaker would be able to do.[55] A first language speaker (a supervisor) may require the same English ability that he or she might have, which is in most instances impossible, and may cause anxiety in the student.[56] Supervisors and examiners may have to rethink what is expected of non-first language English students at doctoral level. If the research is well done, the research methodology is acceptable and if the student is able to convey a coherent and cohesive scholarly message in understandable English while also making an original contribution[57] to science, the question is whether an over-emphasis on the lack of English language ability is not wrong and a colonial or superiority construct of what is to be expected of non-English speakers. That said, mastery of language skills and the ability to convey clear and convincing scholarly messages, orally and in writing, are important at the doctoral level. Carter argues that students should ensure that they make use of a proofreader, if necessary, since the doctoral candidate is ultimately 'the architect of the thesis and must take responsibility for personal shortfalls'.[58]

---

[53] Also see Ting Wang and Linda Y Li, '"Tell Me What to do" vs. "Guide Me Through it": Feedback Experiences of International Doctoral Students' (2011) 12 *Active Learning in Higher Education* 101.

[54] Also see Van Rensburg, Mayers and Roets (n 9).

[55] Nomnian (n 20), 28–29; Phiphawin Suphawat Srikrai and others, 'English language difficulties of non-native English postgraduate students in an English for academic purposes at a Thai university' http://www.fas.nus.edu.sg/cls/CLaSIC/clasic2016/PROCEEDINGS/srikrai_suphawat_phiphawin.pdf accessed 8 July 2019.

[56] See Van Rensburg, Mayers and Roets (n 9).

[57] Gillian Clarke and Ingrid Lunt, 'The Concept of "Originality" in the Ph. D.: How is it Interpreted by Examiners?' (2014) 39 *Assessment & Evaluation in Higher Education* 803 explore the 'elusiveness' of the concept of originality in doctoral research and how its interpretation differs from one discipline to the next and in some instances from one institution to the next.

[58] Carter (n 16), 368.

OBSERVATIONS

Part 1 of this chapter on doctoral research in environmental law makes a case for the nurturing of postgraduate students in the field. Doctoral researchers keep the field of environmental law alive by adding to the existing knowledge base in many ways. A diversity of research methods and a variety in the thematic areas studied are critical if we (those in academia) have any hope of adding value to the process of seeking solutions to the most critical of environmental challenges posed by the Antropocene. This said, the demands of doctoral study are high. As we have pointed out, the doctoral journey often does not follow a straightforward or linear track; there are many challenges along the way, which students and supervisors in the field of environmental law should acknowledge, deliberate, face head-on and constructively help address.

In the next chapter (Part 2) we turn to the dynamics of the relationship between doctoral candidates and their supervisors. We look at this relationship in an attempt to determine how it can add value to the field of environmental law research as well as to personal development among a next generation of environmental law scholars.

15. Doctoral research in environmental law (Part 2): the student-supervisor relationship

Anél du Plessis and Willemien du Plessis

INTRODUCTION

In the previous chapter (Part 1) on doctoral research in environmental law, we explored the rationale informing and the challenges that accompany student research at this level. In this chapter (Part 2) we turn the focus onto the dynamics of the student-supervisor relationship and a number of aspects that seem to characterise many such relationships, in general, but specifically in the field of environmental law. Since this chapter is of an introductory kind, we conclude with a number of observations and pointers towards areas that may require further research.

The literature on the supervisor-student relationship (by some referred to as the 'learning alliance')[1] focuses on what the role of a supervisor should involve[2] and emphasises in some instances the need for training in supervision and mentoring.[3] It also reveals that there may be different expectations of what

---

[1]   See Christine Halse and Janne Malfroy, 'Retheorizing Doctoral Supervision as Professional Work' (2010) 35 *Studies in Higher Education* 79, 83.
[2]   Michael Samuel and Renuka Vithal, 'Emergent Frameworks of Research Teaching and Learning in a Cohort-Based Doctoral Programme' (2011) 29 *Perspectives in Education* 76, 78 indicate that many of the studies available 'are usually characterised by categories of student discontent'.
[3]   Also see Eli Bitzer, 'Postgraduate Research Supervision: More at Stake than Research Training' (2010) 1 *Acta Academica* 23.

the role of a supervisor should be, and what it is in fact.[4] De Beer and Mason[5] indicate, for example, that supervision includes performing an advisory role and a quality role, engaging in a supporting relationship and offering guidance, while a study by Wright *et al* identifies five qualitatively different functions of doctoral supervision ranging from quality assurer, supportive guide, researcher trainer and mentor to knowledge enthusiast.[6]

Van Rensburg, Mayers and Roets[7] state that: 'Supervision requires professional commitment, as it is an intensive form of educator-student engagement. The multiple layers of the supervisor-student relationship need to be recognised and engaged with for a successful outcome to be achieved.'

Samuel and Vithal[8] further state that:

> [...] the PhD research journey is one which shifts over time and that at different phases of the doctoral study the kind of support being offered to PhD students should alter in relation to the evolving stages of doctoral study. A pedagogical model of research learning therefore must take cognisance of different kinds of support offered at different levels of the student's journey. However, like all journeys the trajectory is never linear, even though planned and directed to attain some degree of systemisation. Research learning must include opportunities for multiple sources of influence, especially at doctoral level which aims to produce new theoretical, methodological and contextual knowledge.

In our view, the 'research learning' referred to hinges to a large degree on the dynamics, quality and cultivation of meaningful relationships between doctoral students and their supervisors.

---

[4]   April Wright, Jane P Murray and Patricia Geale, 'A Phenomenographic Study of What it Means to Supervise Doctoral Students' (2007) 6 *Academy of Management Learning & Education* 458, 459 states that, at least initially, '(a) a supervisor's own experience as a doctoral student, particularly the student-supervisor relationship, constitutes an initial socialization into the practice of supervision'.

[5]   Marie De Beer and Roger B Mason, 'Using a Blended Approach to Facilitate Postgraduate Supervision' (2009) 46 *Innovations in Education and Teaching International* 213, 214; Tricia Vilkinas, 'The PhD Process: the Supervisor as Manager' (2002) 44 *Education + Training* 129, 130–36.

[6]   See Wright, Murray and Geale (n 4), 463–8.

[7]   G H Van Rensburg, P Mayers and L Roets, 'Supervision of Post-Graduate Students in Higher Education' (2016) 3 *Trends in Nursing* 4.

[8]   Samuel and Vithal (n 2), 78.

IMPORTANT ASPECTS OF THE PHD STUDENT-SUPERVISOR RELATIONSHIP

The student-supervisor relationship is one between two or more people with a keen interest in the same scholarly field, that of environmental law. This does not however automatically translate in the doctoral candidate and supervisor having the same approach to solving an environmental law problem or to the way in which knowledge and skills transfer should take place. With a doctoral study, the student and supervisor adopt different roles with significant emphasis on the responsibility of the student albeit with the support and guidance of the supervisor. In the section below we identify and explain a number of aspects that form part of most doctoral student-supervisor relationships. It is our objective to highlight some of the views captured in existing literature and to add to the discussion by way of references to our experience with the supervision of environmental law doctoral students. Our experience is admittedly limited to the South African context and the need remains for more extensive comparative research in this field.

A.   Expectations

It is very possible for students and supervisors to have unrealistic expectations of each other in the context of the student-supervisor relationship. The research of Franke and Arvidsson has found that supervisors in Faculties of humanities and social sciences tend to stress doctoral students' independent work, and often downplay their own importance.[9] Löfström and Pyhältö[10] state, for example, that supervisors tend to focus on activities and tangible progress while students relate to their experiences in relation to supervision. To avoid these problems supervisors and students should from the beginning set their expectations of the study (in terms of thematic and procedural aspects)

---

[9]   Anita Franke and Barbro Arvidsson, 'Research Supervisors' Different Ways of Experiencing Supervision of Doctoral Students' (2011) 36 *Studies in Higher Education* 7, 8.

[10]   Erika Löfström and Kirsi Pyhältö, '"I Don't Even Have Time to be Their Friend!" Ethical Dilemmas in Ph. D. Supervision in the Hard Sciences' (2015) 37 *International Journal of Science Education* 2721, 2721. Also see Jitka Linden, 'The Contribution of Narrative to the Process of Supervising PhD Students' (1999) 24 *Studies in Higher Education* 351, 360, which provides a summary of supervisor and student perspectives.

and come to an agreement or a plan of action.[11] According to Herman[12] the supervisor may have to explain 'the financial, emotional and intellectual commitment required to complete a doctorate', including the fact that it may entail a (sometimes radical) change in the doctoral candidate's lifestyle. Some universities require formal agreements and regular (as often as monthly) feedback from both the doctoral supervisor and the student on the progress made or the experience of supervision.[13] It follows that at an institutional level there are expectations that direct supervisors and students.

Supervisors may prefer a hands-off approach in the relationship, while students (especially in Africa) at times refer to their supervisors as their 'mothers' and 'fathers', as they may enjoy (or desire) academic, social and emotional support and experiencing the supervisor's interest in the student as a person.[14] Students, however, also need to show appreciation for the fact that their supervisors fulfil many different roles in a Faculty or school, relating to

---

[11]   Sara Davis and others, 'Fielding Challenges, Finding Strengths: Supervisors and Students Voice their View on Giving and Taking Supervision' (2010) *The New Social Worker* 6. Also see Pia Bøgelund, 'How Supervisors Perceive PhD Supervision – And How They Practice it' (2015) 10 *International Journal of Doctoral Studies* 39; Peace Kiguwa and Malose Langa, 'The Doctoral Thesis and Supervision: The Student Perspective' (2009) 27 *Perspectives in Education* 50, 50; Søren Bengsten, SE, 'Review of the Handbook Literature on Doctoral Supervision' http://phd.arts .au.dk/fileadmin/grads.au.dk/AR/Review_doctoral_supervision.pdf   accessed   8 July 2019; H Friedrich-Nel and J L Mackinnon, 'Expectations in Postgraduate Supervision: Perspectives from Supervisors and Doctoral Students' (2013) 12 *Interim: Interdisciplinary Journal* 1, 1.

[12]   Chaya Herman, 'Obstacles to Success - Doctoral Student Attrition in South Africa' (2011) 29 *Perspectives in Education* 40, 44.

[13]   Also see Löfström and Pyhältö (n 10), 2735; De Beer and Mason (n 5). Van Rensburg, Mayers and Roets (n 7), propose that the agreement should relate to accessibility, regular meetings, the preparation and submission of drafts, records of meetings, expected targets and timelines as well as assistance from other facilities at the university, e.g. writing schools etc. There should also be minutes of the meeting compiled by the student and approved by the supervisor – also see Salim Latib, 'Decolonisation and Scholarship Through Evidence-based Research Supervision in Public Administration' (2017) 52 *Journal of Public Administration* 199, 206.

[14]   In Germany reference is also made to the supervisor as the student's 'Doctor Vater' (doctor father). Also see Löfström and Pyhältö (n 10), 2724, 2734; Lesley Johnson, Alison Lee and Bill Green, 'The PhD and the Autonomous Self: Gender, Rationality and Postgraduate Pedagogy' (2000) 25 *Studies in Higher Education* 135; Viviene E Cree, '"I'd Like to Call You My Mother." Reflections on Supervising International PhD Students in Social Work' (2012) 31 *Social Work Education* 451; Booi Hon Kam, 'Style and Quality in Research Supervision: the Supervisor Dependency Factor' (1997) 34 *Higher Education* 81. Mainhard Tim and others, 'A Model for the Supervisor-Doctoral Student Relationship' (2009) 58 *Higher Education* 359 provides a valuable questionnaire for use in establishing this relationship.

undergraduate lectures, assessment and curriculum development, management responsibilities, research projects and community engagement, to mention a few.[15] A supervisor may have large numbers of students who work under his/her supervision while the student often only has one supervisor. The intensification of institutional pressures on academics to perform at increasingly high levels in both teaching and research are reported to have 'prompted supervisors to be more disciplined and structured about how they manage their time and interaction with students'.[16] Doctoral students may at times demand and expect more direct involvement in their studies than what supervisors can reasonably be expected to provide.

Supervisor styles differ but it is in the interest of the doctoral study, the supervisor and doctoral candidate to maintain a relationship between the latter that is founded on mutual respect, openness and professionalism. Understanding each other's circumstances, committing in full to the demands of the thesis-writing process and setting reasonable expectations may accordingly enhance the student-supervisor relationship. Doctoral candidates should, for example, understand that for the sake of objectivity and unbiased scholarly feedback supervisors cannot be their close confidantes in relation to their intimate personal life and that there has to be some distance.[17] While the human factor may never be negated, students should also guard against using personal circumstances as a reason for the lack of progress and should be encouraged to plan ahead for problems. Doctoral studies tend to make it hard to live a balanced life and inevitably interfere with ordinary relationships at work and at home. When committing to a doctoral study the student should be aware of the physical and psychological demands he or she will unavoidably have to face during the course of completing the thesis and making deadlines. A doctoral study cannot be compared to writing an ordinary book where the only person involved in the process and with a direct stake in the outcome, is the author. Many universities have support services for student well-being and in some Faculties one will find that doctoral students organise themselves in small and informal peer-based support groups.

---

[15] Also see Newman Wadesango and Severino Machingambi, 'Post Graduate Students' Experiences with Research Supervisors' (2011) 2 *Journal of Sociology and Social Anthropology* 31 which indicates that supervisors are sometimes too busy to give effective feedback, or are not committed or have no interest in the students' studies, and provide conflicting feedback at different stages of the study, and that some of the examiners' feedback should have been dealt with by the supervisor earlier, during the supervision process – that could, e.g., relate to methodology or the background to the study. Vilkinas (n 5), also refers to the need for academics to generate additional funding from sources other than government.

[16] Halse and Malfroy (n 1), 84.

[17] Also see Van Rensburg, Mayers and Roets (n 7).

B.   Critique

For a doctoral study in environmental law as in any other field, it is important that its substance and the student researcher's skill be refined through critical reading and the supervisor's engagement with the student's work. Supervisors should assist students with understanding the value of, and interpreting critique – not as failure but as an attempt to improve the doctoral study and to develop sophisticated research skills. As one colleague once stated, 'we (as researchers) do not always explain to our students that we also have to write, rewrite and in the end still receive criticism from unknown peer assessors on our work, resulting in a rework of what we have done'.[18] Once doctoral students understand that the supervisor is also fallible as a researcher, they are more inclined to deal with (often very critical) supervisors' comments and feedback.[19] In a similar vein it is critical that the student trust the judgment of the supervisor who is likely to have a few more years of experience in scholarly environmental law research, student supervision and doctoral examination processes.

In providing critique of work, supervisors should also address possible issues before they become barriers or stumbling blocks not only in relation to the study itself, but also in the supervisor-student relationship.[20] Davis *et al*[21] state that 'interventions [are] to be done with the student, not to the student', allowing the student to raise his or her concerns or to provide alternatives to a specific challenge. Supervisors also need to realise that students may have different circumstances, and different needs and skills, and that these have to be addressed individually. Löfström and Pyhältö[22] refer to justice in supervision as meaning 'fairness, impartiality, reciprocity and equality'. This does

---

[18]   Also see Claire Aitchison, 'Writing the Practice/Practise the Writing: Writing Challenges and Pedagogies for Creative Practice Supervisors and Researchers' (2015) 47 *Educational Philosophy and Theory* 1291, 1297–300 stating that the participants in her study recognised 'that writing developed through numerous iterations of cycles of continuous critique and feedback – aspects that characterize both creative and writing practice'. According to her, supervisors employ different techniques when students have the writer's block – first asking them to write smaller pieces not necessarily related to the study, or to summarise their reading in bullet points, and then to rewrite the material in simple and clear language. She states further (1301) 'I am suggesting that we take great care to explicitly tend to writing, rather than leaving it submerged as an unrecognized layer of supervision practice.'

[19]   Also see ibid.

[20]   Davis and others (n 11). Latib (n 13), 204 indicates that students move between supervisors if issues of quality, e.g., are indicated – the student then cites 'tenuous grounds, such as murmurings on race or the embedded ideological and substantive orientation of the research'.

[21]   Davis and others, ibid., 7.

[22]   Löfström and Pyhältö (n 10), 2724.

not mean that all students should receive the same attention or that supervisors should tiptoe around sub-standard work. Instead, fairness dictates that critique be given and received in the light of the objectives of doctoral level research and that sufficient time be spent on students who seem to need more direction and assistance.

C.   Writing Skills

In a study on creative writing, Aitchison[23] finds that 'far from being invisible or incidental, writing was an integral component of supervisory practice' – it forms part of the 'process of writing', assisting the student in theory development or finding his or her own voice.[24] The supervisor can typically not be expected to act as a proofreader or language editor, but through engagement should assist the student to formulate logical and coherent arguments. Instead, the supervisor may be expected to focus attention on a doctoral candidate's scientific writing skills, including reasoning and formulating scientifically sound arguments.[25] The supervisor accordingly ensures that the student does not only produce (or reproduce) knowledge. In the words of Van Rensburg, Mayer and Roets, supervision 'also entails the development of a new scholar in a specific profession or work environment'. The supervisor of a doctoral study in environmental law acts as a mentor for the student and has to lead him or her towards confidence and independence as a writer.[26] In a similar vein, Qureshi and Vazir[27] state that '[supervision] is a complicated and intensive form of one-on-one teaching of research'. For a doctoral student in environmental law it is helpful to realise from the outset that study at this level is as much about making a new contribution to the scholarly field (in terms of substance and answering complex questions of law) as it is to master the art of research and writing.

---

[23]   Aitchison (n 18), 1297.

[24]   Also see Anne Lee and Rowena Murray, 'Supervising Writing: Helping Postgraduate Students Develop as Researchers' (2015) 52 *Innovations in Education and Teaching International* 558, 559–68, which provides valuable insights with regard to the supervisor's role in writing.

[25]   Van Rensburg, Mayers and Roets (n 7).

[26]   Ibid.

[27]   Rashida Qureshi and Neelofar Vazir, 'Pedagogy of Research Supervision Pedagogy: A Constructivist Model' (2016) 6 *Research in Pedagogy* 95. They also indicate that supervisors mostly follow the example of how they were supervised, and do not necessarily adapt their supervision to the needs of the specific student(s) 96.

D.   Networking

Doctoral candidates in environmental law should be supported to establish networks and speak with like-minded students and colleagues.[28] Conversations beyond those between the supervisor and student are extremely valuable. Castelló *et al*[29] found that students who work in groups, Centres or research groups are also less inclined to experience a feeling of isolation. The Environmental Law Association of South Africa (ELA) and the South African Research Chair in Cities, Law and Environmental Sustainability (CLES), for example, host annual postgraduate student conferences where students from across South Africa can share their research and pose questions to academics and external professionals that participate in these gatherings. We are aware of similar kinds of conferences in the USA, the UK and Germany. These conferences provide a 'safe space' for doctoral students in the field of environmental law who may feel overwhelmed by or may not even otherwise get the opportunity to participate in typical academic meetings. Attendance of academic conferences, especially international conferences (of the kind we had pre-Covid), may also be costly. In the circles of environmental law, we have found that supervisors or their Faculties are often generous enough to financially support a doctoral student to present a paper abroad during the course of his or her studies. In general, students cannot claim such support.

E.   Students' Challenges with Supervisors

Students also experience challenges with supervisors who are absent or do not provide (timeous) feedback, who are incompetent, or abusive, or exploit the supervisor-student relationship. Having two supervisors may bring new and fresh perspectives to a student's study. Less experienced supervisors should first supervise with a more experienced supervisor. However, if the supervisors have a difference of opinion it may also add to the student's stress levels.[30]

---

[28]   Also see Kiguwa and Langa (n 11), 55–6.

[29]   Montserrat Castelló and others, 'Why Do Students Consider Dropping out of Doctoral Degrees? Institutional and Personal Factors' (2017) 74 *Higher Education* 1053, 1056.

[30]   Van Rensburg, Mayers and Roets (n 7); Wadesango and Machingambi (n 15), 35. Also see the study by Herman (n 12), 49–50; Janne Malfroy, 'Doctoral Supervision, Workplace Research and Changing Pedagogic Practices' (2005) 24 *Higher Education Research & Development* 165; Sofie Kobayashi, Brian W Grout and Camilla Østerberg Rump, 'Opportunities to Learn Scientific Thinking in Joint Doctoral Supervision' (2015) 52 *Innovations in Education and Teaching International* 41.

The fact that a supervisor is a well-established researcher does not necessarily translate into him or her being a good supervisor.[31] Some supervisors may abuse his or her 'power' and try to force their ideas on the student, while the student, given the fact that he or she is meant to possess academic freedom, should in fact be encouraged to express his or her independent views and to develop and tender his or her own scholarly approach to the doctoral study. Supervisors should accordingly see themselves as part of another's own development of 'an academic identity'.[32] Co-supervision needs to be managed carefully as it can, as indicated above, also impact on the student's well-being. If co-supervisors on a doctoral thesis are from different backgrounds (e.g., the natural or social sciences or law) they need to agree beforehand on the study's scope and the specific methodological approach to be followed. A legal (environmental law) scholar is not necessarily a natural or social scientist, while similarly natural or social scientists are not lawyers. This requires mutual agreement and 'scholarly negotiation' between two or more supervisors and the student from the design up to the completion of the doctoral thesis. Such agreement is necessary even if they are all from law (as supervisors from different branches of law may also differ on the approach to the study) and even if they are all from the field of environmental law.

F.   Language Barriers

Van Rensburg, Mayer and Roets indicate that in a South African context where English may be neither the student's nor the supervisor's first language, written remarks, electronic feedback or emails may be misunderstood.[33] Sometimes face-to-face feedback with subsequent exchange of minutes may provide a more conducive and understanding environment for student-supervisor communication. Where this is not possible, it may be necessary to conduct discussions via electronic media.[34] Feedback should as far as possible be phrased in a generally accepted kind and polite manner. Despite the benefits of direct communication, Van Rensburg, Mayer and Roets propose that oral feedback

---

[31]   Qureshi and Vazir (n 27), 95.

[32]   See Sonja Loots, L Ts'ephe and Melanie Walker, 'Evaluating Black Women's Participation, Development and Success in Doctoral Studies: A Capabilities Perspective' (2016) 30 *South African Journal of Higher Education* 110, 119.

[33]   Also see Linlin Xu, 'Written Feedback in Intercultural Doctoral Supervision: a Case Study' (2017) 22 *Teaching in Higher Education* 239.

[34]   De Beer and Mason (n 5), 214–25 indicate that the student and supervisor should have access to the same computer programme or platform and should conduct pilot testing of the use of the specific medium that is going to be used. The use of electronic media and supervision can immediately provide a record of what is done. It may also prevent comebacks at a later stage or allegations of non-supervision.

should be reduced to writing (written feedback and minutes following personal feedback meetings) to avoid subsequent misunderstandings between the supervisor and the student. Collins[35] indicates that supervisors who have students with additional learning (language) needs will have to be flexible, listen to the student, communicate clearly and ensure that the student is able to access additional assistance and support where needed.

G.   Publication

Some studies report that supervisors publish their students' work under their (the established academics') own names.[36] There are several issues in this regard. One is the supervisor drawing on the student's work to inform a larger piece of work or research project, another is the supervisor simply taking and publishing the work of a student without accreditation. A third issue is students being required to work as research assistants and having the work produced in that context published/otherwise used without accreditation. Although universities indicate that doctoral studies should be published and that the university may publish the relevant work if the doctoral candidate does not do so, it remains ethical in our view to publish any articles forthcoming from a doctoral thesis under the name of the student only, alternatively with the supervisor as second author. We acknowledge that the practice may differ from one country or university to another. As second author, the supervisor may be expected to have contributed to the article in a substantial way. In support of our views on the importance of doctoral study for the development of environmental law as a scholarly field, doctoral students should be strongly encouraged to publish their doctoral research and to widely disseminate their research findings. This rings particularly true for students who intend to follow an academic career path.

---

[35]   Bethan Collins, 'Reflections on Doctoral Supervision: Drawing from the Experiences of Students with Additional Learning Needs in Two Universities' (2015) 20 *Teaching in Higher Education* 587, 598. Also see Cree (n 14), 459 – referring to technical, broader intellectual, administrative and management support.

[36]   Löfström and Pyhältö (n 10), 2723. Also see Lindsay Clowes and Tamara Shefer, '"It's Not a Simple Thing, Co-publishing": Challenges of Co-authorship Between Supervisors and Students in South African Higher Educational Contexts' (2013) 10 *Africa Education Review* 32 who indicate that 'co-authorship between individuals who are clearly in unequal positions in relation to academic resources and institutional power raises a range of ethical and political issues'. Co-publication may also be fulfilling when the supervisor assists the student to overcome his or her fear of publishing. Supervisors may also need to assist students to accept critique from the peer reviewers in relation to their first publications – ibid., 36–7, 43.

provided in a respectful manner and without being demeaning. It is important that supervisors and doctoral candidates attend to examiners' feedback. In some instances, a university's regulations will require a decision as to whether the award of the doctoral degree can be made without amendments, subject to minor amendments, subject to major revision or not at all. In the middle two options, in some countries, this will require the student to revise and resubmit their work to one or more examiners for further assessment (either on the written work alone or with another viva, if a viva has already been held).[47]

I.   Challenges of the Supervisor in Supervising Environmental Law Themes

The role of a supervisor in environmental law studies is even more complex than in other fields. Over and above addressing the issues already mentioned, the supervisor must keep track of the latest developments in the field, often in very specialised areas of environmental law. Yet the supervisor (and/or examiner) should always remember that he or she is not the one pursuing a student's doctoral study; the candidate must be allowed to gradually build his or her knowledge base and to personally discover new information and knowledge. The supervisor may be expected to lead the candidate to the knowledge or sources of knowledge, but it is the student that needs to explore and assess the knowledge base.[48] This is the part of the thesis-writing process for which the student must take full responsibility. In the same vein, the supervisor (and/ or examiner) cannot expect a doctoral candidate to have the vast amount of knowledge and research experience they might have gained over many years of supervision and research. The field of environmental law is complex and it will have taken the established academic many years to grasp only some of its concepts. It is impossible to be an expert in all the possible branches of environmental law. As mentioned earlier, in assessing a student's work, we must always consider what the set objectives and formal requirements of the

---

nical issues (these are things that can be corrected) but the contents of the thesis should determine the outcome of the assessment. It does not however relinquish the student from ensuring that the thesis is technically accurate.

[47]   See in this regard Vijay Kumar and Elke Stracke, 'Examiners' Reports on Theses: Feedback or Assessment?' (2011) 10 *Journal of English for Academic Purposes* 211.

[48]   Van Rensburg, Mayers and Roets (n 7), propose that a supervisor should pose questions to encourage critical thinking. A study by Grant, Hackney and Edgar further indicates that supervisors should not 'over supervise the student' but should instead 'build the confidence' of the student. See Kevin Grant, Ray Hackney and David Edgar, 'Postgraduate Research Supervision: An "Agreed" Conceptual View of Good Practice Through Derived Metaphors' (2014) 9 *International Journal of Doctoral Studies* 43, 54.

doctoral study are, and reflect on our own knowledge base and experience at the time of writing of our own doctoral theses. That is, we may have to put ourselves in the shoes of the doctoral researcher. Only then would we be able to objectively assess the student's work and not expect more than should actually be expected of them.

CONCLUSION

Education in general is a crucial part of human development. It is also, however, a 'capability generator' that underpins development through the stimulation of reasoning, imagination and critical thought. Tertiary education and postgraduate research (in environmental law and other fields) can be described as central to bringing about change and empowerment in individuals as well as in political, social and other contexts.[49] The two chapters dealing with the topic of doctoral studies and supervision (Parts 1 and 2) set out to explore: (a) the need for doctoral studies and specialised research in the environmental law context; (b) some of the challenges posed by doctoral supervision in this field; and (c) the dynamics of the student-supervisor relationship. The inquiry was set against the backdrop of our understanding that the scholarly field of environmental law has to develop and become more refined to help curb the immensity of the environmental crisis the world finds itself in. In addition, the environmental law scholars of today will become the researchers of tomorrow. Doctoral candidates, in partnership with their supervisors, and arguably also as part of larger teams of researchers, play an important role as agents of knowledge generation and communication in this regard.

In these two chapters on doctoral study and supervision we have merely scraped the surface of the role of doctoral studies and supervision in the advancement of environmental law. The need for doctoral studies and specialised research in the environmental law context hinges on the complexity of the environmental, social, cultural and economic problems the world faces as well as the fact that a scholarly field is being kept alive by those actively exploring its strengths, weaknesses and real life impact. Full-time and part-time doctoral students face many obstacles along the path to achieving the title of doctor. It is a small minority of students that will be able to say that the doctoral journey was easy and pleasing. It is important for supervisors, funders, government bodies and universities to recognise and address those problems which they may inadvertently be helping to create.

The job of the supervisor is similarly not always easy. It is a multifaceted task and requires an understanding of scholarly subject matter and (often,

---

[49]   Also see Loots, Ts'ephe and Walker (n 32), 110, 115.

a younger generation of) people. There may be a need for a research supervisors' handbook on the topic of doctoral supervision in the field of environmental law specifically, which is in line with the thinking of Grant, Hackney and
Edgar, who claim that 'perhaps a new supervisory pedagogy is needed' where
the emphasis falls on inter alia supporting learners 'in the development of their
ability to hold paradoxes and not be overwhelmed by complexity, ambiguity,
conflict, uncertainty and difference'.[50] In the words of Lee, '(w)e are educating
early stage researchers in the age of supercomplexity''.[51]

Engaging in a doctoral study generates several relationships between
the doctoral candidate and others. The most significant of these is arguably
the relationship between the supervisor and the student. As in most other
inter-personal relationships, that between the doctoral candidate and the
student needs to be based on mutual trust, good faith, commitment, open communication and professionalism. From our experience, the student-supervisor
relationship contributes significantly to the success of the individual doctoral
study, but also, over time, to the establishment of environmental law research
communities in a single Faculty or country but certainly also beyond.

---

[50] Grant, Hackney and Edgar (n 48), 57.
[51] Anne M Lee, 'Developing Effective Supervisors: Concepts of Research
Supervision' (2007) 21 *South African Journal of Higher Education* 680.

PART V

Challenges for teaching environmental law

16. Of density and decline: reflections on environmental law teaching in the UK and on the co-production of environmental law scholarship

Steven Vaughan[1]

The following are the co-authors of this chapter. For technical production reasons, it was not possible to list all 14 co-author names in the Table of Contents: Steven Vaughan, Alexandru Baltag, Ryan Brun, Rory Buttle, Caoimhe Creed, Arianne Delos Santos, Nia Evans, Jekilyah Gibson, Milon Goh Wei Ming, Etta Grilli, Kiran Makwana, Cassie Steiert, Kathryn St John, and Alexandra Weiner.

INTRODUCTION

We are the University College London's LLB Environmental Law class of 2018: its module convenor (Steven) and 13 of his final-year undergraduate students. This chapter is about a piece of research we undertook together: about the methodology of that co-production exercise; and about the state of teaching of environmental law in the UK. For the latter, we draw on a dataset we created which was generated through data taken from the top 100 UK law school websites, and survey responses from 49 UK-based environmental law scholars. We use the data to ask some hard questions about if, how, and where the teaching of environmental law has stagnated or been marginalised. This is, in effect, a 'state of the nation' account. We situate the exposition of our website data with the perceptions held by UK environmental law educators about environmental law teaching, what they feel to be the perceptions of the subject by their students, the challenges educators think the subject currently

[1] We are grateful to Maria Lee, Richard Moorhead, Eloise Scotford, and Elen Stokes for comments on an earlier draft. The usual disclaimer applies. An earlier version of this research was published as an online working paper. See: Steven Vaughan and others, 'Of Density and Decline: State of the Nation Reflections on the Teaching of Environmental Law in the UK' (UCL Working Paper Series, No.5/2019).

faces, and the challenges it might face going forward. Our chapter unfolds in five parts. It begins by situating what we did in the wider scholarship in the UK on environmental law teaching. Part 2 sets out the methodology of our co-production. Part 3 summarises what we found. Part 4 looks at why teaching environmental law might be challenging. Finally, we conclude with some reflections on our data.

1.   SCHOLARSHIP ON ENVIRONMENTAL LAW TEACHING IN THE UK

Scholars of UK environmental law have reflected on the 'field' relatively frequently (though also relatively recently). They have debated its contours and framed its limits; traced its origins and analysed its development; compared and contrasted their scholarship with that of others in different areas of law.[2] Those scholars appear to be both hesitant and introspective about environmental law as a discipline and about the quality, quantity, and coherency of environmental law scholarship. There is, however, strikingly little written about the teaching of environmental law in the UK.[3] The primary reference point is work undertaken in the early 2000s by Stuart Bell, Donald McGillivray, Andrea Ross-Robertson, and Sharon Turner on behalf of the UK Centre for Legal Education (hereafter, the 'UKCLE Report').[4] One of the prompts for their interest and for the study undertaken was the (at that time) 'deafening silence coming from the literature' reflecting on the teaching of environmental law.[5] The intervening 17 years have been equally quiet, punctuated by the infrequent noise of a mere handful of papers.[6] Whatever the underlying reasons

---

[2]   See Colin Reid, 'Environmental Law: Sifting Through the Rubbish' (1998) *Juridical Review* 236; Elizabeth Fisher and others, 'Maturity and Methodology: Starting a Debate about Environmental Law Scholarship' (2009) 21 *JEL* 213; Ole Pedersen, 'The Limits of Interdisciplinary and the Practice of Environmental Law Scholarship' (2014) 26 *JEL* 423; Gavin Little, 'Developing Environmental Law Scholarship: Going Beyond the Legal Space' (2016) 36 *Legal Studies* 48; Ole Pedersen, *Perspectives on Environmental Law Scholarship: Essays on Purpose, Shape and Direction* (CUP 2018).

[3]   The notable exception is the work of Jane Holder. See Jane Holder, 'Identifying Points of Contact and Engagement Between Legal and Environmental Education' (2013) 40 *JLS* 541; and Jane Holder, 'Doing the Sustainable Development Dance: Tracing a Critical Route from the Education for Sustainable Development Movement to Environmental Justice in Legal Education' (2012) 65 *CLP* 145.

[4]   Stuart Bell, Donald McGillivray, Andrea Ross-Robertson and Sharon Turner, 'UKCLE Subject Survey – Environmental Law' (UKCLE Report 2002).

[5]   Ibid., 8.

[6]   In her work on education for sustainable development, Jane Holder (n 3) uses the UKCLE Report as an introduction to a wider discussion on the problems encountered

for the lack of interest, engaging in careful and critical debate about the teaching of environmental law has value. Failing to reflect on teaching indicates a blindness to the role of teaching as generative of cutting-edge research.[7] Such failure privileges what academics do with writing over what academics do with students, and this cannot be right. We might further suggest that some form of ethical obligation is at play. If part of what academics do with their students is to teach them how to problematise environmental harms, and if some of those students go on to tackle these problems as environmental lawyers or activists or policymakers, then where, how, and why we teach environmental law can have significant purchase beyond the classroom. As Eloise Scotford and Steven Vaughan have argued elsewhere, 'In the way that we frame, phrase and organize our environmental law classes, we are defining the approach to our subject for future environmental lawyers and future citizens, and also expressing a (usually unarticulated) view on the role played by a law school.'[8] Finally, teaching is part and parcel of the everyday experiences of environmental law scholars. As Fiona Cownie and Anthony Bradney have put it, 'Whatever else legal academics do, one matter that should concern them is the nature of their lives.'[9] Thinking hard and deep about environmental law teaching can benefit us all. And that is one of the reasons why this topic was chosen for the research co-production exercise underpinning this chapter.

2.   WHAT WE DID

There are two methodologies at play in this chapter. The first relates to the data we draw on in the sections that follow. The second relates to the writing of the chapter as a pedagogic co-production enterprise. With respect to the data we use, we have adopted a mixed-methods approach; exploring website

---

in environmental law scholarship and methodology, as well as in the teaching of sustainable development. There is also a grouping of papers that explore embedding sustainability into legal education. See, e.g., Colin Reid and Nadeem Ali, *ESD and the Professional Curriculum* (HEA Academy Interdisciplinary Project Report 2010/11); and Jason Lowther and Joanne Sellick, 'Embedding Sustainability Literacy in the Legal Curriculum: Reflections on the Plymouth Model' (2016) 50 *The Law Teacher* 307.

    [7]   See generally Alisa Miller and others, *What is Research-Led Teaching? Multi-Disciplinary Perspectives* (GuildHE 2012).

    [8]   Eloise Scotford and Steven Vaughan, 'Environmental Law and the Core of Legal Learning' OUP Blog (15 October 2018).

    [9]   Fiona Cownie and Anthony Bradney, 'An Examined Life: Research into University Legal Education in the United Kingdom and the Journal of Law and Society' (2017) 44 *JLS* 129.

data and survey responses.[10] Information on the teaching of undergraduate environmental law options was taken from UK top 100 university websites in late 2017. A second data set was created for postgraduate modules using information sourced from the websites of the same universities in early 2018. In mid-May 2018, we then launched an online survey aimed at those with current or previous experience of teaching environmental law in the UK. The link to the survey was distributed via: (1) emails to individual academics whose contact details were sourced from the university websites detailing the relevant environmental law modules; and (2) professional associations. In total, 49 responses were received from those teaching environmental law at 38 separate universities. We use anonymised markers below (namely 'R1', 'R22') to identify qualitative data taken from the survey responses.

As a pedagogic enterprise, this chapter is the product of a research co-production exercise between a module leader and 32 of his undergraduate LLB students on an optional final-year Environmental Law module. Such an approach dovetails with UCL's 'Connected Curriculum' strategy which aims for students 'to learn through participating in research and enquiry', framed around six strands of 'connectivity'. The purpose of the Curriculum is for students to not only learn how to do what we do as academic researchers, but to do it with us as well.[11] As an initial task, all 32 students in the class were allocated three universities in October 2017 by Steven and asked to complete a spreadsheet with information on any undergraduate environmental law modules those universities offered. Thereafter, in the run-up to Christmas 2017, the cohort split into four roughly equally sized groups: collecting data on postgraduate modules; conducting a literature review; reviewing and analysing the undergraduate data; and working on framing questions for an online survey. All of this work was compulsory, extra-curricular (in addition to seminar preparation work), and non-assessed. After February 2018, participation in the exercise was optional and 15 of the 32 students agreed to carry on working on the project.[12] These students then divided their time between checking the data spreadsheets; summarising the literature; contacting academics to complete the survey; and later writing and commenting on drafts of the paper.

---

[10] Burke Johnson and Anthony Onwuegbuzie, 'Mixed Methods Research: A Research Paradigm Whose Time Has Come' (2004) 33 *Educational Researcher* 14.

[11] For deeper accounts of how the Connected Curriculum works in practice, see Dily Fung, *A Connected Curriculum for Higher Education* (UCL Press 2017); and Vincent Tong and others, *Shaping Higher Education with Students: Ways to Connect Research and Teaching* (UCL Press 2018).

[12] Two dropped out at a later date without any further contributions, which explains why there are only 14 authors of this chapter.

3.   WHAT DID WE LEARN ABOUT THE TEACHING OF ENVIRONMENTAL LAW IN THE UK?

Our website data shows that at 47 of the top 100 UK universities some form of environmental law is taught at the undergraduate (UG) level inside a law school.[13] At no university in the UK is it compulsory to study environmental law during a UG law degree. This number (n=47) is lower than that found in the 2002 UKCLE Report, where 59 universities offered UG environmental law in 2002.[14] Of the 47 universities offering UG environmental law modules, 34 of them offer only one module in the subject (and the other 13 only two modules). 67 per cent of UK UG environmental law modules are offered in the final year of study only; 13 per cent in second year only; and the rest in either or both of those two years. This is broadly comparable to the picture in 2002.[15]

One of the reasons we wanted to do the online survey alongside the web searches was to add some detail about who teaches environmental law in the UK. In the survey we asked respondents not only about themselves but also about others teaching environmental law in their universities. Table 16.1 shows two peaks of when our respondents began teaching environmental law: one grouping with under five years of experience; and the other over 21 years of experience (with a couple having taught environmental law since the early 1980s). Such clusters may reflect different corollary peaks of interest in environmental law issues.[16] The UKCLE Report identified the mid-1990s as the main start of environmental law teaching in the UK, with sporadic courses having begun in the 1960s, 1970s, and 1980s.[17] Interestingly, eight of those taking our survey indicated that their environmental law courses had begun in the last two years.

---

[13]   We did not explicitly look for data on environmental law taught elsewhere in the university. This may be worthy of further study.

[14]   UKCLE Report, 14. As far as we can tell, the most recent similar survey in the US was conducted in the early 1970s and has not been updated since. It found 64 universities offering environmental law. See Frances Irwin, 'The Law School and the Environment' (1972) 12 *Natural Resources Journal* 278.

[15]   UKCLE Report, 29.

[16]   This is the same hypothesis put forward by the UKCLE Report authors; UKCLE Report, 20.

[17]   UKCLE Report, 20.

Table 16.1   *Length of time teaching environmental law*

0–5 years	6–10 years	11–15 years	16–20 years	21+ years
14 (29%)	7 (14%)	5 (10%)	7 (14%)	15 (31%)

Note: One survey respondent did not complete this question. This means that the percentages add up to 98 per cent.

In total, 109 individual teachers of environmental law were named in our 2018 survey; 88 of these had been identified in 2002 in the UKCLE Report.[18] The 109 split, fairly evenly, between those in 'old' and those in 'new' universities (the same as in 2002). Of the 109, 66 (61 per cent) were women. This is a statistically significant change since the UKCLE Report.[19] Of the 38 universities covered in our survey, seven had only one teacher of environmental law and eight had five or more. This is also a change since 2002, where there were more environmental law teachers on their own in university law schools.[20]

In only three instances did university websites indicate average environmental law UG class sizes. At the LSE this was 20 students; at UCL 24 students; and at Leeds 75 students. When we asked our survey respondents whether they thought the numbers of students taking environmental law at UG level was changing over time, the majority of those who replied (20 out of 36) thought there was no change; eight thought numbers were increasing; and eight thought numbers were decreasing. When we asked why our respondents thought their students chose (or did not choose) environmental law as an optional module of study, replies centred around three factors. The first went to topicality, or the increase in 'front page environmental issues' [R33], the sense that environmental harms and challenges are now more in the minds of undergraduates than before: 'news coverage around the Paris Agreement seems to have encouraged sign up on my climate course' [R1]. The second went to employability, and the negative referents associated with taking environmental law over other options. The comments here were voluminous:

> It is not so attractive for students selecting their courses based on employment prospects and salary [R18].

> [Students] do not see immediate job prospects [R29].

> Some students may be put off the subject because it is seen as less serious and corporate than other modules. Perceived as wishy washy, a subject for lefties and those consumed by wanderlust, perhaps? [R34]

---

[18] UKCLE Report, 16.
[19] We performed a chi square test on the underlying raw data, with the chi square value of 3.9452 and a p value of 0.047.
[20] UKCLE Report, 17.

Students are interested but they don't see it as an area that leads to employment [R46].

The shared impression among our respondents was that many of their students wanted well-paying, City of London lawyer jobs and that their students thought that taking environmental law would not help in securing those jobs. Here, employability is as much an organising force of modern day universities as our survey respondents seem to think it is of student preferences.[21] Though the extent and operationalisation of the narratives differ, the modern UK university is keen to demonstrate 'value for money' for its students which in part comes from those students leaving the university employable (and hopefully already with employment offers).[22] Rebecca Boden and Maria Nedeva ask whether, 'employability discourses may be adversely affecting pedagogies and curricula, to the disbenefit of students, institutions, employers, social justice and civil society'.[23] Our survey respondents certainly seem to think those discourses are impacting on environmental law student numbers. In this context, the nature and extent of how environmental law is valued or not valued (and in what ways) at different universities may be expressed in institutional attitudes to environmental law which shape, in turn, what students think of the subject. This institutional preferencing might be seen in hiring and promotion decisions, in which centres and institutes are allocated university funding, and in which modules get (and do not get) institutional approval to run.

> The third theme among respondents as to why their students had chosen to study environmental law concerned the perception of the difficulty of the subject matter. 'When I asked why they studied environmental law, a majority responded it was because of the reputation of the module as "easier" than some of the others [R22].

> Its "soft" appearance to some [R28].

> That environmental law was seen as 'soft' was spoken to by the majority of survey respondents. Only one respondent said that the module was perceived as 'hard' (which, they said, impacted negatively on student numbers). Another commented that: 'An interesting bit of feedback we sometimes get is that students found the module more challenging than they imagined [R34].

---

[21]   Sheila Slaughter and Gary Rhoades, 'The Neo-Liberal University' (2000) 6 *New Labor Forum* 73.

[22]   Margaret Thornton, *Privatising the Public University: The Case of Law* (Routledge 2011); Chris Lorenz, 'If you're so smart, why are you under surveillance? Universities, neoliberalism, and new public management' (2012) 38 *Critical Inquiry* 599.

[23]   Rebecca Boden and Maria Nedeva, 'Employing discourse: Universities and Graduate Employability' (2010) 25 *J of Education Policy* 37.

We have three ideas to why environmental law might be seen as 'soft'. One possibility might be that the hesitancy that is sometimes seen in environmental law scholarship (discussed earlier on in this chapter) bleeds through into how environmental law scholars present and frame the subject. A form and practice of reflexivity by some environmental law scholars might be perceived as 'softness' by students. This, of course, depends in part on students knowing something about environmental law scholarship and environmental law scholars before choosing or not choosing to study the subject. Another response might be that environmental law may have thought to be seen as soft because of the liberal connotations of being 'an environmentalist'. That is, and to use Daniel Farber's language, is there a perception among law school students that there are more 'tree huggers' than 'bean counters' in environmental law?[24] Our third, and related, response is that a perception of 'softness' may be linked to an idea that environmental law is more about values and less about (doctrinal) law. Here, we had also asked our survey respondents about how their students found studying environmental law. While we might need to take student feedback with a (decent) pinch of salt,[25] a recurring theme was that while students of environmental law enjoyed the issues, the ideas, and the topicality, they found the law less enticing. 'They are less keen on the dense and technical statutory material' [R8]. 'Students tend to focus on the environmental issues generally and not so much on the law' [R29]. 'In general they don't like dull regulation, but who does?' [R43].

One respondent commented that, in their feedback, one student had asked him for 'more environment and less law' [R36]. Our discussion so far has in some way taken for granted that 'softness' is a negative referent. But it may also be the opposite. Put another way, some students may stay clear of environmental law because they dislike its perceived 'softness'; and others may actively take the subject because of that same perceived quality (because they are interested in values and/or because they would like what they think is a law-lite module to study). Putting the reflexive liberalism of some environmental law scholars to one side, we would argue that the 'law' element of

---

[24]   Daniel A Farber, *Eco-pragmatism: Making Sensible Environmental Decisions in an Uncertain World* (University of Chicago Press 1999).

[25]   We note here the various studies which show how women, BAME academics, and LGBT+ academics are rated less well than straight, white men in student teaching evaluations. See the annotated bibliography maintained by the LSE here: Danica Savonic and Cathy Davidson, 'Newly Updated for International Women's Day – Gender Bias in Academe bibliography' (The London School of Economics and Political Science 2017) https://blogs.lse.ac.uk/impactofsocialsciences/2017/03/08/newly-updated-for-international-womens-day-gender-bias-in-academe-bibliography/ accessed 20 April 2021.

environmental law is just as dense, complex, and challenging as in many other fields. What perhaps distinguishes environmental law is the extent to which in studying the subject one needs to unpick, unpack, and become immersed in a complex of dynamic and often unstable legal, social, economic, and political processes.[26] As Liz Fisher might put it, environmental law is not soft, it is 'hot'.[27] If students think otherwise, that is an error worth correcting.

4.   THE CHALLENGES IN TEACHING ENVIRONMENTAL LAW IN THE UK

The subject seems to have overwhelmed us. Virtually every law teacher – however broad his or her outlook – wants to introduce students to the specific material in the field and to provide some experience and familiarity with it. Yet every such attempt is an encounter with statutes of numbing complexity and detail.

The above quotation from an environmental law scholar could easily have come from our survey data. It did not. It was written in 1989.[28] The challenges in teaching environmental law seem to have elements of universality through time. In the 2002 UKCLE Report, respondents identified the following as the four most significant challenges in teaching environmental law: (1) the rapid pace of change in law and policy; (2) the selection of appropriate course content; (3) the interdisciplinary dimension to the subject;[29] and (4) the polycentric nature of the subject.[30] Our survey respondents raised similar issues: the 'quintessentially interdisciplinary' [R49] nature of environmental law; 'understanding the science behind the law' [R3]; and 'introducing students to the complexity of environmental problems' [R7]. The pace of environmental law was a common challenge: 'it changes so quickly, requires constant updates' [R12]; 'impossible to keep up with all areas within the field anymore' [R17]. Although, again, comments on pace have been made of environmental law since the 1980s,[31] and so there are elements of continuity and change at play.

---

[26]   Elizabeth Fisher, 'Environmental Law as "hot" law' (2013) 25 *JEL* 347.

[27]   Ibid.

[28]   S Joseph Sax, 'Environmental Law in the Law Schools: What We Teach and How We Feel About It' (1989) 19 *Envtl L Rep* 10251. See also: Joel Mintz, 'Teaching Environmental Law: Some Observations on Curriculum and Materials' (1983) 33 *J Legal Educ* 94, 96.

[29]   This, admittedly, has been recognised since at least 1981 as a challenge. See: Guillermo Cano, 'Education in Environmental Law' (1981) 1 *The Environmentalist* 259.

[30]   UKCLE Report, 36.

[31]   Mintz (n 28), 94.

However, not everyone agreed that the challenges in teaching environmental law were any different to teaching in other areas of law. A minority pushed back as to any distinctiveness: 'Although there are always arguments put forward about coherence, complexity and definition, it really is no different to any other subject' [R16]. Such comments, and those that follow, made us reflect on the extent to which the scholarship exploring the nature and boundaries of environmental law is possibly over-egging the pudding.[32]

> Where does the subject begin and end? Different course tutors prioritise different issues, but both these challenges are found elsewhere too [R19].

> I don't buy the argument that environmental law is necessarily any more challenging than e.g., tort, contract. And even 'sleepy subjects' (if I may use that term) like constitutional and public law are presently undergoing dramatic changes [R43].

Almost everyone who completed our survey commented, at some point, about the need to balance breadth of coverage with depth of analysis when teaching environmental law. Once again, little has changed since the UKCLE Report. In both our work and the UKCLE work from 2002, many teachers of environmental law talked about reducing the number of topics they covered to include more depth.[33] This is worth thinking about. Is there an irreducible core to environmental law which students must cover and without which one cannot properly be said to have studied environmental law? The table of contents of the main environmental law textbooks would seem to indicate common areas of interest, but do these speak to a 'core'? Our data would suggest not, given how many academics regularly change their syllabi and how many have reduced the number of topics studied over time. As one respondent put it: 'As I have gotten older, I have realized that I can do what I like (within limits) and that there doesn't have to be a neat intellectual coherency to what the students study with me in environmental law' [R33].

In terms of the detail of the content covered, only 16 of the 47 universities offering UG environmental law put some form of topic list or detailed module overview onto their webpages. Analysis of these lists showed a wide approach to content, with common overlaps including climate change, regulation/governance, pollution control, international issues, and enforcement. However, given the small sample size, we would be wary of taking much from this grouping save that most of our survey respondents also indicated that climate change had taken on a great prominence in their teaching over time. A smaller number of our survey respondents commented (in addition to the increase in

---

[32]   On which, see Elen Stokes, 'Review of Eloise Scotford, Environmental Principles and the Evolution of Environmental Law, Oxford: Hart, 2017' (2018) 81 *MLR* 920.

[33]   UKCLE Report, 45.

focus on climate change) on the rise of 'human rights and rights for nature' [R8] in recent years.[34] What also seemed common was a move from teaching UK environmental law ('definitely less purely national law' [R37]) to teaching environmental regulation at other scales and in other places. We were struck by how few respondents mentioned planning law as part of what they teach, given planning law teaching was the origin of many of the early environmental law courses.[35]

5. FINAL THOUGHTS

Let us end with some reflections on our data. There are two points that we have nibbled at the edges in our discussions but not explicitly addressed. The first is what the popularity of a discipline in teaching terms otherwise means for the health of that discipline. And the second is what our data and our responses to that data might require of environmental law educators. On the first, environmental law is rather marginal in a number of ways, depending on how one slices and dices marginality.[36] For example, we know that when UK practising lawyers are asked directly to list the subjects they think are most important to practice, environmental law does not feature at all.[37] Data from The Law Society shows that just 1.9 per cent of solicitors put environmental law as their primary area of specialism.[38] We also know that only 2.1 per cent of submissions to REF2014 (the UK's government-led assessment of research quality in universities) were for environmental law: by contrast, 11.6 per cent were for company or commercial law; 9.7 per cent for legal theory; and 7.7 per cent for international law.[39] And our own data shows a decline in provision of environmental law teaching and static student numbers. Whether we like it or not, size can matter and there may be radiating effects of environmental law being taught in fewer places with fewer students. Popularity might impact on health. One effect might be that fewer people in turn specialise in environmental law, either as academics or as lawyers. Another might be

---

[34] See: John Knox, 'Report of the Special Rapporteur on the Issue of Human Rights Obligations Relating to the Enjoyment of a Safe, Clean, Healthy and Sustainable Environment' (United Nations 2017).

[35] UKCLE Report, 7 and 26.

[36] On this, see: Fisher and others (n 2), 221–223.

[37] LETR, 'Setting Standards: The Future of Legal Services Education and Training Regulation in England and Wales' (LETR Final Report 2013), 34.

[38] The Law Society, 'Categories of Work Undertaken by Solicitors' (January 2017), 2.

[39] Mark Davies, 'Changes to the Training of English and Welsh Lawyers: Implications for the Future of University Law Schools' (2018) 52 *The Law Teacher* 100, 115.

that universities make hiring, firing, and promotion decisions based on what they perceive to be the 'value for money' from environmental law education provision. Here, increasing emphasis in the UK on government assessments of 'research quality' might also be crowding out time and energy on teaching in favour of time and energy on scholarly outputs. The number of environmental law scholars and the provision of environmental law teaching on their own are not determinative of the health of the discipline, but our data contained some elements of existential angst. We seem to be at a place where environmental law educators and scholars are asking: do we matter?; where will our voices be heard and by whom?

We want to end by asking what the data we have set out requires of us as environmental lawyers (students and scholars). If we see legal education as a vehicle for regulatory and social change,[40] and if we accept the multiple harms from our use of environment, then should we in the environmental law community be doing more to market environmental law as a subject of universal importance and worthy of study? This may seem like a special pleading for environmental law. And, in a way, it is. We are not, to be clear, saying that environmental law is more or less 'important' than other legal subjects. But we are asking what it might say about audiences for expertise, and about commitment to public service,[41] if environmental law scholars primarily research environmental law but mostly (or only) teach subjects that are not environmental law (as our data showed in some instances). As Elen Stokes has observed, the teaching of environmental law is one of the 'more mundane ways in which the discipline gets made'.[42] We may be disciplining the discipline if we have been in any way complicit in the decline in provision of environmental law teaching and static student numbers, or if we do not act in response to the data we have set out.

---

[40]   Stanley Fish (and others) might disagree. See: Stanley Fish, *Save the World on Your Own Time* (OUP 2012).

[41]   Maria Lee, 'Public Service, Environmental Law Academics and Brexit' 2010 https://ssrn.com/abstract=3267300 accessed 2 April 2021.

[42]   Elen Stokes, 'Normal Chaos of Environmental Law' (Reimagining Environmental Law Conference Paper, University of Birmingham, January 2019).

17. Never mind the platform, here's the pedagogy: e-learning in environmental law

Amanda Kennedy and Amy Cosby

INTRODUCTION

Over the last two decades, the combination of technological advances and shifting student priorities and demands has led to significant changes in the delivery of higher education.[1] Students can now access learning material around the clock through virtual learning environments,[2] and there are a growing number of entire degree offerings that can be completed online at universities across the globe.[3] In the authors' home country alone (Australia), off-campus enrolments are increasing at a higher rate than on-campus enrolments, with one-in-five students now studying online.[4] It is fair to say that online learning, or 'e-learning', is 'now in the mainstream'.[5]

While legal education is no exception to this trend, the uptake of e-learning in law has lagged behind other disciplines and is arguably still in its 'infancy'.[6]

---

[1]   Crawford, R., and Jenkins, L. (2017). Blended learning and team teaching: Adapting pedagogy in response to the changing digital tertiary environment. *Australasian Journal of Educational Technology* 33(2).

[2]   Steventon, B., Panesar, S., and Wood, J. (2014). Moving the law school into the twenty-first century–embedding technology into teaching and learning. *Journal of Further and Higher Education* 38(1), 107–28.

[3]   Eom, S. B., Wen, H. J., and Ashill, N. (2006). The determinants of students' perceived learning outcomes and satisfaction in university online education: An empirical investigation. *Decision Sciences Journal of Innovative Education* 4(2), 215–35.

[4]   Norton, A., Cherastidtham, I., and Mackey, W. (2018). Mapping Australian higher education 2018. Grattan Institute.

[5]   Huffman, M. (2015). Online learning grows up-and heads to law school. *Indiana Law Review*, 49, 57.

[6]   Schwartz, M. (2020). Towards modality-less model for excellence in law school teaching. *Syracuse Law Review* (70)1, 115–42, 116. See also Kohn, N. A. (2020). Online Learning and the Future of Legal Education: Symposium Introduction. *Syracuse*

In some cases, this has been due to particular barriers, from technological limitations (e.g., lack of an institutional learning management system, or slow bandwidth), to law school accreditation requirements imposed by legal profession admission bodies which may limit or even prohibit online learning within the qualifying degree.[7] Some have argued, however, that the e-learning lag in law is due to resistance from the legal academy itself: law schools are seen generally as 'conservative'[8] and 'wedded to a Langdellian view' of pedagogy,[9] preferring casebook and Socratic methods which are perceived as less suitable for online delivery.

Nonetheless, there is growing evidence of e-learning adoption and innovation in law schools, ranging from blended or hybrid approaches which combine online and face-to-face formats, to wholly online subjects as well as entire degree programs. This steady increase in e-learning in law is being driven by a number of stakeholders: firstly, students, who require flexibility to balance study with family and work responsibilities; second, industry and professional bodies, who seek law graduates with technological skills; and finally, universities, who are under pressure to develop 'work-ready' graduates for a digital world, and who anticipate cost savings to flow from teaching at a larger scale than permissible in face-to-face mode.[10] Importantly, stakeholders across each of these groups also see the potential for e-learning in law to enhance student learning experiences, through new opportunities for engagement and content interaction.[11]

For law schools not already embracing some form of e-learning, the COVID-19 pandemic in early 2020 forced an abrupt transition to online teaching the world over, in order to ensure continuity of study for students during this unprecedented crisis. The post-COVID-19 pivot to online teaching

---

Law Review (70)1, 1–12; Swift, K. R. (2018) The seven principles for good practice in [asynchronous online] legal education, *Mitchell Hamline Law Review* (44)1, Article 4; Steventon et al, above n 2; Colbran, S., and Gilding, A. (2013). E-learning in Australian law schools. *Legal Education Review* (23)201.

[7] Kohn, above n 6, 3; Dutton, Y. M., Ryznar, M., and Long, K. (2018). Assessing online learning in law schools: Students say online classes deliver. *Denver Law Review* (96)493, 498–502; Lipton, J. D. (2020). Distance legal education: lessons from the virtual classroom, *IDEA* (60)71.

[8] Spisto, M., and Lee, C. (2018). Virtual online teaching in transport law. *Victoria University Law and Justice Journal* (8)35.

[9] Huffman, above n 5.

[10] Corbin, L., and Bugden, L. (2018). Online teaching: The importance of pedagogy, place and presence in legal education. *Legal Education Review*, 28; Kohn, above n 6; Spisto and Lee, above n 8; Bennett, S. C. (2014). Distance learning in law. *Seton Hall Legislative Journal* (38)1.

[11] Dutton, Ryznar and Long, above n 7; Kohn, above n 6; Swift, above n 6.

has seen e-learning quickly become the norm at many law schools, though somewhat predictably, the necessary haste with which online teaching was implemented resulted in mixed reviews from law students (as to the quality and effectiveness of teaching),[12] and faculty (in terms of workload and technological challenges)[13] alike. While this feedback has fuelled ongoing debates about whether online or face-to-face learning is more effective in law, we would argue that simply replicating classroom content electronically is not an exemplar of effective online pedagogy.[14] As O'Neil succinctly puts it, online instruction is more than simply 'slapping classroom content online'.[15] While commendable, what was generally evident in the wake of COVID-19 could best be described as 'emergency online pedagogy' or 'emergency remote

---

[12] International Association of Law Schools, *Transitioning to online legal education: The Student Voice,* July 2020 (copy on file with the authors); Dutton, Y., and Mohapatra, S. (2020). COVID-19 and law teaching: guidance on developing an asynchronous online course for law students. *St. Louis University Law Journal* (forthcoming).

[13] Crawford, B. J, and Simon, M. S. (2020). Law faculty experiences teaching during the pandemic, *St. Louis University Law Journal* (forthcoming); Dutton and Mohapatra, ibid.

[14] Dutton and Mohapatra, ibid.; Kohn, above n 6; Schwartz, above n 6; Corbin and Bugden, above n 10; see also Smith, C. T. (2002). Technology and legal education: negotiating the shoals of technocentrism, technophobia, and indifference. *Journal of the Association of Legal Writing Directors* 1, 247. Kohn (above n 6, 2) notes that the 'literature on the impact of online education in law schools is limited', while Colbran and Gilding (above n 6, 233) have similarly argued, at least in the Australian law school context, that 'e-learning practice is generally simplistic and lacking a systemic strategy of scholarship and development of teaching practices designed to move the entire law discipline forward'. However, there are many examples of the pedagogical benefits of e-learning in law to be found in the literature. A detailed summary of approaches may be found in Dutton and Mohapatra, above n 12 and Corbin and Bugden (above n 10.), but see also Lipton, above n 7; Bennett, above n 10; Sutton, V. (2020). Asynchronous, e-learning in legal education: a comparative study with the traditional classroom. *Syracuse Law Review* 70, 143; Wall Sweany, N. (2020). From theory to practice: evidence-based strategies for designing & developing engaging online courses. *Syracuse Law Review* 70, 167; Colombo, R. J. (2020). Teaching a synchronous online business organizations course to jd students: a case study. *Hofstra Law Review,* forthcoming; Hess, G. F. (2013). Blended courses in law school: The best of online and face-to-face learning. *McGeorge Law Review* 45, 51; Beck, R. J. (2010). Teaching international law as a partially online course: The hybrid/blended approach to pedagogy. *International Studies Perspectives* 11(3), 273–90; Podgor, E. S. (2006). Teaching a live synchronous distance learning course: a student focused approach. *University of Illinois Journal of Law, Technology and Policy* 263.

[15] O'Neil, C. A. (2014). Introduction to teaching and learning in online environments. In O'Neil, C. A., Fisher, C. A., and Rietschel, M. J. (2013). *Developing online learning environments in nursing education.* Springer Publishing Company. 1–13.

teaching'[16] – implemented abruptly, involuntarily, and with variable access to appropriate technological infrastructure, staff training and support.[17]

Whether adopted out of choice or necessity, e-learning will undoubtedly be a feature of the future law school landscape. This requires law teachers – including environmental law teachers – to think quite deliberately about what it means to teach online. In this chapter, we explore e-learning as a specific approach to teaching and learning that may prove useful for environmental law – but the modality, we argue, is secondary to good instructional design. As alluded to in our chapter title, our discussion focuses less on e-learning as a platform, and more on its 'pedagogical soundness'.[18]

In our own teaching of environmental and natural resources law, we have both enjoyed positive experiences with e-learning, and we have found, like others, that 'no sacrifice in educational quality necessarily accompanies online legal education'.[19] Our aim in this chapter however is not to suggest that e-learning is preferable to face-to-face instruction. We hope to demonstrate that, with careful planning and selection based on learning theory and desired learning outcomes, online learning can be used to deliver a pedagogically-robust environmental law course. We begin this chapter by briefly canvassing the tools and benefits of e-learning, before focusing in detail on its pedagogical value. We then discuss some of the challenges and constraints experienced with e-learning, and offer some commentary as to how these might be traversed. Ultimately, we contend that by viewing e-learning as a distinct pedagogy, rather than just a set of technological tools to replicate face-to-face teaching practice, environmental law lecturers can draw upon an effective educational approach grounded in social collaboration, active learning and authentic assessment.

E-LEARNING AND ITS BENEFITS

E-learning – the 'use of internet technologies for the delivery of content and … the construction of learning communities using both asynchronous and, to a lesser extent, synchronous, communication and collaboration technologies'[20]

---

[16] Fisher, W. (2020), 'Emergency online pedagogy', online at: http://182.fab.mwp.accessdomain.com/emergency-online-pedagogy/ accessed 14 August 2020; Dutton and Mohapatra, above n 12.

[17] See International Association of Law Schools, above n 12; Dutton and Mohapatra, above n 12; Ryznar, M. (2020). Common mistakes in online teaching (24 June, 2020). Available at: https://ssrn.com/abstract=3634399.

[18] Colombo, above n 14, 4.

[19] Ibid., 1.

[20] Colbran and Gilding, above n 6, 202.

– is used to varying degrees in law schools across the globe. It is implemented to support face-to-face teaching, as well as to teach complete subjects (and even entire courses) online. It is the latter instance with which we are predominantly concerned in this chapter, and we include both asynchronous (delayed) and synchronous (simultaneous, real-time) interactions in our discussion.

A variety of tools and systems now exist which may be used to facilitate online teaching and learning. A learning management system (LMS), such as Blackboard, Canvas or Moodle, may be used to deliver teaching materials, including course outlines and learning resources, and may integrate other features such as asynchronous discussion forums, online assessment and electronic assignment submission.[21] Lecture capture systems may also be housed within the LMS, allowing for lecture content to be recorded (either during a live lecture or at the academic's desktop), edited and stored for student access. Synchronous interaction tools, such as Zoom, Microsoft Teams, Blackboard Collaborate and Adobe Connect, may be utilised to facilitate live instruction, which enable a typical lecture or tutorial format to be delivered online (possibly accompanied by the simultaneous screen sharing of slides or other visual aids). Other tools usually housed within an LMS include email and messaging; document sharing services; audio-visual material, both developed by the lecturer or obtained from open access sources (e.g., YouTube); and digital marking tools (such as Turnitin and Grademark), which provide a variety of methods for academics to provide feedback to students on their submitted work, as well as prevent and detect plagiarism.[22]

Some e-learning tools enable the academic to go beyond simply digitising traditional face-to-face content, facilitating a 'systematic redesign'[23] of traditional teaching approaches. At the most basic level, presentation platforms (such as Microsoft Sway, and other tools inbuilt within an LMS such as Moodle's 'Book' function) enable the sequenced combination of text and rich media (e.g., videos, images and documents) to modularise content. Digital collaboration tools allow groups to brainstorm and visually organise information and concepts in real-time.[24] Interactive quizzes and 'gamification' tools provide another form of feedback, using game mechanics to engage with learners,[25] while adaptive learning tools (such as Smart Sparrow) allow distinct

---

[21]   Ibid., 206.

[22]   Ibid; Corbin and Bugden, above n 10.

[23]   Colbran and Gilding, above n 6, 206.

[24]   See, e.g., Popplet (https://popplet.com); Miro (https://miro.com); MindMeister (https://www.mindmeister.com); and Padlet (http://padlet.com).

[25]   Ferguson, D. M. (2016). The gamification of legal education: why games transcend the Langdellian model and how they can revolutionize law school. *Chapman Law Review* 19, 629; Bouki, V., Economou, D., and Kathrani, P. (2014). 'Gamification' and

pathways to be built into course design to personalise learning experiences according to individual student capabilities.[26] Finally, role-play simulation game software, such as SecondLife, enable the creation of immersive online learning environments,[27] and even virtual field trips.[28]

Distinct from its pedagogical value (which will be discussed in the following section), e-learning offers a number of advantages for legal education. Most obviously, for students who are managing work and family responsibilities alongside study, online learning can increase flexibility and convenience, allowing the learner to access study materials at a time that suits them.[29] E-learning also exposes students to digital technologies, assisting them to develop hands-on online communication and collaborative skills that are increasingly vital as employers turn to remote working and virtual offices.[30] Some argue that the use of learning technologies also offers an economic benefit to universities, allowing more learners to be accommodated with fewer labour and infrastructure overheads,[31] and potentially reducing the cost of a legal education for the student.[32] However, whether significant savings are realised in practice will vary, depending on the need to engage technological and other support.[33]

Another advantage of online learning is its ability to improve access to legal education, acting as an 'agent of social change'[34] by increasing diversity among

---

legal education: A game based application for teaching university law students. In *2014 International Conference on Interactive Mobile Communication Technologies and Learning (IMCL2014)* (pp. 213–16). e.g., Law Dojo (http://www.lawschooldojo.com/); Kahoot (https://kahoot.com/schools-u/); and Socrative (https://www.socrative.com).

[26]   Isaias, P., and Lima, S. (2018). Collaborative design of case studies applying an adaptive digital learning tool. In *EdMedia+ Innovate Learning* (pp. 1473–82). Association for the Advancement of Computing in Education (AACE).

[27]   Butler, D. (2018). Utilising second life machinima-facilitated narratives to support cognitive and imaginative engagement across an undergraduate curriculum. In *Authentic Virtual World Education* (pp 153–73). Springer, Singapore; Butler, D. (2012). Second Life machinima enhancing the learning of law: Lessons from successful endeavours. *Australasian Journal of Educational Technology* 28, 3.

[28]   Mathews, S., Andrews, L., and Luck, E. (2012). Developing a Second Life virtual field trip for university students: An action research approach. *Educational Research* 54, 1, 17–38.

[29]   Bennett above n 10; Colombo, above n 14; Corbin and Bugden, above n 10.

[30]   Colombo, above n 14; Corbin and Bugden, above n 10.

[31]   Corbin and Bugden, above n 10; Lohmann, S. (2005). The economic imperative for teaching with technology. *Issues in Science and Technology* 22(1), 51.

[32]   Colombo, above n 14.

[33]   Janus, E. S. (2020). The 'worst idea ever!' lessons from one law school's pioneering embrace of online learning methods. *Syracuse Law Review* 70, 1, 13–48.

[34]   Perlin, M. L. (2011). Online, distance legal education as an agent of social change. *Pacific McGeorge Global Business and Development Law Journal* 24, 95.

law graduates. For example, e-learning may be used to provide alternative accessible learning materials to students with disabilities, as well as removing the obstacle of needing to be physically present on campus.[35] This may also be of benefit to students residing in rural and remote locations, who may not otherwise be able to access higher education opportunities, or who may have to relocate at significant cost and inconvenience in order to do so.[36] Remote access has been a distinct advantage of online learning approaches following the COVID-19 pandemic, where physical campus access has been restricted for many law students at institutions around the globe. Online learning may also be used to ease the transition to study for non-traditional or academically underprepared students, providing a platform to disseminate further resources and complementary academic support programs.[37] It can also encourage students 'whose shyness and averseness to the potential humiliation inherent (or perceived to be inherent) in classroom exchanges (both with faculty and other students) leads them to be "back-benchers"'[38] to become more active, emboldened by relative anonymity in the online realm.

Finally, and of particular relevance to environmental law teachers, is the ability to 'walk the talk' of sustainability through online learning. Face-to-face teaching and learning activities consume energy, from the production of hard copy printed educational materials (e.g., textbooks, printed papers), to the use of physical campus facilities (lighting, heating and cooling of large buildings), as well as travel to and from campus. While many universities are consciously undertaking efforts to reduce their on-campus greenhouse gas emissions (e.g., greening campus buildings via the installation of more energy efficient equipment, or renewable energy technologies), online teaching can further contribute to sustainability efforts by cutting down the need for travel, printed materials and the use of on-campus facilities.[39] One study by The Open University (UK) has estimated that the production and provision of e-learning consumes an average of 90 per cent less energy, producing 85 per cent fewer

---

[35]   Ibid.; see also Colombo, above n 14.
[36]   McGrath, J., and Morriss, A. P. (2020). Online legal education and access to legal education and the legal system. *Syracuse Law Review* 70(1), 49–72; Kohn, above n 6.
[37]   Landrum, S. D. (2015). Drawing inspiration from the flipped classroom model: An integrated approach to academic support for the academically underprepared law student. *Duquense Law Review* 53, 245.
[38]   Perlin, M. L. (2006). Ain't no goin' back: teaching mental disability law courses online. *New York Law School Law Review* 51, 991, 995.
[39]   Spisto and Lee, above n 8; Huffman, above n 5.

CO2 emissions per student, when compared with conventional face-to-face learning.[40]

ONLINE LEARNING PEDAGOGY

Having briefly considered the nature and benefits of e-learning in law, we turn now to explore online learning from a pedagogical perspective. Pedagogy refers not only to the methods and techniques of teaching, but also to the theories of learning which underpin them. However, when it comes to instructional design in law, pedagogical practice is all-too-frequently driven by a 'rose-colored image of what happens when students and their professors are in the same rooms'.[41] Legal academics tend towards uncritical replication of their own learning experiences, preferring lengthy lectures and other didactic methods,[42] despite being 'largely of unknown efficacy'.[43] The Socratic method in particular is viewed as superior to other forms of instruction in law, and considered unable to be replicated via online delivery.[44] However, as Janus observes: '…the advantages of live education are assumed, not proved. And there is good reason to be skeptical, in the absence of proof, that the assumed advantages are actually a characteristic of the Socratic Method, or of face-to-face teaching more generally'.[45]

---

[40] Of course, there is scope for variability here, depending on when individual students access learning (e.g., is additional heating or lighting utilised in the home for night-time study), and whether students choose to print materials. See Roy, R., Potter, S., Yarrow, K., and Smith, M. (2005). Towards sustainable higher education: Environmental impacts of campus-based and distance higher education systems. Final Report: Factor 10 Visions Project Higher Education Centre, The Open University (UK). Available online at: http://www3.open.ac.uk/events/3/2005331_47403_o1.pdf, accessed 10 August 2020.

[41] Schwartz, above n 6, 116.

[42] Keyes, M., and Johnstone, R. (2004). Changing legal education: Rhetoric, reality, and prospects for the future. *Sydney Law Review* 26(4), 537–64; Matthew, A. F., and Butler, D. (2017). Narrative, machinima and cognitive realism: Constructing an authentic real-world learning experience for law students. *Australasian Journal of Educational Technology* 33, 1.

[43] Janus, above n 33, 30; see also Chemerinsky, E. (2008). Rethinking legal education. *Harvard Civil Rights-Civil Liberties Law Review* 43, 595; Sullivan, W. M., Colby, A., Wegner, J. W., Bond, L., and Shulman, L. S. (2007). *Educating lawyers: Preparation for the profession of law* (Vol. 2). John Wiley & Sons.

[44] Lipton, above n 7.

[45] Janus, above n 33, 26.

Ideally, learning theory should first guide the decision of what teaching methods and tools are to be employed in a given subject.[46] Teaching methods – whether face-to-face activities or e-learning tools – should not define pedagogical practice; rather, they should be seen as a mechanism to implement 'the best pedagogy for that course or topic'.[47]

There are three predominant theories of learning – behaviourism, cognitivism and constructivism – which describe how learners acquire knowledge.[48] These theories exist on somewhat of a continuum which moves from passive to active learning, and from teaching to facilitation.[49] One approach is not necessarily better than any other – their appropriateness depends on the desired learning objectives, with behaviourist and cognitivist approaches helpful for learning foundational concepts, and constructivist approaches more suited to comprehending advanced subject matter.[50]

Behaviourism sees knowledge acquired from low-level stimulus-response tasks, generally in a passive manner reinforced by the teacher.[51] The focus is on remembering key points through repetition and reinforcement, and the role of the educator is to devise a teaching approach to strengthen the stimulus-response connection.[52] Behaviourist approaches are ideal for teaching foundational concepts, which in law might include identifying and finding legislation.[53] Alternatively, cognitivism views knowledge as more actively constructed by learners as they are required to process what they know, with the teacher acting more as a facilitator guiding student discovery.[54] Specifically, this theory holds that learning is not simply due to external stimuli, but also developed through the learner's mental processes of thinking, observing and problem solving. Learners become more active participants in the learning process, drawing on their prior knowledge and linking this to new information. The role of the educator under cognitivism is to help students strengthen these

---

[46]   Corbin and Bugden, above n 10; Wall Sweany, above n 14; Ertmer, P. A., and Newby, T. J. (2013). Behaviorism, cognitivism, constructivism: comparing critical features from an instructional design perspective. *Performance Improvement Quarterly* 26(2), 43.

[47]   Lynch, M. M., and Roecker, J. (2007). *Project managing e-learning: A handbook for successful design, delivery and management.* Routledge. 6.

[48]   Corbin and Bugden, above n 10; Wall Sweany, above n 14; Ertmer and Newby, above n 46.

[49]   Ertmer and Newby, above n 46.

[50]   Corbin and Bugden, above n 10; Wall Sweany, above n 14.

[51]   Ertmer and Newby, above n 46, 55.

[52]   Wall Sweany, above n 14.

[53]   Corbin and Bugden, above n 10.

[54]   Ertmer and Newby, above n 46, 58.

structural and evaluative connections.[55] In law, cognitivist approaches might be applicable where students need to process what they know, such as applying the law to a hypothetical fact scenario.[56] Finally, constructivism views knowledge as constructed through interactions within a knowledge community, where learners collaborate and co-develop knowledge through experience.[57] Knowledge is contextualised by the learner, who brings their own experiences and interpretation to make sense of information and propose a solution to a problem.[58] In law, constructivist approaches might include students analysing and devising new law reform solutions.[59]

There is abundant evidence of the ways in which e-learning approaches align with these theories of learning. The following sub-sections detail several examples of how online learning tools and technologies might be used to support environmental law teaching, in order to meet both lower- and higher-order learning requirements.

Behaviourist and Cognitivist E-Learning Approaches

For lower-order learning of foundational concepts (behaviourism and cognitivism), there are various e-learning approaches which can effectively transfer knowledge from teacher to student, as well as assess student comprehension and application of knowledge. The emphasis here is on effective knowledge transfer; while it is possible to record lengthy lectures via video as well as deliver these synchronously via videoconferencing platforms, these passive forms of teaching can lead to feelings of boredom and isolation in the online environment.[60] Current research suggests that student attention wanes after 15–20 minutes;[61] thus, lectures spanning multiple hours may be less effective due to competing distractions and the inability of students to manage cognitive load.[62]

---

[55]　Ibid., 60–61; Wall Sweany, above n 14.

[56]　Corbin and Bugden, above n 10.

[57]　Ertmer and Newby, above n 46, 65–6; Wall Sweany, above n 14.

[58]　Ibid.

[59]　Corbin and Bugden, above n 10.

[60]　Wall Sweany, above n 14.

[61]　Ibid., 10; Merritt, D. J. (2008). Legal education in the age of cognitive science and advanced classroom technology. *Boston University Journal of Science and Technology Law* 14, 39–72; Ryznar above n 17; see also Chapter 6 in this volume.

[62]　Cooper, A. Z., and Richards, J. B. (2017). Lectures for adult learners: breaking old habits in graduate medical education. *The American Journal of Medicine* 130(3), 376–81; Dutton, Ryznar and Long, above n 7. Schwartz, above n 6.

In the online learning environment, content does not need to be delivered according to the rigid logistics of campus timetabling requirements.[63] Learning management systems include design features which allow content to be scaffolded into 'short, manageable, readily attainable bursts'[64] for students to work through at their own pace. In our experience, such an approach is incredibly effective for navigating the complexity and interdisciplinarity which characterises environmental law. 'Chunking' of content respects student cognitive limitations and increases the chance that knowledge will be retained over the long term.[65] Student attention can also be effectively captured and maintained in the online learning environment through the ease of integration of multiple resources to suit different learning styles (e.g., visual, audial).[66] Studies suggest the use of video in particular has strong learning benefits, assisting students to 'increase their interest in a subject, stimulate critical thinking, enliven lectures and … stay focused'.[67] Videos enable students to work at their own pace, allowing them to 'pause and rewind the professor'[68] and control their own learning.[69] Shorter videos which combine footage of the teacher talking to the camera with slides or text / graphic tablets engage multiple mental channels, and have been rated as particularly effective by students.[70]

Most LMS platforms facilitate the streamlined display of text, diverse multimedia content (including pictures, audio and video content both from the lecturer as well as external sources e.g., YouTube, TED talks), and even

---

[63]   Janus, above n 33, 34.

[64]   Major, A., and Calandrino, T. (2018). Beyond chunking: microlearning secrets for effective online design. *Distance Learning* 15(2), 27–30, 28.

[65]   Dutton and Mohapatra, above n 12; Dutton, Ryznar and Long, above n 7; Major and Calandrino, ibid.

[66]   Ryznar above n 17.

[67]   Aravopoulou, E., Stone, M., and Weinzierl, L. (2017). Modernising the curriculum and pedagogy–to be or not to be? Using film and online video to engage students and enhance learning. *International Journal of Higher Education Management* 4(1), 1–18, 3; Kay, R. (2012). Exploring the use of video podcasts in education: A comprehensive review of the literature. *Computers in Human Behavior* 28(3), 820–31; Dutton, Ryznar and Long, above n 7.

[68]   Slomanson, W. R. (2014). Blended learning: A flipped classroom experiment. *Journal of Legal Education* 64, 93, 97.

[69]   Fyfield, M., Henderson, M., Heinrich, E., and Redmond, P. (2019). Videos in higher education: Making the most of a good thing. *Australasian Journal of Educational Technology* 35(5), 1–7.

[70]   Noetel, M., Griffith, S., Delaney, O., Sanders, T., Parker, P., del Pozo Cruz, B., and Lonsdale, C. (2020). Video improves learning in higher education: A systematic review. https://doi.org/10.31234/osf.io/kynez; Meseguer-Martinez, A., Ros-Galvez, A., and Rosa-Garcia, A. (2017). Satisfaction with online teaching videos: A quantitative approach. *Innovations in Education and Teaching International* 54(1), 62–7.

animation.[71] While the use of multimedia in teaching is not limited to the online realm, it is certainly easy to curate and integrate relevant resources within an e-learning system, weaving shorter excerpts in with other content and resources using an LMS or digital presentation solution.[72] There is an abundance of freely-available (and rapidly growing) online multimedia relevant to environmental issues and problems in general, and environmental law specifically, which can be incorporated within content modules.[73]

Online learning also offers a range of assessment mechanisms to determine student understanding and provide formative feedback to reinforce learning consistent with behaviourist and cognitivist paradigms. Inbuilt learning analytics within an LMS can provide insight into student progress, and track student completion of content. Tools such as electronic voting and 'pop quizzes' can be integrated within lesson modules to test student comprehension and provide instant feedback.[74] Such tools can even be utilised to pose Socratic-style questions, either asynchronously or during live sessions.[75] Lengthier multiple choice quizzes enable automatic assessment and feedback, and have been 'tried and tested' in learning law as a means of motivating student engagement with content and checking progress.[76] In environmental law, multiple choice quizzes may prove particularly helpful where there is a need to comprehend and master statutes and other rules.[77] Again, while multiple choice testing is not limited to online teaching, LMS platforms provide 'many interesting facilities for the design and use of multiple-choice questions with a wide range of options relating to release of answers and effective feedback'.[78]

---

[71] Adobe Captivate, Articulate Storyline and Powtoon are examples of tools which may be used to create animation for use in online teaching: Corbin and Bugden, above n 10, 8.

[72] We have used Moodle 'Books' and Microsoft 'Sway' which are platforms to collate text content with multimedia resources (including short video lectures from the teaching staff, as well as externally-sourced video and audio content) in a sequential manner that students can work through self-paced.

[73] Kleinhenz, P. N., and Parker, M. S. (2017). Video as a tool to increase understanding and support for the Endangered Species Act. *Applied Environmental Education and Communication* 16(1), 41–55.

[74] Seah, D. (2020). Using Kahoot in law school: differentiated instruction for working adults with diverse learning abilities. *International Journal of Mobile Learning and Organisation* 14(1), 36–48; Schacter, D. L., and Szpunar, K. K. (2015). Enhancing attention and memory during video-recorded lectures. *Scholarship of Teaching and Learning in Psychology* 1(1), 60.

[75] Schwartz, above n 6.

[76] Steventon et al, above n 2, 109; Dutton, Ryznar and Long, above n 7.

[77] Lipton, above n 7.

[78] Steventon et al, above n 2, 109; McGrath and Morriss, above n 36.

Online discussion forums may be used to capture lengthier responses to test more complex cognition, and can incorporate peer and self-review (moderated by the lecturer).[79] As Huffman notes, discussion boards 'permit fuller and broader student participation, create artifacts for student review and instructor evaluation, and allow for more careful instructor assessment of student performance'.[80] Feedback can be provided through direct comments, rubrics and even short oral / video feedback, the latter of which is highly rated by students as effective for learning.[81] For a more structured approach to assessment and feedback, adaptive learning tools can be built into the online lesson interface, acting as a further form of feedback for students. These mechanisms prove particularly useful as the required level of knowledge acquisition advances; as students access content, they may be required to make decisions regarding (for example) a legal fact scenario. Incorrect answers might serve to pause student progress through the lesson, requiring them to undertake further review before moving forward.[82]

Constructivist E-Learning Approaches

Moving to the deeper learning associated with higher level knowledge acquisition, online learning can also foster the reflection, collaboration and connection that is characteristic of the constructionist paradigm. As the role of the lecturer moves beyond teaching towards facilitation, instruction focuses on 'how to construct meaning, as well as how to effectively monitor, evaluate, and update those constructions; and to align and design experiences for the learner so that authentic, relevant contexts can be experienced'.[83] Synchronous video lessons may be a useful e-learning approach where real-time interaction is required to assist students in navigating, evaluating and synthesising knowledge. These may be supported either synchronously or asynchronously with other online activities, such as mind-mapping,[84] student-led content creation (such as e-portfolios, videos or animation) and live simulations to allow students to more actively process and apply knowledge.[85]

---

[79] McNamara, J., and Burton, K. (2009). Assessment of online discussion forums for law students. *Journal of University Teaching and Learning Practice* 6, 2, 6; Corbin and Bugden, above n 10; Dutton and Mohapatra, above n 12; Dutton, Ryznar and Long, above n 7.

[80] Huffman, above n 5, 82.

[81] Corbin and Bugden, above n 10, 7.

[82] Ibid., 10.

[83] Ertmer and Newby, above n 46, 59.

[84] See above n 24 for examples.

[85] Corbin and Bugden, above n 10; Dutton and Mohapatra, above n 12; Butler (2018) and Butler (2012), above n 27; Matthew and Butler, above n 42.

Authentic assessment is increasingly recognised as critical to developing higher order cognition and skills, such as problem solving and critical analysis.[86] One of the distinct pedagogical advantages of online instruction is the ability to create authentic situated learning opportunities at scale.[87] As Lipton explains:

> In many parts of the curriculum that mimic actual legal practice, technology can be a useful tool … because it mimics what many of our students will be doing in the real world as attorneys. For example, attorneys often work remotely on documents with other attorneys when they're drafting and redrafting in the transactional context and maybe in the course of settlement negotiations, drafting documents to put the terms on *digital* paper. Thus, using technology to learn how to share and mark-up documents in these contexts can be very useful.[88]

'Practice ready' assignments, such as videoed oral arguments in response to a hypothetical scenario, electronic filing of documents, synchronous role play negotiation or dispute resolution activities, or a policy submission, provide opportunities for students to practise advocacy and research skills with the added benefit of building the digital competencies they will rely on in the future.[89] These approaches to assessment are all easily administered via an LMS.

The online learning environment can also be used to cultivate a 'community of practice'[90] or 'community of inquiry', where: '…students listen to one another with respect, build on one another's ideas, challenge one another to supply reasons for otherwise unsupported opinions, assist each other in drawing inferences from what has been said, and seek to identify one another's assumptions'.[91]

---

[86]   See Warnock et al, Chapter 8 in this volume, for further discussion of authentic assessment in environmental law.

[87]   Matthew and Butler, above n 42; Herrington, J., Oliver, R., and Herrington, A. (2007). Authentic learning on the web: Guidelines for course design. In Khan, B. (ed.), *Flexible learning in an information society* (pp. 26–7). Hershey, PA: Information Science Publishing.

[88]   Lipton above n 7, 80.

[89]   Nolon, S. F. (2013). Using distance learning to teach environmental problem solving skills and theory. *Journal of Environmental Law and Litigation* 28, 211; Dutton and Mohapatra, above n 12.

[90]   Wenger-Trayner, E., and Wenger-Trayner, B. (2015). Communities of Practice: A Brief Introduction, [online] Available at: https://wenger-trayner.com/introduction-to -communities-of-practice/. A 'community of practice' is defined as: 'groups of people who share a concern or a passion for something they do and learn how to do it better as they interact regularly'.

[91]   Lipman, M. (2003). *Thinking in education*. Cambridge University Press, 20.

This is consistent with the constructivist approach to learning, which acknowledges the learner's social context as a source of knowledge.[92] Critical to establishing such a community however is presence – cognitive presence, social presence and teaching presence.[93] Cognitive presence refers to communication which facilitates the critical thinking from which students construct and confirm meaning; social presence is the extent to which participants identify with their community and develop interpersonal relationships, their ability to 'project themselves socially and emotionally as "real" people';[94] while teacher presence refers to the design and management of cognitive and social processes to realise learning outcomes.[95] Corbin and Bugden observe that 'deep learning happens when the three elements interact',[96] and there are various ways in which this can be achieved in the online learning environment.

Discussion forums,[97] digital collaboration and productivity tools,[98] social media platforms, individual and group blogs,[99] and video / graphic design tools[100] can foster both social and cognitive presence by cultivating 'a culture of knowledge and resource sharing'.[101] Each of these tools can be used to create active learning opportunities where students develop their own content to be shared via the LMS. Socially-mediated learning through reflection and discourse – even simply reading other student's posts – has been consistently found to boost learner engagement with content.[102] Because students are able

---

[92] Corbin and Bugden, above n 10, 12; Wall Sweany, above n 14.

[93] Ibid.; Garrison, D. R., Anderson, T., and Archer, W. (1999). Critical inquiry in a text-based environment: Computer conferencing in higher education. *The Internet and Higher Education* 2, 87, 87–105.

[94] Garrison, D. R., and Anderson, T. (2003). *E-learning in the 21st century: a framework for research and practice.* New York, Routledge, 28.

[95] Ibid.; Garrison, Anderson and Archer, above n 93.

[96] Corbin and Bugden, above n 10, 18.

[97] Xynas, L. (2011). Approaching legal education in the online teaching and e-learning environment: a case study-taxation law. *Journal of the Australasian Law Teachers Association* 4, 81–97; Wall Sweany, above n 14.

[98] For example, Slack (https://slack.com/intl/en-au/about); Yammer (https://www .microsoft.com/en-au/microsoft-365/yammer/yammer-overview); Discord (https:// discord.com); VoiceThread (https://voicethread.com).

[99] Canick, S. (2014). Infusing technology skills into the law school curriculum. *Capital University Law Review* 42, 663, 696; McNamara and Burton, above n 79; Corbin and Bugden, above n 10. See also Flipgrid (https://info.flipgrid.com).

[100] For example, Adobe Spark (https://spark.adobe.com/); Canva (https://canva .com).

[101] Keppell, M., Suddaby, G., and Hard, N. (2015). Assuring best practice in technology-enhanced learning environments. *Research in Learning Technology*, 23.

[102] Dixson, M. D. (2010). Creating effective student engagement in online courses: What do students find engaging? *Journal of the Scholarship of Teaching and Learning*, 1–13; Levy, Y. (2008). An empirical development of critical value factors (CVF) of

to 'carefully and deliberately choose what subject matter they wish to present', and have time to consider responses and seek clarification, asynchronous discussion forums can be particularly effective at increasing the quality of student engagement.[103] Encouraging students to post contemporary news reports on issues relating to course content, as well as share relevant personal information (a profile photograph, or even a video introduction incorporating family and pets), can foster interactions that will enable students to feel 'legitimated and supported by university learning communities'.[104] Linking discussion posts on content to assessment activities – especially those which require students to respond to the posts of other students – can further build student interaction and engagement.[105]

Carr notes however that the most effective method of increasing student engagement online is 'instructor visibility'[106] – in other words, teacher presence. Teacher presence in the online realm requires demonstrating that the 'instructor/facilitator "is there" or has a strong function in the learning process',[107] and a lack of physical presence need not be a barrier to this. Posting introductory discussion posts or videos, addressing students individually by name and learning about their backgrounds, regularly initiating and contributing to discussion threads and participation in synchronous sessions can humanise the lecturer and build teacher presence through 'direct and intimate' connections between instructors and students.[108] Oral feedback which 'talk[s] to the students in a personal way' and uses a tone of voice which conveys 'a sense of encouragement' can also be delivered through digital marking software to add a more personal touch.[109] The key to achieving teacher presence in e-learning is to use digital tools to communicate in ways that demonstrate

---

online learning activities: An application of activity theory and cognitive value theory. *Computers & Education* 51, 1664–75; Gayton, J., and McEwen, B. C. (2007). Effective online instructional and assessment strategies. *The American Journal of Distance Education* 21(3), 117–32.

[103] Xynas, above n 97, 86; see also Huffman, above n 5; McNamara and Burton, above n 79.

[104] Coates, H. (2007). A model of online and general campus-based student engagement. *Assessment and Evaluation in Higher Education* 32(2), 121–41; Dutton and Mohapatra, above n 12.

[105] Huffman, above n 5.

[106] Carr, M. (2014). The online university classroom: one perspective for effective student engagement and teaching in an online environment. *Journal of Effective Teaching* 14(1), 99–110, 107.

[107] Corbin and Bugden, above n 10, 18.

[108] Huffman, above n 5, 38; Xynas, above n 97; Hess, above n 14.

[109] Corbin and Bugden, above n 10, 20.

enthusiasm and interest in the subject content and student progress, and which creates an environment that is comfortable and non-intimidating for students.[110]

Developing a space 'where students will linger, re-examine and reconstruct their understandings by interacting, by talking or corresponding, with others'[111] is central to place-based pedagogy, which is especially pertinent for environmental law. Place-based pedagogy seeks to foreground students' lived experiences as context to their learning,[112] and is gaining traction in environmental law as scholars seek innovative and critical teaching methods to help reveal the operation of law in its wider social, political and economic context. Graham, for example, has recently argued that 'context-free pedagogy reproduces the abstractness of law and detaches it from material conditions';[113] while Van Wagner, in Chapter 4 of this volume, similarly observes that 'too often legal education filters out the broader material and social relations in which legal cases are embedded'.[114] Van Wagner discussed earlier in this book how place-based pedagogy in environmental law might be achieved in the face-to-face teaching setting, exposing law students to 'multiple intelligences'[115] and critical perspectives that are essential for meaningful reform; similarly, Bork and Burmeister have detailed how field-based courses can provide context and interdisciplinary perspectives on environmental law.[116] However, digital tools may also be harnessed to facilitate interdisciplinary and contextual learning about environmental law, particularly where travel to specific sites of legal contestation and relevance might not be possible. At a minimum, e-learning can connect students to a wide range of textual and rich multimedia resources from a variety of disciplines and non-Western knowledges;[117] while innovation in interactive online mapping tools, augmented and virtual reality

---

[110] Ibid.; Huffman, above n 5; Xynas, above n 97.

[111] Corbin and Bugden, above n 10, 16.

[112] Ibid.

[113] Graham, N. (2020). Learning sacrifice: legal education in the anthropocene. In Anker, K., Burdon, P., Garver, G., Maloney, M., and Sbert, C. (eds.), *From environmental to ecological law* (forthcoming), (pp. 429–39). Abingdon, UK: Routledge.

[114] Van Wagner, Ch 4, p. 61. See also Van Wagner, E. (2017). 'Seeing the place makes it real': place-based teaching in the environmental and planning law classroom. *Environment and Planning Law Journal* 34, 522.

[115] Jones, E. (2017). One size fits all? Multiple intelligences and legal education. *The Law Teacher* 51(1), 56–68.

[116] Bork, K., and Burmeister, K. (2018). Cases and places: a field-based approach to teaching natural resource and environmental law. *Journal of Legal Education* 68, 338.

[117] Berg, P. E. (2003). Using distance learning to enhance cross-listed interdisciplinary law school courses. *Rutgers Computer and Technology Law Journal* 29, 33.

technology demonstrates the potential to create immersive experiences for learning about the material and social contexts of environmental law.[118]

While a complete summary of the vast literature concerning online learning approaches is beyond the scope of this chapter, this brief assessment serves to illustrate that the tools and techniques of e-learning are grounded in learning theory. Prioritising pedagogy first in instructional design thus promotes the selection of tools that will best enhance the learning experience, catering to learning styles and needs regardless of whether there is physical proximity between the lecturer and students. For environmental law teaching, the intentional use of e-learning technologies may facilitate dynamic engagement with subject content, provide opportunities for authentic assessment and foster meaningful interaction among students and with staff in order to achieve particular learning outcomes.

CHALLENGES AND CONSTRAINTS

While there may be clear pedagogical justification for the use of e-learning approaches in environmental law, it would be naïve to suggest that online learning is without challenges and constraints. From our own experience teaching environmental law wholly online to both undergraduate and postgraduate cohorts, we offer some brief observations as to how these might be navigated.

First, while there may be a temptation to use synchronous e-learning activities to replicate 'in-person' learning, these should only be used where there is a clear pedagogical imperative for live instruction. For one, a requirement that all students and staff be online at the exact same time contradicts the flexibility that might have seen online instruction chosen in the first instance.[119] As Colombo notes, the need for such flexibility and convenience should not be underestimated; it 'goes beyond merely saving time, money, and energy, and extends to enabling a student to achieve key educational and life objectives'.[120] Additionally, where synchronous technologies are used to interact with large cohorts, class management can become cumbersome for the lecturer who may

---

[118] Mentzelopoulos, M., Parrish, J., Kathrani, P., and Economou, D. (2016). REVRLaw: an immersive way for teaching criminal law using virtual reality. In *International Conference on Immersive Learning* (pp. 73–84). Springer, Cham.; see also The University of Oklahoma College of Law's use of virtual reality machines to take students 'virtually' to significant sites such as oil rigs when learning about oil and gas law: https://books.apple.com/us/book/ou-law-a-leader-in-law-school-innovation/id1488544482.

[119] Dutton, Ryznar and Long, above n 7.

[120] Colombo, above n 14, 51.

have to 'multitask between delivering instruction and monitoring a growing chat feed'.[121] It may be difficult to detect when students seem confused, or have lost interest due to other competing distractions.[122] Accordingly, we would recommend revisiting the pedagogical considerations which underpin live instruction to determine if it is the most appropriate medium in the circumstances. Others have suggested limiting class sizes for synchronous activities to ensure that an instructor can monitor aspects such as facial expressions and body language,[123] as well as establishing norms for engagement during live instruction to ensure participation runs as smoothly as possible.[124]

Further, the more 'sophisticated' the technology employed to engage synchronously (e.g., live video), the more likely students will experience technological issues (e.g., bandwidth, lack of technical support).[125] Identifying appropriate sources of support, or an alternative plan in the event of technological failure, is critical. Some students may simply lack access to video technologies, or even a location they feel comfortable in being visible to their peers and professors via video.[126] Synchronous participation fatigue is also emerging as a side-effect of the current post-COVID-19 intensification of videoconferencing.[127] Once again, synchronous online activities should not be chosen simply for their ability to replicate the face-to-face setting, but because there is a clear pedagogical rationale for live instruction.

Academic integrity is often raised as a concern with e-learning, though in our experience the perception of misconduct looms larger than the reality. If exam-based assessment is determined to be the most pedagogically appropriate assessment activity, online exam systems exist where student identity can be verified via camera, and proctors can monitor use of prohibited materials.[128] For non-exam assessments which require text responses to be submitted, there are plagiarism detection tools (e.g., Turnitin) which compare student submissions to online databases to check for similarity. While it is not possible to use these tools to determine if a student has self-authored a text-based submission (e.g., whether a student has used a 'ghostwriting' service),[129] the same concern exists in face-to-face settings. As Schwartz notes, there is no evidence to

---

[121] Dutton, Ryznar and Long, above n 7, 512.
[122] Dutton and Mohapatra, above n 12.
[123] Colombo, above n 14.
[124] Dutton and Mohapatra, above n 12.
[125] Lipton above n 7.
[126] Dutton and Mohapatra, above n 12.
[127] Ibid.
[128] Schwartz, above n 6.
[129] Lines, L. (2016). Ghostwriters guaranteeing grades? The quality of online ghostwriting services available to tertiary students in Australia. *Teaching in Higher Education* 21(8), 889–914.

suggest that cheating occurs more in the online context than in a conventional classroom,[130] and we have certainly not experienced a marked increase in student misconduct in our online teaching. If anything, the requirement for students to submit text-based assessments through plagiarism detection software has played an educative role, increasing student awareness of academic integrity and scholarly writing requirements.[131]

Ensuring student participation in online learning activities is perhaps the most frequently reported challenge of e-learning, particularly in the asynchronous setting where professors are competing with other distractions.[132] Providing learning resources, discussion forums and the like does not necessarily guarantee that students will access them. While it is possible to track student access of online activities through online metrics, and even build in adaptive learning pathways to direct student progress, there are 'ways around being monitored' and students who will inevitably 'lurk' without making a contribution.[133] One commonly-employed strategy to promote co-operative learning (that we have utilised in our own practice) is to make discussion forum posts assessable, drawing on student extrinsic motivation.[134] However, this too does not guarantee genuine interaction, or prevent the use of 'throw-away responses' (e.g., 'I agree with what has been said already').[135] To ensure that discussions have 'coherence and depth' it is necessary for instructors to plan and actively facilitate forums.[136] This includes organising discussion forums into relevant 'threads' to establish structure and avoid repetition, and providing structured guidance and feedback as to how students should use the forums. It is also advisable to provide a criterion-referenced assessment rubric for students to understand how such attributes as critical thinking and writing quality will be graded.[137] Leveraging intrinsic student motivators, such as an

---

[130] Schwartz, above n 6.

[131] See also Graham-Matheson, L., and Starr, S. (2013). Is it cheating–or learning the craft of writing? Using Turnitin to help students avoid plagiarism. *Research in Learning Technology*, 21; Mphahlele, A., and McKenna, S. (2019). The use of Turnitin in the higher education sector: Decoding the myth. *Assessment and Evaluation in Higher Education* 44(7), 1079–89.

[132] Ryznar, M, and Dutton, Y. M. (2020). Lighting a fire: The power of intrinsic motivation in online teaching. *Syracuse Law Review* 70(1), 73–114.

[133] Lipton above n 7, 90.

[134] Ryznar and Dutton, above n 132.

[135] Huffman, above n 5.

[136] McNamara and Burton, above n 79.

[137] See ibid., for an example of criterion referenced assessment for online discussion posts. See also Huffman, above n 5; and Giacumo, L. A., and Savenye, W. (2020). Asynchronous discussion forum design to support cognition: effects of rubrics and instructor prompts on learner's critical thinking, achievement, and satisfaction. *Educational Technology Research and Development* 68, 37–66.

interest in justice and equality, may prove even more fruitful, because '[c]aring about a topic or the course content is a significant intrinsic motivator to learn the course material'.[138] For environmental law students, this might include appealing to broader student interest in guarding against ecological collapse.

Despite an instructor's best efforts to create an engaging e-learning environment, some students still may simply not enjoy or wish to actively participate in online activities.[139] However, disengagement does not necessarily mean that students are not learning; on the contrary, 'a level of inactivity may leave room for reflexivity and a high level of emotional and cognitive engagement with the subject'.[140] Accordingly, some 'online passivity' may also be conducive to learning, particularly in postgraduate courses, and lecturers must also be cognisant of providing space for this. Students may also gravitate towards their own online spaces for learning, such as social media sites – arguably akin to a group of on-campus students forming a study group and meeting in a physical space.

As noted earlier, the most critical factor in increasing student engagement in learning is strong teacher presence. This leads many to argue that online teaching is more demanding on the academic as they are required to engage in more frequent interpersonal communications than they would in a face-to-face setting.[141] However, these interactions may not necessarily be any more time-consuming than activities undertaken in person to demonstrate care and respect for students, and enthusiasm for the subject matter.[142] As Dutton et al observe, this is not surprising because 'a successful live classroom experience also depends on a professor's level of preparation for class and ability to manage the classroom environment in a way that encourages student learning and interest'.[143] Well-designed authentic collaborative learning activities (e.g., a role play), or detailed feedback containing individualised commentary and suggestions for improvement, take time to prepare, irrespective of the modality.

Nonetheless, we acknowledge that online communication does remove the typical boundaries imposed by a physical classroom, potentially making the lecturer accessible at any time. We have found that establishing clear expectations around communication, including times of availability, and typical

---

[138] Ryznar and Dutton, above n 132, 82.

[139] Xynas, above n 97; Dutton, Ryznar and Long, above n 7.

[140] Morgan-Thomas, A., and Dudau, A. (2019). Of possums, hogs, and horses: capturing the duality of student engagement in e-learning. *Academy of Management Learning & Education* 18(4), 564–80.

[141] Dutton, Ryznar and Long, above n 7; Xynas, above n 97.

[142] Schwartz, above n 6.

[143] Dutton, Ryznar and Long, above n 7, 515.

response times to student comments and questions, can assist in minimising encroachment into non-work time. Further, and particularly with more constructivist learning activities, the lecturer should remember their role is more of facilitator of learning rather than information provider.[144] Accordingly, it might be the case that one is in fact 'over-servicing' students by responding to each and every communication, which reinforces the need to articulate expectations in order to empower students to self-regulate their own learning.[145]

CONCLUSION

In the early 1980s, Clark observed that electronic media technologies used in teaching were merely 'vehicles' for delivering instruction, and were not responsible for influencing student learning outcomes 'any more than the truck that delivers our groceries causes changes in our nutrition'.[146] While much has changed in terms of online learning technology in the intervening decades, this fundamental proposition remains the same – that the achievement of learning objectives is not so much influenced by the use of technology, but rather by the design of instructional strategies and approach to learner engagement.[147] The focus must therefore be on pedagogy first, and technology second.[148]

Should environmental law teachers be faced with the option (or indeed the requirement, as many have in the wake of COVID-19) to teach online, we echo Corbin and Bugden's assessment that 'there is much more to moving to an online teaching environment than using the same teaching strategies as those employed in face-to-face teaching'.[149] Selecting e-learning tools purely on their ability to replicate a physical classroom setting may see learning 'lost in translation',[150] and online teaching efforts viewed as 'mere shadows of the real thing'.[151] Instructors should decide first what learning needs and outcomes

---

[144]   Xynas, above n 97.

[145]   Ibid., 91; Schwartz, above n 6; Ryznar and Dutton, above n 132.

[146]   Clark, R. E. (1983). Reconsidering research on learning from media. *Review of Educational Research* 53, 445–9, 445.

[147]   Simonson M., Smaldino S., and Zvacek S. M. (2015). *Teaching and learning at a distance: Foundations of distance education* (6th ed.). Charlotte, NC: Information Age.

[148]   Ko, S., and Rossen, S. (2017). *Teaching online: A practical guide.* Taylor & Francis, 16.

[149]   Corbin and Bugden, above n 10, 20.

[150]   Lipton above n 7, 78.

[151]   Suk Gersen, J. (2020). Finding real life in teaching law online. *The New Yorker.* 23 April 2020. Online at: https://www.newyorker.com/culture/personal-history/finding -real-life-in-teaching-law-online, accessed 1 September 2020.

must be met, before turning to the suite of e-learning tools and techniques to select the best approach for their teaching purpose.

Throughout this chapter, we have attempted to illustrate that various e-learning approaches to content delivery, assessment and student engagement are grounded in learning theory. We hope that this encourages environmental law teachers to consider the use of online learning tools in their own practice, guided by pedagogy and their own instructional and student engagement requirements. While e-learning is not without challenge or indeed effort on the part of the educator, in our experience we have found that online teaching can facilitate equally rich interaction and collaboration between students and lecturers, as well as provide alternative and scalable options for authentic assessment.

18. Teaching environmental law in Thailand

Chacrit Sitdhiwej and Rob Fowler

INTRODUCTION

Environmental law has been part of law and other tertiary programmes in Thailand for several decades. This chapter aims to share the experiences and challenges that Thai scholars have faced when they have introduced environmental law into law and other programmes in different regions of Thailand. It begins with a summary of the legal system in Thailand and the development of legal education in the country. It then outlines the current state of environmental law teaching in the country, giving examples of creative initiatives in a number of institutions. It also describes a 'Train the Teachers' programme in environmental law delivered to 24 Thai legal scholars in 2017, in which the authors were involved as trainers. The final section describes the difficulties that have arisen with respect to the delivery of environmental law programmes in Thai law schools and offers some proposals for how to address these. The experience described here with the teaching of environmental law in Thailand may provide some insights with respect to the problems likely to arise in the same context in other countries with developing economies, in both Asia and elsewhere.

THE LEGAL SYSTEM IN THAILAND[1]

The development of the Thai alphabet in 1319 facilitated the first recording of laws in the country. These laws possibly had their root in the Hindu Code of

---

[1]   This brief account of the Thai legal system draws upon the historical account provided in Ariyanuntaka, V., 'Thailand: Legal Research and Legal Education in Thailand' in Institute of Developing Economies, Japan External Trade Organization (IDE-JETRO), *Doing Legal Research in Asian Countries China, India, Malaysia, Philippines, Thailand, Vietnam* (2003): available at http://hdl.handle.net/2344/00014998, accessed 28 April 2021.

Manu,[2] but the prescription of laws and administration of justice remained for many centuries the prerogative of the King.[3] In 1782, King Rama I developed the Basic Law of the Judiciary, which was then used for more than a century.[4]

With the colonisation of adjacent countries by the British and the French, numerous royal family members, nobles and high officials were sent to England and Europe during the nineteenth century to study law, bringing back with them expertise in both the common and civil law systems.[5] In 1891, King Rama V established a Ministry of Justice to reform the Thai judiciary and enhance the legal system.[6] Despite the strong influence of the English legal system on Thai law at this time (particularly in areas such as commercial law, procedural law and evidence), ultimately a civil law system was adopted. This system also took Thai customs and culture into account, to a considerable extent, and continues to the present day to provide a systematic and diverse body of legal codes.[7]

A further dynamic in the operation of the legal system in Thailand has been the instability of its political and constitutional system since the establishment of a constitutional monarchy in 1932 as the result of a military coup. Since that time, there have been 13 successful military coups, the latest in 2014, and 20 charters or constitutions, the most recent having been adopted in 2017.[8] Following a general election in March 2019, the Parliament voted to make the leader of the 2014 military coup, Prayut Chan-o-cha, the Prime Minister.[9] International assessments have accorded Thailand poor global rankings on

---

[2]   Patrick Olivelle, *Manu's Code of Law*, (Oxford University Press, 2005) 3–4.

[3]   Ariyanuntaka (n 1) 148.

[4]   Ibid., 149.

[5]   Ibid., 152.

[6]   A strong incentive for reform of the Thai legal system arose from treaty arrangements entered into by Thailand with the colonial powers that exempted foreign nationals located within Thailand from the jurisdiction of the Thai courts and instead rendered them subject to the extra-territorial jurisdiction of the relevant foreign courts. These arrangements did not cease entirely until 1938: see ibid., at 150–52.

[7]   Ibid., 146.

[8]   Harding, A.J. and Leelapatana, R., 'Constitution-Making in 21st Century Thailand: The Continuing Search for a Perfect Constitutional Fit' (2019) 7(2) *The Chinese Journal of Comparative Law* 266–284.

[9]   For a discussion of the conduct of this election and its likely repercussions, see Siripan Nogsuan Sawasdee, 'Electoral Integrity and the Repercussions of Institutional Manipulations: The 2019 General Election in Thailand' (2020) 5(1) *Asian Journal of Comparative Politics* 52–68.

account of human rights violations,[10] corruption[11] and shortcomings in the operation of the rule of law.[12]

THE LEGAL EDUCATION SYSTEM IN THAILAND

Prince Rapee (known as the father of modern Thai law) established the first law school in Thailand in 1897 as an arm of the then recently established Ministry of Justice. This institution was modelled on the Inns of Court in England and included both English and French law subjects within its curriculum.[13] In 1933, following the military coup, the Law School of the Ministry of Justice was transferred by royal decree to the Faculty of Law and Political Science at Chulalongkorn University. It was transferred one year later to the University of Moral and Political Sciences (renamed Thammasat University in 1952).[14] This remained the only institution for legal study in Thailand until Chulalongkorn University re-established its own department of law in 1951 (which subsequently became the Faculty of Law in 1958).[15]

From the late 1950s onwards, other tertiary institutions (both public and private) began to introduce law programmes. By 2000, there were 21 publicly accessible law schools and a further 16 law schools had been established in private universities.[16] Since then, there has been a rapid expansion in the

---

[10]   For a critique of the current human rights regime in Thailand, see Human Rights Watch, World Report 2020, *Thailand: Events of 2019*, available at https://www .hrw.org/world-report/2020/country-chapters/thailand, accessed 28 April 2021; Tyrell Haberkorn, *In Plain Sight: Impunity and Human Rights in Thailand,* (The University of Wisconsin Press, 2018).

[11]   The Corruption Perception Index maintained by Transparency International ranked Thailand in 2019 at 101/180 countries: available at https://www.transparency .org/country/THA, accessed 28 April 2021. See further, Connors, M.K., 'Anticorruption Politics in Thailand', in Chen, C. and Weiss, M.L., *The Political Logics of Anticorruption Efforts in Asia*, (State University of New York Press, 2019).

[12]   The Rule of Law Index produced by the World Justice Project ranked Thailand at 71/128 countries in 2020: available at https://worldjusticeproject.org/sites/default/ files/documents/WJP-ROLI-2020-Online_0.pdf, accessed 28 April 2021. For a recent account of the difficulties that have been experienced in maintaining democratic government in Thailand, see Chambers, P.W., 'Democratization Interrupted: The Parallel State and the Demise of Democracy in Thailand', in Croissant, A. and Hellman, O., *Stateness and Democracy in Asia,* (Cambridge University Press, 2020).

[13]   Ariyanuntaka (n 1) 145.

[14]   *Thammasat University Act 1952*, ss.3–4. The term 'Thammasat' is a variation of the term 'Dharmasastra' in Sanskrit, which means 'jurisprudence'.

[15]   Ariyanuntaka (n 1) 157.

[16]   Ibid., 167. The term 'law school' used in this chapter may refer to a faculty of law or a school of law that is a unit of a university (e.g., Faculty of Law, Thammasat University and School of Law, Chiang Rai Rajabhat University) or to a department,

number of law schools, particularly in the growing private university sector, but also as a result of the conversion of former teachers and technology public colleges to the status of universities.[17]

There is no authoritative source of information concerning the total number of law schools currently operating in Thailand. However, a survey conducted in 2017 in connection with an IUCN Academy of Environmental Law and Asian Development Bank-funded programme to train Thai legal scholars to teach environmental law – the 'Train the Teachers' programme (TTT) – indicated that there were 56 law schools within 82 public tertiary institutions and 42 law schools within 43 private tertiary institutions.[18] This more than doubling in the number of law schools over a relatively short period may have impaired the overall quality of law graduates, especially as many law teachers are only part-time and do not have postgraduate qualifications. However, in recent years, leading universities in Thailand have begun to require new law teachers to have a Masters' degree in Law, and preferably a PhD/LLD, and to pressure their existing staff to pursue higher degrees.

ENVIRONMENTAL LAW TEACHING IN THAILAND

Environmental and natural resources laws have been steadily developed in Thailand since the 1970s. The principal legislation governing environmental protection and environmental impact assessment is the *Enhancement and Conservation of National Environmental Quality Act, 1992.* In 2019, three new laws concerning biodiversity protection were adopted.[19] In addition, environmental divisions have been created in the Courts of Justice and the Administrative Courts and there has been contemplation of a 'one-stop-shop' judicial forum embracing civil, criminal and administrative jurisdictions.[20]

---

which is a unit within a particular faculty (e.g., Department of Law, in the Faculty of Social Science, Kasetsart University).

[17] *Rajabhat Universities Act 2004*, s.4; and *Rajamangala Universities of Technology Act 2005*, s.5.

[18] Survey conducted by the Thai participants in the IUCNAEL-ADB Train-The-Trainers Programme, June 2016 (file with first co-author).

[19] *Wildlife Preservation and Protection Act 2019* (replacing a 1992 law); *National Park Act 2019* (replacing a 1961 law); and *Community Forest Act 2019*; see further, Boonrueang, S., 'Terrestrial Biodiversity Conservation Law in Thailand: A Preliminary Illustration of Applicable Laws and Their Limitations' (2019) 12(1) *Naresuan Law Journal* 23.

[20] Pring, G. and Pring, C., *Environmental Courts and Tribunals: A Guide for Policy Makers,* United Nations Environment Programme, Nairobi (2016) 87 (available at https://wedocs.unep.org/bitstream/handle/20.500.11822/10001/environmental-courts-tribunals.pdf?sequence=1, accessed 28 April 2021). However, as is common

Hence, there is a solid body of material suitable for coverage in a domestic environmental law course within the Thai legal curriculum.

Environmental Law as an Elective Within the LLB Curriculum

Many Thai law schools include environmental law as an elective subject within their LLB curriculum, with the first courses having been introduced several decades ago. There is no authoritative record of the number of law schools that currently list environmental law as an elective in their undergraduate programme, but participants in the TTT programme conducted in 2017 indicated that most law schools now do so.[21]

A more extensive array of environmental law-related electives has been offered by the Law Department within the Faculty of Social Science at Kasetsart University since 2003.[22] Its LLB programme is unique in aiming to produce graduates specialising in agrarian law, natural resources law, environmental law and intellectual property law.[23] Unfortunately, student demand for this unique programme did not prove to be strong, with most students preferring to choose their major in the so-called 'four-pillar' fields of law, discussed further below. As a result, since 2017, the LLB curriculum at Kasetsart University has allowed students the freedom to mix-and-match elective subjects of their choice. This adjustment has succeeded in attracting more

---

in many Asian countries, most members of the Thai judiciary have little or no familiarity with environmental law and may encounter difficulties in interpreting and applying it rigorously; in an effort to address this common problem, the Asian Development Bank established the Asian Judges Network on the Environment in 2010 (see Asian Development Bank, *Environmental Governance and the Courts in Asia: An Asian Judges Network on the Environment,* Law and Policy Reform, Brief No.1, 2012, available at https://www.adb.org/sites/default/files/publication/29827/2012-brief-01 -environmental-governance.pdf, accessed 28 April 2021) and has since conducted a number of environmental law roundtables and similar events for members of the judiciary in Asian countries.

[21]   See above n 18.

[22]   Kasetsart University was established in 1943 as Thailand's then first and only tertiary institution in agriculture and has always included law subjects within the curricula of all its faculties. A Law Department was established in the Faculty of Social Science, upon the approval of an LLB programme in 2003.

[23]   *Kasetsart University Bachelor of Law Curriculum 2012.* The Thai text is available at https://eduserv.ku.ac.th//academics%202008/PDF/ku/soc/CS_LL.B._55.pdf, accessed 30 September 2019. Alongside a core of conventional LLB subjects, the elective subjects include Agrarian Law, Agricultural Welfare Law, Energy Law, Environmental Law, Fishery Management Law, Forestry Management Law, Land Management Law, Natural Resources Law, Plant Variety Law and International Environmental Law.

enrolments by students in the agrarian, natural resources and environmental law electives.[24]

Environmental Law as a Compulsory Subject Within the LLB Curriculum

Two law schools have gone further by making environmental law a compulsory subject within their LLB programmes. At Chiang Mai University Law School, the subject Law and the Environment is a compulsory unit in the fourth year of one of two streams of study available to its LLB students from the third year onwards.[25] Also, the School of Law at Chiang Rai Rajabhat University, one of the 38 provincial-focused universities in Thailand, made environmental law a compulsory subject within its LLB programme in 2019. Unfortunately, a new requirement by the Ministry of Education of Thailand for law schools to reduce the number of credits required to complete an LLB programme[26] has necessitated the combination of the new environmental law subject with a land law subject, thereby making it extremely difficult to provide a comprehensive coverage of the environmental law component.[27]

Teaching Environmental Law in Faculties Other than Law

One of the very first environmental law courses to be taught in Thailand was not offered in an LLB programme but rather as a compulsory subject in an undergraduate degree in environmental science that was established at Thammasat University (TU) in 1985.[28] This predated by nine years the introduction of an LLM programme in natural resources and environmental law in the Faculty of Law at TU, which is discussed further below. It should also be noted that the Department of Environmental Science at TU was the first of its

[24] Interview with Dr Worapoj Suebprasertkul, Secretary of the 2020 LLB Programme Development Committee, Department of Law, Faculty of Social Science, Kasetsart University, 27 September 2019 (record with the first co-author).

[25] See https://www.law.cmu.ac.th/en/study-program-llb.pdf, accessed 28 April 2021. The subject, International Environmental Law, is also offered as an elective within the LLB curriculum.

[26] *Notification of the Ministry of Education on LLB Degree Standard, 2018.* The Thai text is available at http://www.ratchakitcha.soc.go.th/DATA/PDF/2561/E/319/T _0007.PDF accessed 30 September 2019.

[27] Interview with Mr Vorranat Boonchareon, Assistant Dean, School of Law, Chiang Rai Rajabhat University, 3 July 2019 (record with the first co-author).

[28] *Thammasat University Environmental Science Curriculum 1985,* at 36 (file with the first co-author). It should also be noted that the Department of Environmental Science at TU was the first of its kind in Thailand.

kind in Thailand. Its establishment was met with strong resistance at the time, both within and outside the university, by those who felt science education should be focused solely on pure science areas such as physics, chemistry and biology.[29]

From the outset, the delivery of the compulsory environmental law subject relied on academic staff members from the Faculty of Law at TU. When this was not possible at one point, the Department of Environmental Science had no choice but to make the subject an elective (and hope that no student would enrol!).[30] It was only after the first co-author was invited to teach the subject for the department in 2012 that the Department encouraged its students to enrol in the subject again. With the growing importance of environmental law in Thailand, and increased student demand for the subject, the Department has recently made its environmental law subject compulsory once again.[31]

It is likely that environmental law is being taught in programmes other than law at other Thai universities, particularly those that have an interdisciplinary focus on environmental studies, but there is no authoritative source of information on the number of such courses being delivered.

Teaching Environmental Law at the Postgraduate Level

A number of Thai law schools have established coursework LLM and LLD degrees, and some of these include an environmental law subject within the curriculum. However, there is no reliable information as to how many of these programmes are offering an environmental law subject within these degrees.

Until recently, only one law school in Thailand has offered a postgraduate degree focused specifically on environmental law. TU Faculty of Law has conducted a Natural Resources and Environmental Law LLM Programme for some 20 years, with an enrolment of approximately 20 students each year.[32] This programme was established at the initiative of Professor Dr

---

[29] Interview with several staff members of the Department of Environmental Science, Faculty of Science and Technologies, Thammasat University, 1 July 2019 (record with the first co-author).

[30] Ibid.

[31] Ibid.

[32] *Thammasat University LLM Curriculum, 2013*. The Thai text is available at https://reg.tu.ac.th/en/Picture/AttFile/c113296d-c2c6-4641-8c13-c0f1b28479be accessed 30 September 2019. At present, the compulsory subjects offered are Advanced Environmental Law, International Environmental Law, Natural Resources and Environmental Law Seminar, Natural Resources Law and Policy, Selected Problems in Natural Resources and Environmental Law, while the compulsory-elective subjects offered include Comparative Environmental Law and Energy Law. The elective subjects offered include Energy Law, Environmental Issues in International

Amnat Wongbandit, the then Director of the Graduate School of TU Faculty of Law, as part of a wider scheme to strengthen postgraduate studies in the Law School.[33] Despite opposition from some senior academic staff members, the modernisation of the LLM programme was approved by the University in 1999. As a result, the Department of Natural Resources and Environmental Law was established alongside seven other specialist Departments and put in charge of the offering of both LLM and LLD degrees in natural resources and environmental law. The Department has recently been renamed the Natural Resources and Environmental Law Centre.

In 2019, a second, specialised LLM programme focused on agricultural, natural resources and environmental law was established by the Faculty of Law Pridi Banomyong of Dhurakij Pundit University, one of Thailand's major private law schools.[34] This new programme was strongly supported by both the Law School academic staff and the University's senior executives. However, limits on the staff development budget of the University have prevented the recruitment of sufficient academic staff members with expertise in the field of environmental law to enable the programme to be fully delivered yet.[35]

This recent experience illustrates a wider problem with respect to the teaching of environmental law in Thailand, namely the lack of legal scholars with appropriate expertise in this field. This and other challenges will be discussed in the following section.

Transactions, Legal Problems in Agriculture and Agricultural Institution, Legal Problems in Environmental Assessment, Problems in Environmental Litigation and Tourism and Cultural Heritage Law.

[33]   Interview with Prof Dr Amnat Wongbandit, former Head of the Natural Resources and Environmental Law Centre, Faculty of Law, Thammasat University, 28 June 2019 (record with the first co-author).

[34]   *Dhurakij Pundit University LLM Curriculum 2019.* The Thai text is available at http://www.dpu.ac.th/llm/course-plan.html accessed 30 September 2019. The core subjects offered are Advanced Civil Law, Advanced Criminal Law, Advanced Public Law and Legal Research Methodology, while the major subjects offered are Advanced Environmental Law, Law of Agriculture and Agricultural Institution and Law of Natural Resources. The elective subjects offered include Energy Law, Land Resources Law, Plant Genetic Resources Law, Fishery Resources Law, Forestry Resources Law and Water Resources Law.

[35]   Interview with Assistant Professor Dr Somchai Ratanachueskul, Dean, Faculty of Law Pridi Banomyong of Dhurakij Pundit University, 1 July 2019 (record with the first co-author).

CHALLENGES IN UNDERTAKING THE TEACHING OF ENVIRONMENTAL LAW IN THAILAND

Lack of Legal Academic Staff with Expertise in Environmental Law

Despite the various initiatives described above, environmental law remains a relatively niche element of the LLB and LLM curricula in Thai law schools, even though the country faces a wide range of environmental problems that require firm legal and policy responses.[36] There has been a strong policy emphasis within the national government on the promotion of resource exploitation and economic development, with economic objectives often taking precedence over environmental considerations. The legal education system has largely reflected this preference, by focusing the curriculum on the delivery of what are referred to as the 'four pillars' of law (civil, criminal, civil procedure and criminal procedure laws).[37]

This focus also has been prompted by the strong desire of Thai law graduates to gain employment either as judges or as public prosecutors in the Office of Public Prosecutors. As a result, the law curriculum has been directed towards educating students in the areas of law that are most connected to these occupations.[38] Most academic staff within Thai law schools seek to teach in these fields and have shown little interest in other emerging areas such as environmental law. The result is that there has been, and remains, a significant lack of legal academic staff with sufficient expertise to teach environmental law in Thai law schools. To a considerable extent, there also has been a corresponding lack of interest across the law student body in Thailand in taking up the study of environmental law.

It is not possible to accurately report on the current number of Thai legal scholars with expertise and teaching experience in environmental law, but some indication was able to be gained from the survey of the 24 legal scholars who participated in a five-day TTT programme conducted at Chiang Mai University Law School in 2017. This programme was presented by trainers

---

[36]   See Open Development – Thailand, *Environment and Natural Resources*: 'Thailand faces increasing environmental degradation in many regions, including the loss of biodiversity and declining wildlife populations, deforestation, desertification, water scarcity, climate change, and air and water pollution.' Available at https://thailand.opendevelopmentmekong.net/topics/environment-and-natural-resources/, accessed 28 April 2021.

[37]   Ariyanuntaka (n 1) 186.

[38]   Ibid.

from the IUCN Academy of Environmental Law (IUCNAEL)[39] and five Thai environmental law scholars, with the financial support of the Asian Development Bank (ADB).[40] The surveys taken during that programme indicated that most law schools in Thailand have no academic staff with expertise in environmental law and that, in most instances, the environmental law elective listed in their curricula has never been presented. Furthermore, it appears that even the institutions whose innovative initiatives have been described above are limited in most instances to just one or two scholars with environmental law expertise.[41]

Even where an environmental law elective has been offered, this has often involved the use of contracted teachers from outside the particular law school. This is consistent with a widespread practice within Thai law schools over many years of relying on 'outsiders' (e.g.. academic staff from the larger law schools, judges, public prosecutors, public servants or private practitioners) to deliver courses on a contract basis. However, even this means of presenting an environmental law elective is now under threat, as a result of a directive in 2015 by the Ministry of Education, through its Office of the Higher Education Commission, that no more than 50 per cent of the workload of any subject may be assigned to outside staff. The majority of the teaching workload is to be handled by the in-house academic staff in charge of each subject.[42] This directive has presented an additional impediment to the delivery of an environmental law elective by many, if not most, law schools.

---

[39] For further information concerning IUCNAEL and its activities, see https://www.iucnael.org/en/, accessed 28 April 2021.

[40] See https://www.teachenvirolaw.asia/, accessed 28 April 2021.

[41] See interviews previously cited above n 24, 27, 28, 33 and 35.

[42] *Notification of the Ministry of Education on Undergraduate Degree Standard, 2015*, clause 10.1.3; and *Notification of the Ministry of Education on Postgraduate Degree Standard, 2015*, clause 10.2.3. The Thai text is available at http://www.ratchakitcha.soc.go.th/DATA/PDF/2558/E/295/2.PDF and http://www.ratchakitcha.soc.go.th/DATA/PDF/2558/E/295/12.PDF, respectively, both accessed 19 July 2019. It should be noted that since 2 May 2019, the Ministry of Higher Education, Science, Research and Innovation of Thailand (MHESI) has been established to take over a range of duties and powers from the Ministry of Education, specifically those concerning the higher education affairs discussed above. Office of the Higher Education Commission was also transferred to be under MHESI: see *Reorganisation of Ministry, Sub-Ministry and Department Act, 2002 as amended by the Reorganisation of Ministry, Sub-Ministry and Department Act (No 19), 2019*, sections 5(6/1), 17/1, 17/2, 40; and *Reorganisation of Ministry, Sub-Ministry and Department Act (No 19), 2019*, sections 9–16.

Promoting Academic Staff Development in the Field of Environmental Law

An obvious response to the lack of environmental law scholars in Thailand would be to provide training and other staff development activities that can enable new or existing scholars to engage in teaching and research in this field. However, the challenge here is to find the resources to undertake such activities – from within the national government, the university sector, or elsewhere. In the absence of any current resources from the Thai national government for this purpose, it necessarily falls to the universities or their law schools to take up this challenge.

Unfortunately, apart from the small number of well-established law schools such as TU Faculty of Law, most law schools in Thailand lack the financial resources to directly finance staff development themselves, especially in fields of knowledge that are not mainstream. However, it can be argued that, given the 2015 Ministry of Education direction to universities to substantially reduce the use of outside teachers, it is incumbent upon them to find the means to invest in the development of their academic staff, including in the field of environmental law. This argument is reinforced by the fact that, in recent years, many Thai universities have been tightening up their standards for the employment of scholars by demanding higher level qualifications.

One form of staff development therefore could be the offering of scholarships to competent academic staff members to pursue a higher degree at a prominent domestic or overseas university. In the long run, if Thai legal scholars could pursue a coursework LLM or a PhD by research in the field of environmental law, there would emerge a cohort of appropriately educated academic staff members who could contribute their knowledge, expertise and innovation to the field of environmental law, both domestically and globally.

Meanwhile, a 'fast-track' initiative has been deployed recently to train Thai legal scholars in the teaching of environmental law, with some positive outcomes. The IUCNAEL-ADB TTT programme previously mentioned, was delivered to 24 Thai scholars from across 15 universities in 2017, as part of a broader project by those organisations to deliver similar training in 14 Asian countries.[43] The TTT training programme concentrated particularly on the demonstration to, and practice by, the participants of a wide range of teach-

---

[43] For an account of the history of the development of the TTT course by IUCNAEL and its subsequent development and delivery in a number of Asian countries with the financial support of ADB, see Fowler, R.J., 'The Role of the IUCN Academy of Environmental Law in Promoting the Teaching of Environmental Law', IUCNAEL e-Journal, Issue 8, 2017, available at https://www.iucnael.org/en/e-journal/previous-issues/86-journal/issue/640-issue-2017#, accessed 28 April 2021.

ing formats and methodologies that extended beyond the traditional, deeply entrenched lecturing technique. These included various forms of inter-active small group activities, case studies, a drafting exercise, a role play exercise, a field trip and a research assignment.

As in other Asian countries where this programme has been delivered, the Thai participants enthusiastically embraced many of these relatively unfamiliar teaching methodologies and committed to introducing them into their own environmental law courses in the future. Most importantly, the participants subsequently established a Facebook network of Thai environmental law scholars to share information and ideas and undertake collective activities, such as conferences and seminars.

The success of this particular programme, and of similar programmes delivered by IUCNAEL and ADB in other Asian countries between 2015 and 2018, provides a compelling demonstration of how the problems with teaching environmental law that have been identified above with respect to Thailand, and which may be widely shared in developing countries around the world, can be addressed to a reasonable extent through a relatively inexpensive approach. This form of training also has the merit of being highly inclusive of local expertise alongside experienced international trainers and respectful of relevant national laws, culture and customs.

CONCLUSIONS

Despite the substantial challenges and difficulties that have been experienced with the teaching of environmental law in Thailand, it is essential that such teaching expands in the near future. The growing severity of global and national environmental problems (e.g., climate change, biodiversity decline, hazardous substances, pollution and waste), requires that every country has a larger number of environmental law experts, and also a greater ability on the part of these experts to address emerging or disrupting issues and challenges. This change would mean that many more law students would have access to a good quality environmental law course and, hopefully, be inspired by their studies to pursue a career that relates to or involves the drafting, implementation and enforcement of environmental laws.

Thailand is typical in this regard. Many more Thai law graduates should be equipped to assist with tackling the aforementioned issues more effectively, by arming them with an appropriate level of awareness, knowledge and expertise in environmental law. This could be most effectively achieved by making environmental law a compulsory subject in the LLB curriculum in Thailand, as has happened already in three of the most populous nations in the world

(China, India and Indonesia).[44] While there are no firm proposals in this regard at present, it is submitted that every law school should play a significant role in promoting this idea.

Specifying environmental law as a compulsory subject in every LLB programme in Thailand would require a considerably larger cohort of environmental law teachers than currently exists. This would best be achieved through the national tertiary education institution (i.e., the Ministry of Higher Education, Science, Research and Innovation) and the universities and law schools in Thailand cooperatively and jointly investing in the development of legal academic staff in the field of environmental law. In addition, or alternatively should such an initiative not occur, further 'fast-track' training programmes such as the IUCNAEL-ADB TTT course delivered in 2017 could contribute substantially and efficiently to meeting this important staff development challenge.

---

[44] Ibid.

Index

academic expertise
  of environmental lawyers 102
  harnessing & building on 208, 215
  multi-disciplinary 118
  shortage of 3, 7, 17, 284–5
active learning 81, 146
  case studies 91
  challenges 145
  enhancing learning experience 5
  flipped classrooms 93–4
  improving 84
  movement in favour of 145
  pre-lecture reading 85–6
  requirements 146
  self-reflection 87–8
  small-group exercises 93
  structured listening 86–7
  through lectures 84, 85–8
  using LMS tools 267
  see also lectures
Anthropocene 12, 66, 165, 180, 212–13, 215
assessment 113, 125
  authentic 115, 118–19
  case study 114–15, 119
    multi-disciplinary student conferences 122–4
    positive features 126
    refining 126–7
  as controversial 113
  desire for more 126
  emerging forms 119, 120–21
  evaluation 125–7
    final 125
    initial surveys 125
  formative 116
    use of personal reflective essays 127–8
  for learning 116
  outcome-based 115, 117–18
  role of 115–19
    in deep learning 117

influence for teaching & learning 116
  summative 116–17

Buddhist teachings 46
environmental law topics
  atmosphere 172
  biodiversity 171, 173, 174
  climate change 14, 17, 22, 114
    mitigation 123
  contested water use 43
  development 43, 53–4
  ecosystems 172
  fisheries 171
  mass extinctions 48
  oceans/seas 172
  wind farms 43
  world heritage 171
Borrows, John 49–50
bright green future 29

climate change 4, 48
  as complicated issue 125
  and government promises 53–4
  as hot topic 28
  calls for teaching on 114
  impacts 66, 174
  law 14–15
    teaching 17
  mental health challenge of 22, 23, 34
  momentum for global action on 179
  Ottawa Conference on *see* Ottawa Conference on Climate Change
  ozone layer depletion 178
  solutions to 123
  UNFCCC 88, 173
communication
  cognitive presence 267
  expectations 273–4

online 258
open 239
oral 98, 100, 101, 201
     building 207
relatable 32
skills 87, 99
     building 122, 207
student-teacher 233–4, 273–4
Continuing Professional Development
     205
contributory expertise 189
co-production 80, 114, 241–2
     UK environmental law teaching
          study *see* UK environmental
          law teaching study
course design 12–17
     content 15–16
          ethical & philosophical
               dimensions 16
          'foundations' of environmental
               law 15
          normative aspects of
               environmental law 16
          relevant perspectives 15
     and interdisciplinarity 16–17
     purpose 12–14
          pragmatic approach 13–14
          specifics approach 12
          survey approach 12, 13
     scope 14–15
          legal ambit 14
          purpose & objectives 14
          streams of study 14–15
     and teaching challenges 18–19
course-based graduate environmental law
     programs 194–5
courts 62
     design 278
     International Court of Justice 175
     moot 144
     oral submissions before 170
     rules of practice
          Australia 138, 142
          US 135, 142
     specialized environmental 189
     Supreme Court of Argentina 29
     Supreme Court of India 29
COVID-19 pandemic 18, 255–6
     and e-learning *see* e-learning

intensification of videoconferencing
     271

decolonizing 4
decolonizing teaching 49–50
     deep engagement with Indigenous
          law as crucial to 59
     failure of legal education over 50
     natural resource law in 49, 56–60
     place-based teaching 49, 58, 60,
          61–2
          critical pedagogy of place 62
          Indigenous jurisdiction 51,
               54–5, 57–8, 59
          Indigenous ownership 51
          placing self 50–52
     and presumption of Crown
          sovereignty 58–9
     reconciliation 51–2
     TRC Calls to Action
          Recommendation 28 56–7
          Recommendation 50 57
     see also natural resource law
deep ecology 44, 46
     basic tenets 44
deep ecology workshops 35, 44–8
     aim of 45–6
     establishing heart connection to the
          environment 45
     four-part spiral being 46
     as important pedagogical tool 48
     purpose of 46–7
     success of 45
     theory behind 46
     trust exercises 46
     use of silence 47
developing or emerging economies 3,
     11, 276
doctorate 210–11, 224, 238–9
     diverse forms of 211
     examiners 235–7
          choosing 235
          divergent examination reports
               236
          recommendations for 236–7
          subject prejudice 235, 236
     impetus behind 212
     need for research 210, 212, 215
          in Anthropocene era 212–13
          interdisciplinary 213, 214–15

juxtadisciplinary 214
multidisciplinary 213, 214
role of supervisor 210
South Africa 232
  challenges 220–221
  credits system 218
  ethical clearance 218
  external pressures 217–18, 222
  National Research Foundation
    217
  permissions 218–19
  pressure to deliver degrees
    faster 216–17
  qualifications for 219–20
  shortage of qualified
    supervisors 217
student-supervisor relationship 210,
    216, 225–6, 227
  co-supervision 232–3
  handling criticism 230–31
  language barriers 233–4
  multiple layers of 226
  networking 232
  research publication 234
  setting out expectations 227–9
  supervisory functions 226
  writing skills 231
supervisory challenges 210, 215–16,
    237–8
  dearth of literature of 215
  doctoral process 221–2
  institutional 215–16, 216–19
  language 216, 222–3
  nature of environmental law
    216, 219–21
  personal circumstances 216
value of research 212, 213
see also postgraduate education
dynamism
  classroom 30, 93, 150
    dynamic environment 156–8
  of environmental law 10, 11, 77,
    78, 82
  group dynamics 100–101, 125
  intellectual 6
  of real life 148

ecological collapse 4, 273
education as capability generator 238
e-learning 7–8, 253–6, 274–5

and academic integrity 271–2
  plagiarism detection software
    272
advantages 258–60
  economic 258
  exposure to digital technology
    258
  flexibility 258
  improved access to legal
    education 258–9
  increased diversity 259
  increased participation 259
  sustainability 259–60
alignment with learning theory 262
assessment mechanisms 264
asynchronous 257
barriers to 254
behaviourist & cognitivist
    approaches 262–5
  assessment mechanisms 264
  content chunking 263
  discussion forums 265
  effective knowledge transfer
    emphasis 262
  streamlining 263–4
  use of multimedia 264
blended/hybrid approaches 254
challenges
  communication expectations
    273–4
  disengagement 273
  student participation 272
constructivist approach 265–70
  authentic assessment 266
  cognitive presence 267
  community building 266
  discussion forums 267–8
  focus 265
  fostering reflection,
    collaboration and
    connection 265
  importance of teacher presence
    268–9
  place-based pedagogy 269–70
  practice ready assignments 266
  social context as source of
    knowledge 267
  synchronous teaching 265
content chunks 263
and COVID-19 pandemic 254–5

emergency remote teaching
        255–6
definition 256
drivers 254
effective knowledge transfer 262
feedback 265
increase in enrolment 253, 254
learning management systems
        257–8, 263–4
    adaptive learning tools 257–258
    audio-visual 257
    digital collaboration tools 257
    digital marketing tools 257
    document sharing 257
    email & messaging 257
    gamification tools 257
    interactive quizzes 257
lecture capture systems 257
leveraging student motivation 272–3
multimedia 264
not simply replicating classroom
        content 255–6
online discussion forums 265, 272
pedagogy 260–62
presentation platforms
    Microsoft Sway 257
    Moodle Book 257
promotion of co-operative learning
        272
role-play simulation 258
synchronous
    Adobe Connect 257
    Blackboard Collaborate 257
    class management 270–71
    Microsoft Teams 257
    as not replicating in-person
        teaching 270
    participation fatigue 271
    potential for technological
        issues 271
    tech support for 271
synchronous interaction tools
    Zoom 257
and systematic redesign of teaching
        257
video use 263
wholly online 254
emotion
    cognitive/evaluative theory of 37–8

core of dispute resolution 35
emotional skills 33
    self-understanding 36–7, 38
engaging 167
and storytelling 166, 179–80
teaching about 37
transformative potential 35
see also reflection; storytelling
empirical research
    dearth of literature on 215
    in doctoral studies 218
    into game-based teaching 162
    into mental health 24
    need for 142
employability 9, 246–7
    CLE and 130
    as organising force of universities
        247
environmental disputes
    as emotional 35
    contested values in 41–2
    multi-stakeholder 35
    and value assumptions 36
environmental law
    becoming more mainstream 10–11,
        12
    as contestable issue 8
    disconnection from mainstream
        legal scholarship 9
    growing body of publications 11–12
    importance of 8
    intellectual 'diversity' 19
    intellectual 'incoherence' 19
    no agreed definition of 14
    perceived marginality 8–9
    PhD *see* doctorate
    public interest 23
    as value laden 35–36
    values-based nature of 9
environmental law clinics 6, 10, 129–30,
        133–4
    Australia 136–8
        development 136–7
        elective nature of 137
        externship/placement model
            137
        interdisciplinary 138
        NGO partnership model 137–8
        proliferation of 136

Victorian Civil and
Administrative Tribunal
136–7
AU/US comparison 138–42
assessment 139–40
classroom component 139
political interference 140–42
student education levels 138–9
student supervision 140
university oversight 139
definition 133
key components 133
USA 134–6
early clinics 134
focus 136
limitations 135
NGO partnership model 134–5
numbers 134
student education levels 135
student practice rules 135–6
environmental LLM 190, 193
extinction rebellion/XR 48

field trips 47, 48, 63, 66, 194, 209, 287
virtual 258
flexibility
in design of legal curricula 11
of e-learning 258
flexible optimism 33
inflexibility of texts 80
need for 270
of on-line group projects 119
inline learning increasing 258
student 254
of teaching methods 99

Gaia theory 46
game-based learning 144–5, 159
difficulty defining 146–7
as enriching in-class teaching
159–61
games 146, 147–8
gamification 146, 149–50
increased interest in 146
as leading to research opportunities
161–2
offering new perspectives 162

Ottawa Conference on Climate
Change *see* Ottawa
Conference on Climate
Change
research needs 162–3
roots 146
serious games 146, 150–52
simulation games 146, 150
simulations 146, 148–9
student feedback 163

happiness
career 23
cultivating 22, 34
'Foundations of Happiness at Work'
course 25–6
student 24, 34

Innis, Harold
staples theory 53
interactional expertise 189, 190
interactional methods
learning & teaching 100–101
in small-group teaching 103
international environmental law *see*
environmental law
IUCN Academy of Environmental Law
11, 18, 285
Teaching and Capacity-Building
Sub-Committee 11
'training-the-teachers' programme
18, 286–7, 288

land ethic 45
learning
active *see* active learning
blended 79, 197, 204, 209
case reading 85
co-operative 272
deep 117
e- *see* e-learning
experiential 117, 120, 134, 137, 146,
187
definition 130
reinforcing 144
game-based *see* game-based
learning
meaningful 83
student-centred 5, 97

visual 84, 88–93
learning outcomes 98–9, 145, 197
    enhancing 98
    in game-based learning 159, 162
    identifying 114
    need to focus on 117, 123, 200, 208,
        267
    in pedagogy of hope 26, 34
    and place-based teaching 63
    promoting student-centred 4–5
    rationale behind 98–9
    recognising 81
learning theory 146, 256, 261
    behaviourism 261–2
    cognitivism 261, 262
    constructivism 261, 262
    e-learning as grounded in 270, 275
    social
        small-group exercises 84, 91
lectures 83–5, 94–5
    and active learning 84, 85–8
        flipped classrooms 93–4
        pre-lecture reading 85–6
        structured listening 86–7
        student self-reflection 87–8
    social learning
        small-group exercises 84
    and visual learning 84, 88–93
        case studies 91
        role play 90
        small-group exercises 91–3
        videos 89
        visiting lecturers 89–90
    as weak teaching technique 83–4
    see also small group teaching
legal education
    clinical 129, 130–31
        benefits 130–31
        environmental *see*
            environmental law
            clinics
        experiential learning in 130
        specialist 131–2
    lectures *see* lectures
    transmission model 99–100
Leopold, Aldo 45

Macy, Joanna 45–6, 47,
    Work that Reconnects 48
marginalisation 214, 241

marginality of environmental law 1, 7,
    8, 9, 251
mental health 22–3
    burnout 23
    challenges 22, 23, 34
    cultivation of happiness 22
    cultivation of optimism 34
    improving student wellbeing 25–6
        Foundations of Happiness at
            Work course 25–6
    of law students 24
    stresses 23–4
    student wellbeing 25–6
    teaching hope 26–33
        pedagogy of hope 23, 26–7, 34
        success stories 27–33
    see also pedagogy of hope; success
        stories
methodological alternatives 2, 202
mixed cohorts 199, 209
    case study 205–7
    class participation 201
    cultural challenges 200–202
    formative assessment 202–3
    non-law students 202
moot courts 144
multi-disciplinary approaches 5, 113
    advantages of 202–3
    as a form of 'reciprocal elucidation'
        122
    Interdisciplinary Aspects of Climate
        Change course 114–15
    as promoting authenticity 118
    student conferences 122–3
    working groups 123

Naess, Arne 44, 47
natural resource law 4, 49, 52–4
    and Canadian economy 53–4
    and colonialism 52–3, 54–5
        roots in colonial property law
            52, 61
    deep engagement with indigenous
        law 59
        Kunst'aa guu-Kunst'aayah
            Reconciliation Protocol
            59
        Maori law 59
    defining 52
    domination 56

by property law 56
by 'resource-ist, utilitarian
approach' 55–6
and Indigenous relationship to the
land 52–3
Indigenous jurisdiction 54–5
in legal education 54–6
decolonization & reconciliation
56–60
teaching 55
overlay of administrative law 55
and place-based teaching 61–62
traditional approach 58
see also decolonizing teaching
natural resources management 15, 199
co-management 59–60
non-lawyers 199, 202
in ELCs 136
foundational material for 205–6
postgraduate education 190–91
sharing expertise with 189

online learning *see* e-learning
open-learning resources 257
online open access sources 257
open access textbooks 5, 82
open pedagogies 5, 81, 82
textbooks as 82
Ottawa Conference on Climate Change
145, 152
dynamic environment 156–8
debriefing 158
negotiation 157–8
preparation 156–7
four pillars 152
gameful design 155–6
realistic experience of treaty
negotiation 152–5
provision example 153–4
topics opened to negotiation
154–5
simplified representation 158–9
see also game-based learning

participation 201
assessing 86, 101, 105, 106, 117,
206
self-assessment 112
small groups 110–11

challenge 272–3
on discussion boards 265
e-learning increasing 259
encouraging 30, 110
fatigue 271
and games 147
instructor visibility and 268–9
pedagogical innovation 196
pedagogy
doctrinal 201
Langdellian method 117, 254
of online learning *see* e-learning
open pedagogies 5, 81, 82
place-based pedagogy 49, 58, 60,
61–2
Socratic method 84, 117, 201, 254,
260
pedagogy of hope 3, 4, 23, 26–7
postgraduate education 182–4, 197–8,
199–200
best practice 209
critical features 204
doctoral research *see* doctorate
environmental law research 6–7
increasing complexity of
environmental law 199
intensive block teaching 199–200,
203–5
and blended learning 204
challenges 203–4
defining 203
popularity 203
key lessons for 207–9
build classroom community
208
good preparation 208
keep classroom exciting 209
tailor evaluations 208–9
well-structured materials 208
mixed cohort case study 205–7
diverse teaching approaches
207
learning management system
use 205–6
mini-lectures 206
on-campus session 206
reading material 205
role plays 207
scaffolded learning activities
206–7

teamwork exercises 207
mixed cohorts 199, 209
    class participation 201
    cultural challenges 200–202
    formative assessment 202–3
    non-law students 202
    specialist coursework programs *see*
        SPCELs
problem-based teaching 116, 121, 144,
    194
reconciliation 51–2
    decolonization and 56–60
    see also decolonizing teaching;
        decolonization &
        reconciliation
reflection
    deep student learning 39–40
        enabling 40–41
    reflective journaling *see* reflective
        journaling
    self-understanding 36–8
    self-written 87–8, 92
    and trust 40
    see also emotion
reflective journaling 6, 35, 38–41, 48
    assessment 44
    encouraging 42–3
    increasing use of, 38
    in nursing 38–9
    pitfalls 39
    potential of 38
    reading journal 41
    resistance to 42
    student evaluation 44
    therapeutic value of 48
    uses 39, 41–2
risk regulation 14, 17

Seed, John 45
shortage of legal scholars 3, 7, 18
small group teaching 96–8, 108, 111
    basic philosophy 98
    case studies 108–9
    challenges of 100–101
    comparative law exercises 109–10
    and depth of learning experience
        99–100
    drafting assignments 108
    as enhancing student learning 98
    facilitating student discussion 104

feedback 110
    flipped classroom similarities 101
    general benefits 101
    and learning outcomes 98–9
    methodologies 5
    participation assessment 101,
        110–11
    preparing for 103
    rationale for 98, 102–3
    role play 109
    self-assessment form 112
    structured discussion 104–5
        brainstorming 107–8
        free-form 107
        larger classes 106–7
        self-directed 107
        seminars 105
    student presentations 109
    and verbal articulation 100
    see also assessment
socio-constructivism 146
South African National Research
    Foundation 217
SPCELs 183
    and adaptive management 195–6
    culture 194–5
    diplomas/certificates in
        environmental law 183
    mission 184–6
    multidisciplinary masters programs
        183
    non-thesis LLMs 183, 184, 191
    pedagogy
        course format 193–4
        curriculum design 187–8
        diversity 192–3
        interdisciplinarity 189–91
        internationalizing 192
        multiculturalism 191–2
        pedagogical approaches 194
        professional skills training
            188–9
    see also postgraduate education
stagnation 241
stories 6, 164–5
    good 167
    as integral to remembering &
        understanding 166
storytelling 6, 179–80
    coat-hanger structure 165, 168, 169

case study 170–72
  /usual course comparison 171–4
as core cognitive tool 166
course example 174–5
  1945–60 175–6
  1960–80 176–7
  1980–90 177–8
  1990–present 178–9
defining 166
as enriching 167
imaginative education 166
storytelling pedagogy 166–8
prejudice against 166
success stories 27–33
  as aiding problem-solving skills
    31–2
  as building optimism 32–3
  challenges created by 33
  Douglas A Kysar 27–8
  environmental rights revolution 29
  integrating 30
  ozone depletion 29
  purpose of 30–31
  recovery of endangered species 29

teaching and learning 1–2
  lecturing 5
  small group methodologies 5
  teacher training 5–6
teaching challenges 18, 19–20
  technology innovation 19
teaching methodology 4–5
technological innovation 18–19, 214
  consequences of 19
  impact of 18
textbook tradition 71, 72–75, 79–80, 82
  common-law mindset in 72–3
  critique of 69–70
  disciplinary challenges 70, 78–80
    accessibility of relevant primary
      sources 78–9
    changes to modes of learning
      79
    connectivist/constructivist
      approaches to learning
      79
    digital resources 79
    virtual learning environments
      79
  and future learning resources 80–82

inter-disciplinary approach 81
open educational resources
  (OER) 80–81
real-world skill recognition 81
re-structuring texts 81–2
learning resource model 75–8
  innovations 75
significance of 72
textbook writing laws 75
  be brief 77
  be reliable 77–8
  cover the ground, the whole
    ground and nothing but
    the ground 76–7
  keep up to date 77–8
textbooks
  as convenient secondary sources 78
  formative role of 73–4
  as key source of information 70
  market for 74
  multiple purposes of 72
  open access 5
  outdated 70
  as promoting rote learning 79
  sub-standard 69
  undermining innovation 70
  whether fit for purpose 70–71
Thailand 7, 276
  academic expertise
  academic staff development
  Enhancement and Conservation
    of National Environmental
    Quality Act (1992) 279
  environmental law teaching 279–80,
    287–8
  lack of academic expertise
    284–5
  lack of staff development
    resources 286–7
  LLB compulsory component
    281
  LLB elective component
    280–81
  in non-law courses 281–2
  postgraduate 282–3
legal education 278–9
  'Train the Teachers'
    programme 276, 279,
    286–7
legal system 276–8

Basic Law of the Judiciary 277
civil law 277
influence of English legal
system 277
political/constitutional instability
277
transformational practice 56, 57
Truth and Reconciliation Commission of
Canada 56
Calls to Action, Recommendation
28 56–7

UK environmental law teaching study
251–2
2002 UKCLE Report 242, 245, 249
methodology 243–4
potential future 251–2
results 245–9
class sizes 246
decline in courses offered 251
employability issues 246–7
experience levels of teachers
245, 246

institutional attitudes to
environmental law
247–8
lack of planning law teaching
251
number of teachers 246
static student numbers 251
student attitudes 248–9
undergraduate level modules
offered 245
scholarship 242–3
teaching challenges 249–51
course content selection 249,
250–51
interdisciplinarity of subject
249
law & policy changes 249
poly-centricity of subject 249
pushback against 250
United Nations Framework Convention
on Climate Change 88

value-based approach 3